Her Word versus His: Establishing the Underlying Text in 1 Samuel 1:23

AARON D. HORNKOHL
adh44@cam.ac.uk
University of Cambridge, Cambridge, CB2 1TN, UK

The Masoretic version of the book of Samuel is notoriously difficult from a text-critical perspective. Scholars have long suspected that this situation reflects a particularly corrupt scribal tradition. Comparison with ancient textual witnesses, especially the Greek and the relevant Hebrew manuscripts among the Dead Sea Scrolls (particularly 4Q51), has generally served to reinforce this view. Several global explanations for differences between the various textual witnesses to Samuel have been proposed. These general approaches, highlighting either accidental or tendentious changes, can illuminate the development of difficult passages. However, many problem passages are given to more than one possible solution. For this reason and others, difficult sections in the text must be dealt with individually, on a case-by-case basis. The present article offers a detailed treatment of attempts to uncover the primary reading of an oft-discussed crux in 1 Sam 1:23, ultimately explaining and arguing for the superiority of the Masoretic testimony while accounting for the interpretive and ideological factors that may have led to the alternative renditions.

The Masoretic edition of Samuel (M) is known for its many cruxes. These are especially conspicuous when M is compared to the same book's ancient Greek translation (G), which generally makes for a smoother read. In the past, commentators were divided as to the reason for this disparity. Some held that G's translator had worked from a text very similar to M but had altered it for the sake of his readership—leveling, adding, subtracting, and explaining as he deemed necessary. Others attributed the divergences not to G's translator, but to the source text, which, it was argued, must have differed substantially from M.

The restoration of the Dead Sea Scrolls text numbered 4Q51 (so-called 4QSam^a, but see below) has thrown light on this matter. Admittedly fragmentary, it nevertheless exhibits striking similarities to the hypothetical Hebrew text reconstructed by back-translation as the source of G.[1] This is not to say that G is a translation of a text identical to 4Q51—even where G was not revised to conform to M there is significant variance between G and 4Q51[2]—but merely that 4Q51 provides Hebrew documentary evidence for many of the differences between G and M that were previously ascribed to G's translator.[3] While the latter may very well have engaged in the sort of leveling characteristic of the work of many translators, his is nowadays considered a generally faithful[4] and fairly literal[5] testimony to the Hebrew text that lay before him. The aforementioned affinity between G and 4Q51 implies that even where, due to 4Q51's fragmentary nature, there exists no Hebrew textual support for G readings appreciably different from those in M, the possibility that such deviations reflect a non–Masoretic-type Hebrew source text merits serious, albeit cautious, consideration. The question then naturally arises: Which of the ancient Hebrew editions, difficult M or apparently easier 4Q51/G-*Vorlage*, preserves the primary text?

I. Global Approaches to M, 4Q51, and G as Textual Witnesses to Samuel

At the risk of oversimplifying current scholarly opinion, I identify three general—and not necessarily mutually exclusive—approaches to the text of Samuel. According to the first, M is a textual tradition pervasively marred by accidental scribal omissions, whereas the 4Q51/G Hebrew textual tradition, while not entirely

---

[1] Eugene Ulrich, *The Qumran Text of Samuel and Josephus* (HSM 19; Missoula, MT: Scholars Press, 1978); Emanuel Tov, "Textual Affiliations of 4QSam^a," *JSOT* 14 (1979): 42; Frank Moore Cross, Donald W. Parry, and Richard J. Saley, "51. 4QSam^a," in *Qumran Cave 4.XII: 1–2 Samuel* (ed. F. M. Cross et al.; DJD 17; Oxford: Clarendon, 2005), 25.

[2] Tov, "Textual Affiliations," 38–39, 51–52; idem, "Determining the Relationship between the Qumran Scrolls and the LXX," in *The Hebrew and Greek Texts of Samuel, Symposium Vienna, 1980* (ed. Emanuel Tov; Jerusalem: Academon, 1980), 45–67, esp. 53–54, 57, 62–65; idem, "The Contribution of the Qumran Scrolls to the Understanding of the LXX," in *Septuagint, Scrolls and Cognate Writings: Papers Presented to the International Symposium on the Septuagint and Its Relations to the Dead Sea Scrolls and Other Writings, Manchester, 1980* (ed. George J. Brooke and Barnabas Lindars; SBLSCS 33; Atlanta: Scholars Press, 1992), 25; Anneli Aejmelaeus, "Corruption or Correction? Textual Development in the MT of 1 Samuel 1," in *Textual Criticism and Dead Sea Scrolls: Studies in Honour of Julio Trebolle Barrera. Florilegium Complutense* (ed. Andres Piquer Otero and Pablo A. Torijano Morales; JSJSup 157; Leiden: Brill, 2012), 9.

[3] Tov, "Textual Affiliations," 42; Robert P. Gordon, *1 & 2 Samuel: A Commentary* (Exeter: Paternoster, 1986), 58; Martin Abegg Jr., Peter Flint, and Eugene Ulrich, *The Dead Sea Scrolls Bible: The Oldest Known Bible* (Edinburgh: T&T Clark, 1999), 214; Cross, Parry, and Saley, "51. 4QSam^a," 26.

[4] Abegg, Flint, and Ulrich, *Dead Sea Scrolls Bible*, 214.

[5] Tov, "Textual Affiliations," 39.

free of corruption of this sort, seems to have suffered relatively less of it.⁶ Adherents to a second view see M as the product of intentional, ideologically driven revision, whereby problematic details were expunged or modified.⁷ In this case, some differences between M and the text represented by 4Q51/G may be chalked up to accidental corruption, but others are more likely intentional literary adaptations. The 4Q51/G textual tradition is thought to have been less affected by such tendentious alteration. Finally, and conversely, the 4Q51/G Hebrew textual tradition has been characterized as expansive to the point of being midrashic. In other words, the scribe responsible for this edition is accused of having sought to harmonize apparent contradictions, to fill in bothersome omissions, and to explain seemingly problematic details of the story in light of biblical precedent or postbiblical tradition.⁸

These general characterizations can prove instructive when dealing with individual problem passages in Samuel. But caution is in order. While the approaches may in theory be more or less equally valid for the book as a whole, each being operative in a number of specific instances, they cannot all hold in a single given case. Additionally, it is important to bear in mind that global approaches of this sort are in reality no more than distillations of the necessarily subjective treatment of multiple local cases. In other words, the validity of any one recognized tendency is only as great as the combined total of its explanatory power in discrete instances

---

⁶ Henry Preserved Smith, *A Critical and Exegetical Commentary on the Books of Samuel* (ICC; Edinburgh: T&T Clark, 1899), xxix–xxxii; Samuel Rolles Driver, *Notes on the Hebrew Text and the Topography of the Books of Samuel* (2nd ed.; Oxford: Clarendon, 1913), xl; Frank Moore Cross, "The Evolution of a Theory of Local Texts," in *Qumran and the History of the Biblical Text* (ed. Frank Moore Cross and Shemaryahu Talmon; Cambridge, MA: Harvard University Press, 1975), 312; Dominique Barthélemy, "La qualité du Texte Massorétique de Samuel," in Tov, *Hebrew and Greek Texts of Samuel*, 43; P. Kyle McCarter Jr., *I Samuel: A New Translation with Introduction, Notes & Commentary* (AB 8; Garden City, NY: Doubleday, 1980), 5; Ralph W. Klein, *1 Samuel* (WBC 10; Waco: Word, 1983), xxvi; Gordon, *1 & 2 Samuel*, 57; Cross, Parry, and Saley, "51. 4QSamᵃ," 26; Aejmelaeus, "Corruption or Correction?" 6–17. For a less extreme view, see Emanuel Tov, *Textual Criticism of the Hebrew Bible* (3rd ed.; Minneapolis: Fortress, 2012), 189: "somewhat corrupt." Cf. Stephan Pisano, *Additions or Omissions in the Books of Samuel: The Significant Pluses and Minuses in the Massoretic, LXX and Qumran Texts* (OBO 57; Freiburg, Switzerland: Universitätsverlag; Göttingen: Vandenhoeck & Ruprecht, 1984), 283–85.

⁷ Emanuel Tov, "Different Editions of the Song of Hannah," in *Tehillah le-Moshe: Biblical and Judaic Studies in Honor of Moshe Greenberg* (Winona Lake, IN: Eisenbrauns, 1997); idem, *Textual Criticism*, 254, and the references he adduces in n. 99; Aejmelaeus, "Corruption or Correction?" 6–17.

⁸ Barthélemy, "La qualité, du Texte Massorétique," 43–44; Pisano, *Additions or Omissions*, 283–85; Alexander Rofé, "The Nomistic Correction in Biblical Manuscripts and Its Occurrence in *4QSamᵃ*," *RevQ* 14 (1989): 247–54; idem, "4QMidrash Samuel?—Observations Concerning the Character of 4QSamᵃ," *Textus* 19 (1998): 63–74; idem, "Midrashic Traits in 4Q51 (So-Called 4QSamᵃ)," in *Archaeology of the Books of Samuel: The Entangling of the Textual and the Literary History* (ed. Philippe Hugo and Adrian Schenker; VTSup 132; Leiden: Brill, 2010).

of textual difficulty. This means that despite the attractiveness of these broad theories, apparent problem passages in Samuel must be dealt with on their own merits on a case-by-case basis, though the possibility of potentially pervasive textual and/or literary propensities should not be ignored.[9]

II. 1 Samuel 1:23: The Problem

The story of Samuel's birth and dedication for service at Shiloh is well known and need not be rehearsed here. M is replete with nonstandard, unexpected, and difficult locutions. One oft-discussed crux comes in Elkanah's words to Hannah in 1 Sam 1:23. In response to her decision to delay Samuel's dedication for perpetual cultic service until the boy's weaning, Elkanah tells Hannah to do as she sees fit and then adds the puzzling אך יקם יהוה את־דברו, "but may the Lord establish his word." Nowhere in the foregoing text has the writer made reference to divine speech. To which word of the Lord can Elkanah be referring?

The Versions

Before discussing the various ways in which this question has been answered, it will be helpful to examine how the text in question appears in the ancient versions so commonly employed as textual witnesses, including 4Q51. Not unexpectedly, despite a certain expansiveness elsewhere in the verse, the Aramaic translation in *Targum Jonathan*, יקיים יי ית פתגמוהי, "may the Lord fulfill his words," basically supports the Masoretic reading,[10] as does Jerome's more stylized *precorque ut impleat Dominus verbum suum*, "I pray that the Lord fulfill his word," in the Vulgate. Other witnesses, however, present a significantly different reading. For

---

[9] See Eugene Ulrich ("A Qualitative Assessment of the Textual Profile of 4QSam^a," in *Flores Florentino: Dead Sea Scrolls and Other Early Jewish Studies in Honour of Florentino García Martínez* [ed. Anthony Hilhorst, Émile Puech, and Eibert Tigchelaar; JSJSup 122; Leiden: Brill, 2007], 147–61), who sees M and 4Q51 not as different editions of Samuel, but as "exemplars of the same general edition, simply distantly related due to separate transmission, where each has gained numerous innocent and predictable additions, and each has suffered either losses or double renderings or corruption. But they do not represent intentionally produced variant literary editions" (pp. 159–60).

[10] The Targum's rendering of Hebrew דברו ("his word") with plural פתגמוהי ("his words") is unexpected. Possible explanations include: (a) interpretation of the ו- ending as plural in the light of other such instances in the wider context, e.g., the Ketiv-Qere cases in 1 Sam 2:9, 10 (2x), and 3:2; (b) a more general presentation of God's word in the face of the difficulty of locating the specific one in question; (c) reference to the midrashic tradition made explicit in *Midrash Samuel*, according to which the echo of the Lord's voice repeatedly announced the coming birth of the righteous Samuel; (d) the two elements of Hannah's vow fulfilled by the Lord's word (see below). I would like to express my gratitude to Kim Phillips for thoughts on this matter.

example, the Peshiṭta has ܒܪܡ ܢܩܝܡ ܡܪܝܐ ܡܠܬܟܝ, "but may the Lord make firm your [fem. sg.] word," while both G, with ἀλλὰ στήσαι κύριος τὸ ἐξελθὸν ἐκ τοῦ στόματός σου, and 4Q51, with אך יקם יהו[ה היוצא מפיך, read "but may the Lord establish that which comes out of your [fem. sg.] mouth."[11]

The Non-Masoretic Readings

Given the immediate context, those readings according to which Elkanah is reported to have said something along the lines of "may the Lord help you keep your word" appear immensely attractive. They offer no hint of the problem associated with an ostensibly missing "word of the Lord." Moreover, they are psychologically appropriate in terms of what a character in Elkanah's position might be expected to have felt, that is, interpreting Hannah's apparent procrastination as loss of resolve to fulfill her vow. His reminder, "but may the Lord establish your word/what you have said" is, at least at first glance then, somewhat more expected than the alternative, "but may the Lord establish his word." It is thus unsurprising that, even prior to the discovery of 4Q51, commentators, bewildered by M and grateful for the help offered by G and the Peshiṭta, often preferred the readings of the latter versions.

As early as 1689, Louis Cappel reasoned that G's translator had read דברך ("your word"),[12] and in 1753 Charles F. Houbigant argued that the Syriac's ܡܠܬܟܝ pointed to just such an original reading.[13] In 1842, on the basis of G, Otto Thenius proposed the more radical original reading אך תקימי ליהוה את־היוצא מפיך, "but may you [fem. sg.] establish for the Lord that which has come out of your mouth."[14] Dissatisfied with this reconstruction, on the basis of which the Syriac was difficult to explain, in 1864 he put forth the slightly revised אך תקימי את־דברך, "but may you [fem. sg.] establish your word."[15] Finally, in 1871 Julius Wellhausen came down on the side of דברך ("your word") as original,[16] which S. R. Driver, Henry Preserved Smith, and others subsequently adopted in their commentaries.[17] There have also

---

[11] Only in Syriac is the possessive "your" explicitly marked as feminine; neither the Hebrew consonantal tradition nor the Greek permits explicit gender distinction in the case of the relevant particle. Be that as it may, the feminine singular status of the referent is evident from the context and is left implicit in the glosses throughout the remainder of the present discussion.

[12] Ludovicus Cappellus, *Commentarii et notae criticae in Vetus Testamentum* (Amsterdam: P. & J. Blaeu, 1689), 430.

[13] Houbigant, *Biblia Hebraica cum notis criticis et versione latina ad notas criticas* (Lutetia-Paris: A. C. Briasson and L. Durand, 1753), 2:166.

[14] Thenius, *Die Bücher Samuels* (Kurzgefasstes exegetisches Handbuch zum Alten Testament 4; Leipzig: Weidmann, 1842), 6.

[15] Thenius, *Die Bücher Samuels* (2nd ed.; Kurzgefasstes exegetisches Handbuch zum Alten Testament 4; Leipzig: Hirzel, 1864), 7–8.

[16] Wellhausen, *Der Text der Bücher Samuelis* (Göttingen: Vandenhoeck & Ruprecht, 1871), 41.

[17] Driver, *Notes*, 20; Smith, *Books of Samuel*, 13–14.

been conjectural emendations with no documentary support[18] and, of course, scholars who were content with M.[19] It bears mentioning at this point that a crucial factor in the scholarly recourse to non-Masoretic readings was—and remains—desperation in the face of the perceived incomprehensibility of M.

The confirmation of G's ἀλλὰ στήσαι κύριος τὸ ἐξελθὸν ἐκ τοῦ στόματός σου discovered in 4Q51's אך יקם יהו[ה היוצא מפיך, both "but may the LORD establish that which comes out of your [fem. sg.] mouth" has only reinforced scholarly preference for readings referring to Hannah's vow.[20] However, significantly, critics have yet to furnish a satisfactory explanation for the development of the three known readings: M's "his word," Syriac's "your word," and 4Q51/G's "that which comes out of your mouth." While a reference to Hannah's vow may, at first glance, seem more readily intelligible than a reference to God's word, it is significant that the textual witnesses supporting the former do not agree among themselves as to the specific expression employed. The Peshitta's "your word" and 4Q51/G's "that which comes out of your mouth" are, it is true, referentially synonymous, but their verbal dissimilarity should not be glossed over.

It is sometimes argued that the 4Q51/G collocation היוצא מפיך, "that which comes out of your mouth" is original.[21] While this expression is not used exclusively of vows (Josh 6:10; Isa 48:3; 55:11; Esth 7:8), similar votive wording is employed in a number of passages, most notably Numbers 30 (Num 30:3, 24; Judg 11:36; Isa 45:23; Jer 44:17[?]).[22] On the assumption of such a primary reading, however, it is no simple matter to explain the development of Syriac's ܡܠܬܟ ("your word") and M's דברו ("his word"). If Elkanah's words were indeed היוצא מפיך, "that which comes out of your mouth," the Syriac translator's failure to render with the expected ܡܕܡ ܕܢܦܩ ܡܢ ܦܘܡܟܝ, "that which comes out of your mouth" (as in Num 30:3) would be uncharacteristic of the version, given its literal renderings of this and similarly worded phrases elsewhere.[23] Furthermore, in no way is reference to a vow by means

---

[18] See, e.g., Arnold B. Ehrlich, who reconstructed an original נדרך ("your vow") (*Randglossen zur Hebräischen Bibel: Textkritisches, sprachliches und sachliches* [7 vols.; Leipzig: Hinrichs, 1908–14], 3:167).

[19] See, e.g., Carl F. Keil and Franz Delitzsch, *Biblical Commentary on the Books of Samuel* (Clark's Foreign Theological Library, 4th series, vol. 9; trans. J. A. Martin; Edinburgh: T&T Clark, 1866), 27.

[20] McCarter, *I Samuel*, 56; Klein, *1 Samuel*, 2–3; Gordon, *1 & 2 Samuel*, 77; Abegg, Flint, and Ulrich, *Dead Sea Scrolls Bible*, 211; Cross, Parry, and Saley, "51. 4QSamᵃ," 33; Aejmelaeus, "Corruption or Correction?"; Tov, *Textual Criticism* (3rd ed.), 255–56 (hesitantly; cf. Tov, *Textual Criticism of the Hebrew Bible* [2nd rev. ed.; Minneapolis: Fortress, 2001], 176).

[21] McCarter, *I Samuel*, 50, 56; Klein, *1 Samuel*, 2–3, 10; Cross, Parry, and Saley, "51. 4QSamᵃ," 33; Abegg, Flint, and Ulrich, *Dead Sea Scrolls Bible*, 215; Aejmelaeus, "Corruption or Correction?" 8–17; Tov, *Textual Criticism* (3rd ed.), 256 (hesitantly).

[22] Note also מוצא שפתים, "the utterance of the lips," in Num 30:13; Deut 23:24; and Ps 89:35.

[23] In addition to the references in the previous note, see Num 32:24; Deut 8:3; Josh 6:10; 1 Sam 2:3; Isa 48:3; 55:11; Jer 17:16; Job 15:13; 37:2; Lam 3:38; Esth 7:8.

of the bland "your word" an improvement on the idiomatic "that which comes out of your mouth"; on the contrary, as argued below, "your word" here creates, rather than solves, a problem. The Syriac reading must almost certainly have developed from some reading other than היוצא מפיך. It may reflect underlying Hebrew דברך ("your word"), which, if original, would make היוצא מפיך a secondary, explanatory paraphrase. Alternatively, it may derive from דברו ("his word"), which, if primary, would again make היוצא מפיך secondary or, if secondary, would make the Syriac reading "your word" tertiary.

As for M's דברו ("his word"), some see it as a tendentious theological correction to expunge Elkanah's unseemly petitioning of the LORD to establish Hannah's word.[24] This is said to reflect discomfort with the idea of divine fulfillment of human speech. It may also be part of a programmatic attempt to minimize the role of Hannah, a woman, in the narrative, evidence for which has been identified elsewhere in the context.[25] In this case M's reviser took specific issue with Hannah's involvement in Samuel's dedication for ministry.

The question of whether other differences between M and the Hebrew textual tradition represented by 4Q51/G in 1 Samuel 1–2 should be attributed to a given editorial agenda with the goal of rendering Hannah more inert in M than she had been in G's *Vorlage* is beyond the scope of this article. In the case under discussion, however, such a scenario, while not inconceivable, is less convincing than alternative explanations.

The strongest evidence against the claim that M resulted from an attempt to shift credit for Samuel's future status away from Hannah is the exceedingly poor execution of it. Even in M's allegedly retouched edition of the story, with no reference to Hannah's vow in 1 Sam 1:23, her words in v. 11 still come across as binding and efficacious. For purposes of comparison, it may be useful to consider the announcement of Samson's birth and future role in Judges 13, in which Samson's parents are entirely passive. Had M's editor been truly concerned that readers might wrongly associate Samuel's calling with his mother's vow, then he should have eliminated the vow, because the link between it and Samuel's vocation is obvious despite the purported rewording of 1 Sam 1:23.

A revision of the sort just discussed seems more likely with original דברך ("your word") than with original היוצא מפיך, "that which comes out of your mouth." As previously noted, the latter expression hints strongly at a vow. It is difficult to imagine it being understood as anything other than a piously couched reminder to Hannah that she must keep her word. Conversely, the expression אך יקם יהוה את־דברך, "but may the LORD establish your word," is problematic. According to biblical usage, a person can establish God's word (1 Sam 15:11, 13) or his or her own

---

[24] Tov, "Different Editions," 156; idem, *Textual Criticism* (2nd ed.), 176; idem, *Textual Criticism* (3rd ed.), 255–56 (hesitantly; see his n. 102); Aejmelaeus, "Corruption or Correction?" 10–11.

[25] Tov, *Textual Criticism* (3rd ed.), 255–56; Aejmelaeus, "Corruption or Correction?" 1–15.

(Jer 35:15), and God can establish a divine word[26] and even that of the prophets (Isa 44:26; Jer 28:6). None of these situations obtains here. It also seems a rather awkward way of saying "may the Lord help you keep your promise." To sum up: דברך ("your word"), ostensibly reflected in Syriac ܡܠܬܟ, is more plausibly original than 4Q51/G היוצא מפיך, because it is difficult on the basis of primary מפיך היוצא to arrive at either דברך = Syriac ܡܠܬܟ ("your word") or M דברו ("his word"). Conversely, assuming the infelicitous דברך ("your word") to be primary, both 4Q51/G's היוצא מפיך, "that which comes out of your mouth,"[27] and M's דברו ("his word") are obvious improvements.

In this case, the Syriac would offer the most accurate testimony, whereas the 4Q51/G rendition would be a nomistic attempt to improve a difficult text by substituting biblical phraseology more clearly indicative of a vow than דברך ("your word").[28] From the same starting point, M's דברו ("his word") may be variously explained as due to graphic confusion between *waw* and *kaf* or as an intentional, theologically motivated "correction" of the awkward אך יקם יהוה את־דברך, "but may the Lord establish your word," which, though doubtless a reference to Hannah's vow, was deemed an irreverent formulation, perhaps in part because it referred to a woman. In order to resolve this perceived problem, some argue that the offended scribe "elevated" Hannah's word to the level of a divine promise.[29] In so doing,

---

[26] See 2 Sam 7:25; 1 Kgs 2:4; 6:12; 8:20; 12:15; Jer 29:10; 33:14; Neh 9:8; Dan 9:12; 2 Chr 6:10; 10:15.

[27] Aejmelaeus objects to the notion that 4Q51 and G share a secondary, nomistic, reading on the grounds that such close affinity between the two has yet to be established ("Corruption or Correction?" 9). Her argument is based on the approach articulated by Tov, according to which shared primary readings are less significant as evidence of genetic affiliation than shared secondary readings, since the former are quite naturally preserved in multiple text types, while the latter are more likely to betray a special relationship. The logic of the approach is sound, but the determination of whether a given shared reading is primary or secondary is obviously subjective. If the reading common to 4Q51 and G's *Vorlage* discussed in the present article is deemed secondary on the basis of the arguments here adduced, then it would, as Aejmelaeus observes, imply a fairly early nomistic modification. For just such an early harmonization in light of biblical legal requirements, consider the cases of מצבה ("standing stone") in Exod 24:4, in place of which the Samaritan Pentateuch reads אבנים ("stones") and G translates λίθους ("stones," which nowhere else renders מצבה), apparently under the influence of Deut 16:22 "You must not set up a standing stone, which the Lord your God detests" (see Rofé, "Nomistic Correction," 249; Tov, *Textual Criticism* [3rd ed.], 252). More generally, special affinity between 4Q51 and G, including secondary readings, is widely, though by no means unanimously, accepted; in addition to the references in n. 1 above, see Edward D. Herbert, "4QSam^a and Its Relationship to the LXX: An Exploration in Stemmatological Analysis," in *IX Congress of the International Organization for Septuagint and Cognate Studies: Cambridge, 1995* (ed. Bernard A. Taylor; SBLSCS 45; Atlanta: Scholars Press, 1997), 37–55.

[28] Rofé, "Nomistic Correction," 252; idem, "Midrashic Traits," 82–83.

[29] Abegg, Flint, and Ulrich, *Dead Sea Scrolls Bible*, 211.

however, the scribe unwittingly generated a reference to a nonexistent divine utterance.

The foregoing discussion has important ramifications for assessing the value of the 4Q51/G Hebrew textual tradition. If דברך ("your word") is a more logical candidate than היוצא מפיך, "that which comes out of your mouth," for the underlying text of 1 Sam 1:23, the replacement of the former with the latter is indicative of bold literary initiative. The Hebrew scribe responsible for 1 Sam 1:23 in the 4Q51/G tradition is revealed to be less of a copyist and more of a problem solver. Since indications of his penchant for harmonization with biblical and postbiblical tradition have been detected elsewhere, Alexander Rofé has gone so far as to argue against calling 4Q51 "4QSam[a]," suggesting the alternative title "4QMidrash Samuel."[30] Whatever title his text be given, the relevant scribe's willingness to engage in nomistic adaptation necessarily calls into question the reliability of his textual testimony.

With regard specifically to 1 Sam 1:23 it emerges that the scribe's היוצא מפיך is no better evidence for דברך ("your word") as primary than it is for דברו ("his word"). Despite the fact that he wrote in Hebrew, once this scribe's readiness for modification is admitted, it becomes very difficult to establish his source text with anything approaching certainty.

Before returning to M, it is well to reiterate a point made only in passing above, namely, that one of the strongest arguments for the non-Masoretic readings of 1 Sam 1:23 is M's perceived unintelligibility. But what if sense can be made of M? While this may not negate the reasonableness of the alternative readings, it may render them superfluous.[31]

---

[30] Rofé, "4QMidrash Samuel," 64–65; idem, "Midrashic Traits," 75–76.

[31] Some might argue that such an approach uncritically assigns priority to M over other textual witnesses. However, in the case of the ancient non-Hebrew versions this priority is surely warranted, since it is in the nature of translation to adapt a text for a foreign audience. In the case of ancient Hebrew texts, such as the Samaritan Pentateuch or the biblical Dead Sea Scrolls, the situation can be more complicated. Of course, for much of the Hebrew Bible the question is moot, M and derivative traditions being the only Hebrew witnesses. Where, on the other hand, alternative Hebrew editions exist, their overall reliability vis-à-vis M may be evaluated in part on the basis of their penchant for updating linguistic features and leveling linguistic and nonlinguistic discrepancies. For example, there is no doubt but that both the written and reading traditions of the Samaritan Pentateuch have later linguistic profiles than the Masoretic Torah. The Samaritan Pentateuch is also well known for a harmonistic *Tendenz* (see Tov, *Textual Criticism* [3rd ed.], 82–90). These characteristics speak to a willingness on the part of the scribe(s) involved to modify the text and must therefore be taken into account when gauging text-critical reliability. The Dead Sea Scrolls biblical material has yet to be subjected to a comprehensive linguistic analysis but would also appear, on the whole, to exhibit a somewhat later linguistic profile than that preserved in M (despite the fact that the former are approximately a thousand years older than the codices that contain the most authoritative editions of the latter). Be that as it may, as stated above, each individual instance of suspected textual difficulty merits its own examination, which may or may not conform to the recognized tendencies of the various textual witnesses.

III. M

Having excluded 4Q51/G's testimony as ambiguous, it is opportune to revisit M to determine whether it can be read as it stands. Notwithstanding a noticeable scholarly antipathy toward M's דברו ("his word"), might not it be original and Syriac's ܡܠܬܟ ("your word") secondary? It is true that nowhere in the text spanning 1 Sam 1:1–22 is there explicit reference to divine speech. This has been variously— though not always credibly—explained. According to rabbinic tradition, the narrative is simply elliptical.[32] Others argue for a rather general meaning of דברו ("his word"), explaining it to mean something like "God's will."[33] Solutions like these, while perhaps not to be dismissed out of hand, must be judged less convincing than those according to which the deity's word is identified within the text and explained in specific reference to Elkanah's wish that it be fulfilled. In the absence of the latter, readers' frustration with M and recourse to alternative textual traditions are certainly understandable. Thankfully, an explanation exists that simultaneously makes sense of M and accounts for the alternate readings.

As a number of scholars have noted, the only explicit "word" to which דברו ("his word") can possibly refer is Eli's in 1 Sam 1:17: "Go in peace. May the God of Israel give you your request that you have asked of him."[34] The problem is that, at least at first glance, Elkanah's appeal for God to fulfill his own word seems out of place. After all, Hannah has already been granted a child. Here, though, it is well to remember that Hannah's prayer included two elements: both a request for a child and a promise to dedicate him for perpetual service. The child's birth was thus only the first step in realization of the divine promise embodied in Eli's blessing; the child also had to live long enough for Hannah to fulfill her vow. If modern infant mortality rates in less developed nations can be taken as any indication of the situation in antiquity, it could by no means be taken for granted that a newborn child would live long enough to be weaned.[35] Further, given the importance the ancients

---

[32] Consider the Midrash mentioned in n. 10 above and perhaps the Targum as well.

[33] Keil and Delitzsch, *Books of Samuel*, 27; Rofé, "Nomistic Correction," 252; idem, "Midrashic Traits," 82; David Toshio Tsumura, *The First Book of Samuel* (NICOT; Grand Rapids: Eerdmans), 129.

[34] See, e.g., Yehudah Kiel, *Sefer Shmuel I* (Daʿat Miqra; Jerusalem: Mosad Harav Kook, 1981), 13; Dominique Barthélemy, *Critique textuelle de l'Ancient Testament*, vol. 1, *Josué, Juges, Ruth, Samuel, Rois, Chroniques, Esdras, Néhémie, Esther* (OBO 50.1; Fribourg: Éditions Universitaires; Göttingen: Vandenhoeck & Ruprecht, 1982), 141. On this translation, see n. 38 below.

[35] See "Infant Mortality Rate," *World Fact Book 2009* (Washington, DC: Central Intelligence Agency, 2009; accessible at https://www.cia.gov/library/publications/the-world-factbook/fields/2091.html); and United Nations, Department of Economic and Social Affairs, Population Division, *World Population Prospects: The 2010 Revision* (CD-ROM Edition, 2011; accessible at http://esa.un.org/unpd/wpp/Excel-Data/mortality.htm). The celebration in conjunction with a boy's weaning (e.g., Gen 21:8) may also hint at the precariousness of infant life.

attached to the fulfillment of vows,[36] Elkanah's concern lest the child die before Hannah could satisfy hers is perfectly plausible. Hence, "May the LORD establish his word," is to be seen as an invocation that God, having granted a child, would preserve him long enough for the fulfillment of Hannah's vow. Among commentators, a reading incorporating these elements is rare.[37] It should be noted, however, that an interpretation of this sort was suggested by the medieval Jewish commentator David Qimḥi (Radaq): "'may the LORD fulfill his word'—its interpretation: that which [the LORD] spoke through the prophet [Eli], that [the LORD] would 'grant your request,' and it was that *he live and belong to the LORD*" (emphasis added).[38]

M's דברו ("his word") may seem out of place from the limited perspective of 1 Sam 1:23, but it is quite natural in the broader literary and cultural context. For its part, then, Syriac ܡܠܬܟ ("your word") is either a simple mistake or, what is more likely, a "minimalist" attempt to salvage a text not readily understood. Admittedly, choosing between "your word" and "his word" as the underlying text is a subjective enterprise. Nevertheless, three considerations arguably tip the scales in favor of דברו ("his word"). First, though intelligible, this reading is somewhat cryptic. The reader has been left the task of identifying the referent of an admittedly ambiguous allusion to God's word. Failure to do so is precisely what led to the ancient attempts to "improve" the text. Second, because reference to Hannah's vow by means of דברך ("your word"), particularly following יקם יהוה את, "may the LORD establish," is unlikely in view of the full expression's use throughout the Bible, the use of דברך ("your word") is better explained as an ad hoc "correction" of דברו ("his word") influenced by the immediate context but made in ignorance of the unsuitability of the phrase thereby generated. Finally, it bears emphasizing that the reading "your word" is, unlike the other two candidates for underlying reading, evidenced in no extant Hebrew manuscript, but only in translation. As argued above, היוצא מפיך, "that which comes out of your mouth," cannot be taken as unequivocal evidence that "your word" was ever documented in the form of Hebrew דברך. It is thus entirely possible, perhaps even likely, that the reading "your word" only ever existed in Syriac. As for היוצא מפיך, it is exposed as an attempt employing a typically biblical votive expression either to rehabilitate primary but opaque דברו ("his word") or, less likely, to clarify secondary but ambiguous דברך ("your word").

---

[36] Consider the cases of Jephthah and his daughter (Judg 11:30–40) and Saul and Jonathan (1 Sam 14:24–45).

[37] Barthélemy, *Critique textuelle*, 1:141.

[38] See also the commentary by the later Rabbi Levi ben Gershon (i.e., Ralbag or Gersonides). Eli's blessing, לכי לשלום ואלהי ישראל יתן את שלתך אשר שאלת מעמו, is universally translated as a wish, "May the God of Israel grant the request you have made of him." It is worth noting, however, that the verb יתן is not in clause-initial position, that is, the normal word order for modal forms, and that there is no obvious reason for the fronting of the subject אלהי ישראל, "God of Israel." This may be no more than an anomaly, but the syntax is more appropriate for predictive prophecy than for petitionary blessing. Cf. the more cardinally jussive constituent order in אך יקם יהוה את־דברו, "but may the LORD establish his word."

IV. The Possible Motivation Behind 4Q51/G's Modification

Before concluding, a closer examination of the possible interpretive strategy behind the 4Q51/G Hebrew reading היוצא מפיך, "that which comes out of your mouth," is in order. As previously explained, this nomistic modification serves either to clarify דברך ("your word") or, more probably, to "correct" דברו ("his word"). Whatever the case may be, the change probably involved a network of interpretative decisions.

According to M v. 11, Hannah dedicates her child to the Lord "for all the days of his life," adding that "a razor will not touch his head." G also has the latter, reads "until the day of his death" for the former, and connects the two with the plus "and wine and beer he will not drink." On the basis of average column and letter width, though broken in v. 11, 4Q51 resembles G in terms of length and, presumably, content. More significant, at the end of v. 22, against both M and G, 4Q51 has "and I will gi]ve him as a Nazirite forever, all the days of [his life." Samuel's recasting as a Nazirite by means of phraseology borrowed from Numbers 6 and Judges 13,[39] implicit in G and explicit in 4Q51, is considered by most to represent a conscious effort to bring him into conformity with biblical law and postbiblical tradition.[40] A similar concern has been detected in the Chronicler's attempt to paint Samuel as a Levite in the genealogy in 1 Chronicles 6.[41] This strategy is even clearer in postbiblical tradition: Samuel's status as a Nazirite is explicitly discussed in *m. Naz.* 9:5, with pertinent details appearing in Ben Sira 46:13 and Josephus, *Ant.* 5:344, 347 as well.[42]

If this bit of nomistic harmonization cleared up one difficulty, though, it created a new one. For as Dominique Barthélemy astutely notes, according to a tradition recorded in *m. Naz.* 4:6, a Nazirite may be consecrated by his father but not by

---

[39] G's "until the day of his death" is from Judg 13:7; "and wine and beer he will not drink" resembles Num 6:3 and Judg 13:4, 7, and 14; also, under the influence of Num 6:5, 4Q51 uses the verb עבר instead of M's עלה for "(a razor will not) touch (his head)."

[40] Smith, *Books of Samuel*, 9; Driver, *Notes*, 13; Rofé, "Nomistic Correction," 251; idem, "Midrashic Traits," 82–83; Barthélemy, *Critique textuelle*, 1:141; Klein, *1 Samuel*, 3; Matitiahu Tsevat, "Was Samuel a Nazirite?" in *Sha'arei Talmon: Studies in the Bible, Qumran, and the Ancient Near East Presented to Shemaryahu Talmon* (ed. Michael Fishbane, Emanuel Tov, and Weston W. Fields; Winona Lake, IN: Eisenbrauns), 199–202; cf. McCarter, *I Samuel*, 53–54; Aejmelaeus, "Corruption or Correction?" 15–16.

[41] Rofé, "Nomistic Correction," 251; idem, "Midrashic Traits," 83.

[42] Barthélemy, *Critique textuelle*, 1:141; Rofé, "4QMidrash Samuel?" 70. See Tsevat, "Was Samuel a Nazirite?," on the dubious value of the evidence from Ben Sira and Josephus. More generally on the topic of Nazirites and the Nazirite vow in the Second Temple period, see Stuart Chepey, *Nazirites in Late Second Temple Judaism: A Survey of Ancient Jewish Writings, the New Testament, Archaeological Evidence, and Other Writings from Late Antiquity* (Ancient Judaism and Early Christianity [AGJU] 60; Leiden: Brill, 2005).

his mother.⁴³ On any reading of 1 Samuel 1, however, it was Hannah who dedicated Samuel.⁴⁴ The scribe behind the 4Q51/G Hebrew textual tradition devised a brilliant solution for this blatant contravention of tradition. By inserting the phrase היוצא מפיך, "that which comes out of your mouth," he not only clarified the nature of the utterance referred to by Elkanah (i.e., a vow) but unambiguously invoked legal precedent from Numbers 30, a passage dealing specifically with women's vows. According to that section, except in the case of widows and divorcées, such vows are subject to tacit ratification or explicit annulment on the part of the woman's male guardian. However, while Numbers 30 assumes the male's presence, in the narrative in 1 Samuel 1 Elkanah was not present to hear Hannah's vow and so could not endorse it. Thus, though problematic from the perspective of biblical law and in clear violation of postbiblical tradition, Hannah's vow was treated as binding. Elkanah's "May the LORD establish that which came out of your mouth," which provides the necessary masculine legal ratification, is in this way unmasked as a creative and effective solution to perceived ideological and exegetical problems.⁴⁵ A discussion of the ideological issue is beyond the scope of this article. Regarding the exegetical problem thus resolved, in view of the apparent authenticity and readability of M as it stands, the "solution" was wholly gratuitous.⁴⁶

V. Conclusion

Regardless of whether the complex scenario of nomistic revision detailed in the previous section is accepted, the cryptic intelligibility of M as it stands, the difficulty of arriving at the M and Syriac readings on the basis of the primary reading allegedly reflected in the 4Q51/G tradition, and the problems associated with the Syriac reading—that is, the infelicity of the supposedly underlying Hebrew phraseology and the fact that the reading is undocumented in Hebrew manuscripts—combine to support the central claim of the foregoing arguments, namely, that M's דברו ("his word") is the primary reading in 1 Sam 1:23.

---

[43] Barthélemy, *Critique textuelle*, 1:141.

[44] The Mishnah's prohibition of maternal Nazirite vows may very well have come about as a corrective for a popular misconception itself due at least in part to the story of Samuel's dedication. As Tsevat, has observed, while the Mishnah acknowledges the view that Samuel was thought by some to be a Nazirite, its final word on the matter is, in fact, that he was not ("Was Samuel a Nazirite?" 200 n. 5). Thus, the Mishnaic ban in no way contradicts its understanding of Samuel's status. The explicit designation of Samuel as a Nazirite in 4Q51, on the other hand, is problematic from the standpoint of the Mishnah: the scribe responsible would have either to challenge the tradition upheld in the Mishnah, that is, claim the legitimacy of maternal Nazirite dedication, or to find a way around the apparently efficacious nature of Hannah's dedication of Samuel. He opted for the latter.

[45] Barthélemy, *Critique textuelle*, 1:141.

[46] On the potential textual value of 4Q51 and G in general despite their expansionistic tendencies, see Rofé, "4QMidrash Samuel?" 74; and idem, "Midrashic Traits," 88.

Abingdon ACADEMIC

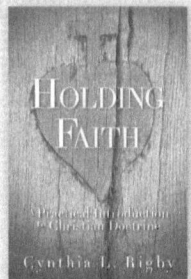

Paul: Apostle and Fellow Traveler
By Jerry L. Sumney
9781426741975

From Crisis to Christ: A Contextual Introduction to the New Testament
By Paul N. Anderson
9781426751042

Holding Faith: A Practical Introduction to Christian Doctrine
By Cynthia L. Rigby
9781426758140

Available February 2015

Available March 2015

Available April 2015

Barnabas vs. Paul: To Encourage or Confront?
By C.K. Robertson
9781630882778

The History of Theological Education
By Justo L. González
9781426781919

Christ and Community: The Gospel Witness to Jesus
By Suzanne Watts Henderson
9781426793080

Abingdon Press
AbingdonPress.com | 800.251.3320

Visit AbingdonAcademic.com to learn more and request an exam copy today.

4QPs^x: A Collective Interpretation of Psalm 89:20–38

MIKA S. PAJUNEN
mika.s.pajunen@helsinki.fi
University of Helsinki, Helsinki FIN-00014, Finland

This study deals with a small, puzzling fragment, 4QPs^x (4QPs89), that has been aptly described in DJD 16 as "one of the most unusual Psalms manuscripts found at Qumran." The fragment has text parallel to MT Ps 89:20–31, but with differences in the form of the text and its order. Most scholars have argued that the text form of 4QPs^x should be seen as a source for, or an early version of, Psalm 89. I offer a different assessment of the manuscript here. First, to determine whether 4QPs^x originally contained the whole of Psalm 89 or only a part of it, several material aspects relating to the actual fragment are considered. Then the contents of the fragment and the text's structure are analyzed. I conclude that a common motif behind the text form of 4QPs^x can account for most of the variants and that the text of the fragment is secondary to MT Psalm 89.

A puzzling fragment (4QPs^x = 4QPs89) containing a text parallel to at least part of MT Psalm 89 was discovered among the manuscripts of cave 4 at Qumran. Although the fragment is small (6.3 cm high, 4.4 cm wide) it has received a fair amount of scholarly attention because of its contents.[1] The fragment has aptly been

[1] The fragment (at the time classified as 4Q236) was preliminarily published in 1966 by József T. Milik, "Fragment d'une source du Psautier (4QPs89) et fragments des Jubilés, du Document de Damas, d'un phylactère dans la Grotte 4 de Qumran," *RB* 73 (1966): 94–106. Subsequently, interpretations of the text were offered by Johannes P. M. van der Ploeg ("Le sens et un problème textuel du Ps LXXXIX," in *Mélanges bibliques et orientaux en l'honneur de M. Henri Cazelles* [ed. A. Caquot and M. Delcor; AOAT 212; Neukirchen-Vluyn: Neukirchener Verlag, 1981], 471–81), Patrick W. Skehan ("Gleanings from Psalm Texts from Qumrân," in Caquot and Delcor, *Mélanges bibliques*, 439–52), Uwe Gleßmer ("Das Textwachstum von Ps 89 und ein Qumranfragment," *BN* 65 [1992]: 55–73), and Peter Flint ("A Form of Psalm 89 [4Q236 = 4QPs89]," in *The Dead Sea Scrolls: Hebrew, Aramaic and Greek Texts with English Translations*, vol. 4A, *Pseudepigraphic and Non-Masoretic Psalms and Prayers* [ed. James H. Charlesworth and Henry W. L. Rietz; Princeton Theological Seminary Dead Sea Scrolls Project; Tübingen: Mohr Siebeck, 1997], 40–45). The official edition of the fragment was published in 2000, prepared by Eugene Ulrich et al., "4QPs^x," in *Qumran Cave 4.XI: Psalms to Chronicles* (ed. Eugene Ulrich et

described as "one of the most unusual Psalms manuscripts found at Qumran" as well as a "battered and isolated bit."[2] It has text corresponding to MT Ps 89:20–31, but with differences in the form of the text and its order.[3] Scholarly estimations of the importance of these variations for understanding the textual development of Psalm 89 vary considerably. At one end of the spectrum are scholars who argue that the fragment is part of an ancient source for the Psalter or at least for Psalm 89.[4] At the other end is the view of Patrick W. Skehan, who argues that the fragment is a random text jotted down from memory by an inept scribe and as such clearly secondary to MT Psalm 89.[5] Some scholars have positioned themselves in the middle by taking the text of the fragment into account only in terms of variant readings and not with regard to the text as a whole, or only in discussions of the importance of the text for understanding Psalm 89 without considering the text-critical importance of the fragment.[6] Thus far only Johannes P. M. van der Ploeg has suggested that the fragment should be viewed mainly as something other than as a text purporting to give a version of Psalm 89. He argues that it belonged to a libretto of messianic testimonia, was intentionally modified for this purpose, and is thus secondary to MT Psalm 89.[7]

---

al.; DJD 16; Oxford: Clarendon, 2000), 163–69. The designation of the fragment was changed in the *editio princeps* to 4QPs^x to account for its perceived status as a Psalms manuscript. Since that publication, two articles have appeared that deal with this fragment in some detail: Klaus Koch, "Königspsalmen und ihr ritueller Hintergrund: Erwägungen zu Ps. 89,20–38 und Ps. 20 und ihren Vorstufen," in *The Book of Psalms: Composition and Reception* (ed. Peter W. Flint and Patrick D. Miller Jr.; VTSup 99; Leiden: Brill, 2005), 9–52; and Matthew Mitchell, "Genre Disputes and Communal Accusatory Laments: Reflections on the Genre of Psalm LXXXIX," *VT* 55 (2005): 511–27.

[2] Ulrich et al., "4QPs^x," 163; Skehan, "Gleanings," 439.

[3] The lists of variant readings found in the Psalms manuscripts from Qumran compiled by Peter W. Flint reveal that two texts stand out because of a large number of variants in a single Psalm (*The Dead Sea Psalms Scrolls and the Book of Psalms* [STDJ 27; Leiden: Brill, 1997]). One is 4QPs^x and the other is a version of Psalm 91 found in 11QapocrPs VI, 3–13. In the case of Psalm 91, most of the variant readings apparently stem from a common motif and mark intentional redactional activity, as I have recently argued in Mika S. Pajunen, "Qumranic Psalm 91: A Structural Analysis," in *Scripture in Transition: Essays on Septuagint, Hebrew Bible, and Dead Sea Scrolls in Honour of Raija Sollamo* (ed. Anssi Voitila and Jutta Jokiranta; JSJSup 126; Leiden: Brill, 2008), 591–605.

[4] See Milik, "Fragment," 102–4; Gleßmer, "Das Textwachstum," 71; Flint, "Form of Psalm 89," 41; Ulrich et al., "4QPs^x," 164; Koch, "Königspsalmen," 26–31.

[5] Skehan, "Gleanings," 439, 441.

[6] See, e.g., Mitchell Dahood, *Psalms*, vol. 2, *51–100* (AB 17; Garden City, NY: Doubleday, 1968), 316–17; Marvin E. Tate, *Psalms 51–100* (WBC 20; Dallas: Word, 1990), 410. Mitchell does not assess the text-critical importance of the text, but his view on the text of 4QPs^x as a whole is revealed by his comments, and these imply that he considers the text secondary to the MT ("Genre Disputes," 512, 520–21).

[7] Van der Ploeg, "Le sens et un problème textuel," 480–81. Cf. Michael Pietsch, *"Dieser ist der Sproß Davids ...": Studien zur Rezeptionsgeschichte der Nathanverheißung im alttestamentlichen,*

It seems that most scholars, when evaluating the importance of this text, have followed the classic rule of textual (and redaction) criticism that the shorter version is the more original one, and there is not much argumentation as to why the text of 4QPs^x should be seen as a source of MT Psalm 89. József Milik proposed this on the basis of language, namely, the orthography and some word forms,[8] but he did not explain the different order of the verses (or the ones missing from 4QPs^x). Uwe Gleßmer compared 4QPs^x, MT Psalm 89, and Nathan's oracle in 2 Samuel 7 and suggested that 4QPs^x might have an earlier form of the text than the other two.[9] Klaus Koch took this line of thought to its limits: he points out that 4QPs^x has clear secondary tendencies in comparison to the MT text of Psalm 89, and he claims that these tendencies are the work of a redactor and that by removing them layer by layer one would eventually get to the original source text of Psalm 89 (and 2 Samuel 7).[10]

In this study I will show that there is a common motif in 4QPs^x that can account for the textual variants without having to posit theoretical stages of textual development between the texts. In fact, it will be demonstrated that 4QPs^x should be seen mainly as something other than a text presenting a version or even a direct quotation of Psalm 89, and hence the rule of a shorter text being more original is not at all applicable to the text of the fragment. It has been assumed that the fragment's text is from a variant version of Psalm 89 rather than the MT. The variants, however, do not attest to textual growth prior to the MT Psalm 89 but are due to later interpretive modifications adapting the oracle to David to a changed cultural setting. These claims are based on an analysis of what the fragment 4QPs^x actually is and how it relates to MT Psalm 89. I approach these questions by first examining several different material aspects (e.g., the fragment itself and the script) that will help in determining whether the manuscript originally contained all of Psalm 89 or only a part of it. Then I consider the actual text and its structure and offer an overall interpretation of the variants and their significance.

I. ANALYSIS OF THE MATERIAL ASPECTS

Skehan argued that the fragment comes from a blank handle sheet of a scroll already in use. The rest of the scroll would have contained another text, unrelated to the text on the fragment, and this short text on the fragment would have been written from memory on the back side of the handle sheet attached to the final sheet of the manuscript.[11] Surprisingly enough, Skehan's suggestion has not

---

zwischentestamentlichen und neutestamentlichen Schriftum (WMANT 100; Neukirchen-Vluyn: Neukirchener Verlag, 2003), 113–15.
    [8] Milik, "Fragment," 95–104.
    [9] Gleßmer, "Das Textwachstum," 71.
    [10] Koch, "Königspsalmen," 20–31.
    [11] Skehan, "Gleanings," 441.

merited comments from other scholars, nor have other materially based suggestions been made as to how much material, if any, there was before this fragment. Milik proposed that the fragment comes from the final sheet of a longer manuscript that would have been a source for the Psalter and ended with this version of Psalm 89,[12] but he does not give arguments relating to the material that would truly support this view. Van der Ploeg's suggestion that the text belongs to a collection of messianic testimonia also presupposes other material (either preceding or following the current text), and Ulrich et al. offer the possibility that a couple of words (אז דברת) found in MT Psalm 89:20 but not fitting in 4QPs^x line 1 might be included "at the end of the previous column," which implies that there were more columns before the text that now survives.[13]

However, Skehan appears to be correct about the fragment belonging to a handle sheet. He argued this on the basis that letters on the fragment are frequently crowded, which implies a limitation of writing space that is hard to account for if the text continued onto another sheet.[14] This is a valid argument but not decisive on its own, as it does not rule out preceding text. A more conclusive factor is usual scribal practice, which was to write the intended text on different sheets and only afterwards sew the sheets together.[15] In this fragment it is evident that the sewing was there before the text, as the scribe obviously had to avoid the stitching present on the left edge of the fragment by placing a few of the last letters above the last word on several consecutive lines (at least lines 5 and 6).[16]

Another point in this regard is the lack of ruling, both horizontal and vertical, on the fragment. There is no ruling visible on the fragment, and it is evident from the way the lines slant—especially as they slant in different directions—that the ruling has not simply faded but was not there in the first place (which is compatible with handle sheets). Finally, if at least some of the reconstructions based on MT Psalm 89 are correct, the original dimensions of the fragment fit a handle sheet very well[17] but would make a strikingly short column (especially as there should normally be at least one centimeter of space left blank at the left edge for the stitching). Thus, unless it is supposed that this fragment is an exception to how things were

---

[12] Milik, "Fragment," 103–4. Gleßmer ("Das Textwachstum," 67) supports Milik's view of the material.

[13] Van der Ploeg, "Le sens et un problème textuel," 481; Ulrich et al., "4QPs^x," 166.

[14] Skehan, "Gleanings," 441.

[15] Emanuel Tov, *Scribal Practices and Approaches Reflected in the Texts Found in the Judean Desert* (STDJ 54; Leiden: Brill, 2004), 37. He also notes a couple of possible exceptions to this practice.

[16] Ulrich et al. also note that the scribe had to avoid the stitching on these lines, but they do not draw any conclusions from this ("4QPs^x," 166–67).

[17] Tov indicates that there is some variance detectable in the preserved handle sheets; for example, some of them are ruled but others are not (*Scribal Practices*, 114–17). The original dimensions of most handle sheets can only be conjectured, but, for example, 11QapocrPs has a seven-centimeter-wide handle sheet. The handle sheet under investigation would be a bit under six and a half centimeters.

usually done, it is likely that the text was written down later than the rest of the scroll it was on (the sewing does indicate that there was something else on this scroll and the fragment is not an isolated piece of leather). There was no material preceding this fragment, and so this text does not have the beginning of Psalm 89 but only a section of it, starting from v. 20. Although the exact original dimensions of the handle sheet, and particularly its height, can only be guessed at, the way that the scribe has written the text would seem to indicate that it probably was not a very tall strip of leather and it is doubtful that the whole ending of the Psalm would have fit the leather even in a shorter text form. Therefore, it is likely that, if the text was covering a coherent whole of the Psalm, it is either an abbreviation or an early form of God's promise to David and his descendants in vv. 20–38.[18]

Skehan did not discuss why the text should have been on the back side of a handle sheet and not the front. This is an important factor because, if the text was written on the back, it would likely have been a secondary text in comparison to the text already present on the scroll. It would have been at the end of the scroll and in the innermost layer, which would not have been visible until the scroll was almost completely rolled open (and even then only partly). On the other hand, if the text is written on the front side, it means that it was written on the handle sheet preceding the material on the scroll and would likely have a connection with the text already there as it would have been the first thing seen when the scroll was opened. The observation by Ulrich et al. that "the writing surface was well-prepared"[19] is a strong argument for the writing being on the front side and consequently on the handle sheet at the beginning of the scroll. Additional confirmation for this can be gathered by analyzing some of the characteristic features of the scribe's style.

There are several recurring problems in the text that have led to criticism of the scribe's skills, and Skehan goes so far as to call him inept.[20] There are many reasons for this assessment in the small amount of text available. First of all, fitting the text to the available space has presented a constant problem for the scribe. The first line is really crammed with letters, and it seems that it was either written later or the scribe initially thought that he would need considerably more space for writing the intended text than is available on the fragment. This crowding of letters continues in other lines, but, on the other hand, the script in these is quite large in comparison with most of the Qumran manuscripts and the text would have fitted well if the scribe had written a bit more neatly. As the text now stands, space is not always left between words (e.g., מזשמן in line 3) and half the lines end with crowding at the left edge (esp. lines 4–7). Furthermore, there are many small mistakes corrected later by the same scribe, and, for example, the use of the final form of

---

[18] This appears to be a distinct section in Psalm 89, and, according to Frank Lothar Hossfeld and Erich Zenger, there has long been a consensus about the division of Psalm 89 into three parts: vv. 2–19, 20–38, and 39–52 (*Psalms 2: A Commentary on Psalms 51–100* [Hermeneia; Minneapolis: Fortress, 2005], 402).

[19] Ulrich et al., "4QPs^x," 163.

[20] Skehan, "Gleanings," 441–42.

mem varies (mostly the scribe also uses the medial form in final position, but the final form does appear once in תכנבם in line 4). In view of the large number of mistakes, and especially the spacing of the text, it is unlikely that an experienced scribe would have written this even in haste. Therefore, this is likely the work of a beginner who was still learning his trade.[21]

Skehan used the scribe's errors and the Aramaic influence found in the text as indicators that the scribe was not following a written prototype.[22] If the mistakes had been left uncorrected, his view would be easier to accept. However, the scribe has corrected his errors by inserting supralinear (lines 6–7) and infralinear (line 1) letters, dotting out an extra word (line 4) and apparently also changing a letter from *yod* to *reš* (line 2).[23] In addition, if the first line was written later, as might well be the case,[24] this would seem to indicate that there was a written prototype rather than a text put down from memory, because it is hard to imagine that the scribe would have started from the middle of a verse and then later put in the first part as an afterthought, as Skehan suggests.[25] The possible Aramaic influence in the text can be explained just as well (if not better) by its presence in the exemplar rather than as a characteristic of the scribe. These indicators might not make it a certainty that the scribe had a written prototype, but they do point in that direction. If this is the case, the text is probably not a random text written down on the back side of a handle sheet at the end of a scroll where it would not have been seen unless the scroll was turned over. Rather, the effort put into using a written prototype and correcting scribal errors suggests that the text had some specific purpose and that it was thus copied on the front side of the handle sheet rather than the back.

The paleographical dating of the fragment is made difficult by the lack of material and consistency. Two paleographic dates have previously been suggested: Milik dated the script between 175 and 125 B.C.E., which was later followed by Ulrich et al.,[26] but van der Ploeg posited a substantially later date, in the second half of the first century B.C.E.[27] Although no definitive answers can be given on this question, it appears that both of these dates might be incorrect and that the fragment should rather be dated roughly to the middle of the Hasmonean period.

The script is Hasmonean with many semicursive elements.[28] There are no evident Herodian forms (see esp. *ʾalep, he, ḥet, zayin, mem, nun*). There are several

[21] See van der Ploeg, "Le sens et un problème textuel," 475.
[22] Skehan, "Gleanings," 441.
[23] Ulrich et al., "4QPs^x," 166.
[24] So Milik, "Fragment," 95–96; Skehan, "Gleanings," 440; Flint, "Form of Psalm 89," 42; Ulrich et al., "4QPs^x," 163.
[25] Skehan, "Gleanings," 440–41.
[26] Milik, "Fragment," 95, 102. Ulrich et al. accept this dating ("4QPs^x," 163).
[27] Van der Ploeg, "Le sens et un problème textuel," 475
[28] The script is analyzed in accordance with the typology established by Frank Moore Cross, "The Development of the Jewish Scripts," in *The Bible and the Ancient Near East: Essays in Honor of William Foxwell Albright* (ed. G. Ernest Wright; Garden City, NY: Doubleday, 1961), 133–202.

early Hasmonean features in the letters, but also some more developed forms. *Waw* and *yod* are generally distinguishable from each other, but the leg of *yod* has lengthened so that several times the letters are of similar size (see line 5 יד, line 7 אני). *Zayin* and the vertical of *lamed* are made with single strokes with no enlargement of the top (line 8 יעזבו, line 6 לענותו). The letters with semicursive features agree closely with those found in 4QDan[c] (esp. final *mem*, *nun*, final *nun*), which is dated to ca. 100–50 B.C.E. A development toward uniformity of letter size is discernible in ʾ*alep*, *dalet*, *mem*, *nun*, ʿ*ayin*, and *taw*. The form of *taw* follows the formal tradition, not the looping *taw* typical of the semicursive script. Its legs are of equal length and the left leg ends with a smooth curve into an angular base, not a curved flourish (line 5 שמתי, line 7 את).

A more coherent view of the text has been gained by the analysis of these material aspects. The fragment is part of the handle sheet preceding a scroll that was already written and sewn together before this text was put on it. The text consists of some verses of Psalm 89 starting from v. 20 and likely not going beyond v. 38. Thus, this fragment is not a part of a version of the whole Psalm 89. There are two possible reasons for inserting this bit of text before another composition. Either it is part of the composition already on the scroll and was accidentally left out when the scroll was first inscribed, or it was inserted as a fitting introduction to the text previously written on the scroll. The contents of the manuscript and its connection with MT Psalm 89 are analyzed next in order to illuminate the message of the text, which should in turn establish a basis for any future attempts to place this fragment as part of a particular composition.

II. Text and Translation

4QPs[x]   MT Psalm 89:20–31

top margin

1 [בחזון ל]בֿחריך תאֿמר שתעו[זר על   20 אז דברת בחזון לחסידיך ותאמר שויתי
  גב]וֿר[ ]   עזר על גבור הרימותי בחור מעם 21 מצאתי
2 [הרימותי ב]חרֿ מן עֿם מצתי[ו [דוד עבדי בשמן קדשי משחתיו 22 אשר ידי
3 [ומשחתיו]מֿזֿשמן קדשי *vacat*   תכון עמו אף זרועי תאמצנו 23 לא ישא אויב
4 [יהוה אשֿ]רֿ {שמן} ידו תכנכם   בו ובן עולה לא יעננו 24 וכתותי מפניו צריו
   ת   ומשנאיו אגוף 25 ואמונתי וחסדי עמו ובשמי
5 [ותאמצכם ו]שֿמתי בים יד בנהר   תרום קרנו 26 ושמתי בים ידו ובנהרות ימינו
   יֿ   וֿ   27 הוא יקראני אבי אתה אלי וצור ישועתי
6 [ימין לא יוסיף] אואב ובן על לענות   28 אף אני בכור אתנהו עליון למלכי ארץ
   נ   29 לעולם אשמור לו חסדי ובריתי נאמנת
7 [יקראני א]בֿי את אני בכור אֿתֿנ[ו]   30 ושמתי לעד זרעו וכסאו כימי שמים
8 [עליון למלכי א]רֿץֿ אם יעזבו   31 אם יעזבו בניו תורתי

1. [In a vision to] your chosen ones you will say: "a hel[per] has been appointed [upon] a migh[ty one]
2. [I have exalted one ch]osen from the people. I have found [him]
3. [and anointed him] with some of my holy oil." vacat
4. [It is Yhwh who]se {oil} hand will establish you (pl.)
5. [and support you (pl.): "And] I will set the hand on the sea and on the rivers
6. [the right hand. No more will] the enemy and the son of iniquity oppress him.
7. [He will cry to me:] 'You are my [fa]ther,' I will make [him] my firstborn
8. [the highest among the kings] of the earth. If they forsake

20 Once you spoke in a vision to your devoted ones, and said: "I have set help on a mighty one, I have exalted one chosen from the people. 21 I have found David my servant, with my holy oil have I anointed him. 22 My hand will remain with him, and my arm will strengthen him. 23 No enemy will rise up against him, and the son of iniquity will not oppress him. 24 I will crush his enemies before him, and strike down those who hate him. 25 And my faithfulness and steadfast love are with him, and in my name his horn is exalted. 26 And I will set his hand on the sea and his right hand on the rivers. 27 He will cry to me: 'You are my Father, my God, and the Rock of my salvation!' 28 Also, I will make him the firstborn, the highest among the kings of the earth. 29 Forever I will keep my steadfast love for him, and my covenant will stand firm for him. 30 I will establish his seed forever, and his throne as long as the days of heaven. 31 If his sons forsake my law, and do not walk according to my ordinances,

III. Textual Notes

The letters on the fragment have, for the most part, been read in similar ways by scholars, and the reconstructions offered are also quite close because they are based on MT Psalm 89. Where there are differences in readings, scholars basically follow one of two interpretations. One way of reading the disputed letters is argued by Milik (followed by Gleßmer and in most cases also by van der Ploeg),[29] but the readings offered by Skehan (followed by Peter Flint and Ulrich et al.) fit the remaining traces of the letters better in every case, and the text presented here agrees in all these instances with the latter group of scholars.[30] Sufficient arguments for these

---

[29] Milik ("Fragment," 96–98), van der Ploeg ("Le sens et un problème textuel," 476), and Gleßmer ("Das Textwachstum," 60–66) read the text differently in the following cases. In line 2 instead of בחר they read בחיר. In line 4 they read ידי instead of ידו. Line 6 is read and reconstructed quite differently by them: ימין לו ישאו] אבו בן על לוענוה. Milik reconstructs הוא at the beginning of line 7 following the MT, and the last word of the line is read as אתנן.

[30] Skehan, "Gleanings," 442–43; Flint, "Form of Psalm 89," 42–44; Ulrich et al., "4QPsˣ," 165–66.

readings,³¹ and reconstructions stemming from them, have been given by the above-mentioned scholars, and consequently the following notes cover only issues where the reading or reconstruction offered here differs from all the previous editions.³²

Lines 1–2. The earliest PAM photo, 40.620, has the clearest image of these lines, and some of the first letters in line 1 can be more confidently identified from this photograph. There is also a small piece of leather in the upper left corner of the fragment that broke off between the taking of this photo and PAM 41.438 and has gone unnoticed before this. It shows the infralinear *gimel* in גּבֿ[ור completely, part of the apparent *bet* following it, as well as nearly all of the *yod* at the end of line 2. Unfortunately, most of the surface of this piece is gone, as is evident from the way both *bet* and *yod* break off, and it cannot help with verifying the rest of the reconstructions offered to complete these lines.

Lines 2–3. David is explicitly mentioned in v. 21 of MT Psalm 89, and because of this, the name David (דוד) has been reconstructed in the lacuna preceding line 3 by most who have dealt with the fragment in detail.³³ But from the point of view of content (see below), it is doubtful whether David would be explicitly mentioned in 4QPsˣ. There are three features in the text of the fragment that support this view. First is the spacing used by the scribe for the last word in line 2 (מצתי). The spacing between the letters in this word is markedly larger than elsewhere on the fragment and indicates that this was most likely the last word the scribe intended to write on the line and because of that he spread the letters to fill out most of the line.³⁴ However, the word דוד is short and would almost (but not quite) fit the end of line 2 even with the current spacing. If the scribe had written מצתי in his usual way, דוד would have fit well at the end of the line. Thus, it is likely that the scribe intended to write a longer word next that had no possibility of fitting at the end of line 2. Second, the reconstruction of דוד at the beginning of line 3 is unlikely because of the change of preposition from ב to מן in v. 21. Starting a new colon with מן would be quite awkward; the verb should come before it. Last, and most important, the reconstruction משחתיו אשר generally suggested for the lacuna preceding line 4 is

---

³¹ There is one exception that has to be noted. Ulrich et al. argue that the supralinear letter near the end of line 7 cannot be meant as the final letter of the word because it is medial in form ("4QPsˣ," 167). This is not a decisive argument since at least in 1QIsaᵃ medial forms are used in supralinear corrections even when meant as a final letter. More important for deciding this issue is the placement of the supralinear letter. It is not written at the end of the line as are the supralinear letters in the previous two lines. Therefore, it is not to be read as the final letter of the word but as a medial one.

³² I have studied the available PAM photos of the fragment (40.620, 41.438, 43.399) and the original fragment for the readings.

³³ Milik, "Fragment," 98; Skehan, "Gleanings," 442; Gleßmer, "Das Textwachstum," 58–66; Flint, "Form of Psalm 89," 44; Ulrich et al., "4QPsˣ," 165.

³⁴ See Tov, *Scribal Practices*, 106–8.

much too long for it.³⁵ This plainly argues in favor of a different place for the verb, and in light of all these considerations, I suggest that משחתיו should be reconstructed in the lacuna at the beginning of line 3, and not in the lacuna in line 4, and that a suffix (3rd masc. sg.) should therefore be reconstructed in the lacuna at the end of line 2.

Line 3. This line ends in a *vacat*, that is, an empty space left intentionally by the scribe. It is quite large (ca. 1.2 cm) in comparison with the overall scale of the fragment, and there are two plausible reasons for it. The first possibility is that there was a long word beginning line 4 that would not have fit the end of line 3, and the second is that the *vacat* signifies a break in the composition.³⁶ Both are valid options, and there is no certainty as to which might be the correct one. If the scribe wrote the last word of the previous line with larger spaces between letters to cover most of the empty space left on the line, the same has not been done in this line. Furthermore, the penultimate word is written together with the preceding word, which could indicate that the *vacat* is meant as a compositional break because writing the words together would not have been necessary otherwise. This view is supported by the content, as there is a clear break in the text at this point, and consequently I hesitantly prefer this alternative.

Line 4. The reconstruction יהוה אשר is suggested as a tentative solution because it fits the lacuna perfectly, makes the evident change in address clear, and retains the sense and almost exact wording found in the MT. The accidental שמן in line 4 could in this case be explained by postulating that the scribe still had the previous verse in mind and hence first wrote יהוה אשר שמן ("Yʜᴡʜ whose oil …") before realizing that he should have written ידו ("his hand") instead.

Line 6. There have been many hypotheses and linguistic arguments as to why the *waw* was not written in the middle of על even though it is in a consonantal

---

³⁵ Almost all of the reconstructions offered by Skehan ("Gleanings," 442), Flint ("Form of Psalm 89," 44), and Ulrich et al. ("4QPsˣ," 165) make the lines practically the same length (as they should be). There are two notable exceptions: this reconstruction would make the line nearly one centimeter longer than the other lines, and the reconstruction in line 6 (ימין לא יוסיף) is slightly longer than the others. Reconstructing both אשר and משחתה or משחתיו in line 4 (thus Milik, "Fragment," 98; Flint, "Form of Psalm 89," 44; Ulrich et al., "4QPsˣ," 165) is obviously too long for the lacuna. On the other hand, reconstructing only משחתיו (thus Skehan, "Gleanings," 442) would make the line a bit short in comparison with the other lines, and, moreover, *waw* is not compatible with the ink traces of the final letter preserved at the edge of the lacuna. The reconstruction in line 6 fits the available space, albeit barely, if the gap between the words is similar to the spacing at the end of the same line (and not, e.g., line 4) and the letters are written quite tightly. Thus, the reconstruction of line 6 is still a real possibility, and, because of a lack of convincing alternatives, I accept it, although with some hesitation.

³⁶ The use of *vacats* to indicate compositional breaks is well attested in the Qumran corpus; see, e.g., 1QpHab. For further examples and the practice of marking compositional breaks in general, see Tov, *Scribal Practices*, 143–66.

position in the word,[37] but it appears to have been there all along as a supralinear correction. The vertical stroke of *lamed* in עֹל changes to a shape closely resembling the head of ו/י at the very top, and careful observation reveals that the vertical stroke is not completely continuous. It seems that the stroke breaks off and an extralinear *waw* is written above it. The identification is not certain, but the trace is definitely ink and not a shadow. It must also be noted that, if the only other preserved *lamed* in this fragment is correctly drawn (line 6, ולענותו), the vertical stroke of *lamed* did not have a broadened top in this hand.

IV. The Content of 4QPs[x] and Its Relation to MT Psalm 89:20-31

4QPs[x] has numerous differences from the Masoretic version of Ps 89:20-31,[38] and there has been much discussion about which reading is in each instance the more original one.[39] Thus far, no one has offered a single, coherent explanation that would account for most of the variants, but there does seem to be one. The suggested motive is found most clearly presented in lines 4-5 of the Qumran text (v. 22). There it can clearly be observed that God's promises to David are adapted to a collective use. The collective reinterpretation of earlier passages in the MT Psalter is a phenomenon of the postexilic period and is present explicitly in some passages of the MT Psalter and implicitly in many more. These are passages where a reference to an individual has later been interpreted in a collective way and the text has been changed to accommodate this interpretation. Marko Marttila has analyzed these references in the MT Psalter, and Psalm 89 is one of the psalms included in his study.[40] For some reason, however, he does not deal with 4QPs[x]. This is unfortunate, because 4QPs[x] explicitly demonstrates that someone in the Second Temple period did interpret Ps 89:22 in a collective way. Koch noticed this tendency in 4QPs[x] and correctly judged it to be a secondary feature in comparison with the MT tradition, but he did not pursue it beyond giving one possible example

---

[37] Milik, "Fragment," 102; Dahood, *Psalms*, vol. 2, *51–100*, 316; van der Ploeg, "Le sens et un problème textuel," 480; Skehan, "Gleanings," 441–42; Flint, "Form of Psalm 89," 43; Ulrich et al., "4QPs[x]," 166.

[38] The LXX supports the MT in all but one of these cases (for this variant see n. 52 below). For a thorough study of MT Psalm 89, its literary layers, colometrical structure, *Sitz im Leben*, and connections with other texts, see Timo Veijola, *Verheißung in der Krise: Studien zur Literatur und Theologie der Exilszeit anhand des 89. Psalms* (AASF B 220; Helsinki: Suomalainen tiedeakatemia, 1982).

[39] E.g., Milik, "Fragment," 94–106; Dahood, *Psalms*, vol. 2, *51–100*, 316–17; Tate, *Psalms 51–100*, 410. For a full list of the variants, see Ulrich et al., "4QPs[x]," 167.

[40] Marttila, *Collective Reinterpretation in the Psalms: A Study of the Redaction History of the Psalter* (FAT 2/13; Tübingen: Mohr Siebeck, 2006), 135–44. For collective aspects in Psalm 89, see also Veijola, *Verheißung in der Krise*, 135; Pietsch, *"Dieser ist der Sproß Davids,"* 113, 115, 119, 121.

of it (line 1, עוזר). Furthermore, he claimed that the text of 4QPs^x is more original than MT Psalm 89 after this tendency is removed from it as a later redaction layer.[41] However, when the textual variants are seen from this perspective, it is obvious that this is the central reason behind the Qumran version. It is a collective interpretation of the core of God's promise to David,[42] which has been both edited and abbreviated.[43]

In the following discussion, the text is viewed from this angle; that is, I assume that MT Psalm 89 presents the earlier version of the text.[44] In v. 20, the recipients of the oracle have been changed into the "chosen" of God. This might denote a specific group at some point in time, but it is nonetheless a more general name than the חסידיך ("your faithful ones") in the MT, which is a term that might also have had some political implications.[45] Another alteration in v. 20 is the time frame of the oracle. It is brought from a past event to a future/present one by leaving out אז דברת ("once you spoke"). After this setting comes what God has said and will say to his chosen ones. It is likely that the rarer verbal root שוה of the MT is here changed to the much more common שית.[46] The verb is likely used here in the passive sense in line with בחר in the next colon, but Skehan's suggestion that the form is due to Aramaic influence is also a possibility.[47] The change from noun to participle in עוזר ("helper") is, in Koch's view, part of the democratization tendency of 4QPs^x, and this is quite possible.[48] But the noun is used many times in the Hebrew Bible in the meaning "one who helps" (see Gen 2:18, 20; Deut 33:7; Pss 33:20; 115:9–11), so the slight change from noun to participle might simply reflect that the noun had already been read in this meaning and was at some point accidentally changed to the participial form that has the exact same sense. As this idea of a heavenly helper is here connected with divine election, which is explicitly present in both the preceding and following colons, it means that God's election includes here the promise of a helper for the chosen person or group. Whether this is God or an agent of God is open to question.

---

[41] Koch, "Königspsalmen," 26–31.

[42] That is, the core of the promise from a collective point of view; for an individual like David, the promise of a dynasty would have been part of the core.

[43] The tendency of 4QPs^x to abbreviate the text of MT Psalm 89 was noted already by Skehan, "Gleanings," 443.

[44] I present the material in this way instead of first giving the results of the analysis inductively in order to save space and to preserve the clarity of the argumentation. All major differences between the texts are noted.

[45] See Tate, *Psalms 51–100*, 410.

[46] So also van der Ploeg, "Le sens et un problème textuel," 479. Milik interpreted the word as a Hebrew form with ancient orthography, but, especially in view of the whole text, this seems unlikely.

[47] Skehan, "Gleanings," 442.

[48] Koch, "Königspsalmen," 28.

It is doubtful whether David is mentioned in the Qumran text in v. 21 (see above). Although this is not certain since the text is in a lacuna, it is more likely that there would have been a more general reference than a mention of the specific figure of David. Anointing could be understood in a collective way in the post-exilic period. This has been shown by Marttila's study of the term משיח ("anointed") in some of the postexilic psalms.[49] It appears, therefore, that the reference to the choosing of David in MT Psalm 89 is here modified to a more general remark about God electing chosen individuals (or groups) from the people.

After v. 21 there is a break in 4QPs[x] that has not been noted previously. Skehan, followed by Flint and Ulrich et al., claims that 4QPs[x] would have said that the hand establishing the chosen in v. 22 would actually be David's, not God's, as in the MT.[50] Without going into the theological implications of this reading, it is to be noted that it does not fit the sense of the passage. There is a change of address here: it is not God speaking to David but a reader leading the audience to a new point in the oracle (the same voice that addresses God in v. 20 and recites the text). This is more probable than the voice of God being directed suddenly to the audience in the present day and then turning back again to David in the historical scene.[51] The promises made to David in v. 22 are directed to the chosen ones in the Qumran fragment. Moreover, at least the first promise has a slightly different meaning: in it the past promise of God to remain with David from that point onward is changed by a small alteration in verb form into a future promise to establish the chosen (cf. 2 Sam 7:13). If the suggested reconstruction is correct, the second part of v. 22 has

---

[49] Marttila, *Collective Reinterpretation*, 177–91.

[50] Skehan, "Gleanings," 442; Flint, "Form of Psalm 89," 41; Ulrich et al., "4QPs[x]," 164. Mitchell interprets the verse in 4QPs[x] in a fashion similar to these scholars and concludes that this feature and the absence of the word חסד in 4QPs[x] bring the emphasis of Psalm 89 as a whole and its original *Gattung* as an angry lament into sharper focus ("Genre disputes," 320–21, 326). Mitchell's argumentation presumes that the word חסד would have been in the text but was removed at some point because otherwise its absence in a text does not mean anything; that is, if a word was never part of a composition, its absence cannot in itself be used as an argument for anything. In order for the absence of a word to be meaningful for understanding a version of a text, the word needs to have been present in the *Vorlage* of the version that does not have it anymore. If then the word would have been removed from a version of Psalm 89 at some point, it is not evident how this new version of the psalm could be used to argue on behalf of the *original* setting of Psalm 89. More importantly, there is nothing present in the text of 4QPs[x] itself that would make the psalm a lament, nor is there anything in it that might be termed angry. On the contrary, it plainly looks forward to a time when God's eternal promise will be made a reality again in the fate of God's new chosen ones.

[51] The setting of vv. 20–38 in the MT tradition also makes evident that the psalm is reciting a promise once made by Yhwh to David and his descendants that is, in the final section of the Psalm (vv. 39–53), contrasted with the present situation; see Hossfeld and Zenger, *Psalms 2*, 410. MT Psalm 89 does not give the promise to anyone at the moment of recitation, which the Qumran text explicitly does.

the same meaning as in the MT, but it has been abbreviated. This collective interpretation of the verse has a foundation already in the MT text. If one reads עמו as "his people" instead of "with him," one can establish the interpretation in the text. What this interim speech directed to the audience promises is that God will establish the chosen and support them after that.

Proof of the promise that was just recited is then given by continuing the oracle once more in a more direct quotation and with a return to the first person speech of God. Verse 26 has been moved to after v. 22 in 4QPs[x] because it states the first part of the promise just given to the audience: God will establish you, namely, give you control of the land. The verb כון that is used in v. 22 is often connected with establishing a kingdom or throne (e.g., 2 Sam 5:12; 7:12; 1 Chr 28:7), and v. 26 speaks about God stretching the hand of his chosen one from the sea to the rivers, that is, establishing the kingdom by giving the land. Verse 23, which follows next, does the same thing for the second part of the received oracle.[52] It gives the promise of God's support a concrete frame. Verse 27a continues with the same theme, and v. 28 comes back to the idea of establishing, rounding out the promise God has given to all his chosen: the land and his support.[53]

The verses that are left out of 4QPs[x] are the ones most clearly relating to the Davidic dynasty and throne (vv. 29–30) and thus would not fit well within a collective framework. This makes better sense of the absence of these verses than the thesis by Gleßmer and Koch that these verses are later insertions to the original oracle traceable through 4QPs[x].[54] Verses 24–25 continue the message of v. 23 in MT Psalm 89, and, considering the fact that all the verses preserved in 4QPs[x] have been at least slightly abbreviated, these verses were probably cut out to avoid unnecessary repetition. Verse 27a might be a similar case, or the reason might be related to the language, which reflects the close relationship between God and king. Finally, the section turns to a warning about what will happen to the chosen ones if they fail to do God's will. They will lose the protection and the land. If the fragment contained something else from Ps 89:20–38, it is plausible that it might have

---

[52] In v. 23, 4QPs[x] is likely working with a text form close to the LXX (οὐ προσθήσει τοῦ κακῶσαι αὐτόν), which is probably dependent on 2 Samuel 7. The most straightforward explanation for this shared variant reading is that the text form from which the author of 4QPs[x] created his composition was in this instance the same as the *Vorlage* of the LXX translator. This connection with 2 Samuel 7 is more easily explained in this way than by positing, on the basis of this textual connection, that 2 Samuel 7 was dependent on this version (or a core behind the current version). See Gleßmer, "Das Textwachstum," 67; Koch, "Königspsalmen," 26. For arguments on behalf of Psalm 89 being dependent on 2 Samuel 7, see, e.g., Veijola, *Verheißung in der Krise*, 60–69; Marttila, *Collective Reinterpretation*, 139.

[53] Marttila has correctly noted that the term בכור ("firstborn") in v. 28 actually fits better as a collective term than as referring to the king, inasmuch as Ps 89:27 is the only instance in the Hebrew Bible where the term is connected with the king (*Collective Reinterpretation*, 143).

[54] Gleßmer, "Das Textwachstum," 67; Koch, "Königspsalmen," 26.

continued the list of admonitions (vv. 31–33) and made reference to God's mercy and fidelity (v. 34), but this can only be a matter of conjecture.

To put the structure of 4QPs^x in a short form:

1. A promise is presented that God will choose his elect from the nation. This is proven by God's words to David when he was chosen. The use of the same term (בחר) for David and for the audience is significant because it creates a conscious link between the two settings.

2. God's promises to establish and support his chosen ones are related. Again, God's own words are given as proof. The chosen will get the land, and God will support them in keeping it as long as they act in accordance with the divine will.

The text of the Qumran fragment is an abbreviation of Ps 89:20–31 and aims to present the core of God's promise to his chosen ones. It transposes this promise from applying only to David and his descendants, as is clear from the missing verses dealing with the dynasty, and attaches it to the new chosen of God, namely, the group addressed in vv. 20 and 22. An audience versed in earlier traditions would have known that the original recipient of the promise was David, so what is new is the interpretation that such a promise applies also to the audience as the chosen people. Another Qumran text demonstrates that the reinterpretation of the oracle of Nathan in 4QPs^x is not a unique phenomenon. Parts of it have been reinterpreted also in 4Q174 (frgs. 1–2 and 21, col. i, 1–13).[55] The reinterpreted verses are 2 Sam 7:10–14, and they are taken, for example, as referring to the "latter days," the future savior of Israel, and the Sons of Light instead of David and his descendants. These texts show that a way around the seeming problem presented by the contradiction of the eternal promise of God to David and his descendants in the oracle of Nathan and the historical reality (which Psalm 89 takes up) was developed at some point in the late Second Temple period. By reinterpreting the promise, the texts exhibit a belief that the promise itself is truly eternal and no longer applies (only) to David and his descendants because of their bad deeds, but to new chosen individuals and/or groups. These will in turn be the heirs of the eternal promise as long as they act in accordance with the will of God.

It is evident that more than one Jewish group from around 150 B.C.E. onward thought of itself as the sole elect of God in the nation (see Psalm 154, 1QS, 1QS^b, 4QNon-Canonical Psalms B, 4QBeautitudes, the *Barkhi Nafshi* hymns, and the *Psalms of Solomon*), though this particular oracle was not employed in all instances. Each of these groups viewed itself as the only one interpreting the Torah and other earlier traditions correctly and believed, therefore, that a special destiny awaited its members. These groups sought justification for this self-identification in God's

---

[55] I am grateful to Professor George Brooke for bringing this passage to my attention.

promises to his elect in the past and consequently reinterpreted such passages as referring to themselves. Such a group was also behind the composition on 4QPs^x. While the group responsible for 4QPs^x and some other movements reinterpreted Nathan's oracle from a collective perspective, others still looked forward to the appearance of a Davidic messiah figure who would fulfill the promise (see particularly the Gospel of Matthew [3:13–17] and the baptism of Jesus as divine anointment and election, including language of adoption similar to, e.g., Ps 89:21, 28). Therefore, it seems safe to say that the promises of God were seen as eternal (as they were assured to be), but how they should be interpreted in a specific historical context was a matter of interpretation, which in turn depended on how different groups and powerful individuals saw themselves and their group in relation to other similar groups and the Jewish people as a whole.

V. Conclusions

This brief study of the fragment 4QPs^x has provided an idea of the probable length of the original text of the fragment and its relation to MT Psalm 89. Consideration of the material aspects suggests that the fragment is part of a handle sheet preceding a composition already written on the scroll proper at the time of the writing of this text. Consequently, I argued that 4QPs^x did not have the beginning of Psalm 89, but an abbreviated version of the text beginning from v. 20 and likely not going beyond v. 38.

I suggested several new readings and reconstructions and pointed to a motive behind the variant readings between 4QPs^x and MT Psalm 89. Nearly all of the variants between the versions can be explained if one views 4QPs^x as an abbreviated collective interpretation of the oracle to David and his descendants in Psalm 89:20–38. 4QPs^x probably does not contain a more original reading than MT Psalm 89, since the text on the fragment is not meant to present a direct quotation of Psalm 89 at all, but rather a later interpretation of it, which shows it to be mostly secondary to the MT version. Before claiming a reading in this fragment as more original than a reading in the MT one would first have to prove that it cannot be explained by the characteristic features of the editing process used in creating this interpretation, such as eliminating repetition or making the text more general to fit the collective aspect.

I have shown that the shorter version of a text is not always necessarily the more original one. There are other things that need to be considered besides the length of the text, and if these offer a simpler solution than what is otherwise available then they should be preferred over complex theories involving hypothetical intermediary stages. To put it slightly differently: if a text form can be explained by existing versions and an editorial theme that is attested also as a theme elsewhere during the same time period, it is to be favored over positing several theoretical stages of textual development of which no evidence survives. In fact, it has been demonstrated that the rule of a shorter text cannot be automatically relied on and that it is necessary carefully to judge the relationship between the two texts before making use of such an axiom. Therefore, I concluded that 4QPs^x is secondary to the MT version and should be seen mainly as something other than a text presenting a version or even a direct quotation of Psalm 89. Thus, the grouping of this fragment by the official editors with biblical manuscripts should be reconsidered. It is possible that the text to which this fragment originally belonged will never be firmly identified, unless the fragment can be materially joined to a specific manuscript, but the characteristic features of the text and their connections with other compositions would nevertheless merit some further consideration in the future.

top scholarship from
BAYLOR UNIVERSITY PRESS

by **RICHARD B. HAYS**

"With his characteristic blend of biblical and literary scholarship, Hays opens new and striking vistas on texts we thought we knew."

—N.T. WRIGHT

B
Books for Good | baylorpress.com

Nebuchadnezzar's Affliction: New Mesopotamian Parallels for Daniel 4

HECTOR AVALOS
HectorAvalos@aol.com
Iowa State University, Ames, IA 50011

In an article in this journal, Christopher B. Hays argued that Nebuchadnezzar's affliction is best understood in the context of netherworld imagery ("Chirps from the Dust: The Afflictions of Nebuchadnezzar in Daniel 4:30 in Its Ancient Near Eastern Context," *JBL* 126 [2007]: 305–25). On the other hand, Matthias Henze believes that Nebuchadnezzar's affliction follows the trope of the uncivilized man akin to Enkidu in the Epic of Gilgamesh (*The Madness of King Nebuchadnezzar* [1999]). Hays appealed to the supposed lack of evidence that such a primal status could result from the curse of a deity. But magico-medical Mesopotamian texts known as the dingir.šà.dib.ba incantations do provide clear evidence that a primal earthly status could result from a divine curse. Accordingly, those texts support Henze's interpretation while validating Hays's argument that Mesopotamian prayer genres can illuminate Daniel 4.

The literary sources and sociohistorical context for the story of Nebuchadnezzar's affliction in Daniel 4 have attracted enough attention to be the subject of a monograph, *The Madness of King Nebuchadnezzar: The Ancient Near Eastern Origins and Early History of Interpretation of Daniel 4*, by Matthias Henze.[1] Therein, Henze argues that Nebuchadnezzar's madness "is modeled on a trope we find in the mythic lore of the ancient Near East, the notion of the wild man."[2] For Henze, Gilgamesh's friend, Enkidu, would be a principal example of that trope.[3]

---

[1] JSJSup 61; Leiden: Brill, 1999.
[2] Henze, *Madness of King Nebuchadnezzar*, 3.
[3] See further Gregory Mobley, "The Wild Man in the Bible and the Ancient Near East," *JBL* 116 (1997): 217–33; Peter W. Coxon, "Another Look at Nebuchadnezzar's Madness," in *The Book of Daniel in the Light of New Findings* (ed. A. S. van der Woude; BETL 106; Leuven: Leuven University Press, 1993), 211–22.

On the other hand, Christopher B. Hays argues that the passage about Nebuchadnezzar's affliction is best understood in the context of netherworld imagery.[4] In particular, Hays focuses on Dan 4:30 [Eng. 4:33], which reads:

בה שעתא מלתא ספת על נבוכדנצר ומן אנשא טריד ועשבא כתורין יאכל ומטל
שמיא גשמה יצטבע עד די שערה כנשרין רבה וטפרוהי כצפרין

> Immediately the sentence was fulfilled against Nebuchadnezzar. He was driven away from human society, ate grass like oxen, and his body was bathed with the dew of heaven, until his hair grew as long as eagles' feathers and his nails became like birds' claws. (NRSV)

Hays argues that the collection of animals mentioned had underworld associations. He also claims that "the type of animal imagery found in this passage frequently symbolized those who were afflicted by divine powers."[5] Overall, Hays believes that the proper context for this story is not in the mythical epics but in prayer genres (e.g., lament and thanksgiving prayers).

In addition, Hays specifically rejects Henze's parallel in a Sumerian story, known as *The Dispute between Cattle and Grain*, which describes the primitive nonurban living conditions of human beings:

> Mankind of that time (i.e., primordial times)
> Knew not the eating of bread
> Knew not the wearing of garments;
> The people went around with skins on their bodies.
> They ate grass with their mouths like sheep,
> Drank water from ditches.[6]

According to Hays, "in order to show that such a text is comparable to Dan 4:30, it would help to have some evidence that such a primal status could result from the curse of a deity, but that is not the case."[7]

In this article, I show that a group of magico-medical Mesopotamian texts collected by Wilfred G. Lambert and known as the dingir.šà.dib.ba incantations do provide clear evidence that a primal earthly status could result from the curse of a deity.[8] Accordingly, Henze is probably more correct in situating the context of the

---

[4] Hays, "Chirps from the Dust: The Afflictions of Nebuchadnezzar in Daniel 4:30 in Its Ancient Near Eastern Context," *JBL* 126 (2007): 305–25.

[5] Ibid., 305.

[6] Henze (*Madness of King Nebuchadnezzar*, 95) is citing the edition in Jeffrey H. Tigay, *The Evolution of the Gilgamesh Epic* (Philadelphia: University of Pennsylvania Press, 1982), 203. For an accessible version, see "The Debate between Grain and Sheep," *Electronic Text Corpus of Sumerian Literature* (Faculty of Oriental Studies, University of Oxford), lines 19–25. Online: http://etcsl.orinst.ox.ac.uk/cgi-bin/etcsl.cgi?text=t.5.3.2# (accessed October 17, 2013). For an older translation, see Samuel N. Kramer, *The Sumerians: Their History, Culture, and Character* (Chicago: University of Chicago Press, 1963), 220–21.

[7] Hays, "Chirps from the Dust," 306–7.

[8] Lambert, "dingir.šà.dib.ba Incantations," *JNES* 33 (1974): 267–322. Since Lambert published

story in the motif of an earthly (as opposed to netherwordly) wild man, while Hays is correct in seeing that Mesopotamian prayer genres are one key to the interpretation of Daniel 4.

In addition, I intend to demonstrate the utility of Mesopotamian magico-medical literature in illuminating the book of Daniel.[9] The link between Mesopotamian magico-medical literature and Daniel is evidenced already in the book of Daniel itself.[10] For example, the MT of Daniel (2:10, 27; 4:4; 5:7, 11, and 15) mentions that Nebuchadnezzar summoned many types of magico-medical consultants, including the *āšipu* (אשף), a well-known Mesopotamian ritual specialist who worked with incantations.[11] Pseudo-Danielic traditions in the Dead Sea Scrolls similarly exhibit connections with magico-medical literature. In particular, 4QprNab ar (4Q242), otherwise known as the *Prayer of Nabonidus*, mentions a magico-medical consultant (גזר) that is found also in the MT of Daniel (2:27; 4:4; 5:7, 11).[12]

---

his study, we have more comprehensive studies of other Mesopotamian prayer genres, including Christopher G. Frechette, *Mesopotamian Ritual-Prayers of "Hand-lifting" (Akkadian Šuillas): An Investigation of Function in Light of the Idiomatic Meaning of the Rubric* (AOAT 379; Münster: Ugarit, 2012), which, however, does not treat dingir.šà.dib.ba incantations. See also Anna Elise Zernecke, *Gott und Mensch in Klagegebeten aus Israel und Mesopotamien: Die Handerhebungsgebete Ištar 10 und Ištar 2 und die Klagepsalmen Ps 38 und Ps 22 im Vergleich* (AOAT 387; Münster: Ugarit, 2011); Donna Lee Petter, *The Book of Ezekiel and Mesopotamian City Laments* (OBO 246; Fribourg: Academic Press; Göttingen: Vandenhoeck & Ruprecht, 2011).

[9] In general, the dingir.šà.dib.ba incantations have been used very briefly and often in connection with prayers in the Psalms. See further Alan Lenzi, "Invoking the God: Interpreting Invocations in Mesopotamian Prayers and Biblical Laments of the Individual," *JBL* 129 (2010): 303–15; John H. Walton, *Ancient Israelite Literature in Its Culture Context: A Survey of Parallels between Biblical and Ancient Near Eastern Texts* (Library of Biblical Interpretation; Grand Rapids: Zondervan, 1994), 139; Patick D. Miller, *They Cried to the Lord: The Form and Theology of Biblical Prayer* (Minneapolis: Fortress, 2000), 80, 371 n. 76; Karel van der Toorn, *Sin and Sanction in Israel and Mesopotamia: A Comparative Study* (SSN 22; Assen: Van Gorcum, 1985), esp. 61–67; idem, "Scholars at the Oriental Court: The Figure of Daniel against Its Mesopotamian Background," in *The Book of Daniel: Composition and Reception* (ed. John J. Collins and Peter W. Flint; VTSup 83; Leiden: Brill, 2011), 37–54. On the other hand, some works specializing in connections between the Bible and Assyria lack any indexed reference to them, e.g., Mark W. Chavalas and K. Lawson Younger, *Mesopotamia and the Bible: Comparative Explorations* (Grand Rapids: Baker Academic, 2002).

[10] For the argument that Egyptian analogues for the biblical Danielic stories are as significant as those of other areas of the ancient Near East, see Tawny L. Holm, "Daniel 1–6: A Biblical Story Collection," in *Ancient Fiction: The Matrix of Early Christian and Jewish Narrative* (ed. Jo-Ann A. Brant, Charles W. Hedrick, and Chris Shea; SBLSymS 32; Atlanta: Society of Biblical Literature, 2005), 149–66, esp. 161–66.

[11] For a general treatment of the work of the *āšipu*, see Cynthia Jean, *La magie néo-assyrienne en contexte: Recherches sur le métier d'exorciste et le concepte d'āšipūtu* (SAAS 17; Helsinki: Neo-Assyrian Text Corpus Project, 2006); Markham J. Geller, *Ancient Babylonian Medicine: Theory and Practice* (Ancient Cultures; Malden, MA: Wiley-Blackwell, 2010), esp. 43–55.

[12] 4QprNab ar, line 4. For the Aramaic text, I depend on John J. Collins, "Prayer of

I. Problems with the Netherworld Theory

In order to illustrate the benefits of using the dingir.šà.dib.ba incantations for understanding Daniel 4, it is necessary to understand why the theory of Hays is less satisfactory than that of Henze. First, the set of animals in Dan 4:30 does not demand a netherworld explanation. It is true that birds (including the eagle, or vulture), lions, and oxen could be depicted as underworld creatures.[13] Hays specifically cites "The Netherworld Vision of an Assyrian Prince" to show that, of the fifteen gods described therein, "six have birdlike features."[14] But as Jeremy Black and Anthony Green aptly note when speaking of this text, "Even in the Assyrian period these iconographic elements were not confined to underworld denizens, since they are shared by beneficent and magically protective figures."[15] So, it would help Hays's case to have a set of animals that are specific only to the netherworld, and clearly lions, birds (e.g., eagles or vultures), and oxen are not such a set, whether in composite form (e.g., Anzu) or not.

Second, the description of Nebuchadnezzar's banishment seems most consistent with an earthly existence. For example, Dan 4:22 [Eng. 4:25] states that Nebuchadnezzar's "dwelling shall be with the wild animals" (cf. OG 4:33b: γυμνὸς περιεπάτουν μετὰ τῶν θηρίων τῆς γῆς, "I went about naked with the beasts of the earth"), which is fully consistent with describing our world, not the netherworld.[16] In fact, even *The Descent of Ishtar*, which Hays cites to support his interpretation, describes what is available to netherworld denizens for consumption as follows: "dust is their sustenance and clay their food."[17] So, eating grass like an ox is perfectly

---

Nabonidus," in *Qumran Cave 4.XVII: Parabiblical Texts, Part 3* (ed. J. C. VanderKam; DJD 22; Oxford: Clarendon, 1996), 83–84 + pl. VI. For an earlier edition, see Frank Moore Cross, "Fragments of the Prayer of Nabonidus," *IEJ* 34 (1984): 260–64.

[13] For discussions of whether *nešer* is an eagle or a vulture, see Jehuda Feliks, *The Animal World of the Bible* (Tel Aviv: Sinai, 1962), 68.

[14] Hays, "Chirps from the Dust," 313. The edition of "The Netherworld Vision of an Assyrian Prince" being cited is that of Alasdair Livingstone, *Court Poetry and Literary Miscellanea* (SAA 3; Helsinki: Helsinki University Press, 1989), 72.

[15] Black and Green, *Gods, Demons and Symbols of Ancient Mesopotamia: An Illustrated Dictionary* (Austin: University of Texas Press, 1992), 44. Hays cites this work for his statistics, but he does not note that Black and Green explicitly see the talon/wing combination as unrepresentative of underworld iconography. See also Salvatore Viaggio, "Birds in Ešnunna and Other Old Babylonian Texts," *JSem* 16 (2007): 786–840; Nili Wazana, "Anzu and Ziz: Great Mythical Birds in Ancient Near Eastern, Biblical, and Rabbinic Traditions," *JANES* 31 (2008): 111–35.

[16] Following the translation of Tim J. Meadowcroft, *Aramaic Daniel and Greek Daniel: A Literary Comparison* (JSOTSup 198; Sheffield: Sheffield Academic Press, 1995), 300. For connections between the bestial image and the story of Ahiqar, see Henze, *Madness of Nebuchadnezzar*, 91.

[17] Hays ("Chirps from the Dust," 310) provides the relevant extract from Benjamin R. Foster,

consistent with an earthly existence, but not with the netherworld described by the *Descent of Ishtar*. In addition, being bathed with the "dew of heaven" (מטל שמיא) implies that Nebuchadnezzar is living in our ordinary environment. Hays explains that this "rain of heaven" may be symbolic of divine judgment, but that does not render it incompatible with an earthly judgment for Nebuchadnezzar.[18]

Third, there are no explicit indicators of Nebuchadnezzar's descent into, or existence in, a netherworld. The lack of such indicators is one reason why Hays's parallel with the story of Ahiqar is not the most apt. True enough, there is a passage in which the protagonist, Ahiqar, is placed in a pit beneath his house to hide him from those who seek to kill him. His friends pretend that he is dead. After being delivered from the pit, Ahiqar's condition is described as follows in the Syriac version:

> The hair of my head had grown down to my shoulders,
> and my beard reached my breast, and my body was foul with the dust,
> and my nails were grown long like eagles'.[19]

In this story there is an explicit simulation of death, and there are explicit references to descending and ascending from a literal underground pit. For example, the Syriac version says of Ahiqar, "he is cast into a darksome pit [*bgwbʾ*] where he seeth no light."[20] Then, when he is rescued, Ahiqar says: "I ascended [*slqt*]."[21]

However, Ahiqar's physical condition is not so much the result of his underground or symbolic netherworld location as it is of the time he spent in that location. Prior to his extraction from the pit, it is said that it was "a few days" (*qlyl ywmtʾ*) before Ahiqar, who was initially left with some food, was given additional food.[22] More time passed until he was actually discovered because, between his placement in the pit and the eventual extraction, Pharaoh wrote a letter to Sennacherib, the king of Assyria, after hearing of the apparent death of Ahiqar.[23] A letter from Egypt

---

From Distant Days: Myths, Tales, and Poetry in Ancient Mesopotamia (Bethesda, MD: CDL, 1995), 78–79.

[18] Hays ("Chirps from the Dust," 313) prefers "rain of heaven," following *HALOT*, 374, and Zech 8:12.

[19] This part of the story of Ahiqar is not attested in the oldest witness (fifth century B.C.E.) from Elephantine; however, it is extant in Syriac. I follow Hays in using the standard edition of the Syriac text by F. C. Conybeare, J. Rendel Harris, and Agnes Smith Lewis, *The Story of Ahikar* (2nd rev. and corr. ed.; Cambridge: Cambridge University Press, 1913), 116; Syriac text c. V.11–12. For a recent study of the Elephantine version, see Michael Weigl, *Die aramäischen Achikar-Sprüche aus Elephantine und die alttestamentliche Weisheitsliteratur* (BZAW 399; Berlin: de Gruyter, 2010). For a standard English introduction and translation, see James M. Lindenberger, *OTP* 2:479–507.

[20] Conybeare, *Story of Ahikar*, 114; Syriac text c. IV.19.
[21] Conybeare, *Story of Ahikar*, 116; Syriac text c. V.11.
[22] Conybeare, *Story of Ahikar*, 114; Syriac text c. IV.18.
[23] Conybeare, *Story of Ahikar*, 114.

would have taken weeks to reach Assyria.[24] If Ahiqar had hidden anywhere else, whether in a tower or in a pit, his hair and nails might have been in a similar condition.

No such explicit mentions of simulated death, pits, descending, or ascending are present in the Nebuchadnezzar story in Daniel 4. More importantly, Nebuchadnezzar's initial transformation seems to be immediate in Dan 4:30 [Eng. 4:33]: "Immediately the sentence was fulfilled against Nebuchadnezzar." At least part of Nebuchadnezzar's bestial condition (e.g., eating grass like an ox) is the result of a predicted curse now apparently imposed instantaneously and not so much the result of any elapsed time.

Fourth, and in agreement with Henze, the wild man motif is more consistent with the context of the story. Nebuchadnezzar is the epitome of the civilized man living in splendor, the builder of the famed city of Babylon. As Dan 4:27 [Eng. 4:30] phrases it: "Is this not magnificent Babylon, which I have built as a royal capital by my mighty power and for my glorious majesty?" A just punishment might be to de-civilize him and return him to the nonurban domain, which is where animals dwell.[25] In fact, Nebuchadnezzar's punishment is applied immediately after he utters this boast about building the urban center of his power.

As mentioned, Henze cites *The Dispute between Cattle and Grain*, where activities attributed to uncivilized people (e.g., eating grass) offer a better parallel to Nebuchadnezzar's situation than any netherworld analogues that Hays offers. In such contexts, acting like a beast is a symptom of a more fundamental lack of the wisdom and intelligence associated with urban and civilized people.[26] The entire canonical Danielic corpus focuses on the frailty of the wisdom of those who do not acknowledge the Hebrew God as superior (see Dan 1:20; 2:20–23; 5:14; 9:22; 11:33).

---

[24] Albertine Hagenbuchner discusses some detailed trip calculations for a trip between Amarna in Egypt and Hattusa in modern Turkey and concludes that "die Strecke Ḫattuša–Amarna in 45 + bis 35 + (27+) Tagen zu bewältigen war" (*Die Korrespondenz der Hethiter* [Texte der Hethiter 15; Heidelberg: Winter, 1989], 1:26). See further Cord Kühne, *Die Chronologie der internationalen Korrespondenz von El Amarna* (AOAT 17; Neukirchen-Vluyn: Neukirchener Verlag, 1973), 105–24.

[25] For a study of the civilized/uncivilized contrast in Mesopotamian animal imagery, see Chikako E. Watanabe, *Animal Symbolism in Mesopotamia: A Contextual Approach* (Wiener Offene Orientalistik 1; Vienna: Institut für Oientalistik der Universität Wien, 2002), 150–56. For an anthropologically oriented interpretation of Nebuchadnezzar's transition to and from the animal world, see Alec Basson, "'A King in the Grass': Liminality and Inversion in Daniel 4:28–37," *JSem* 18 (2009): 1–14. A general study of how Nebuchadnezzar is portrayed in biblical texts is provided by Ronald H. Sack, "Nebuchadnezzar and the Old Testament: History versus Ideology," in *Judah and the Judeans in the Neo-Babylonian Period* (ed. Oded Lipschitz and Joseph Blenkinsopp; Winona Lake, IN: Eisenbrauns, 2003), 221–33.

[26] For the view that Enkidu actually is a "noble savage," whose story functions also as a critique of civilization, see Aage Westenholz and Ulla Koch-Westenholz, "Enkidu—the Noble Savage?" in *Wisdom, Gods and Literature: Studies in Assyriology in Honour of W. G. Lambert* (ed. Andrew R. George and Irving L. Finkel; Winona Lake, IN: Eisenbrauns, 2000), 437–51.

Accordingly, transforming Nebuchadnezzar into a beast is an appropriate punishment for one who prides himself on his wisdom.

II. The dingir.šà.dib.ba Incantations

While both Henze and Hays are correct to avoid medical retro-diagnostic approaches that have been applied to Nebuchadnezzar's condition,[27] Mesopotamian magico-medical writings can still provide some fresh perspective on biblical literature. The dingir.šà.dib.ba incantations are so named because they contain the longer Sumerian rubric inim.inim.ma dingir.šà.dib.ba, which can be translated as "incantation for appeasing an angry god."[28] The texts collected by Lambert belong to late Assyrian and late Babylonian libraries.

These incantations show that assuming a bestial nature could be one of the curses that gods could impose on a human being for insolence and for violating the temple. Here is an illuminating passage:

> I am an ox, I do not know the plants I eat
> I am a sheep, I do not know the absolution rite in which I take part
> I am river water, I do not know where I am going
> I am a ship, [I do not know] at which quay I put in
> The iniquities of mankind are more numerous than the hairs on his head
> I have trodden on my iniquities, sins, and transgressions, [which] were heaped up [like leaves]
> On this day let them be released and absolved …[29]

This passage shows that, contrary to Hays's claim, an individual could be cursed as an earthly animal in order to illustrate a lack of common sense. The patient eats grass like an ox (*alpu*), just as Nebuchadnezzar was eating grass like an ox in the field. The imagery of the long hair is bestial in Daniel 4, and the incantations show that abundant hair and the multiplicity of sins are found also in Mesopotamian literature.

---

[27] Typically, such approaches seek to diagnose a condition mentioned in the Bible in precise modern medical terms. In the case of Nebuchadnezzar, Henze (*Madness of King Nebuchadnezzar*, 92–93) discusses the long tradition in biblical commentaries of diagnosing Nebuchadnezzar with a medical condition known as "zooanthropy." For a more a systematic application of a retro-diagnostic approach to ancient Mesopotamia, see JoAnn Scurlock and Burton R. Andersen, *Diagnoses in Assyrian and Babylonian Medicine: Ancient Sources, Translations, and Modern Medical Analyses* (Urbana: University of Illinois Press, 2005). Critiques of retro-diagnostic approaches are now numerous, and these include Hector Avalos, *Illness and Health Care in the Ancient Near East: The Role of the Temple in Greece, Mesopotamia, and Israel* (HSM 54; Atlanta: Scholars Press, 1995); Joel S. Baden and Candida R. Moss, "The Origin and Interpretation of ṣāraʿat in Leviticus 13–14," *JBL* 130 (2011): 643–62, esp. 659 n. 55.

[28] Lambert, "Incantations," 267.

[29] Ibid., 285, lines 2–8.

That such a humbling experience is part of a divine curse or punishment imposed by divine beings is clear because the patient states, "Your hand is terrible. I have experienced your punishment."[30] It is also clear that this dehumanizing experience is regarded as part of an illness because of the patient's complaint: "Palsy [*munga*] has seized my arms, impotence has fallen on my knees, I moan like a dove night and day. I am inflamed, weeping bitterly."[31]

In the Hebrew Bible, a principal reason for Nebuchadnezzar's bestial condition is that he had uttered some insolent and arrogant words. Note again Dan 4:27 [Eng. 4:30], where Nebuchadnezzar states, "Is this not magnificent Babylon, which I have built as a royal capital by my mighty power and for my glorious majesty?" Daniel 4:28 says that the bestial nature was imposed while he was uttering such an arrogant claim (עוד מלתא בפום מלכא).

The reasons for imposing such a beastlike condition in the dingir.šà.dib.ba incantations also parallel the reasons that the Hebrew God punished Nebuchadnezzar. The Mesopotamian patient indicates that his condition has "come upon me because of the raging of the wrath of my god and goddess.... I repeated [what should not be uttered], improper things were on my lips. In innocence I went too far."[32] Nebuchadnezzar, of course, is the Babylonian king who looted and destroyed the temple of Jerusalem. This sort of desecration is also part of the reason that the Mesopotamian patient is cursed with his bestial nature. The patient states:

> I spoke improper things, you know them all.
> I committed offence against the god who created me.
> I did an abomination, ever doing evil.
> I coveted your abundant property.
> I desired your precious silver.
> I raised my hand and desecrated what should not be so treated.
> In a state of impurity I entered the temple [é-kur].[33]

The desecration of the temple is not mentioned in the MT as a reason for Nebuchadnezzar's affliction. However, it is mentioned in the OG version in v. 22:

καθότι ἐξερήμωσας τὸν οἶκον τοῦ θεοῦ τοῦ ζῶντος ἐπὶ ταῖς ἁμαρτίαις τοῦ λαοῦ τοῦ ἡγιασμένου.

How you desolated the house of the living God, on the occasions of the sins of the holy people.[34]

---

[30] Ibid., 275, line 33/274, line 33: *dan-na-at qat-ka a-ta-mar še-ret-ka*.

[31] Ibid., 275, lines 10–12. While Lambert uses "palsy" to translate *munga*, it is best not to attempt a precise medical diagnosis because there are too many uncertainties and possibilities. Indeed, Scurlock and Andersen (*Diagnoses in Assyrian and Babylonian Medicine*, 249) mention that *mungu* could also be used to describe "a pointing abscess ... and hydrocele."

[32] Lambert, "Incantations," 281, lines 118–27.

[33] Ibid., 283, lines 138–44.

[34] Following the translation of John J. Collins, *Daniel: A Commentary on the Book of Daniel* (Hermeneia; Minneapolis: Fortress, 1993), 211.

It remains puzzling why the OG mentions this desecration of the temple when the MT does not. But the mention of temple desecration by the OG should at least raise the possibility that this reflects the preservation of another Mesopotamian tradition rather than being an OG expansion of the MT.[35]

The number seven forms another commonality between the sentence imposed on Nebuchadnezzar and the number of transgressions ascribed to the Mesopotamian patient in the dingir.šà.dib.ba incantations. The Mesopotamian patient says, "Though my transgressions be seven [sebe gíl-la-tu-ú-a], let your heart rest, though my sins be many show great kindness and cleanse [me]."[36] The divine sentence on Nebuchadnezzar specifies: "let seven times [שבעה עדנין] pass over him" (Dan 4:13 [Eng. 4:16]). This number is repeated in vv. 20, 22, and 29 of the MT. Likewise, 4QPrNab (line 3) specifies that the king was ill for seven years [שנין שבע].

Since the number seven forms a common trope in the Bible, one cannot claim literary dependence on the dingir.šà.dib.ba incantations based on the occurrence of this trope alone. However, it does show that those incantations represent instances where that numerical trope is combined with bestial imagery, temple desecration, and the penalty imposed on a transgressive individual.

It is important also to recognize differences between dingir.šà.dib.ba incantations and Daniel 4, and so the parallels must not be pressed too far. In the dingir.šà.dib.ba incantations, the patient complains, "Like a bird, my pinions have been cut off, I have shed my wings and am unable to fly."[37] Such imagery, which here represents impotence, is the reverse of what one sees in Daniel 4, where having wings and talons represents being uncivilized. Nevertheless, this shows that the earthly patient saw himself as a bird while healthy, but not while in the underworld.[38] In another instance, a bird represents being unhealthy (mourning like a "dove" above). In each case, the context must tell us whether any particular animal feature (or combination of features) is being viewed positively or negatively.

III. Illuminating Redactional Histories

The dingir.šà.dib.ba incantations also offer new avenues through which to explore the redactional conundrums that Daniel 4 poses. The problems in Daniel 4 have been rehearsed extensively by, among others, Henze, T. J. Meadowcroft,

---

[35] For example, Collins (*Daniel*, 229) states that "the OG expands on the hubris of the king." On the reference to temple desecration in the OG, as compared to Theodotion, see Hans-Dieter Neef, "Menschliche Hybris und göttliche Macht: Dan 4 LXX und Dan Th im Vergleich," *JNSL* 31 (2005): 59–89, esp. 75–77. See also Robert Timothy McLay, "The Old Greek Translation of Daniel iv–vi and the Formation of the Book of Daniel," *VT* 55 (2005): 304–23.

[36] Lambert, "Incantations," 283, lines 155–56.

[37] Ibid., 275, lines 8–9.

[38] For positive human features symbolized by birds, see Viaggio, "Birds in Ešnunna," esp. 826.

Lawrence M. Wills, and Ernst Haag, and so they will not be repeated here.[39] In general, Sharon Pace correctly concludes that one cannot be prejudiced in favor of the purity or "originality" of any one textual tradition without examining each tradition on its own merits.[40]

For the purposes of this article, what is important is that the authors of these Danielic materials evinced an extensive awareness of Mesopotamian culture and literature. This awareness includes preservation in Dan 9:24–25 of traditions concerning the prophecies of Marduk and temple rededication rituals clearly attested during the time of Esarhaddon.[41] Associated stories of Bel and the Dragon bespeak Mesopotamian settings.[42]

The *Prayer of Nabonidus* also has obvious affinities with Daniel 4 insofar as it deals with a Mesopotamian king who was afflicted for seven years and was assisted by a Jewish healer. Collins states:

> It is evident that Daniel 4 draws on older traditions most dramatically illustrated by 4QPrNab, but whether it is possible to reconstruct the actual sources in the manner attempted by Haag seems doubtful.... It is impossible to be certain, however, at which point the motif of the beast entered the tradition.[43]

---

[39] Henze, *Madness of King Nebuchadnezzar*, esp. 38–49; Meadowcroft, *Aramaic Daniel and Greek Daniel*, 32–55; Lawrence M. Wills, *The Jew in the Court of the Foreign King: Ancient Jewish Court Legends* (HDR 26; Minneapolis: Fortress, 1990); Ernst Haag, *Die Errettung Daniels aus der Löwengrube: Untersuchungen zum Ursprung der biblischen Danieltradition* (SBS 110; Stuttgart: Katholisches Bibelwerk, 1983). For other studies, see Johann Lust, "The Septuagint Version of Daniel 4–5," in van der Woude, *Book of Daniel in Light of New Findings*, 39–53; Rainer Albertz, *Der Gott des Daniel: Untersuchungen zu Daniel 4–6 in der Septuagintafassung sowie zu Komposition und Theologie des aramäischen Danielbuches* (SBS 131; Stuttgart: Katholisches Bibelwerk 1988). For the idea that oral traditions may be responsible for variants, see Edgar Kellenberger, "Textvarianten in den Daniel-Legenden als Zeugnisse mündlicher Tradierung," in *XIII Congress of the International Organization for Septuagint and Cognate Studies, Ljubiljana, 2007* (ed. Melvin K. H. Peters; SBLSCS 55; Atlanta: Scholars Press, 2008), 207–23. Similarly, Neef states, "Vielleicht wurde diese Erzählung damals auch in verschiedenen Fassungen mündlich oder schriftlich uberliefert" ("Menschliche Hybris," 86).

[40] Pace, "The Stratigraphy of the Text of Daniel and the Question of Theological Tendenz in the Old Greek," *BIOSCS* 17 (1984): 15–35, esp. 20; Sharon Pace Jeansonne, *The Old Greek Translation of Daniel 7–12* (CBQMS 19; Washington, DC: Catholic Biblical Association of America, 1988). For a similar view, see Alexander A. Di Lella, "The Textual History of Greek Daniel," in Collins and Flint, *Book of Daniel: Composition and Reception*, 2:586–607. For the view that the *Vorlage* of Daniel 4 was written in Hebrew, see Pierre Grelot, "La Septante de Daniel IV et son substrat sémitique," *RB* 81 (1974): 19–21.

[41] See Hector Avalos, "Daniel 9:24–25 and Mesopotamian Temple Rededications," *JBL* 117 (1998): 507–11. Esther Eshel concentrates on sources from Qumran, not Mesopotamia ("Possible Sources of the Book of Daniel," in Collins and Flint, *Book of Daniel: Composition and Reception*, 2:387–94).

[42] See also Shalom M. Paul, "The Mesopotamian Babylonian Background of Daniel 1–6," in Collins and Flint, *Book of Daniel: Composition and Reception*, 1:55–68.

[43] Collins, *Daniel*, 219.

The dingir.šà.dib.ba incantations, besides offering other benefits, demonstrate that the bestial tradition was already combined with curse and healing elements by late Assyrian and Babylonian times. Therefore, these magico-literary texts may have functioned as templates that offer "pre-combined" features adopted by later writers.

IV. Conclusion

In denying the explanatory power of Henze's primal man interpretation of Nebuchadnezzar's affliction, Hays argued that "it would help to have some evidence that such a primal status could result from the curse of a deity, but that is not the case."[44] The dingir.šà.dib.ba incantations refute that objection because they do offer just such an example of a primal status resulting from a divine curse against a human being. In addition, these Mesopotamian texts support Henze's interpretation, which situates Nebuchadnezzar's primal status in an earthly, as opposed to a netherworld, context.

The dingir.šà.dib.ba incantations can also help modern scholars to recognize preexisting templates where many important features found in Daniel 4 were already combined. For example, a connection between a bestial punishment and desecration of the temple, which some see as an addition in the OG relative to the MT and Theodotion, was already combined in dingir.šà.dib.ba incantations. Thus, modern redactional theories should consider such preexisting combinations before declaring some tradition to be independent or added in the Daniel traditions.

Nonetheless, it should be emphasized that appeal to the dingir.šà.dib.ba incantations here is not meant to solve any redactional problems. Rather, such an appeal aims to provide another Mesopotamian literary tradition from which the ancient authors/editors of Daniel 4 could have drawn inspiration, templates, and pre-combined elements. Therefore, Hays is correct about the benefits of those prayer genres when interpreting Daniel. In addition, the dingir.šà.dib.ba incantations exemplify the potential of the rich and extensive magico-medical literature of Mesopotamia to illuminate biblical texts.

---

[44] Hays, "Chirps from the Dust," 306–7.

NEW FROM B&H ACADEMIC

A THEOLOGY FOR THE CHURCH, REV. ED.
ed. by Daniel L. Akin, Bruce R. Ashford, and Kenneth Keathley

"*A Theology for the Church* ably unpacks the great doctrines of the faith with sound exegesis, historical perspectives, careful synthesis, and warm applications."

—Christopher W. Morgan, Dean and Professor of Theology, California Baptist University

9781433682131 • 770 pgs • hardcover • $54.99

ILLUSTRATED LIFE OF PAUL
Charles L. Quarles

"*Illustrated Life of Paul* is a well-written, beautifully illustrated, and accurate basic introduction to the apostle Paul."

—Douglas J. Moo, Professor of New Testament, Wheaton College

9780805494532 • 300 pgs • paperback • $29.99

THE TESTING OF GOD'S SONS
Gregory S. Smith

"This is a thoughtful and suggestive study of an issue of enormous enduring significance. Smith valuably combines careful philology with constructive theology."

—Walter Moberly, Professor of Theology and Biblical Interpretation, Durham University

9780805464184 • 240 pgs • hardcover • $24.99

INTRODUCTION TO GLOBAL MISSIONS
Zane Pratt, M. David Sills, and Jeff K. Walters

"Pratt, Sills, and Walters have provided their readers with a marvelous overview of global missions. I highly recommend this outstanding, capably researched, and highly applicable volume."

—David S. Dockery, President, Trinity International University

9781433678752 • 288 pgs • hardcover • $34.99

 bhacademic.com
blog.bhpublishinggroup.com/academic

Idols כתבונם: A Note on Hosea 13:2a

STUART A. IRVINE
sirvine@lsu.edu
Louisiana State University, Baton Rouge, LA 70803

The MT of Hos 13:2a criticizes Israelites for producing idols "according to their skill" (כתבונם). The grammatical difficulty of the Hebrew phrase, the evidence of the ancient versions, and Mesopotamian analogues to the Israelite understanding of cult images all support emending כתבונם to כתבניתם, "according to their [the idols'] model." This reading makes good sense in the context of Israel's renewed revolt against Assyria in 721–719 B.C.E. Israelites sought to ensure divine aid for the revolt by manufacturing new cult images according to the model of images they had lost earlier in 722 B.C.E.

Hosea 13:2a criticizes Israelites for manufacturing cult images. The MT reads: "And now they sin more. They have made for themselves a cast image [מסכה], idols from their silver according to their skill [מכספם כתבונם עצבים]. All of it [כלה] is the work of artisans." The mixture here of singular and plural references—"cast image," "idols," and "all of it"—is peculiar. The singulars might have a collective sense, since the continuation of the criticism in v. 2b assumes the production of multiple statues in calf form. Scholars debate whether the calf images represent Baal or YHWH or a syncretistic blend of the two.[1] Either way, v. 2 sets forth three main points. (1) The manufacture of the images is a continuation of Israelite sin. (2) The images are entirely human-made, and thus they are not divine. (3) The

---

I dedicate this article to the late John H. Hayes. He was a creative scholar, an encouraging teacher, and a loyal friend. He could also tell a good story.

[1] Compare Ziony Zevit, *The Religions of Ancient Israel: A Synthesis of Parallactic Approaches* (London: Continuum, 2001), 29 n. 28; Tryggve N. D. Mettinger, "Israelite Aniconism: Developments and Origins," in *The Image and the Book: Iconic Cults, Aniconism and the Rise of Book Religion in Israel and the Ancient Near East* (ed. Karel van der Toorn; CBET 21; Leuven: Peeters, 1998), 181; Herbert Niehr, "In Search of Yahweh's Cult Statue," in van der Toorn, *Image and the Book*, 82; Wesley I. Toews, *Monarchy and Religious Institution under Jeroboam I* (SBLMS 47; Atlanta: Scholars Press, 1993), 165; Youn H. Chung, *The Sin of the Calf: The Rise of the Bible's Negative Attitude toward the Golden Calf* (Library of Hebrew Bible/Old Testament Studies 523; New York: T&T Clark, 2010), 109–80, esp. 125–34.

509

veneration of the calf images, which includes kissing the images and perhaps human sacrifice, is stupid, if not offensive.[2]

The phrase כתבונם merits close attention. It consists of the preposition -כ and what appears to be the feminine noun תבונה (from the root בין, "discern, understand") with the third person plural possessive suffix. The great majority of recent scholars adhere closely to the MT and translate v. 2a as a statement about Israelites making idols "according to their understanding/skill."[3] The accusation supposedly reflects the aniconic tradition in texts such as Exod 20:4–6 and 34:17, and it fits with Hosea's other denunciations of cult images (e.g., 8:6). It also appears to match the polemic against idols in the preaching of other prophets, for example, Second Isaiah, who ridicules craftsmen for presuming to "fashion a god" (see Isa 40:18–20; 41:6–7; 44:9–20; 46:1–7).[4]

In contrast, previous generations of scholars were more inclined to emend the MT in Hos 13:2a. Julius Wellhausen and William Rainey Harper changed כתבונם to כתמונתם, "according to their [the idols'] image/model."[5] Heinrich Ewald, George A. Smith, and Henrik S. Nyberg preferred to read כתבניתם or כתבנתם, "according to their [the idols'] form/type."[6] Artur Weiser, following the suggestion of *BHK*, omitted the possessive suffix and read כתבנית or כתמונת in construct with עצבים: "according to the idols' form."[7]

---

[2] In the MT of v. 2b, the phrase זבחי אדם likely means, "those who sacrifice people." See Francis I. Andersen and David Noel Freedman, *Hosea: A New Translation with Introduction and Commentary* (AB 24; Garden City, NY: Doubleday, 1980), 624, 632; and Hans Walter Wolff, *Hosea: A Commentary on the Book of the Prophet Hosea* (Hermeneia; Philadelphia: Fortress, 1974), 219, 225; but compare the NRSV and also Douglas K. Stuart, *Hosea–Jonah* (WBC 31; Waco: Word, 1982), 198–99, 202.

[3] J. Andrew Dearman, *The Book of Hosea* (NICOT; Grand Rapids: Eerdmans, 2010), 316; Andrew A. Macintosh, *A Critical and Exegetical Commentary on Hosea* (ICC; Edinburgh: T&T Clark, 1997), 522; Graham I. Davies, *Hosea: Based on the Revised Standard Version* (NCB Commentary; Grand Rapids: Eerdmans, 1992), 287; Jörg Jeremias, *Der Prophet Hosea* (ATD 24.1; Göttingen: Vandenhoeck & Ruprecht, 1983), 159; Stuart, *Hosea–Jonah*, 198–202; Andersen and Freedman, *Hosea*, 631–32; James Luther Mays, *Hosea: A Commentary* (OTL; Philadelphia: Westminster, 1969), 171. See also the NRSV, NIV, NJPS, JB, and REB.

[4] See Michael B. Dick, "Prophetic Parodies of Making the Cult Image," in *Born in Heaven, Made on Earth: The Making of the Cult Image in the Ancient Near East* (ed. Michael B. Dick; Winona Lake, IN: Eisenbrauns, 1999), 1–53.

[5] Wellhausen, *Die kleinen Propheten übersetzt und erklärt* (3rd ed.; Berlin: Reimer, 1898; repr., Berlin: de Gruyter, 1963), 19, 131; Harper, *A Critical and Exegetical Commentary on Amos and Hosea* (ICC; New York: Scribner's Sons, 1905), 395.

[6] Ewald, *Commentary on the Prophets of the Old Testament* (trans. J. Frederick Smith; 5 vols.; London: Williams & Norgate, 1875–81), 1:293; Smith, *The Book of the Twelve Prophets* (2nd ed.; 2 vols.; London: Hodder & Stoughton, 1896), 1:304; Nyberg, *Studien zum Hoseabuch* (Uppsala: A. B. Lundequistska, 1935), 100–101.

[7] Weiser, *Der Buch der zwölf kleinen Propheten* (ATD 24.1; Göttingen: Vandenhoeck & Ruprecht, 1949), 79–80; compare Wolff, *Hosea*, 219.

The purpose of this note is to defend one of these emendations. The grammatical difficulty of the MT's כתבונם, the evidence of the ancient versions, and Mesopotamian analogues to the Israelite understanding of cult images all favor seeing in Hos 13:2a a reference to the "form" or "model" of idols.[8] The article will conclude with brief remarks on the historical significance of the emended reading.

The feminine noun תבונה occurs forty-two times in the Hebrew Bible. It is especially frequent in wisdom literature (nineteen times in Proverbs and four times in Job), where it generally means "understanding, discernment" and often functions as a synonym of חכמה, "wisdom" (see, e.g., Prov 3:10; 10:23). In Exod 31:3; 35:21; and 1 Kgs 7:14, the noun refers to an artisan's expertise in metal-, stone-, and woodwork, and this meaning appears to be the precise sense of כתבונם in Hos 13:2. However, the form in 13:2 is peculiar. One would expect the possessive suffix to attach to the feminine construct תבונת, thus yielding כתבונתם. The noun תבונה with a possessive suffix occurs seven other times in the Hebrew Bible, and in each instance the suffix attaches to the ת-ending of the feminine construct (e.g., לתבונתי in Prov 5:1; ובתבונתך in Ezek 28:4; and לתבונתו in Ps 147:5).

Scholars have made various arguments in defense of the MT's כתבונם or a reading close to it. (1) The medieval commentators Abraham Ibn Ezra and David Qimḥi contend that the form is an unusual but legitimate variant of כתבונתם. They point to an analogue in Ps 49:15, where the Qere צורם appears to substitute for צורתם, "their form."[9] (2) According to GKC §91e, there is a remote possibility of shortening when suffixes attach to feminine singular nouns. In the case of כתבונם in Hos 13:2, the normal ending תָ-ם perhaps was reduced to ם-. (3) According to James L. Mays, the form in 13:2 might simply be a scribal miswriting of כתבונתם. The right translation remains "according to their understanding."[10] (4) Francis I.

---

[8] Mesopotamian ideas about cult images have received considerable scholarly attention in recent years. See the several essays in three anthologies: *The Image and the Book* (1998; see n. 1 above); *Born in Heaven, Made on Earth* (1999; see n. 4 above); and *Cult Image and Divine Representation in the Ancient Near East* (ed. Neal H. Walls; ASOR Books 10; Boston: ASOR, 2005). See also Edward M. Curtis, "Images in Mesopotamia and the Bible: A Comparative Study," in *The Bible in the Light of Cuneiform Literature* (ed. William Hallo, Bruce William Jones, and Gerald L. Mattingly; Ancient Near Eastern Texts and Studies 8; Scripture in Context 3; Lewistown, NY: Mellen, 1990), 36–56; Angelika Berlejung, *Die Theologie der Bilder: Herstellung und Einweihung von Kultbildern in Mesopotamien und die alttestamentliche Bilderpolemik* (OBO 162; Freiburg, Switzerland: Universitätsverlag, 1998); Christopher Walker and Michael B. Dick, *The Induction of the Cult Image in Ancient Mesopotamia: The Mesopotamian mis pî Ritual* (SAA Literary Texts 1; Helsinki: Neo-Assyrian Text Corpus Project, 2001); Victor A. Hurowitz, "The Mesopotamian God Image, from Womb to Tomb," *JAOS* 123 (2003): 147–57; Christopher E. Woods, "The Sun-God Tablet of Nabu-apla-iddina Revisited," *JCS* 56 (2004): 23–103. Commentators on Hosea have not exploited the Mesopotamian analogues for the illumination of the prophet's preaching against idols, especially in 13:2.

[9] See מקראות גדולות (Warsaw: n.p., 1860–68).

[10] Mays, *Hosea: A Commentary*, 171.

Andersen and David Noel Freedman suggest that the noun in 13:2 might be תבון, a masculine form to which a suffix would connect directly. If so, the MT's כתבונם could be perfectly grammatical. Hosea perhaps coined the masculine noun by fusing the features of תמונה ("likness, form") and תבנית ("pattern, construction") and the ideas they express.[11]

None of these ideas is convincing. As a variant of כתבונתם, כתבונם lacks the support of even one other attestation of the form. The reading is hardly strengthened by the supposed analogue in Ps 49:15, since צורם there is also text-critically doubtful.[12] As for the explanation of כתבונם as an instance of shortening when a suffix attaches to a feminine noun, even GKC voices skepticism, concluding that the examples of such shortening are "for the most part uncertain." One may emphasize again that in the seven other cases of suffixes attaching to תבונת, no such shortening occurs.

Andersen and Freedman's proposal to see the coined word תבון in 13:2 is ingenious but impossible to test. One would not expect additional attestations of a word especially invented by a single writer or speaker. However, even if Hosea coined תבון in the way that Andersen and Freedman imagine, the sense of the new word presumably would derive from the two nouns that it fuses. The meaning of the noun thus would be "form, model, pattern," not "skill," as Andersen and Freedman render it. One might reasonably ask, too, why the prophet bothered to coin תבון instead of simply using תמונה or תבנית. The semantic plus of the new word is hard to discern.

The explanation of כתבונם as a miswriting of כתבונתם is certainly possible, and it has the virtue of simplicity. However, there is no textual evidence to support it. The LXX speaks of the Israelites making a molten silver image κατ' εἰκόνα εἰδώλων ("according to the form of idols"). The Greek phrase is matched exactly by the Vulgate's *quasi similitudinem idolorum* ("according to the pattern/likeness of idols"). Both readings appear to reflect a Hebrew construct chain: כתבנית/כתמונת עצבים.[13] In contrast, the Targum's כדמותהון צלמניץ ("according to their likeness/model, idols [they made]") and the Peshitta's *bdmwthwn ptbrʾ* ("in their likeness, idols [they made]") adhere to the syntax of the MT. However, like the LXX and Vulgate, the Aramaic and Syriac texts assume the Hebrew noun תבנית or תמונה.

---

[11] Andersen and Freedman, *Hosea*, 631–32.

[12] The form צורם is the Qere in v. 15; the Ketiv is צירם, apparently the masculine noun ציר ("image") with the pronominal suffix (compare צירים in Isa 45:16). Hans-Joachim Kraus describes the whole of v. 15 as "irreparably corrupt" (*Psalms 1–59: A Commentary* [trans. Hilton C. Oswald; Minneapolis: Augsburg, 1988], 480).

[13] Elsewhere in the LXX, the noun εἰκών renders צלם (twenty-six times), סמל (three times), פסל (twice), and דמות (once). Why the Greek translator chose to use εἰκών in 13:2 remains unclear, but perhaps he did so with an eye to Deut 4:15–17. In that text, תבנית, תמונה, and סמל occur together as near synonyms, and there the LXX renders סמל as εἰκών. As for the Latin noun *similitudo*, it translates תמונה in Exod 20:4; Deut 4:15–17, 23, 25, and תבנית in Deut 4:17.

All of the ancient versions thus support the emendation of the MT in Hos 13:2a. The verse originally referred to the production of idols according to their תבנית or תמונה. The former noun might be the better reading, since it can convey the specific idea of a *prescribed* form, that is, a plan or model to be followed. For example, in Exod 25:9, Yhwh orders Moses, "According to all that I show you, the plan [תבנית] of the tabernacle and the plan [תבנית] of all its furniture, so you shall make it." In 1 Chr 28:11–18, David gives Solomon the "plan" (תבנית) that was "in his mind" for all the details of the temple. The review of specific items concludes with David's statement in v. 19: "All this, in writing at the hand of Yhwh's direction, he [Yhwh] made clear to me—the plan [תבנית] of all the works."[14] Finally, in 2 Kgs 16:10, when King Ahaz sees an altar in Damascus, he sends to Uriah the priest in Jerusalem "the likeness of the altar and its plan [תבניתו], exact in its details." Subsequently, Uriah builds the altar "according to all that King Ahaz sent to him" (v. 11).

The passages in Exodus 25 and 1 Chronicles 28 both suggest that the תבנית of a cultic item is supposed to be divinely dictated. The absence of this claim in 2 Kings 16 is noteworthy, since it might reflect the biblical writer's subtle attempt to disparage Ahaz's altar as illegitimate. In any case, in all three texts the noun תבנית designates a prescribed form, that is, a model for making a cultic item.[15] This meaning fits well in Hos 13:2a. If it is correct, the prophet speaks of Israelites making calf images of the deity on the basis of a precise model.

Mesopotamian analogues support this interpretation.[16] The parade example comes from the "Sun Disk" tablet of Nabu-apla-iddina, king of Babylon in the

---

[14] Compare an inscription of the Babylonian king Nabopolassar (625–605 b.c.e.), who speaks of building a temple on the basis of an oracle and in accordance with a copy. The text reads: "I asked the oracle of Shamash, Adad, and Marduk, and the great gods showed me through the decision of an oracle (the place) where I should put my heart and take the measurements into consideration.... I built a temple after the copy of the Ebabbara with joy and jubilation." For this translation, see Tomoo Ishida, *The Royal Dynasties in Ancient Israel: A Study on the Formation and Development of Royal-Dynastic Ideology* (BZAW 142; Berlin: de Gruyter, 1977), 88.

[15] For a detailed discussion of תבנית as a model of a cult object, see Victor Hurowitz, *I Have Built You an Exalted House: Temple Building in the Bible in the Light of Mesopotamian and Northwest Semitic Writings* (JSOTSup 115; Sheffield: JSOT Press, 1992), 168–70; and Siegfried Wagner, "*bānāh*," *TDOT* 2:179–81; compare Andersen and Freedman, *Hosea*, 631. See also Silviu N. Bunta's discussion of the phrase חתם תבנית ("imprinted by the pattern"), which he restores in Ezek 28:12 ("Yhwh's Cultic Statue after 597/586 B.C.E.: A Linguistic and Theological Reinterpretation of Ezekiel 28:12," *CBQ* 69 [2007]: 222–41).

[16] For discussions of the examples presented below, see Christopher Walker and Michael Dick, "The Induction of the Cult Image in Ancient Mesopotamia: The Mesopotamian *mis pî* Ritual," in Dick, *Born in Heaven, Made on Earth*, 147–57; Christopher Walker, "The Sun-God Tablet of Nabu-apla-iddina Revisited," *JCS* 56 (2004): 23–103; Michael Dick, "The Mesopotamian Cult Statue: A Sacramental Encounter with Divinity," in Walls, *Cult Image and Divine Representation*, 43–67.

mid-ninth century B.C.E.[17] The text tells that two centuries earlier, in the reign of Simbar-Sihu (1025–1009 B.C.E.), the Suteans raided the sanctuary of Shamash in Sippar and destroyed the cult statue of the god. As a result, the cult ordinances of Shamash were forgotten and his "appearance and appurtenances" were lost. Simbar-Sihu inquired (through divination?) about Shamash's appearance, but the god was angry at the land and refused to "turn his face" to the king. The king then enshrined a sun disk in place of the cult statue. During the rule of Kassu-nadin-ahhe (1008–1006 B.C.E.), famine and starvation brought an end to the sacrificial cult of Shamash. However, the reign of Nabu-apla-iddina (ca. 887–855 B.C.E.) established new conditions that placated the wrath of Shamash, and so the deity allowed a clay replica of his image to be found on the west bank of the Euphrates across from Sippar. A new cult statue was then produced and consecrated through the "Washing of the Mouth" (*mis pî*) ritual.

The Sun Disk tablet suggests or implies four important beliefs. (1) The god Shamash is present in his cult statue. (2) The statue of Shamash ranks higher than the sun disk; the latter is only a temporary substitute. (3) The new statue of the deity can be made only if there is a model to follow. (4) The model for the cult statue is divinely revealed.

A second example comes from the Erra Epic, an eighth-century B.C.E. text consisting largely of speeches by the gods Erra, Ishum, and Marduk.[18] The dialogue tells that the cult statue of Marduk has deteriorated and so Marduk has abandoned it and left his temple. Erra proposes to rule in Marduk's place, and Marduk apparently agrees. He then explains that his new cult statue ultimately will be the work of divine craftsmen, "the Seven Sages of the Apsu, the holy carp, who are perfect in lofty wisdom like Ea their lord, who can make my body (the statue) holy." The materials for the statue, furthermore, are divinely prescribed, for example, the "pure" *azgindura*-stone and the *elmesu*-stone and the *mesu*-wood, which is the "flesh of the gods." Although the text does not refer explicitly to a prescribed model of Marduk's statue, one may reasonably speculate that such a model is also in mind. One thing is clear: the details of the statue are not left entirely to the discretion of human artisans. The materials of the statue, and perhaps also its form, must conform to divine wisdom.

A seventh-century B.C.E. inscription of the Assyrian king Esarhaddon offers a third analogue. It tells that, on the basis of answers to oracular inquiries, the king plans to refurbish the cult statues of Marduk and other deities and to return them to their restored sanctuaries in Babylon. Esarhaddon, however, first prays to the high gods Marduk and Ashur.

> Whose right is it, O great gods, to create gods and goddesses in a place where man dare not trespass? This task of refurbishing (the statues), which you have constantly been allotting to me (by oracle) is difficult! Is it the right of deaf and

---

[17] See *COS* 2.135:364–68.
[18] See *COS* 1.113:404–16.

blind human beings who are ignorant of themselves and remain in ignorance throughout their lives? The making of (images of) the gods and goddesses is your right, it is in your hands; I beseech you, create (the gods), and in your exalted holy of holies may what you yourselves have in your heart be brought about in accordance with your unalterable word. Endow the skilled craftsmen whom you ordered to complete this task with as high an understanding as Ea, their creator. Teach them skills by your exalted word; make all their handwork succeed through the craft of Ninshiku (= Ea).[19]

In the continuation of the text, Esarhaddon reports the confirmation of the selection of the artisans through divination, the provision of the precious materials for the making of the statues and sanctuaries, the "birth" of the gods (that is, the production of their images), and their adornment "exactly as the great lord Marduk wanted and as pleased queen Sarpanitu (the goddess)." Again, while the inscription does not refer explicitly to the models of the statues, it might hint at such models when it speaks of what the great gods have "in their hearts" and of "their unalterable word" and of the adornment of Marduk's statue "exactly as the great lord Marduk wanted."[20]

Hosea's statement about the production of images "according to their model" fits the circumstances of the northern kingdom in the late 720s B.C.E.[21] When the Israelite king Hoshea revolted against Assyria in 727–726, the Assyrian king Shalmaneser V responded by attacking Samaria and arresting Hoshea. Shalmaneser and the Assyrian army then withdrew from the area to subjugate Tyre. During their absence the Israelite rebellion resumed. In late 725 or early 724, Assyrian forces returned to Samaria and placed the city under siege. It fell to Shalmaneser in the fall of 722. If the provincialization of the northern kingdom had not been decreed already in 725, certainly it was ordered in 722.[22] No doubt also, with the fall of the capital city, Shalmaneser confiscated the calf icon(s) that was central to the national cult. The spoliation of cult images was a standard Assyrian practice, intended to discourage future rebellion by depriving a conquered state of its gods and thus quelling its hope for divine aid.[23] During the siege of Samaria the prophet

---

[19] For this translation, see Walker and Dick, "Mesopotamian *mis pî* Ritual," 64–65.

[20] According to Hurowitz (*Exalted House*, 170), two Babylonian inscriptions of Nabonidus (556–539 B.C.E.) also attest the idea of a divinely revealed model for a cultic object. In one text, the model is for the production of a chariot for the god Sin; in the other text, it is for the making of the regalia of a priestess.

[21] For the following historical reconstruction, see John H. Hayes and Jeffrey K. Kuan, "The Final Years of Samaria (730–720 BC)," *Bib* 72 (1991): 153–82; compare Nadav Na'aman, "The Historical Background of the Conquest of Samaria (720 BC)," *Bib* 71 (1990): 206–25; M. Christine Tetley, "The Date of Samaria's Fall as a Reason for Rejecting the Hypothesis of Two Conquests," *CBQ* 64 (2002): 59–77; and Sung Jin Park, "A New Historical Reconstruction of the Fall of Samaria," *Bib* 93 (2012): 98–106.

[22] Hosea 13:1b might allude to the events of 722 B.C.E. when it speaks of Israel's "death."

[23] See Mordechai Cogan, *Imperialism and Religion: Assyria, Judah and Israel in the Eighth and Seventh Centuries B.C.E.* (SBLMS 19; Missoula, MT: Scholars Press, 1974), 22–41. Cogan

Hosea anticipated this practice and predicted the loss of the calf image: "They shall tremble for the calf of the iniquitous temple [לעגל בית און], the one that dwells in Samaria [שכן שמרון].... It too shall be carried to Assyria as tribute to the great king" (10:5a, 6a).[24]

With the death of Shalmaneser V in late 722 B.C.E., the Assyrian army abruptly left Palestine and returned home. At the time of their departure, the process of provincializing Israel probably was unfinished. The new Assyrian king, Sargon II, spent the early part of his reign suppressing military rebellion in the Assyrian homeland and fighting the king of Elam. The circumstances encouraged Israel and other Syro-Palestinian states to revolt again.[25] Only at the end of his second regnal year was Sargon free to campaign westward against the rebel states and cities. One of his early inscriptions, the so-called Nimrud Prism, describes in detail the king's conquest of Samaria in late 720–719 B.C.E.:

> The Samarians, who with a king [hostile to] me had consorted not to do service and not to bring tribute—and they did battle: in the strength of the great gods, my lords, I clashed with them, [2] 7,280 people with their chariots and the gods they trust, as spoil I counted, 200 chariots (as) my royal muster I mustered from among them. The rest of them I caused to take dwelling in the midst of Assyria. The city of Samaria I repopulated, and greater than before I caused it to become. People of lands conquered by my two hands I brought within it; my officer as prefect over them I placed, and together with the people of Assyria I counted them.[26]

Two details of this account are especially noteworthy:

1. Sargon refers to a king who had led "the Samarians" in revolt. Although the identity of this figure remains obscure, the most straightforward reading of the text suggests that he was an indigenous king. Apparently the Israelites replaced Hoshea with a monarch who led their rebellion in 721–719 B.C.E.[27]

---

explains that Assyrian kings often deported confiscated cult statues to various locations within Assyria. This transfer of the statues symbolized the abandonment of a state by its own gods. Understandably, rebel states often took special steps to prevent the capture of their cult statues.

[24] For the emendation of the MT's עגלות ("calves") to the singular עגל, see *BHS*. Most modern translations and commentators construe שכן שמרון as the subject of the Hebrew sentence: "The inhabitants of Samaria tremble for the calf of Beth-aven [= Bethel]." The rendering proposed here suggests that the capital city Samaria had a temple with a calf icon sometime during Hosea's career, probably in the late 720s B.C.E. See John Van Seters, *The Life of Moses: The Yahwist as Historian in Exodus–Numbers* (Louisville: Westminster John Knox, 1994), 299.

[25] Thus Hos 13:15a speaks of Ephraim hoping to "flourish among allies," even after the nation's "death" in 722 B.C.E. (13:1).

[26] See Cyril J. Gadd, "Inscribed Prisms of Sargon II from Nimrud," *Iraq* 16 (1954): 180.

[27] Hosea 13:10a perhaps taunts Israel for depending on this ruler: "Where is your king, where, that he might save you in all your cities?" The speech continues in v. 11: אתן־לך מלך באפי ואקח בעברתי, "I [Yhwh] shall give you a king in my anger, and I shall take away (a king) in my

2. Sargon lists "the gods they trust" among the spoil he took from Samaria in late 720–719 B.C.E. The reference is certainly to the cult statues of the Israelite god(s), presumably housed in the sanctuary of the city. These probably were the calf images mentioned in Hos 13:2. The production of the calf images was part and parcel of Israel's renewed rebellion in 721–720. The images were viewed as essential to the war effort, since they guaranteed the protective presence of the god(s).[28] Hosea opposed the revolt and expected its failure (14:1), and thus he disparaged the calf icons as human-made and a continuation of the nation's religious/political sin. Most Israelites, however, believed in the divinity of the cult images, in part because they had been made "according to their model," that is, according to the prescribed design of the calf figurine(s) previously confiscated by Shalmaneser V. Only in this way could the images foster the Israelite hope in divine aid against Assyria.

---

wrath." The dual threat here may anticipate Sargon's conquest of Samaria and the deportation (or execution) of the last Israelite monarch.

[28] A similar link between cult images and political revolt is apparent in Hos 8:4–10, which probably dates to 725 B.C.E. See Stuart A. Irvine, "Politics and Prophetic Commentary in Hosea 8:8–10," *JBL* 114 (1995): 292–94.

The most comprehensive volume ever produced in defense of the Gospels and Acts.

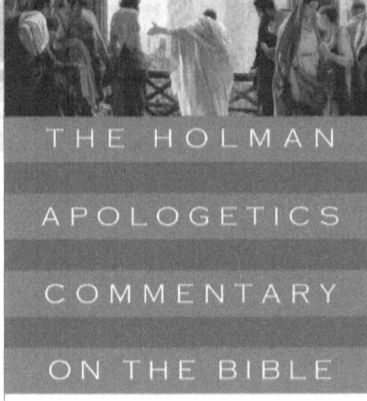

Jeremy Royal Howard
General Editor

Michael J. Wilkins
Matthew

Craig A. Evans
Mark

Darrell L. Bock
Luke, Acts

Andreas J. Köstenberger
John

The primary purpose of the *Holman Apologetics Commentary on the Bible* is to equip readers to defend the reliability of Scripture and the historic evangelical understanding of its teachings. It is designed for use by general readers, though scholars will find it a probing and welcome resource as well. A secondary purpose is to encourage awareness and discussion of Bible difficulties that are not commonly mentioned from the pulpit or even the seminary lectern.

Now available at your favorite bookstore.

BHPublishingGroup.com

HOLMAN REFERENCE

Cutting Off "Kith and Kin," "Er and Onan"? Interpreting an Obscure Phrase in Malachi 2:12

JONATHAN M. GIBSON
gibson_jonny@yahoo.com
University of Cambridge, Cambridge, CB3 9BA, UK

The participial phrase ער וענה in Mal 2:12 has been a *crux interpretum* since the earliest versions of the Hebrew Bible. A comprehensive search reveals that at least ten distinct interpretations have been proposed for the obscure phrase by translators and commentators. Retroversion of ancient versions to a different Hebrew *Vorlage*, conjectural emendation, or various etymological and philological considerations of the homonymic verbs עור and ענה (some on the basis of cognate languages) do not yield a clear understanding of how to interpret the obscure phrase. This article therefore proposes a different methodological approach. By comparing the construction כרת + ל + two coordinated participles/nouns (often displaying alliteration and/or assonance) with other biblical texts, some progress is possible on discerning the meaning of this difficult phrase, even if an exact rendering remains beyond our grasp. Having established that the phrase is most likely a grammatical hendiadys, which constitutes an idiom for "offspring"— one's own "kith and kin"—this article engages with a recent proposal for an innerbiblical allusion to Genesis 38, and the sons of Judah, עֵר and אוֹנָן.

יַכְרֵת יְהוָה לָאִישׁ אֲשֶׁר יַעֲשֶׂנָּה עֵר וְעֹנֶה מֵאָהֳלֵי יַעֲקֹב וּמַגִּישׁ מִנְחָה לַיהוָה צְבָאוֹת׃

May Yhwh cut off for the man who does this "kith and kin" from the tents of Jacob, though he offers a gift to Yhwh of hosts. (Mal 2:12)

The participial phrase ער וענה has long puzzled translators and commentators, ancient, medieval, and modern alike. The Cairo (895 C.E.), Aleppo (925 C.E.), and Leningrad codices (1008 C.E.) all display the reading ער וענה,[1] whereas 4QXII[a]

I am grateful to Professor Emeritus Robert P. Gordon for his helpful comments on an earlier draft of this article.

[1] Benjamin Kennicott records one medieval manuscript that has ד instead of ר in the first hand: "עד primo עד 99" (*Vestus Testamentum Hebraicum: Cum Variis Lectionibus* [Oxford: Clarendon, 1776], 304).

(4Q76) reads עד ועננה.[2] The LXX seems to have read signs similar to 4QXII[a] in its Hebrew *Vorlage*.

The obscurity of the phrase and the textual variant in 4QXII[a] and the LXX have produced a variety of translations and interpretations and show that the earliest translators knew of no tradition behind the meaning of the phrase. The various translations and interpretations may be categorized as follows, with some overlap between them.

I. Early Translations and Interpretations

1. *Humiliation (LXX).* The LXX betrays a textual variant to the MT, reading עד (temporal preposition ἕως) for ער and translating ענה from the verb "be humbled": ἕως καὶ ταπεινωθῇ ἐκ σκηνωμάτων Ιακωβ ("until he has even been humiliated from the tents of Jacob"; NETS).[3]

2. *Legal (4QXII[a]).* In Mal 2:12 in 4QXII[a], although the ink is faint, the *dalet* on עד is certain. *The Dead Sea Scrolls Bible* translates the phrase "one who witnesses or answers."[4] Russell Fuller reads the Qumran text as presenting a legal context: "The implication would be that the guilty party [that is, the one who intermarries] would no longer be allowed to participate in legal proceedings within the community."[5]

3. *Familial (Targum Nebiʾim and Peshitta).* The *Tg. Neb.* and Syriac interpret the phrase along familial lines. *Tg. Neb.* renders עד וענה as בר ובר בר ("son and grandson"), presumably in connection with the Hebrew expression נין ונכד (e.g., Gen 21:23; etc.).[6] The idea is that the family line would eventually become extinct.

4. *Educational (Talmud and Vulgate).* The Talmud and Vulgate explanation is distinct again. The Talmud reads the phrase as referring to a wise teacher among

---

[2] Beate Ego et al., eds., *Biblia Qumranica*, vol. 3b, *Minor Prophets* (Leiden: Brill, 2005), 191. The Hebrew text of Malachi is attested in two biblical manuscripts (4QXII[a] and 4QXII[c] [4Q78]) and one *pesher* (5QpMal [5Q10]). 4QXII[c] and 5QpMal are of little interest or text-critical value, whereas "4QXII[a] is a somewhat idiosyncratic witness which is unaffiliated with either the Masoretic Text or the LXX" (Russell Fuller, "Minor Prophets," in *Encyclopedia of the Dead Sea Scrolls* [ed. Lawrence H. Schiffman and James C. VanderKam; 2 vols.; Oxford: Oxford University Press, 2000], 1:557). 4QXII[a] is a Hebrew biblical manuscript from Qumran consisting of twenty-one fragments and part of a scroll of the Minor Prophets.

[3] This reading assumes ענה II *pual*: וְעָנָה.

[4] Martin G. Abegg Jr. et al., eds., *The Dead Sea Scrolls Bible: The Oldest Known Bible* (Edinburgh: T&T Clark, 1999), 477.

[5] Fuller, "Text-Critical Problems in Malachi 2:10–16," *JBL* 110 (1991): 51.

[6] Kevin J. Cathcart and Robert P. Gordon, *The Targum of the Minor Prophets* (ArBib 14; Wilmington, DE: Glazier, 1989), 233 n. 18.

the sages and a student who knows how to answer.⁷ The interpretation refers to the practice of learning by memorizing: the one who awakes (ער) is the teacher who excites through questions, and the one who answers (ענה) is the pupil. This reading appears to have influenced the Vulgate: *magistrum et discipulum*.⁸

II. MODERN TRANSLATIONS AND INTERPRETATIONS

5. *Nomadic (Duhm; Keil)*. Bernhard Duhm and others relate the phrase to a nomadic custom of a watchman keeping guard in a camp, the one who awakes (ער) and who answers (ענה) to any problem.⁹ In a similar vein, Carl F. Keil understands the phrase to derive from the Aramaic for night watchman (עִיר; cf. Dan 4:10[13], 14[17]) and so translates *vigil et respondens* ("the one awake and answering").¹⁰ The interpretation seems to fit with the prepositional phrase "from the tents of Jacob" (מאהלי יעקב).¹¹

Along similar lines, Wilhelm Rudolph takes ער as a participial substantive of the Hebrew verb עיר ("protect"; cf. Deut 32:11; Job 8:6),¹² thus, "protector (Beschützer), defender (Behüter)." He reads ענה as "call, react, appeal," thus, "interlocutor" (Gesprächspartner).¹³ Rudolph understands that the offender will be cut off from the community in a social and cultic sense, left without any protection.

---

⁷ *B. Sanh.* 82a: "If he is a scholar, he shall have none awakening [i.e., teaching] among the sages and none responding among the disciples"; *b. Šabb.* 55b: "If an Israelite, he shall have none awakening [i.e., teaching] among the sages and none responding among the disciples"; followed by Rashi and Qimḥi (A. J. Rosenberg, ed., *Mikraʾoth Gedoloth: Twelve Prophets. A New English Translation* [New York: Judaica, 1992], 409).

⁸ Followed by Martin Luther, *Lectures on the Minor Prophets*, vol. 1, *Hosea, Joel, Amos, Obadiah, Micah, Nahum, Zephaniah, Haggai, Malachi* (ed. Jaroslav Pelikan; Luther's Works 18; Saint Louis: Concordia, 1975), 404. Cf. the AV (original 1611 version): "the Master and the Scholler" (Cathcart and Gordon, *Targum of the Minor Prophets*, 233).

⁹ Duhm, *Anmerkungen zu den Zwölf Propheten* (ZAW Sonderabdruck 31; Giessen: Töpelmann, 1911), 93: "der da wacht (auf Anruf) antwortet" ("the one who stays awake [on call] responds"). Similarly, Theodor Lescow, "Dialogische Strukturen in den Streitreden des Buches Maleachi," *ZAW* 102 (1990): 109–10: "Wachender und Antwortender" ("watchman and respondent"); and S. R. Driver, *The Minor Prophets* (2 vols.; Century Bible; Oxford: Oxford University Press, 1906), 314.

¹⁰ Keil, *The Minor Prophets* (1866; Commentary on the Old Testament 10; repr., Peabody, MA: Hendricksen, 2001), 650–51. He thinks that it also carries the sense of *vivus quisque* ("everyone living").

¹¹ "The tent is the essence of the nomadic way of life" (Klaus Koch, "אֹהֶל," *TDOT* 1:120).

¹² *HALAT* (3:758, s.v. עוּר II *qal*) also raises עִיר as a possibility for the root verb in Mal 2:12.

¹³ Rudolph, *Haggai, Sacharja 1–8, Sacharja 9–14, Maleachi* (KAT 13.4; Gütersloh: Mohn, 1976), 269. Similarly, Henning Graf Reventlow, *Die Propheten Haggai, Sacharja und Maleachi* (ATD 25.2; Göttingen: Vandenhoeck & Ruprecht, 1993), 146: "Wächter und Verteidiger" ("guardians and defenders"); Dominique Barthélemy, *Critique textuelle de l'Ancien Testament*,

6. *Legal (Wellhausen et al.).* Julius Wellhausen suggests a retroversion similar to the presumed Hebrew *Vorlage* behind the LXX, except that עד is taken as the noun "witness/accuser" rather than the preposition "until" (ἕως); וענה is rendered "and who answers," as in the phrase קרא וענה.[14] For Wellhausen, the phrase concerns two opposing parties: "a (hostile) witness [Kläger] and a (defending) counsel [Verteidiger]."

Albin van Hoonacker understands the two words to be synonyms—rather than two opposing categories—which are used to accentuate the idea of a "defense" with regard to the one who had committed the abuse of intermarriage: "witness and respondent" ("témoin et répondant").[15] Coordinating מגיש with עד וענה, he translates the former as "cult minister" ("le ministre du culte"), suggesting that the accused person was deprived of all legal and cultic support before Yhwh.[16]

Also envisaging a legal context, but without Wellhausen's retroversion to a different Hebrew *Vorlage*, Julia M. O'Brien suggests that עד may derive from the Aramaic עֲרָר.[17] She notes that עד means to enter into a lawsuit with someone,[18] and, in various rabbinic texts, עֲרָר refers to protest and objection (e.g., *y. Ketub.* VII, 31c).[19] Although the masoretic vocalization is against it, the consonantal text of Mal 2:12 could support the derivation of עד from עֲרָר.[20]

Continuing with the witness theme but in a different context, Martin A.

---

vol. 3, *Ézéchiel, Daniel et les 12 Prophètes* (OBO 50.3; Fribourg: Editions Universitaires; Göttingen: Vandenhoeck & Ruprecht, 1992), 1029: "À l'homme qui commettra cela, le Seigneur retranchera appelant et réagissant hors des tentes de Jacob" ("To the person who commits it, the Lord will cut off the one calling and responding from the tents of Jacob").

[14] Wellhausen, *Skizzen und Vorarbeiten*, vol. 5, *Die kleinen Propheten* (4th ed.; Berlin: de Gruyter, 1892), 198. Similarly, D. Ernst Sellin, *Das Zwölfprophetenbuch übersetzt und erklärt* (KAT 12; Leipzig: Deichert, 1929), 550: "'Bürgen' und Zeugen" ("'guarantors' and witnesses"); Wilhelm Nowack, *Die kleinen Propheten* (HAT; 3rd rev. ed.; Göttingen: Vandenhoeck & Ruprecht, 1922), 435: "Ankläger und Verteidiger" ("[commercial] attester and [judicial] witness"); Andrew E. Hill, *Malachi: A New Translation with Introduction and Commentary* (AB 25D; New York: Doubleday, 1998), 221: "witness or respondent"; Douglas K. Stuart, "Malachi," in *The Minor Prophets: An Exegetical and Expository Commentary* (ed. Thomas Edward McComiskey; 3 vols.; Grand Rapids: Baker, 1998), 3:1334: "witness and testifier"; idiomatically, "one who says this and one who says that." Stuart believes that it is almost certainly an idiom for "every single one."

[15] Van Hoonacker, *Les douze Petits Prophètes* (EBib 4; Paris: Victor Lecoffre, 1908), 724, though in his translation van Hoonacker has the opposite order, and "répondant" is in scare quotes. The NRSV reads עד instead of עַר: "any to witness or answer."

[16] Van Hoonacker, *Les douze Petits Prophètes*, 724.

[17] O'Brien, *Priest and Levite in Malachi* (SBLDS 121; Atlanta: Scholars Press, 1990), 71–72. In Dan 4:16, עָר signifies an adversary.

[18] See A. Cowley, *Aramaic Papyri of the Fifth Century B.C.* (Osnabrück: Otto Zeller, 1923), no. 8, line 27.

[19] Jastrow, 1123–24, s.v. עֲרָר.

[20] עֵר is the participle form of עוּר, while the participle of עָרַר (stative) is עָר (contra O'Brien, who suggests עָר [*Priest and Levite*, 72 n. 98]).

Shields follows the reading of 4QXII[a] and the LXX but takes עד וענה to be a description of the goddess in v. 11 (בת־אל נכר): "a witness and one who bears testimony."[21] He explains, "This rendering would have the prophet calling upon Yahweh to cut off the one who makes the goddess 'a witness.'"[22] The idea is that people were putting the goddess in the place of Yhwh as the arbiter of right and wrong (cf. Mal 2:14; 3:5).[23]

7. *Cultic (Matthews).* J. G. Matthews interprets the phrase in the MT as "inciter and respondent," reading it in a cultic sense: "an admirable characterization of those who take part in the dance or in the antiphonal responses in Tammuz worship."[24]

8. *Sexual (Glazier-McDonald et al.).* Overlapping with the cultic view is Beth Glazier-McDonald's "novel" interpretation: "the one who is aroused (from sexual inactivity, i.e., the aroused one) and the lover."[25] She suggests that ער and ענה bear a sexual connotation that relates to a fertility rite.[26] Based on the sexual connotations of the *qal* participle of עור ("awake, arouse") in Song 4:16 and 5:2, Glazier-McDonald argues that the meaning of ער in Mal 2:12 may be sexual.[27] In addition, she reads ענה to mean "express sexual intercourse by mutual consent" (cf. Hos 2:16–17[14–15]), from ענה III *qal*.[28] Seeing both terms as veiled synonyms of זנה, "play the harlot, commit fornication"[29] (see Hos 1:2; 2:7[5]; 3:3; 4:10; 5:3; 9:1), she believes that they help to highlight the syncretistic worship that

---

[21] Shields, "Syncretism and Divorce in Malachi 2:10–16," *ZAW* 111 (1999): 73–75. Shields understands עשה to have a double accusative: the feminine suffix on יעשנה refers back to בת־אל נכר and עד וענה. Shields does not name the goddess but implies that she was of Babylonian origin (72 and n. 9).

[22] Ibid., 75.

[23] Ibid., 76. Shields suggests that this may explain the significance of the question in Mal 2:17: "Where is the God of justice?"

[24] Matthews, "Tammuz-Worship in the Book of Malachi," *JPOS* 2 (1931): 46.

[25] Glazier-McDonald, "Malachi 2:12: *ʿēr wĕʿōneh*—Another Look," *JBL* 105 (1986): 297. Glazier-McDonald claims that a sexual connotation of the two words "has never been examined" (p. 296), but L. Levy had previously suggested the connotation ("Der Prophet Maleachi," in *Festschrift zum 75. jährigen Bestehen des Jüdisch-theologischen Seminars der Fraenckelscher Stiftung* [2 vols.; Breslau: M. & H. Marcus, 1929], 2:273–84).

[26] Glazier-McDonald, "Malachi 2:12," 296.

[27] Glazier-McDonald is dependent on Marvin H. Pope (*Song of Songs: A New Translation with Introduction and Commentary* [AB 7C; Garden City, NY: Doubleday, 1977], 498), who translates the verbs in Song 4:16 and 5:2 in this way. The *hiphil* and *polel* of עור are used in Song of Songs to mean "rouse, excite love" (2:7; 3:5; 8:4).

[28] Glazier-McDonald, "Malachi 2:12," 296. See the *piel* of ענה III in legal contexts, where the idea of forced sexual intercourse or rape is in mind (Gen 34:2; Deut 21:14; 22:24, 29).

[29] W. Gesenius, *Gesenius's Hebrew and Chaldee Lexicon to the Old Testament Scriptures* (trans. S. P. Tregelles; London: Samuel Bagster & Sons, 1857), 249.

Malachi is addressing as a result of the intermarriages in postexilic Judah.³⁰ Thus, for Glazier-McDonald,

> What Malachi is opposing are the syncretistic phenomena that have entered the Yahweh cult through intermarriage. The sexual connotations of ʿēr and ʿōneh support the suggestion that these rites have to do with fertility. The man (ʾîš) who performs them is a fornicator, a prostitute (zōneh, ʿēr, ʿōneh). The overwhelming fertility, sexual imagery finds its antithesis in Mal 2:15. The fornicator will be barren (i.e., without spirit); his seed will not germinate.³¹

Steffan Schreiner also opts for a sexual reading but arrives at his proposal via different homonym roots of עור and ענה.³² He proposes that the phrase is a reference to the man who has intermarried: he has committed "shame" ("Schande")³³ and "fornication" ("Unzucht").³⁴

Similar to the sexual connotation proposed by Glazier-McDonald is David L. Petersen's repointing of the consonantal text to read עָר וְעֹנֶה ("anyone … involving nakedness and improper habitation"), practices acquainted with the veneration of a foreign deity such as Asherah.³⁵

9. *All-inclusive (S. R. Driver et al.).* Some scholars read the phrase ער וענה as an alliterative proverbial expression for "everyone." So S. R. Driver: "him that waketh and him that answereth" means "everyone"; or Conrad von Orelli: "him that calls and him that gives reply" means "all active in the house."³⁶ For Theodore F. K. Laetsch, it may mean "the entire body of people, the whole nation," while Eugene H. Merrill describes it as a merism consisting of opposing categories intended to include everyone: "the awake and the asleep, who together make up all of mankind."³⁷

---

³⁰ A couple of factors draw Glazier-McDonald in this direction. Aspects of fertility are suggested by the verb בעל (Mal 2:11), which recalls Baal, the god of rain and fertility, and Mal 2:13 alludes to weeping as part of a fertility rite (Gösta W. Ahlström, *Joel and the Temple Cult of Jerusalem* [VTSup 21; Leiden: Brill, 1971]) or as part of mourning over the death of a goddess's lover (בעל) (Flemming Friis Hvidberg, *Weeping and Laughter in the Old Testament: A Study of Canaanite-Israelite Religion* [Copenhagen: NYT Nordisk Forlag, 1962]) (Glazier-McDonald, "Malachi 2:12," 298).

³¹ Glazier-McDonald, "Malachi 2:12," 298. On this epexegetical reading, the phrase ער וענה is in apposition to לאיש, serving as a further explanation of the man who will be cut off.

³² Schreiner, "Mischehen–Ehebruch–Ehescheidung," ZAW 91 (1979): 211.

³³ From עור II qal, "be exposed," or from ערה, "lay bare."

³⁴ From ענה II qal, "be occupied, busied with."

³⁵ Petersen, *Zechariah 9–14 & Malachi* (OTL; Louisville: Westminster John Knox, 1995), 194, 201.

³⁶ S. R. Driver, *Minor Prophets,* 314; von Orelli, *The Twelve Minor Prophets* (trans. John Shaw Banks; Edinburgh: T&T Clark, 1897), 394. The NIV interprets the phrase as qualifying איש: "whoever he may be." Similarly, Pieter A. Verhoef, *The Books of Haggai and Malachi* (NICOT; Grand Rapids: Eerdmans, 1987), 271: "irrespective of the person, whoever he may be."

³⁷ Laetsch, *Minor Prophets* (Concordia Commentary Series 3; St. Louis: Concordia, 1956), 524; Merrill, *Haggai, Zechariah, Malachi: An Exegetical Commentary* (1994; repr., LaVergne, TN:

10. *Familial (Torrey et al.).* According to C. C. Torrey, an accident in one of the early manuscripts rendered the text partially illegible. He suggests that where the two troublesome words stand one should expect the equivalent of "all his house, remembrance, posterity," or some such phrase, that is, "everyone." Through comparison with Mal 3:19, he suggests that the original words were שרש וענף and would thus have read: "Yahwè destroy, for the man who does this, *root and branch* from the tents of Jacob!"[38] Others, while not going along with Torrey's emendation, think that the two words form a proverbial pair whose thrust was to include "everybody" related to the person: "Offenders would have no friends or relatives left at all."[39] Thus, the verse conveys "the extermination of the entire family of the guilty man."[40]

Differing from Torrey's conjectural emendation, other scholars have arrived at the familial interpretation via an etymological and philological approach on the basis of cognate languages. For example, Georg H. A. Ewald proposes a possible cognate for ער in the Arabic root *gharra*, from which several derivatives signify "boy, child"; ענה then carries the sense of a "witness," "probably equivalent to a descendant, child."[41] G. R. Driver links ער וענה with two Arabic roots and renders the phrase: "gad-about and stay-at-home," an ancient saying originally describing

---

Biblical Studies Press, 2003), 361; similarly, Rex Mason, *Preaching the Tradition: Homily and Hermeneutics after the Exile* (Cambridge: Cambridge University Press, 1990), 249.

[38] Torrey, "The Prophecy of 'Malachi,'" *JBL* 17 (1898): 5 n. 12. Similarly, Karl Marti, *Das Dodekapropheton* (KHC 13; Tübingen: Mohr Siebeck, 1904), 470: "Wurzel und Zweig" ("root and branch"); G. Johannes Botterweck, "Schelt und Mahnrede gegen Mischehen und Ehescheidung: Auslegung von Mal. 2:2, 10–16," *BibLeb* 1 (1960): 182. Some years later, upon finding an Arabic parallel, Torrey changed his mind: the MT was correct. He then translated the phrase as "the calling one and the answering one," taking ער as deriving from עור: "the one who begins [lit. arouses] the conversation and the one who answers." The idea, however, was still that of totality: the guilty man would have no one left with whom to converse ("*ʿēr wĕʿōneh* in Malachi ii.12," *JBL* 24 [1905]: 176–78).

[39] David J. Clark, "A Discourse Approach to Problems in Malachi 2:10–16," *BT* 46 (1998): 417. In support, see Georg Heinrich August von Ewald, *Commentary on the Prophets of the Old Testament*, vol. 5, *The Books of Haggai, Zakharya, Malʾaki, Yona, Barûkh, Daniel* (trans. J. Frederick Smith; London: Williams & Norgate, 1881), 81–82; Joyce G. Baldwin, *Haggai, Zechariah, Malachi: An Introduction and Commentary* (TOTC; Leicester: InterVarsity, 1972), 239; Walter C. Kaiser Jr., *Malachi: God's Unchanging Love* (Grand Rapids: Baker, 1984), 68; David J. Clark and Howard A. Hatton, *A Handbook on Haggai, Zechariah, and Malachi* (UBS Handbook Series; New York: United Bible Societies, 2002), 415; Richard A. Taylor and E. Ray Clendenen, *Haggai, Malachi* (NAC 21A; Nashville: Broadman & Holman, 2004), 339; Alviero Niccacci, "Poetic Syntax and Interpretation of Malachi," *SBFLA* 51 (2001): 85: "any living offspring." A. S. van der Woude thinks that the verse is a gloss ("Malachi's Struggle for a Pure Community: Reflections on Malachi 2:10–16," in *Tradition and Reinterpretation in Jewish and Early Christian Literature: Essays in Honour of Jurgen C. H. Lebram* [ed. J. W. van Henten et al.; StPB 36; Leiden: Brill, 1986], 68). NJPSV: "descendants" (with a footnote claiming that the meaning of the Hebrew is uncertain).

[40] John Merlin Powis Smith, *A Critical and Exegetical Commentary on Malachi* (ICC; Edinburgh: T&T Clark, 1912), 51.

[41] Ewald, *Prophets of the Old Testament*, 81–82.

all members of a tent.⁴² He argues that this interpretation is not an "extreme Arabism" since both roots are known in the Hebrew Bible: עָר derives from the same root as עַיִר ("wild ass"), while ענה is translated "dwell" by the LXX in at least one place: Isa 13:22[21]: καὶ ὀνοκένταυροι ἐκεῖ κατοικήσουσιν (MT: וענה איים באלמנותיו).⁴³ Certainly the parallel verbs רבץ and שכן in Isa 13:21[20] lend support to the LXX translation.⁴⁴ Shifting language, Friedrich Horst suggests a cognate for עָר with Akkadian *ajaru* (*āru/ajjaru*), meaning "male offspring" ("männlicher Sproß").⁴⁵

III. Critique

The vast array of translations and interpretations is daunting and leaves one perplexed as to the meaning of עָר וענה in Mal 2:12. Some careful reflection, however, reveals problems with some of the early and modern translations and interpretations.

Regarding option (1), while two independent witnesses (LXX and 4QXIIᵃ) suggest the reading עֵד over עָר, Anthony Gelston, editor of the *BHQ* edition of the Twelve Minor Prophets, writes, "The difficulties of this phrase [עָר וענה] are exegetical rather than textual."⁴⁶ He contends that "the great majority of variations between the Hebrew Bible and the ancient versions originated within the versions themselves rather deriving from a variant Hebrew *Vorlage*."⁴⁷ He draws attention to several factors that limited the ancient translators' understanding of the Hebrew text: (a) the phenomenon of homonyms, words of identical form but different in

---

⁴² G. R. Driver, "Confused Hebrew Roots," in *Occident and Orient: Being Studies in Semitic Philology and Literature, Jewish History and Philosophy and Folklore in the Widest Sense, in Honour of Haham Dr. M. Gaster's 80th Birthday. Gaster Anniversary Volume* (ed. Bruno Schindler; London: Taylor's Foreign Press, 1936), 80. Cf. עור = ערה = ערר. See also idem, review of Joseph Ziegler, *Untersuchungen zur LXXa des Buches Isaias* (1934), *JTS* 36 (1935): 81–83, esp. 82; idem, "Linguistic and Textual Problems: Minor Prophets. II," *JTS* 39 (1938): 272; idem, "Supposed Arabisms in the Old Testament," *JBL* 55 (1936): 104–5. The NEB translates "nomad and settler."

⁴³ In support, see Israel Eitan, "A Contribution to Isaiah Exegesis (Notes and Short Studies in Biblical Philology)," *HUCA* 12 (1937–38): 61–62. Eitan compares ענה to the rare Arabic root *ganiya*, "stay (in a place), inhabit permanently" (cf. Hos 2:17 [possibly]). Both roots are sufficiently rare for their meaning at an earlier date to have been forgotten.

⁴⁴ Although James Barr is correct to point out that ענה is not so rendered in LXX Mal 2:12, he neglects to notice that such a rendering is unlikely given that LXX translates עד as ἕως (*Comparative Philology and the Text of the Old Testament* [Oxford: OUP, 1968], 243). Barr generally cautions against G. R. Driver's Arabisms (165, 243, 250, 333).

⁴⁵ Horst, *Die zwölf kleinen Propheten, Nahum bis Maleachi* (HAT 14; Tübingen: Mohr Siebeck, 1974), 268. See *CAD* 1:230: *ajaru* D = young man; *AHw* 1:25: *ajjaru* = junger Mann.

⁴⁶ Gelston, *The Twelve Minor Prophets* (BHQ 13; Stuttgart: Deutsche Bibelgesellschaft, 2010), 150*.

⁴⁷ Gelston, "Some Difficulties Encountered by Ancient Translations," in *Sôfer Mahîr: Essays in Honour of Adrian Schenker Offered by Editors of Biblia Hebraica Quinta* (ed. Yohanan A. P. Goldman et al.; VTSup 110; Leiden: Brill, 2006), 47.

meaning; (b) the lack of vocalization in biblical Hebrew texts; and (c) the difficulty thrown up by "irregular" verbs. I would suggest that all three difficulties are present in Mal 2:12. First, the verbs עור and ענה exhibit substantial homonymy in the Hebrew Bible.[48] Second, the LXX translation of ἕως for the presumed word עד reveals that "witness" (עֵד) was not necessarily the obvious reading of the consonantal text. And third, on either reading of ער or עד an "irregular" verb is in play.

In addition to these three factors of difficulty for an ancient translator, the variant עד is potentially an example of one of the most common discrepancies that occurs, either in the scribal transmission of the Hebrew *Vorlage* or in the actual process of translation into Greek: a ר has been (mis)read for a ד.[49] Indeed, in Malachi the reverse graphical error occurs four times in the LXX: a ד has been (mis)read for a ר (2:15 [2x]; 3:15, 19).[50] Gelston has observed a similar and frequent confusion in both directions between ר/ד elsewhere in the LXX of the Twelve.[51] As he concludes in a study on the LXX of Amos, "The frequency of confusion between *daleth* and *resh* suggests that the difficulty lay principally in the actual handwriting of the Hebrew text that formed the *Vorlage* used by the LXX translator."[52]

A similar explanation may be given for option (2), the (mis)reading of ד in 4QXII[a].[53] The Hebrew letters ר/ד are graphically similar during all stages of the Hebrew script. As Emanuel Tov comments:

> In certain periods and in the writing of certain scribes, some of these letters were hardly distinguishable. In attempting to distinguish between them when copying their sources, scribes were guided not only by the form of the letters but also by contextual considerations. In practice this meant that scribes sometimes must have pondered whether the word they were about to copy would make more sense when written, for example, with a *daleth* than with a *resh*. Translators must have acted similarly.[54]

Tov continues: "The assumption of such palaeographical maneuvering is objectively conditioned by the occurrence of lexical difficulties,"[55] which is exactly the case in Mal 2:12: ער וענה is an obscure phrase.

---

[48] עור has two entries in *HALAT* and five in *DCH*, while ענה has a standard four entries in the main lexicons, with *DCH* providing a possible thirteen.

[49] Emanuel Tov notes that "there are generally no rules for the *direction* of the interchange" (*Textual Criticism of the Hebrew Bible* [Minneapolis: Fortress, 1992], 243). The ר/ד interchange is one of the most frequent interchanges between the LXX and the MT, along with י/ו.

[50] Malachi 2:15: אחד is (mis)read for אחר (ἄλλος; ἄλλο); Mal 3:15 and 3:19: זדים is (mis)read for זרים (ἀλλοτρίος; ἀλλογενής, respectively).

[51] Gelston, "Some Hebrew Misreadings in the Septuagint of Amos," *VT* 52 (2002): 493–500.

[52] Ibid., 499.

[53] 4QXII[a] is a fragmentary text that exhibits a range of typical transmission errors, such as haplography, metathesis, and confusion of similar letters.

[54] Tov, *The Text-Critical Use of the Septuagint in Biblical Research* (2nd rev. and enlarged ed.; Jerusalem Biblical Studies 8; Jerusalem: Simor, 1997), 163.

[55] Ibid., 164.

In sum, it seems reasonable to suggest that the reading עד in the LXX and 4QXII[a] is an error, made either by a copyist, or, as Gelston suggests, by a translator in reading illegible handwriting in the Hebrew *Vorlage*. Fuller's rejection of the MT reading, on the basis that it is "problematic," leans more toward assertion than argument and ignores the possible authenticity of a text based on the *lectio difficilior*—ער וענה is indeed the harder reading. Moreover, as L. Kruse-Blinkenberg states, "there are no weighty arguments against literal translation and understanding of the MT."[56]

Tg. Neb.'s rendering of "son and grandson" in option (3) above is repeated for the expression שרש וענף ("root and branch") in Mal 3:19, which does not "inspire confidence in *Tg.*'s philological competence."[57] Option (4) is problematic from a contextual perspective: prima facie, the educational idea is foreign to Malachi's immediate concerns. Moreover, the prophet does not suggest that he is speaking only of priests, who would, in this case, be the teachers who "awake"; the whole nation is being addressed (v. 10). Option (5) raises the question as to how cutting off a watchman in the camp becomes a curse on the man who has intermarried.

Wellhausen's proposal (6) of a hostile witness and a defending counsel, followed in various ways by others, is based on the (questionable) presupposition that the original text read עד. But even if this reading is granted, עד does not have the technical meaning that Wellhausen attaches to it: עד means "witness," for or against, depending on the context, but it is never used of an actual human plaintiff or accuser, although it is used of YHWH.[58] Indeed, one is led to ask why YHWH would cut off the accuser of the man who intermarries. Surely YHWH would be on his side, rather than choosing to remove him. The participle ענה can also have a legal meaning and may be used for an accusing or defending witness, though more frequently for the former.[59] The context, however, does not suit these meanings for either word, since עד and ענה are to be cut off "from the tents of Jacob" (מאהלי יעקב) and not from the courtroom.[60] Attending to this context also counters the legal proposals of van Hoonacker and O'Brien. G. R. Driver's comment that ordinary people

---

[56] Kruse-Blinkenberg, "The Pesitta [sic] of the Book of Malachi," *ST* 20 (1966): 101.

[57] Cathcart and Gordon, *Targum of the Minor Prophets*, 233 n. 18.

[58] Glazier-McDonald, "Malachi 2:12," 295. Note the meanings "bear witness for" (Isa 43:9, 10; 44:8, 9; Job 29:11; Lam 2:13) and "bear witness against" (1 Kgs 21:10, 13). Neither *HALAT* nor *DCH* gives this technical meaning to עד when used of a human. *HALAT* (3:745) has the meaning of accuser when used of YHWH: "Richter bzw. Ankläger" ("judge or prosecutor") (Gen 31:50; 1 Sam 12:5, 6; 20:12; Jer 29:23; 42:5; Mic 1:2; Mal 3:5). *DCH* (6:271–72) is less certain and mentions only Isa 55:4 and Mal 3:5 as possibilities for the meaning "judge." In each of these cases, however, "witness" is an equally good rendering, as most English translations demonstrate.

[59] For "accuse," see Exod 20:16; Num 35:30; Deut 19:18; 2 Sam 1:16; for "defend," see Gen 30:33. *DCH* (6:495) suggests that ענה in Mal 2:12 means "respond (as a witness), bear (witness), testify," but also gives ענה II *qal*, "oppress," and ענה VII *qal*, "stay," as other possibilities.

[60] Torrey, "Prophecy of 'Malachi,'" 5 n. 12. Marti argues that if the courtroom is the context we would expect "gates of his city" (שערי עירו) (*Das Dodekapropheton*, 470).

would be little concerned with legal matters and would not be so commercialized as to be able to afford a legal defense further weakens the judicial angle.⁶¹

Shields follows the questionable reading of the LXX, but his attempt to assign the phrase to a goddess who bears witness breaks down also from a gender perspective: it is unlikely that the goddess (בת־אל נכר) (feminine) would be described with two masculine participles (ער וענה). However, Shields's interpretation, along with Matthews's (7) and Petersen's (8), may be ruled out also on the basis that the cultic reading for Mal 2:10–16 does not hold; a literal reading that understands the pericope to be about human marriage between a man and a woman makes more sense in the context.⁶²

The problem with Glazier-McDonald's "novel" interpretation (8) is that the sexual connotation of עור *qal* is found only in Song 4:16 and 5:2;⁶³ all other occurrences in the *qal* stem simply mean "awake, arise, arouse" (Judg 5:12; Isa 51:9; 52:1; etc.). This is not to say that a sexual connotation is automatically ruled out in Mal 2:12; but it is weakened by the fact that the partner term ענה unlikely expresses "sexual intercourse by mutual consent," as Glazier-McDonald proposes.⁶⁴ The only other text that possibly carries this meaning is Hos 2:17[15], and even then other renderings are far more plausible.⁶⁵ Moreover, Glazier-McDonald's claim that both terms (עור and ענה) are veiled synonyms of זנה is problematic: in the Hebrew Bible the verb זנה is attributed "properly and chiefly to a woman,"⁶⁶ which creates problems with attributing such connotations to the man here. Besides, strictly speaking, the curse in Mal 2:12 is not for fornication with a foreigner but for marriage to a foreigner. Furthermore, Glazier-McDonald's epexegetical construction of the clause goes against the normal punishment formula of כרת + ל, where the two accompanying participles/nouns serve as the main object of the verb (see below).

Option (9) lacks specificity: does Yhwh desire the cutting off of "the whole nation" or "all mankind" as the result of *one* man who intermarries? A more specific group that is related to the man (לאיש) is surely intended. Finally, while some of the etymological and philological proposals for rendering the phrase in a familial sense in option (10) may appear to be attractive, they are based on guesswork and conjecture.

---

⁶¹ G. R. Driver, "Confused Hebrew Roots," 80.

⁶² Petersen's repointing of the consonantal phrase to עֵר וְעֹנָה is too awkward to be credible (*Zechariah 9–14 & Malachi*, 194, 201): grammatically, עֵר is an infinitive construct of ערר, while עֹנָה is a feminine noun (used elsewhere only in Exod 21:10). The alliteration at least suggests that the phrase was an idiom, and thus more grammatical balance would be expected.

⁶³ Though, interestingly, *HALAT* and *DCH* do not give this sense in the *qal* stem.

⁶⁴ Therefore Schreiner's proposal above also runs into the same problem.

⁶⁵ *DCH* (6:501) suggests ענה I, "answer," ענה III, "sing," or ענה XII, "attend," as alternatives to ענה XIII, "have intercourse." *HALAT* does not supply the root ענה with the meaning "have intercourse."

⁶⁶ Gesenius, *Gesenius's Hebrew and Chaldee Lexicon*, 249.

IV. Toward an Answer

In moving toward a solution for the difficult phrase ער וענה, a few things may be affirmed with at least some level of certainty. First, the obscurity of the alliterative proverbial expression suggests that it is best viewed as an idiom of some kind. Second, the meaning of the phrase should be deduced in relation to כרת, either as a qualification of the degree of the cutting off (e.g., socially and/or religiously), or as an extension of judgment against those guilty of such crimes (e.g., some kind of punishment of their descendants).[67] Third, in this regard the interpretation of ער וענה is influenced by how one reads the prepositional ל on איש. The common understanding is that it marks the object of the verb כרת.[68] But ל may introduce a complement, the so-called *dativus incommodi* (cf. 1 Sam 2:33; 1 Kgs 14:10; 21:21; 2 Kgs 9:8).[69] On this reading, the object of the verb כרת becomes ער וענה, with איש as the indirect object: "may Yhwh cut off for the man who does this ער וענה." Finally, any understanding of the phrase must be closely associated with some aspect of community life, since the prepositional phrase מאהלי יעקב is integral to the main sentence.[70]

V. Textual Comparison

As I have demonstrated above, retroversion of the LXX to a different Hebrew *Vorlage*, conjectural emendation of ר to ד, or various etymological and philological considerations of the homonymic verbs עור and ענה (some on the basis of cognate languages) do not yield a clear understanding of how to interpret the obscure phrase ער וענה. This is not to disparage any of these approaches; it is, however, to suggest that in this particular case another methodological approach is required in order to advance the discussion. I propose that a textual comparison of relevant biblical passages containing the formula כרת + ל + two coordinated participles/nouns (often displaying alliteration and/or assonance) may prove helpful for the interpretation of ער וענה.

---

[67] Hill, *Malachi*, 235. Jacob Milgrom argues that in Mal 2:12 the verb כרת expresses a divine penalty that involves "extirpation of the offender's entire line" (*Leviticus 1–16: A New Translation with Introduction and Commentary* [AB 3; New York: Doubleday, 1991], 459).

[68] GKC §117n: a "solecism [a grammatical mistake or absurdity] of the later period is … the introduction of the object by the preposition ל" (cf. Gen 17:12).

[69] GKC §119s.

[70] The complete phrase harks back to Israel's nomadic days in the wilderness (see Exod 12:15, 19; 31:14; Lev 7:20, 21, 25, 27; 19:8; 20:18; 22:3; Num 9:13; 15:31; 19:13, 20) (Merrill, *Malachi*, 361); contra Hill, who views it as simply an alternative way to describe a home (*Malachi*, 235).

Malachi 2:12	1 Kings 14:10
יַכְרֵת יְהוָה לָאִישׁ אֲשֶׁר יַעֲשֶׂנָּה עֵר וְעֹנֶה מֵאָהֳלֵי יַעֲקֹב וּמַגִּישׁ מִנְחָה לַיהוָה צְבָאוֹת׃	לָכֵן הִנְנִי מֵבִיא רָעָה אֶל־בֵּית יָרָבְעָם וְהִכְרַתִּי לְיָרָבְעָם מַשְׁתִּין בְּקִיר **עָצוּר וְעָזוּב** בְּיִשְׂרָאֵל וּבִעַרְתִּי אַחֲרֵי בֵית־יָרָבְעָם כַּאֲשֶׁר יְבַעֵר הַגָּלָל עַד־תֻּמּוֹ׃
	1 Kgs 21.21
	הִנְנִי מֵבִי אֵלֶיךָ רָעָה וּבִעַרְתִּי אַחֲרֶיךָ וְהִכְרַתִּי לְאַחְאָב מַשְׁתִּין בְּקִיר **וְעָצוּר וְעָזוּב** בְּיִשְׂרָאֵל׃
	2 Kgs 9:8
	וְאָבַד כָּל־בֵּית אַחְאָב וְהִכְרַתִּי לְאַחְאָב מַשְׁתִּין בְּקִיר **וְעָצוּר וְעָזוּב** בְּיִשְׂרָאֵל׃
	Isa 14:22
	וְקַמְתִּי עֲלֵיהֶם נְאֻם יְהוָה צְבָאוֹת וְהִכְרַתִּי לְבָבֶל **שֵׁם וּשְׁאָר וְנִין וָנֶכֶד** נְאֻם־יְהוָה׃
	Jer 44:7
	וְעַתָּה כֹּה־אָמַר יְהוָה אֱלֹהֵי צְבָאוֹת אֱלֹהֵי יִשְׂרָאֵל לָמָה אַתֶּם עֹשִׂים רָעָה גְדוֹלָה אֶל־נַפְשֹׁתֵכֶם לְהַכְרִית לָכֶם **אִישׁ־וְאִשָּׁה עוֹלֵל וְיוֹנֵק** מִתּוֹךְ יְהוּדָה לְבִלְתִּי הוֹתִיר לָכֶם שְׁאֵרִית׃
	Jer 47.4
	עַל־הַיּוֹם הַבָּא לִשְׁדוֹד אֶת־כָּל־פְּלִשְׁתִּים לְהַכְרִית לְצֹר וּלְצִידוֹן כֹּל **שָׂרִיד עֹזֵר** כִּי־שֹׁדֵד יְהוָה אֶת־פְּלִשְׁתִּים שְׁאֵרִית אִי כַפְתּוֹר׃

In the texts cited above where the punishment formula כרת + ל appears a common pattern emerges.[71] In these texts the word prefixed by ל marks the evildoer, but only as the indirect object of the verb; the object comprises a word pair, in some cases two word pairs or a collocation of terms. Four features of the coordinated word pairs in these texts are noteworthy. (1) In nearly every case the word pair exhibit alliteration and/or assonance. (2) Each word pair form either a hendiadys (the word pair convey one specific societal component, e.g., עצור ועזוב, "bond and free") or a merism (the word pair convey totality via the extension of opposites on one plane, e.g., איש ואשה, "man and woman").[72] (3) In most cases, read in context, the word

---

[71] In each case, the *hiphil* stem of כרת is used.

[72] Shemaryahu Talmon and Weston W. Fields define hendiadys as "a double-barrelled expression, or a form of parataxis, which expresses or refers to one specific societal component only, defining it by juxtaposition of two designations. In such instances, in fact, the two terms mutually illuminate each other, or else one explains the other." They give the following examples: עצור ועזוב (ruler/leader); גר ותושב (resident alien); נע ונד (wanderer); תהו ובהו (disorder);

pair denote the *offspring* of the evildoer. (4) The common idea in the surrounding contexts of each text is that the offspring will be completely wiped out as a result of Yhwh's punishment—there will be no remnant.

Examination of the details of Mal 2:12 suggests that similar features are present. First, the word pair exhibit alliteration with the initial ע and assonance in the final vowel sound. Second, the word pair form either a hendiadys or a merism.[73] Most commentators propose that the phrase ער וענה is a merism, a polar expression, conveying a "totality" of sorts. However, A. M. Honeyman's distinction between hendiadys and merism perhaps suggests that ער וענה is a hendiadys: "The essential difference between the two figures is that hendiadys describes an object by alluding to its qualities or attributes under two or more different categories, while merismus sets forth its extension on one plane."[74] That is, hendiadys emphasizes a specific category or component (A + B = Z), while merism spotlights the totality of that category or component (A to B and everything in between = Z).

Of the known homonyms for the two roots עור and ענה, there are no obvious

---

יין ושכר (intoxicating drink); כסף וזהב (riches) ("The Collocation משתין בקיר ועצור ועזוב and Its Meaning," *ZAW* 101 [1989]: 87–88). Interestingly, Talmon and Fields place ער וענה in this category of hendiadys (p. 88 n. 14). A. S. Yahuda suggests that ער וענה is a parallel expression to עצור ועזוב ("Ueber עצור ועזוב und ער וענה im Alten Testament," *ZA* 16 [1902]: 261).

Joze Krašovec defines merism as "the art of expressing a totality by mentioning the parts, usually the two extremes, concerning a given idea, quality and quantity; consequently polar expression is the most usual form of merism" ("Merism—Polar Expression in Biblical Hebrew," *Bib* 64 [1983]: 232). He explains that merism is a substitution for the abstract words "all," "every," and the like. The mentioned parts are figurative or metaphorical, not literal; and merism should not be confused with antithesis. Examples in the OT of merismus are: טוב ורע ("good and evil"; Gen 3:5); מוצאך ומבאך ("your going out and your coming in"; 2 Sam 3:25); ראש וזנב ("head and tail"; Isa 9:13[14]); שם ושאר ונין ונכד ("name and survivors, offspring and descendants"; Isa 14:22); צדיק ורשע ("righteous and wicked"; Ezek 21:8[3]); שרש וענף ("root and branch"; Mal 3:19[4:1]).

[73] It is sometimes tricky to differentiate between hendiadys and merism, as can be seen from the overlap in the lists above, and scholars differ over which phrases belong to which category. For example, H. A. Brongers comments, "Neben den reinen Hendiadysen gibt es nun auch eine ganze Reihe von Wortpaaren, Kombinationen von zwei Substantiven oder zwei Adjektiven, die zwar die Form des Hendiadys aufweisen, inhaltlich aber keine Hendiadyse sind" ("Besides the pure hendiadyses there are now a number of word pairs, combinations of two nouns or adjectives that indeed show that they have the shape of the hendiadys, but are not hendiadys in content") ("Merismus, Synekdoche und Hendiadys," *OtSt* 14 [1965]: 110). Among these he lists תהו ובהו (Gen 1:2), עצור ועזוב (1 Kgs 14:10; 21:21; 2 Kgs 9:8; 14:26), and שם ושאר (Isa 14:22). In contrast, Talmon and Shields list the first two as instances of hendiadys ("The Collocation משתין בקיר ועצור ועזוב and Its Meaning," 88).

[74] Honeyman, "*Merismus* in Biblical Hebrew," *JBL* 71 [1952]: 17. Honeyman states that merism, "a figure of speech akin in some respects to synecdoche, consists in detailing the individual members, or some of them—usually the first and last, or the more prominent—of a series, and thereby indicating either the genus of which those members are species or the abstract quality which characterizes the genus and which the species have in common" (p. 13).

"polar opposites." One possibility is "protector and oppressor,"[75] but this does not directly relate to the familial context. Moreover, for "oppressor" to be the meaning of ענה, the *piel* stem would be required, whereas the *qal* stem is used here. The other possibility is "nomad and settler,"[76] which seems to be more attuned to the familial idea and to the context of "the tents of Jacob"; but, again, this is based on questionable or unknown etymologies for the verbs עור and ענה. It seems more reasonable, therefore, to see the phrase as a hendiadys that refers to two qualities or attributes of the one social component.

Third, the context of Mal 2:12 (marriage) and the accompanying prepositional phrase ("from the tents of Jacob") support reading the idiomatic expression as a reference to offspring. Finally, the idea of a total punishment is evident from the evildoer's offspring being cut off from the community.

The textual comparison of the construction כרת + ל + two coordinated participles/nouns (often displaying alliteration and/or assonance) supports the familial intepretation of ער וענה. In most cases the participial/noun word pair denote *offspring* of the evildoer. As noted earlier, *Tg. Neb.* and some scholars (e.g., Torrey) arrive at this same conclusion, though there are questions about the Targum's "philological competence"[77] and about Torrey's speculative tendencies. While the interpretation presented here agrees with the likes of *Tg. Neb.* and Torrey, my conclusion has been arrived at on firmer grounds: the formal correspondence with other texts suggests that the word pair denote the *descendants* of the person involved, and not simply a general category of "everyone." Malachi 2:12 would appear, then, to be an idiomatic expression for offspring, one's own "kith and kin," which is conveyed by a hendiadys. In short, Mal 2:12 states that the evildoer who has intermarried will be punished by losing his offspring; no remnant will be left to him, recalling the Deuteronomic curse (see Deut 28:15–20).

A number of factors in the surrounding context complement this interpretation: (1) The subsequent phrase מאהלי יעקב ("from the tents of Jacob") suggests that the ער וענה belong to the community of Israel in some way. (2) The later interest in זרע אלהים ("seed of God," v. 15) shows that descendants are within Malachi's conceptual horizon (note also the focus on YHWH as Father [אב] in v. 10). (3) Directing the curse (ל + כרת) against offspring is supported by the use of כרת elsewhere in the Hebrew Bible (e.g., Ps 109:13; Ruth 4:10) and echoes Mal 2:3, where YHWH threatens to "rebuke" (גער) the seed (זרע) of the priests for their own transgressions

---

[75] Participle of עיר I *qal*, "protect"; or noun ער I, "protector" (*DCH* 6:368, 546), and participle of ענה II *qal*, "be afflicted" (*DCH* 6:497).

[76] Participle of עור *qal*, "rouse oneself"; or noun ער II, "nomad, vagabond" (*DCH* 6:314, 546), and participle of ענה VII *qal*, "dwell, stay in a place" (*DCH* 6:500). (*DCH* vol. 6 mistakenly has ער II, "protector," and ער III, "nomad," on p. 314, but then on p. 546 it has ער I, "protector," and ער II, "nomad, vagabond"). *HALAT* (3:829) provides only ער I, "protector" (Beschützer), as a possibility for Mal 2:12.

[77] Cathcart and Gordon, *Targum of the Minor Prophets*, 233 n. 18.

of the sacrificial laws. (4) The idea of offspring bearing the curse of guilty parents is a common feature in covenantal-legal contexts, which is Malachi's context here (cf. v. 10).

VI. Inner-Biblical Allusion to Genesis 38?

Over the last century, some scholars have taken the reading of descendants a step further, suggesting that the words ער and ענה may allude to the names Er (עֵר) and Onan (אוֹנָן), the sons of Judah and grandchildren of Jacob, who were born through Judah's mixed marriage with a Canaanite woman, the daughter of Shua (Gen 38:2–4, 12).[78]

Malachi 2:11–12	Genesis 38:2–4
בָּגְדָה **יְהוּדָה** וְתוֹעֵבָה נֶעֶשְׂתָה בְיִשְׂרָאֵל וּבִירוּשָׁלָםִ כִּי חִלֵּל **יְהוּדָה** קֹדֶשׁ יְהוָה אֲשֶׁר אָהֵב וּבָעַל **בַּת־אֵל נֵכָר**׃ יַכְרֵת יְהוָה לָאִישׁ אֲשֶׁר יַעֲשֶׂנָּה **עֵר וְעֹנֶה** מֵאָהֳלֵי יַעֲקֹב וּמַגִּישׁ מִנְחָה לַיהוָה צְבָאוֹת׃	וַיַּרְא־שָׁם **יְהוּדָה בַּת־אִישׁ כְּנַעֲנִי** וּשְׁמוֹ שׁוּעַ וַיִּקָּחֶהָ וַיָּבֹא אֵלֶיהָ׃ וַתַּהַר וַתֵּלֶד בֵּן וַיִּקְרָא אֶת־שְׁמוֹ **עֵר**׃ וַתַּהַר עוֹד וַתֵּלֶד בֵּן וַתִּקְרָא אֶת־שְׁמוֹ **אוֹנָן**׃

Matthias Krieg notes a point of similarity between the two texts in the name יהודה and his son's name ער.[79] Judah's intermarriage with a Canaanite, according to Krieg, is echoed in the people of Judah's relationship with idolatry (Mal 2:11). The allusion to the tradition recalls Yhwh putting to death the two sons of Judah because of their wickedness (Gen 38:2–4, 7, 10), thus conveying the message that "out of the Canaanite relationship ... no good fruit emerges."[80]

Karl W. Weyde also opts for an inner-biblical allusion to Genesis 38, but thinks that Krieg's analysis does not quite hit the mark. For Weyde, the connection between the two texts is formed on the basis of the "clear allusion" to the names of the two brothers ער and אונן, as well as through the reference to Jacob's tents (אהלי יעקב), which "suggests that perhaps the verbs עֵר וְעֹנֶה should also be related to the Jacob

---

[78] Levy, "Der Prophet Maleachi," 283; Douglas R. Jones, *Haggai, Zechariah, and Malachi: Introduction and Commentary* (Torch Bible Commentaries; London: SCM, 1962), 195; Matthias Krieg, *Mutmassungen über Maleachi: Eine Monographie* (ATANT 80; Zurich: Theologischer Verlag, 1993), 185–86; Karl W. Weyde, *Prophecy and Teaching: Prophetic Authority, Form Problems, and the Use of Traditions in the Book of Malachi* (BZAW 288; Berlin: de Gruyter, 2000), 246; Marvin A. Sweeney, *The Twelve Prophets* (2 vols.; Berit Olam; Collegeville, MN: Liturgical Press, 2000), 2:736–37.

[79] Krieg, *Maleachi*, 185 n. 283. Krieg has not tried to shed light on the meaning of the participial phrase.

[80] Ibid., 185–86: "aus kanaanäischen Beziehungen ... gehen keine guten Früchte hervor."

tradition, to the names of the two brothers Er and Onan."[81] According to him, the allusion works out in the following way: "Judah, the son of Jacob, married the daughter of a foreign god, just as the men of Judah, the descendants of Jacob, are accused of having done, according to Mal 2:11."[82] The names ער and אונן, alluded to in the participles ער וענה, also "bring to mind the punishment of Judah's two sons and their tragic fate: YHWH put them to death."[83] This explains, for Weyde, why the two words ער and ענה are chosen: they are intended as an allusion to the Judah tradition in Genesis. Weyde believes that earlier allusions to the Jacob tradition in Mal 1:2 and possibly 1:9 reinforce the possibility of an intended connection here.

Marvin A. Sweeney likewise proposes that ער וענה refers back to Er and Onan in Genesis 38.[84] According to him, Er (ער) is related to the verb ערר, "strip oneself, be destitute, childless" (cf. Gen 15:2; Lev 20:20, 21; Jer 22:30), while Onan (אונן) may be related to the root ענה, which, he argues, appears to have sexual connotations as indicated by the noun עֹנָה, "conjugal rights" (Exod 21:10; cf. Hos 10:10).[85] Although the translation of the statement in Mal 2:12 remains unclear for Sweeney, "it seems to refer to a man who is cut off for such acts as one who is 'childless and destitute/humiliated from the tents of Jacob.'" On this reading, Sweeney understands ער וענה to be epexegetical to לאיש, a further description of the direct object of כרת. That it is inappropriate for such a man to offer YHWH a gift (v. 12c), Sweeney believes, coheres with Deuteronomic laws on the barring of individuals from the assembly of YHWH due to damaged reproductive organs (Deut 23:1), or those born of improper unions (Deut 23:2) or those of foreign ethnicity (Deut 23:3). Sweeney concludes: "In the present case, one who marries a foreign woman is considered as one who will not have children or who in effect becomes a foreigner himself."

VII. Assessment

As alluring as this allusion to Genesis 38 may be, there are significant problems with it. Although there is assonance in the first syllable, the spelling of אונן does not exactly compare with ענה. Weyde's connection to the two sons via ער וענה is therefore immediately strained, as is Sweeney's to the noun עֹנָה via אונן. Krieg, to his credit, makes the connection through the common names יהודה and ער in both texts, but this raises the question of why אונן was left out. Sweeney's proposal

---

[81] Weyde, *Prophecy and Teaching*, 246.
[82] Ibid.
[83] Ibid.
[84] Sweeney, *Twelve Prophets*, 2:736–37.
[85] Sweeney notes that the root ענה can also refer to humiliation, affliction, or rape (e.g., Gen 34:2; Deut 21:14; 22:24; Judg 19:24; 20:5; 2 Sam 13:12, 14; Ezek 22:10, 11; Lam 5:11) (*Twelve Prophets*, 2:737).

that Er relates to the verb ערר may be true, but it does not prove that Mal 2:12 contains an allusion to this individual with the connotation of childlessness.[86] Comparison of texts containing the construction ל + כרת distinguishes indirect object (איש) from direct object (ער וענה), making it unlikely that ער וענה is a description of the man who is to be cut off.[87] The phrase, rather, concerns a distinct social component.

Contextual factors present the main obstacles to proposals for an inner-biblical allusion. In Genesis 38, the intermarriage of Judah with a Canaanite woman is not the cause of Yhwh's punishment of the sons; rather, it is the wickedness of the two sons themselves.[88] In Malachi 2, it is not the wickedness of the offspring that is the cause of Yhwh's punishment but rather that of the איש אשר יעשנה. In this regard, there is no contextual congruence between the texts, making an allusion to Er and Onan less credible. Moreover, contrary to Krieg, there is some "good fruit" that emerges from the mixed marriage of Judah and Tamar: twins are born, one of whom, Perez, is the continuation of the royal line. For these reasons, I remain unconvinced of an inner-biblical allusion to Genesis 38.

VIII. Conclusion

Commenting on the phrase ער וענה, Laetsch concluded that "the two terms used by Malachi can no longer be definitely determined."[89] I have demonstrated here that the pessimism is perhaps unwarranted. While I have not provided a literal rendering of the phrase or the precise etymological root or philological meaning of each word, my textual comparison of the formal correspondence of כרת + ל + two coordinated participles/nouns (often displaying either alliteration and/or assonance) sheds light on this difficult phrase. This fresh approach avoids giving uncertain translations from either guesswork or insecure philological bases.[90] The contention of this article is that the participial phrase ער וענה is an idiom denoting a person's descendants, their own "kith and kin."

Weyde's proposal, among others, of an allusion to "Er and Onan" in Genesis 38 via the familial idiom ער וענה is found wanting on close examination: the

---

[86] It should also be noted that the participle of ערר (active) is עֵרֵר not עֵר.

[87] Contra Glazier-McDonald's epexegetical reading above.

[88] Conceded by Weyde. The fact that the third son, Shelah, is not struck down by Yhwh supports the point.

[89] Laetsch, *Minor Prophets*, 524.

[90] The context of the phrase must ultimately determine the meaning of the words and not their etymological derivation from other cognate languages. Nevertheless, if the understanding of the idiom as relating to offspring is along the right lines, then some of the etymological and philological considerations above are not impossible; though, at this stage, one cannot say anything more.

lexemes do not match exactly and the contexts are different. What is to be "cut off," according to Malachi, is the man's "kith and kin," without any accompanying allusion to Genesis 38. In this case, formal correspondence helps to enlighten one's understanding of an obscure phrase; verbal dependence only serves to heighten one's playful imagination.

However one views the curse of "cutting off"—banishment/ostracism, excommunication, or actual destruction of the evildoer and his descendants—the inherent irony in the terminology should not be missed: those who are "cut into" a covenant are now in danger of being "cut off" from the covenant, they and their descendants.[91] For the sin of mixed marriage Malachi utters a solemn warning: "May Yhwh cut off for the man who does this 'kith and kin' from the tents of Jacob, though he offers a gift to Yhwh of hosts."[92]

---

[91] ל + כרת is how the Hebrew Bible also describes the making of a covenant (Exod 23:32; Deut 7:2; Josh 9:6, 11, 15, 16; 1 Sam 11:1; 2 Sam 5:3).

[92] Following Weyde, who reads the *waw* on מגיש as concessive (*Prophecy and Teaching*, 249). The final clause (ומגיש מנחה ליהוה צבאות) may refer to the evildoer, his offspring, both together, or to the priest who presents the offering on his/their behalf. If the latter, then the man and his offspring are allowed no representative to plead their case; if any of the former options, then he/they are cut off from the cult as well as from the community. In either case, the curse involves a removal of cultic privileges or acceptance.

New from Bloomsbury and T&T Clark

The True Herod
By Geza Vermes
HB | 9780567575449
$35.00

The Israelite Woman
By Athalya Brenner
PB | 9780567657732
$24.95

NOW AVAILABLE IN PAPERBACK

INTERNATIONAL CRITICAL COMMENTARY SERIES

Colossians and Philemon (ICC)
9780567101235 | $42.95

Hosea (ICC)
9780567323286 | $46.95

Isaiah 1-5 (ICC)
9780567473707 | $42.95

Isaiah 40-55 Vol 1 (ICC)
9780567173522 | $42.95

Isaiah 40-55 Vol 2 (ICC)
9780567020000 | $42.95

Jeremiah (ICC)
9780567164902 | $46.95

John 1-4 (ICC)
9780567595669 | $42.95

Lamentations (ICC)
9780567481672 | $42.95

T&T Clark Handbook to Social Identity in the New Testament
Edited by J. Brian Tucker and Coleman A. Baker
HB | 9780567379542
$200.00

Jesus: Evidence and Argument or Mythicist Myths?
By Maurice Casey
HB | 9780567447623
$34.95

All titles will be on display at booth 515 at the annual SBL conference
NOVEMBER 22-25 IN SAN DIEGO

BLOOMSBURY   t&tclark

www.bloomsbury.com • 1-888-330-8477

Reclaiming the Land (1 Maccabees 15:28–36): Hasmonean Discourse between Biblical Tradition and Seleucid Rhetoric

KATELL BERTHELOT
katell.b@free.fr
CNRS – Aix-Marseille University
CPAF – Maison Méditerranéenne des Sciences de l'Homme
13090 Aix-en-Provence, France

The First Book of Maccabees (15:28–36) records a diplomatic exchange over disputed cities and territories between Simon, Judas Maccabeus's brother, and the Seleucid king Antiochus VII. In vv. 33–34, Simon argues that the Jews/Judeans have not seized foreign lands that belonged to others but have simply taken back "the heritage of our fathers." Many scholars have interpreted Simon's reply as a self-evident indication that the Hasmonean dynasty saw itself as reconquering the promised land. However, a closer analysis of the text shows that this claim is exaggerated. Moreover, scholars refer to this passage alone in support of such a theory. Through the analysis of the literary construction of the passage and of its connections with biblical traditions, with Seleucid rhetoric as presented in 1 Maccabees itself, and with Hellenistic arguments used in cases of territorial strife, I argue that "the heritage of our fathers" refers to Judea alone, and that Simon's discourse cannot be interpreted solely through the lens of biblical intertextuality but rather needs to be compared with the ways of arguing about one's legitimate right to possess a territory in the Hellenistic world at large.

The First Book of Maccabees, originally written in Hebrew during the last part of the second century B.C.E.,[1] can be read, among other things, as the story of the

[1] Carl L. W. Grimm indicates the time span for when the book could have been written to be from 105–64 B.C.E. (*Das erste Buch der Maccabäer* [Kurzgefasstes exegetisches Handbuch zu den Apokryphen des Alten Testamentes; Leipzig: Hirzel, 1852], XXIV–XXV); F.-M. Abel dates it from around 100 B.C.E. (*Les livres des Maccabées* [EBib; Paris: Gabalda, 1949], XXVIII–XXIX); Jonathan A. Goldstein connects the work with the reign of Alexander Jannaeus (*1 Maccabees: A New Translation with Introduction and Commentary* [AB 41; Garden City, NY: Doubleday, 1983], 62–64); Stephanie von Dobbeler prefers to date it from the period of Hyrcanus's high priesthood,

539

acts of treachery committed by the Seleucid kings against the Hasmoneans.[2] The fifteenth chapter of the book deals precisely with a betrayal of this kind. It starts with a very friendly letter sent by Antiochus VII Sidetes to Simon and the Judean *ethnos* in 138 B.C.E., when Antiochus was planning to reconquer the Seleucid kingdom against the usurper Trypho and needed the support of the Judeans. The letter runs as follows:

> King Antiochus to Simon, high priest and ethnarch and to the nation of the Judeans, greeting. 3 Since certain traitors have seized power over the kingdom of our fathers, and I am determined to assert my claim to the kingdom in order to restore it to its former state, I have raised a large force of mercenary soldiers and have had warships fitted out; 4 I intend to land in our territory in order to punish those who have ruined our domains and laid waste many cities in my kingdom—5 therefore, I now confirm for you all the exemptions conceded to you by the kings who preceded me, and all other awards which they conceded to you. … 9 When we shall have established our rule over our kingdom, we shall confer great honor upon you and your nation and your temple, so that your glory will become manifest in all the earth. (1 Macc 15:2-9)[3]

---

shortly after 134 B.C.E. (*Die Bücher 1/2 Makkabäer* [Neuer Stuttgarter Kommentar, Altes Testament 11; Stuttgart: Katholisches Bibelwerk, 1997], 46). In general, scholars tend to date the work from the time of John Hyrcanus.

[2] By "Hasmoneans" I mean all of Mattathias's descendants, from Judas until Mattathias Antigonus; 1 Maccabees, though, deals only with the period from the beginning of the revolt to Hyrcanus I's rise to power in 135/134 B.C.E. On the conflict between the Seleucids and the Hasmoneans, the bibliography is extensive; see the classic works of Elias Bickerman, *The God of the Maccabees: Studies on the Meaning and Origin of the Maccabean Revolt* (trans. Horst R. Moehring; SJLA 32; Leiden: Brill, 1979); and Victor Tcherikover, *Hellenistic Civilization and the Jews* (Philadelphia: Jewish Publication Society of America, 1959), part 1; Jonathan A. Goldstein, "The Hasmonean Revolt and the Hasmonean Dynasty," in *The Cambridge History of Judaism*, vol. 2, *The Hellenistic Age* (ed. W. D. Davies; Cambridge: Cambridge University Press, 1989), 292–351. For more recent approaches, see in particular John Ma's analysis of the power balance between the Seleucids and the Hasmoneans in "Seleukids and Speech-Acts: Performative Utterances, Legitimacy and Negotiation in the World of the Maccabees," *Scripta Classica Israelica* 19 (2000): 71–112; idem, "Relire les *Institutions des Séleucides* de Bikerman," in *Rome, a City and Its Empire in Perspective: The Impact of the Roman World through Fergus Millar's Research* (ed. Stéphane Benoist; Impact of Empire 16; Leiden, Brill, 2012), 59–84; and also Erich S. Gruen, "Hellenism and Persecution," in *Hellenistic History and Culture* (ed. Peter Green; Hellenistic Culture and Society 9; Berkeley: University of California Press, 1993), 244–64; Seth Schwartz, *Imperialism and Jewish Society, 200 B.C.E. to 640 C.E.* (Jews, Christians, and Muslims from the Ancient to the Modern World; Princeton: Princeton University Press, 2001); Edward Dąbrowa, *The Hasmoneans and Their State: A Study in History, Ideology, and the Institutions* (Electrum 16; Cracow: Jagiellonian University Press, 2010).

[3] For the Greek text, see Werner Kappler, *Maccabaeorum libri I–IV*, fasc. 1, *Maccabaeorum liber I* (Septuaginta 9; Göttingen: Vandenhoeck & Ruprecht, 1936), 139–43. The translation quoted in the text above and the one used in the article as a whole is based on that of Goldstein (*1 Maccabees*, 510–11) with slight modifications according to my understanding of the Greek text.

Consequently, Simon is said to have sent two thousand men, silver and gold, as well as military equipment to Antiochus. However, after having defeated Trypho, Antiochus turned against Simon and behaved in a hostile way by sending the following message through Athenobius, one of his friends:

> You are holding Joppa and Gazara and the Akra in Jerusalem, cities of my kingdom. 29 You have laid waste their territories and caused grave damage in our domains, and you have seized many districts of my kingdom. 30 Accordingly, deliver over to me the cities you have captured and the taxes of the districts outside the borders of Judaea over which you have seized control, 31 or else pay five hundred talents of silver as compensation for them and five hundred more talents for the damage you have done and for the taxes due from the cities. Otherwise, we shall come and make war on you. (1 Macc 15:28–31)

Then the story goes on as follows:

> 33 Simon replied: "We have not taken land that is not ours nor have we conquered anything that belongs to others. Rather, we have taken the inheritance of our fathers which had been unjustly conquered by our enemies using one opportunity or another [οὔτε γῆν ἀλλοτρίαν εἰλήφαμεν οὔτε ἀλλοτρίων κεκρατήκαμεν, ἀλλὰ τῆς κληρονομίας τῶν πατέρων ἡμῶν, ὑπὸ δὲ ἐχθρῶν ἡμῶν ἀκρίτως ἔν τινι καιρῷ κατεκρατήθη]. 34 Now we, seizing our opportunity, lay claim to the inheritance of our fathers [ἡμεῖς δὲ καιρὸν ἔχοντες ἀντεχόμεθα τῆς κληρονομίας τῶν πατέρων ἡμῶν]. 35 As for Joppa and Gazara, which you demand, those cities were causing grave damage to our people and were laying waste our country. In payment for them we are ready to give a hundred talents." Athenobius gave him no reply, 36 but angrily returned to the king and reported this conversation to him, telling him also of Simon's splendor and of all that he had seen. The king was furious. (1 Macc 15:33–36)

This passage is systematically referred to by modern commentators who argue that the Hasmoneans planned to reconquer the "promised land" and, therefore, deliberately embarked on wars of expansion.[4] Moreover, most of these scholars suppose that the territorial vision of the Hasmoneans was a maximalist one.[5] Doron Mendels, for instance, writes, "Whereas until 140 [B.C.E.] 1 Maccabees never includes the Land as a declared goal of the war of the Hasmoneans (although it emphatically mentions the Torah, the People, and the Temple), from that year the Land is added as a goal of the war," and then he quotes 1 Macc 15:33.[6] Aryeh Kasher argues as follows:

---

[4] The expression "promised land" is not found as such in the Bible or in Jewish literature from the Second Temple period but is commonly used by modern scholars; hence the quotation marks.

[5] Tcherikover, commenting on Simon's answer in 1 Macc 15:33–34, writes, "According to this view, the whole of Palestine was to be united under the rule of the Hasmoneans, and its inhabitants were again to be Jews, as they had been under the kings of the house of David" (*Hellenistic Civilization*, 249).

[6] Mendels, *The Land of Israel as a Political Concept in Hasmonean Literature: Recourse to*

> ... we must not ignore [Simeon's] sincere religious ambition, shared by most of the Jewish population, which was to purge the Land of Israel of the impurities caused by its idolatrous inhabitants; nor may we dismiss the nationalistic and historical motives of liberating portions of the "homeland." ... All of these are indicated in Simeon's reply to the ultimatum presented by Antiochus VII Sidetes regarding the evacuation of Gazara (Gezer) and Joppa (1 Macc. 15.33–35). In my opinion, these motives did not constitute a mere ideological and (given the circumstances) apologetic cover for the economic and demographic needs; rather, they were the most pressing concerns which guided Simeon.[7]

In short, according to several modern scholars, "the inheritance of our fathers" in 1 Macc 15:33–34 designates the whole "promised land," from the Mediterranean Sea to Transjordan at least, a land that the Hasmoneans, since the very beginning of the revolt, dreamed of reconquering. However, how is it that 1 Macc 15:33–34 is the only proof-text found to support this thesis? And does Simon's reply to Athenobius really testify to such an ambitious program?

1 Maccabees 15:1–36 is a complex text that requires careful analysis. First, I will attempt to understand which territories were at stake in the conflict according to the information provided by 1 Maccabees itself. Then, taking into account the use of biblical idioms in the book as a whole, I will analyze the possible biblical background of the expression "the inheritance of our fathers" (ἡ κληρονομία τῶν

History in Second Century B.C. Claims to the Holy Land (TSAJ 15; Tübingen: Mohr Siebeck, 1987), 47–48. See also Dan Barag, who concludes that John Hyrcanus's wars later on were nothing but "the fulfilment of the policy expressed by Simon Maccabee (1 Macc. 15:33–35)" ("New Evidence on the Foreign Policy of John Hyrcanos I," *Israel Numismatic Journal* 12 [1992–93]: 1–12).

[7] Kasher, "The Changes in Manpower and Ethnic Composition of the Hasmonean Army (167–63 BCE)," *JQR* 81 (1991): 344; see also idem, *Jews and Hellenistic Cities in Eretz-Israel: Relations of the Jews in Eretz-Israel with the Hellenistic Cities during the Second Temple Period (332 BCE–70 CE)* (TSAJ 21; Tübingen: Mohr Siebeck, 1990), esp. 105–6. Similarly, Zeev Safrai writes, "We accordingly propose that the Bible profoundly influenced Hasmonean strategy. This hypothesis is based on two arguments: (1) the similarity between the early directives and the policy which was implemented; (2) the deep influence of the Biblical concept of the conquest of the land on the literature of the Hasmonean period, as noted by previous researchers" ("The Gentile Cities of Judea: Between the Hasmonean Occupation and the Roman Liberation," in *Studies in Historical Geography and Biblical Historiography Presented to Zecharia Kallai* [ed. Gershon Galil and Moshe Weinfeld; VTSup 81; Leiden: Brill, 2000], 77). See also Israel Shatzman's conclusion in "Jews and Gentiles from Judas Maccabaeus to John Hyrcanus according to Contemporary Jewish Sources," in *Studies in Josephus and the Varieties of Ancient Judaism: Louis H. Feldman Jubilee Volume* (ed. Shaye J. D. Cohen and Joshua J. Schwartz; Ancient Judaism and Early Christianity [AGJU] 67; Leiden: Brill, 2007), 237–70; according to Shatzman, from Judas down to John Hyrcanus, the same will to reestablish Jewish sovereignty over Eretz Israel manifests itself. Finally, even Uriel Rappaport interprets 1 Macc 15:33–34 as implying that the author "sees *Eretz Israel* as the historical heritage of the people of Israel," and, in another passage of the commentary, Rappaport refers to the divine promise made to Israel (*The First Book of Maccabees: Introduction, Hebrew Translation, and Commentary* [in Hebrew; Jerusalem: Yad Ben-Zvi, 2004], 59, 345).

πατέρων ἡμῶν) in Simon's reply to Athenobius and reassess previous interpretations of Simon's response that claim that Simon and his successors deliberately planned to reconquer the "promised land." As a third step, I will look at the literary and rhetorical dimension of 1 Maccabees 15, paying particular attention to the way Simon's response echoes Seleucid discourse in ch. 15 and in 1 Maccabees as a whole. Finally, I will examine the similarities between Simon's discourse and Seleucid rhetoric (or Hellenistic rhetoric in general) in the context of territorial strife as attested to in both Greek literary texts and inscriptions.

I. The Territorial Strife between the Seleucids and the Hasmoneans

The passage in ch. 15 raises several questions: Which territories does Antiochus allude to in vv. 29–31 when he speaks about the numerous "districts" (τόποι) that the Judeans have seized outside the borders of Judea (ἐκτὸς τῶν ὁρίων τῆς Ἰουδαίας)? What does Simon mean by "the inheritance of our fathers"? Is he really referring to the "promised land"? And, if so, according to which borders?[8] Alternatively, does Simon mean Judea alone?

Let us first try to determine which territories had been taken from the Seleucids by the Hasmoneans. A close reading of 1 Maccabees leads to the following conclusions: Judas led several victorious battles, but he did not permanently conquer any place outside Judea. Concerning the following period under Jonathan's rule, Demetrius I had promised the Hasmonean leader that he would grant the Judeans the right to annex to Judea three districts from Samaria in exchange for Jonathan's political and military support (1 Macc 10:26–39). Jonathan, however, turned down the offer, preferring to remain faithful to Alexander Balas, who had already made peace with him. Alexander had offered the city of Akkaron ('Eqron) and its territory to Jonathan as a personal gift. Both could be considered at that time to be lying outside Judea.[9] In the following years, Demetrius II, son of Demetrius I, after having made peace with Jonathan, wrote to the *ethnos* of the Judeans speaking about them in the third person: "We have confirmed as their possession both the territory of Judea and the three districts of Aphairema and Lydda and Rathamin; the latter, with all the region bordering them, were added to Judea from

---

[8] The biblical texts contain at least three different definitions of the borders of the "promised land." See, in particular, Nili Wazana, *All the Boundaries of the Land: The Promised Land in Biblical Thought in Light of the Ancient Near East* (in Hebrew; Sifriyat ha-Entsiḳlopedyah ha-Miḳra'it 24; Jerusalem: Mosad Bialik, 2007).

[9] According to Josh 15:45, 'Eqron and its territory are included in Judah's lot. However, in 1 Samuel–2 Kings, it represents one of the five cities of the Philistines, together with Ashdod, Ashkelon, Gaza, and Gath. At the time of the Maccabean revolt, it was located outside Judea. See F.-M. Abel, *Géographie de la Palestine* (2nd ed.; EBib; Paris: Gabalda, 1938), 2:50, 319.

Samaria" (1 Macc 11:34). In fact, the real annexation of the three districts probably took place under Demetrius II, since nowhere before in the text are these places said to have actually been annexed by the Judeans.[10] In any case, it should be underlined that so far (up to 1 Macc 11:34) the territorial growth of Judea is the result of Seleucid concessions and not of Hasmonean conquests.[11] Similarly, in 1 Macc 11:57 we read about a fourth district annexed to Judea with the agreement of the Seleucids. Its precise name and location are debated. Following Gustaf Dalman and F.-M. Abel, Jonathan Goldstein suggests that this fourth district (or nome) should be identified with the Akrabattene, which stood next to the districts of Aphairema and Rathamin.[12] This additional district provided Judea with a coherent extended territory.

All in all, Simon is the first among the Hasmoneans to annex territories outside Judea through military conquest. First, according to 1 Macc 11:66, he took over Beth-Zur, an important stronghold on the border between Judea and Idumea that had already been defeated by Judas (1 Macc 4:61) and had been taken back by Antiochus V (1 Macc 6:50).[13] Simon placed a Judean garrison there. Then he took Joppa (on the Mediterranean coast), which had already been forced to surrender to Jonathan (1 Macc 10:76) but had done so for only a short period of time. The author of 1 Maccabees justifies this military operation with an argument about security: "he had heard that they were ready to hand over the stronghold to the men whom Demetrius had sent; and he stationed a garrison there to guard it" (1 Macc 12:33–34). Later on, the author of 1 Maccabees alludes to the economic advantages connected with Joppa's harbor (1 Macc 14:5). Then the reader is told that Simon had strongholds built in Judea and that he gave orders to rebuild Adida and to fortify it (1 Macc 12:38); Adida was actually located in the Shephelah five or six kilometers northeast of Lydda in one of the districts that had recently been annexed to Judea.[14] Finally, in 141–140 B.C.E., when Judea reached independence, Simon conquered Gazara and the Akra, the Seleucid stronghold in Jerusalem (1 Macc 13:43–53). Later on in 1 Maccabees, the conquest of Gazara—whose

---

[10] In 1 Macc 11:28, Jonathan asks for a tax exemption for Judea and for the three Samaritan districts, but maybe this is a way of reminding Demetrius of his father's promises in this respect. See F.-M. Abel, "Topographie des campagnes maccabéennes (5)," *RB* 35 (1926): 206–22.

[11] According to 1 Macc 10:84, Jonathan burns Azot, and according to 1 Macc 11:61–62, he besieges Gaza and plunders its countryside. However, he does not conquer the towns and does not annex them to Judea.

[12] See Abel, *Géographie de la Palestine*, 2:135; Goldstein, *1 Maccabees*, 439.

[13] Concerning Beth-Zur, see Ovid R. Sellers, *The Citadel of Beth-Zur: A Preliminary Report of the First Excavation Conducted by the Presbyterian Theological Seminary, Chicago, and the American School of Oriental Research, Jerusalem, in 1931 at Khirbet et Tubeiqa* (Philadelphia: Westminster, 1933); Robert W. Funk, "The 1957 Campaign at Beth-Zur," *BASOR* 150 (1958): 8–20; idem, "Beth-Zur," in *NEAEHL* 1:259–61.

[14] See Abel, *Géographie de la Palestine*, 2:340–41; and idem, "Topographie des campagnes maccabéennes (5)," 218.

strategic importance cannot be overestimated—is justified by the fact that the garrison in this stronghold caused a lot of trouble to the Judean people and great damage to their land (1 Macc 15:35).[15] Therefore, the main argument put forward by Simon to justify the conquests is about *security*, not the holiness of the land.[16]

When Antiochus Sidetes writes to Simon in 138–137 B.C.E. to claim Joppa, Gazara, and the citadel (Akra) in Jerusalem, the contested conquests are those of Simon and no other leader. The author of 1 Maccabees explicitly praises Simon for these political and military achievements in ch. 14, where we find a passage written in a poetic biblical style:

> The land had rest all the days of Simon. He sought the good of his nation; his rule was pleasing to them, as was the honor shown him, all his days. 5 To crown all his honors he took Joppa for a harbor, and opened a way to the isles of the sea. 6 He extended the borders of his nation [ἐπλάτυνεν τὰ ὅρια τῷ ἔθνει αὐτοῦ], and gained full control of the country [ἐκράτησεν τῆς χώρας]. 7 He gathered a host of captives; he ruled over Gazara and Beth-Zur and the citadel (the Akra), and he removed its uncleanness from it. (1 Macc 14:4–7)[17]

For the author of 1 Maccabees, Simon "extended the borders of his nation," which apparently means that the Judeans started to settle areas that had not traditionally belonged to their territory.

However, Antiochus Sidetes' accusations remain unclear. Beyond the case of Joppa, Gazara, and the Akra, of what do the numerous "districts" he is referring to consist? Could it be that Antiochus did not take into account the previous agreements made between his predecessors and Jonathan, and that he considered the Samaritan districts annexed to Judea an illegal possession? This seems unlikely, since they were not taken by force and Simon could easily have referred to the gifts made by Antiochus's predecessors. Could Antiochus have had Akkaron in mind, a territory given to Jonathan as a personal gift? This is unlikely as well, for the same reasons. The only other cases left, according to 1 Maccabees, are Beth-Zur (located on the border between Judea and Idumea), and Adida, two strongholds whose loss probably displeased the Seleucid king. Two strongholds are not exactly "many

---

[15] See 1 Macc 9:52: Bacchides fortifies Gazara in the context of his fight against Judea.

[16] As correctly noted by Joseph Sievers, who adds, "It is worth noting that territorial claims were not based on biblical precedent, but apparently on recent settlement patterns" (*The Hasmoneans and Their Supporters: From Mattathias to the Death of John Hyrcanus I* [South Florida Studies in the History of Judaism 6; Atlanta: Scholars Press, 1990], 129). On the Hasmonean occupation of Gazara (Gezer), see Joe D. Seger, "The Search for Maccabean Gezer," *BA* 39 (1976): 142–44; Ronny Reich, "Archaeological Evidence of the Jewish Population of Hasmonean Gezer," *IEJ* 31 (1981): 48–52. See also R. A. Stewart Macalister, *The Excavation of Gezer, 1902–1905 and 1907–1909* (3 vols.; London: John Murray, 1912), 1:34, 209–23, 2:276–77; William G. Dever, "Gezer," in *NEAEHL* 2:496–506, esp. 506.

[17] The results of Simon's policy are summarized with great enthusiasm by the author of 1 Maccabees in 14:33–37.

districts," but some rhetorical exaggeration is to be expected in discourses like that of Antiochus.

Let us now look carefully at Simon's answer to Antiochus. First, Simon offers the king a hundred talents for Joppa and Gazara instead of the five hundred talents requested by Antiochus. Simon does not mention the Akra; nor does he address the other parts of Antiochus's request concerning the "damage" caused in the royal domain and the districts outside the borders of Judea, which the Judeans were supposed to have seized and for which Antiochus was asking another five hundred talents. Simon actually distinguishes between two cases that are not equivalent to the distinctions made in Antiochus's discourse: he refers to the territories that belong to "the inheritance of our fathers," on the one hand, and to Joppa and Gazara, on the other. A very important conclusion must, therefore, be drawn: *Joppa and Gazara are not part of "the inheritance of our fathers."* Logically enough, "the inheritance of our fathers" cannot be equivalent to Eretz Israel (from the Mediterranean to the Jordan) as argued by some. On the other hand, that the Akra was not mentioned at all can probably be explained because, from Simon's perspective, it obviously belonged to the "inheritance of our fathers," even if it was a Seleucid stronghold—it was, after all, located in Jerusalem, the capital of Judea! It also makes sense to suppose that Simon considered Beth-Zur to be part of Judea. As far as the Samaritan districts annexed to Judea are concerned, as mentioned previously, they do not seem to have been part of the argument, except maybe in the case of Adida, but this is unclear. Now, concerning the territories that represent "the inheritance of our fathers," the Hasmonean leader argues that the Judeans have a right of property over them, because these territories *already belonged to their ancestors*; it is, therefore, a historical right, based on inheritance (and not a divinely granted right).[18] We will see in the last part of this article that this was a common way of justifying one's right to a land, as has been aptly analyzed by historians of the Hellenistic world such as Elias Bickerman, Jean-Marie Bertrand, and Angelos Chaniotis, among others.[19] The notion of inheritance in itself, however, does not inform us about the nature of the borders of the territory.

We may provisionally conclude that the expression "the inheritance of our fathers" very probably referred to Judea (maybe a slightly extended Judea) or maybe to Judea-Samaria, understood as the biblical kingdom of Judah together with the northern kingdom of Israel. However, it must be underlined that nowhere is the land ruled by the Hasmoneans called "Israel";[20] it is consistently called "Judea" or

---

[18] Rappaport rightly emphasizes this point: Simon does not refer to a right that would be granted by God's promise to give the land of Canaan to the children of Israel, but only to a historical right (see Rappaport, *First Book of Maccabees*, 345). On the different ways to ground property rights over a territory in the Hellenistic and Roman world, see n. 41 below.

[19] See section IV below, "Hellenistic Discourse about Land Property Rights."

[20] The expression "Holy Land" cannot be found either, whereas Jerusalem is sometimes called the "holy city" (1 Macc 2:7).

"country of Judah" (γῆ Ιουδα) throughout the whole book.[21] Its people are frequently called the "sons of Israel," as in the biblical books, where the expression designates either all the descendants of Jacob or the Judeans alone (after the destruction of the northern kingdom); but the land is not called "Israel." This linguistic phenomenon, which can also be found in the book of Judith, has been noticed and analyzed by David Goodblatt, who concludes, "Whatever the reason, the Hasmoneans did not restore the state called 'Israel.' Instead they created a 'Greater Judah.'"[22] However, it is extremely difficult to determine which borders were the legitimate borders of the Judeans' territory from the Hasmoneans' perspective, since 1 Maccabees does not provide any information on this issue.[23]

Now, as is well known, Josephus used 1 Maccabees extensively in his parallel account of the Maccabean revolt in his *Jewish* (or *Judean*) *Antiquities*. Does his work provide further information that might shed light on the territorial conflict between Antiochus Sidetes and Simon? At first glance, the episode of 1 Macc 15:28–36 is lacking in the *Antiquities*.[24] Josephus does indeed refer to Antiochus's

---

[21] See 1 Macc 3:39; 5:45, 53, 68; 6:5; 7:10, 22, 50; 9:1, 57, 72; 10:30, 37; 12:4; 13:1, 12; 14:4; etc. Note also that in ch. 2, Mattathias sees "the blasphemies that were committed in Judah and Jerusalem" (v. 6) and he laments for the city of Jerusalem, saying, "Which nation has not inherited her kingdom [ποῖον ἔθνος οὐκ ἐκληρονόμησεν βασίλεια] and has not seized her spoils?" (v. 10). It could be argued that Simon's answer in ch. 15 echoes Mattathias's initial cry of pain, and that "the inheritance of our fathers" alluded to by Simon is closely connected with the glory of Jerusalem and of the kingdom of Judah.

[22] See Goodblatt, "'The Israelites Who Reside in Judah' (Judith 4:1): On the Conflicted Identities of the Hasmonean State," in *Jewish Identities in Antiquity: Studies in Memory of Menahem Stern* (ed. Lee I. Levine and Daniel R. Schwartz; TSAJ 130; Tübingen: Mohr Siebeck, 2009), 84. The author of the book of Judith mainly uses the expressions "children of Israel" (for the people) and "Judea" (for the land).

[23] Mendels himself acknowledges this (*Land of Israel*, 51). Following the indications found in 1 Maccabees, Seth Schwartz considers that, de facto, "at Simon's death, Jewish Palestine consisted only of the tiny district of Judaea, extending roughly from Beth-Zur, about twenty-five kilometres south-southwest of Jerusalem, to the region of Bethel and Gophna, about twenty kilometres to the city's north, and about thirty kilometres from the eastern desert to the high plain at the foot of the Judean hills" ("Israel and the Nations Roundabout: 1 Maccabees and the Hasmonean Expansion," *JJS* 42 [1991]: 17).

[24] As Etienne Nodet has shown, Josephus uses several sources even when he takes his inspiration from 1 Maccabees, and he stops using the latter almost completely from 1 Macc 13:42 onward (see Nodet, *La crise maccabéenne: Historiographie juive et traditions bibliques* [Collection "Josèphe et son temps" 6; Paris: Cerf, 2005], 407–31). For some scholars who build on the fact that Josephus does not use the last chapters of 1 Maccabees, the section that runs from 1 Macc 14:16 to 16:24 represents a secondary addition dated from the second edition of the book, around 100 B.C.E. See, in particular, David S. Williams, *The Structure of 1 Maccabees* (CBQMS 31; Washington, DC: Catholic Biblical Association of America, 1999), 108–22; idem, "Recent Research in 1 Maccabees," *CurBS* 9 (2001): 172–74. On Josephus's use of 1 Maccabees in general, see Ezra Z. Melamed, "Flavius Josephus Compared to 1 Maccabees" (in Hebrew), *ErIsr* 1 (1951): 122–30; Isaiah M. Gafni, "Josephus and 1 Maccabees," in *Josephus, the Bible, and History* (ed.

change of attitude toward Simon, but he simply states that the Seleucid king "through covetousness and dishonesty forgot the services which Simon had rendered him in his necessity, and giving a force of soldiers to Cendebaeus, one of his Friends, sent him off to plunder Judea and seize Simon" (*Ant.* 13.225). This paragraph of the *Antiquities* actually corresponds to 1 Macc 15:38–41, the verses that *follow* the passage under scrutiny here. On the other hand, the episode of Athenobius's embassy to Jerusalem is implied in another passage of the *Antiquities*, 13.236, where Josephus writes that "Antiochus, being resentful of the injuries he had received from Simon, invaded Judea in the fourth year of his reign and the first of Hyrcanus's rule, in the hundred and sixty-second Olympiad." Nowhere in the *Antiquities* has anything been told about Simon causing "injuries" to Antiochus; this passage is thus unintelligible without the testimony of 1 Maccabees 15. Strangely enough, when Josephus relates the siege of Jerusalem by Antiochus, the latter is suddenly described as pious and full of respect for the sanctuary, as if he was the complete opposite of his impious ancestor Antiochus IV (*Ant.* 13.242–43).[25] The kindness (ἐπιείκεια) and the religious fervor of Antiochus VII are such that John Hyrcanus asks him to allow the Jews to live according to their ancestral laws (*Ant.* 13.245). Antiochus answers in a positive way, refuting those among his counselors who accused the Jews of ἀμιξία (of refusing to mix with non-Jews). However, Antiochus demands that the Judeans "hand over their arms, pay tribute to him for Joppa and the other cities bordering on Judaea [καὶ τῶν ἄλλων πόλεων περίξ τῆς Ἰουδαίας] [or, according to MSS FVE: outside (πάρεξ) Judea], and receive a garrison [that is, in Jerusalem]" (*Ant.* 13.246). The Judeans accept the deal, except for the garrison, in exchange for which they hand over hostages and pay five hundred talents of silver.[26] Although this passage of the *Antiquities* does not refer to the trio "Joppa – Gazara – Akra" as in 1 Maccabees 15, it is clear that the same territorial strife is at stake. For the time being, the conflict comes to an end. However, as *Ant.* 13.259–63 shows, later on Hyrcanus sends envoys to Rome to request on behalf of the Judeans that "Joppa and its harbors and Gazara and Pegae and whatever other cities and territories Antiochus took from them in war, contrary to the decree of

---

Louis H. Feldman and Gohei Hata; Leiden: Brill, 1989), 116–31; Gideon Fuks, "Josephus and the Hasmoneans," *JJS* 41 (1990): 166–76; Bezalel Bar-Kokhva, "On Josephus and the Books of the Maccabees, Philology and Historiography" (in Hebrew), *Tarbiz* 62 (1992): 115–32; Louis H. Feldman, "Josephus' Portrayal of the Hasmoneans Compared with 1 Maccabees," in *Josephus and the History of the Greco-Roman Period: Essays in Memory of Morton Smith* (ed. Fausto Parente and Joseph Sievers; StPB 41; Leiden: Brill, 1994), 41–68.

[25] This has to do with the issue of the sources Josephus used, an issue that cannot be dealt with here.

[26] On Josephus's account of the siege and his sources, see Tessa Rajak, "Roman Intervention in a Seleucid Siege of Jerusalem?" *GRBS* 22 (1981): 65–81; Katell Berthelot, *Philanthrôpia judaica: Le débat autour de la "misanthropie" des lois juives dans l'Antiquité* (JSJSup 76; Leiden: Brill, 2003), 123–41; Bezalel Bar-Kochva, *The Image of the Jews in Greek Literature: The Hellenistic Period* (Hellenistic Culture and Society 51; Berkeley: University of California Press, 2010), 399–439.

the Senate, be restored to them." Therefore, the conflict went on, and this time Gazara was explicitly mentioned alongside Joppa. The Akra, however, was not an issue any more, since, according to Josephus, it had been razed to the ground by Simon (*Ant.* 13.215).

In the end, Josephus's testimony does not allow a direct clarification of the diplomatic exchange between Antiochus VII and Simon in 1 Maccabees 15. However, in spite of the fact that Josephus does not recall Athenobius's embassy to Simon, the *Antiquities* echoes the distinction made by Simon between the territories found in Judea that belong to "the inheritance of our fathers" and the territories located outside its borders.

II. THE BIBLICAL BACKGROUND OF THE EXPRESSION "THE INHERITANCE OF OUR FATHERS"

How do scholars who claim that "the inheritance of our fathers" means the whole "promised land" deal with the distinction made by Simon? From their perspective, since Joppa and Gazara are located within the borders of Eretz Israel, Simon's distinction between "the inheritance of our fathers," on the one hand, and Joppa and Gazara, on the other, has to be understood as a diplomatic or tactical concession to the Seleucids, connected with the fact that Simon was aware that he could not use a divine-right argument in his talks with Antiochus. Goldstein, for instance, evokes "the Jews' claims based on divine promises to their ancestors and on previous conquest," and adds:

> As a good diplomat, Simon does not attempt to argue that Joppa and Gazara lay within the confines of the promised land or once belonged to Solomon (II Chron 2:15; Josh 21:21; I Kings 9:15–17). The Seleucid authorities might not have conceded the validity of the evidence. Simon claims the cities by right of conquest in just wars of retribution, a principle recognized in Greek international law.[27]

The problem with this analysis is that it overlooks the fact that Simon actually acknowledges that there is a problem with Joppa and Gazara, justifies their conquest by an argument about security, and is ready to pay a hundred talents for them.

Let us consider for a second the argument of a diplomatic and tactical concession to the Seleucids' form of argumentation. As we shall see in greater detail later on, Simon's answer is indeed formulated in a language that corresponds to Seleucid and, more generally, to Hellenistic standards. However, one should also keep in

---

[27] Goldstein, *1 Maccabees*, 516. Werner Dommershausen writes, "Simeon weiss sehr wohl, dass auch Jafo und Geser einst zum salomonischen Reich gehörten (2 Chr 2:15; 1 Kön 9:15–17), erachtet es aber im Augenblick für diplomatischer, auf den historischen Beweis zu verzichten und die Geldsumme anzubieten" (*1 Makkabäer, 2 Makkabäer* [NEchtB 12; Würzburg: Echter, 1985], 104).

mind that 1 Maccabees was originally written in Hebrew for a Judean audience. Even in the Greek translation, the book contains numerous echoes of the biblical style used in Joshua, Judges, 1–2 Samuel, 1–2 Kings, and 1–2 Chronicles, which were meaningful only to a Jewish audience familiar with the traditions found in the "historical" books that were about to become the Bible. The fact that Simon uses the expression "the inheritance of our fathers" and not "the land given by God to our ancestors" is, therefore, significant. Obviously, it is difficult to determine whether in 1 Maccabees 15 we hear something that comes close to Simon's *ipsissima verba* or a later reformulation of them that may have been very different from the original. Rappaport, for instance, is quite confident that we are dealing with a fair report of Simon's answer to Antiochus.[28] In any case, the text is carefully crafted from a literary point of view, and the formulation has not been chosen by chance.[29]

In order to understand the way the author uses biblical traditions in 1 Maccabees, one must recall that, in contrast to 2 Maccabees, 1 Maccabees does not refer to God very often, especially from Jonathan's rule onward. Rappaport convincingly argues that the author of 1 Maccabees develops a kind of historiography that differs from the biblical one in that it is much more profane and emphasizes the great deeds of the Hasmoneans rather than God's miraculous interventions. Contrary to Kasher and Goldstein, Edward Dąbrowa writes that, from Jonathan and Simon onward, "religious purposes and motivations clearly gave way to political aims."[30]

---

[28] Rappaport, *First Book of Maccabees*, 344.

[29] On the literary construction of 1 Maccabees, see in particular John R. Bartlett, *1 Maccabees* (Guides to the Apocrypha and Pseudepigrapha 5; Sheffield: Sheffield Academic Press, 1998), 21–35; Williams, *Structure of 1 Maccabees*, 72–95, 108–27.

[30] See Dąbrowa, *Hasmoneans and Their State*, 42. This phenomenon has been aptly analyzed by Uriel Rappaport in "A Note on the Use of the Bible in 1 Maccabees," in *Biblical Perspectives: Early Use and Interpretation of the Bible in Light of the Dead Sea Scrolls. Proceedings of the First International Symposium of the Orion Center for the Study of the Dead Sea Scrolls and Associated Literature, 12–14 May 1996* (ed. Michael E. Stone and Esther G. Chazon; STDJ 28; Leiden: Brill, 1998), 175–79; see also idem, *First Book of Maccabees*, 34–35, 52–54. This does not contradict the description of the Hasmoneans as eager to defend the law and to purify the temple and the conquered places where Judeans are going to settle. The Hasmoneans' commitment to the law of Moses and their role as defenders of the law and of the people are the basis of their legitimacy. The question of the exact nature of their faithfulness to the law and the connected issue of the hellenization of the Hasmoneans is too vast to be dealt with here; see, e.g., Tessa Rajak, "The Hasmoneans and the Uses of Hellenism," in *A Tribute to Géza Vermès: Essays on Jewish and Christian Literature and History* (ed. Philip R. Davies and Richard T. White; JSOTSup 100; Sheffield: JSOT Press, 1990), 261–80; Uriel Rappaport, "The Hellenization of the Hasmoneans," in *Jewish Assimilation, Acculturation, and Accommodation: Past Traditions, Current Issues, and Future Prospects. Proceedings of the Second Annual Symposium of the Philip M. and Ethel Klutznick Chair in Jewish Civilization Held on Sunday–Monday, September 24–25, 1989* (ed. Menachem Mor; Studies in Jewish Civilization 2; Lanham, MD: University Press of America, 1991), 2–13; Erich S. Gruen, "Hellenism and the Hasmoneans," in *Heritage and Hellenism: The Reinvention of Jewish Tradition* (Hellenistic Culture and Society 30; Berkeley: University of California Press,

In accordance with these remarks, one should recall that the author of 1 Maccabees never refers to the "promised land" or to the "holy land"; that he does not recall the conquest of the land by Joshua, even when he mentions him among the great men of Israel;[31] and that he never explicitly addresses the issue of the borders of the land.[32]

Once these general observations have been made, can a precise biblical background, nevertheless, be identified behind the expression ἡ κληρονομία τῶν πατέρων ἡμῶν? In biblical literature, the notion of נחלה/κλῆρος or κληρονομία is mainly used in the context of God's covenant with the people; in particular, the terms נחלה/ κληρονομία sometimes designate the land that is given by God to Israel as an inheritance (e.g., Deut 12:8–10).[33] Nevertheless, occurrences of κληρονομία in connection with the "fathers" or the ancestors are not very numerous and actually tend to designate the land owned by a tribe, a family, or an individual, not the land of the people of Israel as a whole.[34] Thus, Num 33:54, which refers to the lots (of land) granted to each tribe, concludes in the following terms: "wherever the lot falls to any man, that shall be his; according to the tribes of your fathers you shall inherit" (למטות אבתיכם תתנחלו, κατὰ φυλὰς πατριῶν ὑμῶν κληρονομήσετε). In Num 36:7–9, the issue of the daughters' inheritance is addressed; the problem raised is whether part of a tribe's lot could be integrated into another tribe's lot. This must not happen: "The inheritance of the people of Israel shall not be transferred from one tribe to

---

1998), 1–40; and the recent book by Eyal Regev, *The Hasmoneans: Ideology, Archaeology, Identity* (Journal of Ancient Judaism Supplements 10; Göttingen: Vandenhoeck & Ruprecht, 2013).

[31] Thus, in Mattathias's discourse about the great deeds of the patriarchs and the ancestors of the people of Israel, he says about Joshua that "for fulfilling the word he was made a judge in Israel" (Ἰησοῦς ἐν τῷ πληρῶσαι λόγον ἐγένετο κριτὴς ἐν Ἰσραηλ) (2:55). When one compares this sentence with the celebration of the military deeds of Joshua in Ben Sira (46:1–10), who starts by recalling that Joshua was the one who had the tribes inherit the land, one grasps the extent to which the author of 1 Maccabees refrains from promoting the fighting Joshua as a model for the Hasmonean dynasty. On the absence of the model of Joshua in 1 Maccabees, see Katell Berthelot, "The Biblical Conquest of the Promised Land and the Hasmonean Wars according to *1* and *2 Maccabees*," in *The Books of Maccabees: History, Theology, Tradition. Papers of the Second International Conference on the Deuterocanonical Books, Pápa, Hungary, 9–11 June, 2005* (ed. Geza G. Xeravits and József Zsengellér; JSJSup 118; Leiden: Brill, 2007), 45–60.

[32] See n. 23 above; and Mendels, *Land of Israel*, 47–48 n. 3, 51. The only passage that Mendels is able to quote in order to justify that, after 140, "the Land is added as a goal of the war" (according to undefined borders!), is none other than 1 Macc 15:33–35. The same tension can be found in W. D. Davies, *The Territorial Dimension of Judaism* (Berkeley: University of California Press, 1982), 62–67.

[33] For the people of Israel as God's κληρονομία, a very common use of the term, see, e.g., 3 Kgdms 8:53; Isa 19:25; 47:6; and Jer 12:7, among others. Conversely, in Ezek 44:28, God declares that he himself is the κληρονομία of the priests.

[34] There may be an exception to this: in Isa 58:14, the country as a whole seems to be designated by the expression "the inheritance of your father Jacob" (τὴν κληρονομίαν Ιακωβ τοῦ πατρός σου). However, the reference is only to one father, Jacob, who is the ancestor of the whole nation.

another; for every one of the people of Israel shall cleave to the inheritance of the tribe of his fathers" (v. 7, כי איש בנחלת מטה אבתיו ידבקו בני ישראל; ὅτι ἕκαστος ἐν τῇ κληρονομίᾳ τῆς φυλῆς τῆς πατριᾶς αὐτοῦ προσκολληθήσονται οἱ υἱοὶ Ισραηλ). The daughters who inherit pieces of land shall marry a man from their father's tribe, "so that every one of the people of Israel may possess the inheritance of his fathers [נחלת אבתיו; τὴν κληρονομίαν τὴν πατρικὴν αὐτοῦ]" (v. 8). The obligation to respect the original boundaries between the lots of the children of Israel is also vigorously recalled in Deut 19:14.

In 1 Maccabees itself, two other occurrences of κληρονομία can be found, which are both connected with lands owned by individuals or families. In one case, reference is made to the territory that Caleb received in Canaan as a reward for his faithfulness during the episode of the spies (Numbers 13–14 and Josh 15:13–14; 1 Macc 2:56); the other case has to do with the property of the impious Judeans, which Judas and his men took from them (1 Macc 6:24). These two cases tend to corroborate the interpretation of ἡ κληρονομία τῶν πατέρων ἡμῶν in 1 Macc 15:33–35 as a legal category probably designating the territories of the tribes of Judah and Benjamin, the ancestors of the Judeans *stricto sensu*, which together formed the kingdom of Judah.[35] By using the term κληρονομία, the text introduces a biblical dimension into the diplomatic exchange between Simon and Antiochus that refers back to the repartition of the lots of land between the tribes of Israel and strongly emphasizes the inalienable character of the Judeans' right to their ancestral land.

Finally, the use of the expression ἡ κληρονομία τῶν πατέρων ἡμῶν could also point to a specific biblical episode, the story of Naboth's vineyard in 1 Kings 21 (LXX 3 Kingdoms 20), an allusion to which only people familiar with the biblical texts could have understood. The story describes how the evil king Ahab wanted to possess Naboth's vineyard in order to extend his garden. Naboth was a simple man, a commoner who nevertheless refused to sell his vineyard to the king or give it in exchange for another piece of land, arguing, "The Lord forbids that I should give you the inheritance of my fathers [נחלת אבתי, κληρονομίαν πατέρων μου]" (1 Kgs 21:3). Together with Num 36:8 (MT rather than LXX, which uses the adjective πατρικός), this passage from 1 Kings contains the expression that is most similar to the one used in 1 Maccabees 15. The story of Naboth again illustrates the fact that κληρονομία, when it is associated with "fathers," generally designates the territory of a tribe, a family, or an individual. Moreover, it is indeed possible that 1 Maccabees 15 contained a deliberate and ironic allusion to the biblical story of Ahab and Naboth, suggesting that Antiochus Sidetes was comparable to the evil and impious Israelite king, whereas Simon was defending the legitimate rights of the Judeans, who were, therefore, comparable to Naboth and, far from seizing the lands of others, asked for nothing more than the right to keep their ancestral estate.

---

[35] The borders of the territory attributed to Judah are described in Joshua 15; those of Benjamin, whose territory adjoins that of Judah and includes both Jerusalem and Jericho, are found in Josh 18:11–28. See also Abel, *Géographie de la Palestine*, 2:46–50, 53–56.

This interpretation, if it is correct, tends to belie the theory according to which Simon's answer implies that the Hasmoneans saw the reconquest of the whole "promised land" as their program and their religious duty. Finally, even if the connection with the story of Naboth is considered far-fetched, the philological observations made above show that understanding the expression ἡ κληρονομία τῶν πατέρων ἡμῶν as referring to the maximalist territorial definition of the "promised land" is far from self-evident. The ancestral estate of the Judeans was Judea alone.[36]

III. Literary Context and Rhetorical Patterns: Seleucid Language in 1 Maccabees

In order to be interpreted correctly, 1 Maccabees 15 needs to be read not only with a possible biblical background in mind but also with an eye on its literary construction and the rhetoric of the chapter and of the book as a whole. The author of 1 Maccabees reproduces Seleucid discourse in several instances and deliberately introduces numerous echoes between Simon's answer and Antiochus's discourse in ch. 15 and elsewhere.[37] Moreover, Antiochus's letter in vv. 28–31 also echoes the first letter sent to Simon in 1 Macc 15:2–9. These linguistic similarities help to underline the contradiction between the two letters, Antiochus's unjustifiable change of attitude toward Simon and the former's wickedness. In ch. 15, the three letters or messages have elements in common. In v. 3, Antiochus complains that "traitors have seized power over the kingdom of our fathers" (κατεκράτησαν τῆς βασιλείας τῶν πατέρων ἡμῶν). It parallels the use of κατακρατέω in v. 28 (κατακρατεῖτε) as well as in v. 33 (Simon's answer: κεκρατήκαμεν; τῆς κληρονομίας τῶν πατέρων ἡμῶν ὑπὸ δὲ ἐχθρῶν ἡμῶν ... κατεκρατήθη). Moreover, in vv. 3–5, Antiochus also declares that he wants to punish "those who have ruined our domains and laid waste many cities in my kingdom" (τοὺς ἠρημωκότας πόλεις πολλὰς ἐν τῇ βασιλείᾳ μου). There are parallels in v. 28 (πόλεις τῆς βασιλείας μου) and in v. 29 (τὰ ὅρια αὐτῶν ἠρημώσατε ... καὶ ἐκυριεύσατε τόπων πολλῶν ἐν τῇ βασιλείᾳ μου) as well as in v. 35, if one follows Abel's plausible correction and reads τὴν χώραν ἠρήμων (a mistake for ἠρήμουν) instead of καὶ τὴν χώραν ἡμῶν. Considering all the echoes and parallels in wording between these discourses, one can plausibly conclude that the expression "the inheritance of our fathers" (ἡ κληρονομία τῶν πατέρων ἡμῶν), which is not used in Antiochus's letters as such or in other instances of Seleucid discourse in 1 Maccabees, echoes the formula "the kingdom of our fathers" (ἡ

---

[36] There were of course other views of the land of Israel and its borders during the second century B.C.E. The book of *Jubilees*, for instance, followed the maximalist definition of the borders of the land found in Genesis. I deal with these different views in my forthcoming book on the Hasmonean wars of conquest and the paradigm of the "reconquest of the promised land."

[37] See Abel, *Les livres des Maccabées*, 272–73.

βασιλεία τῶν πατέρων ἡμῶν) in the speech of the Seleucid king. The reference to "the inheritance of our fathers" in ch. 15 has to be understood not only in connection with biblical texts, but also with Seleucid discourse as it is reproduced by the author of 1 Maccabees himself. To the best of my knowledge, after Abel, the only author who fully noticed the similarities between vv. 3–4 and vv. 33–35 is Robert Doran, who writes, "Antiochus VII had claimed that he was acting to regain control of the kingdom of his ancestors (15:3–4), and likewise now Simon reacts to Antiochus by claiming that he also only took back control of the inheritance of his ancestors (v. 33)."[38] The mirror effect is striking, but it has, nevertheless, been overlooked by most commentators.

Finally, the connection between Simon's reply and Antiochus's discourse is further corroborated by a study of 1 Maccabees as a whole, which leads to the conclusion that the expressions "the land of our/my/his fathers," "the kingdom of our/my fathers," and "the throne of my fathers," are exclusively to be found in the mouths of the Seleucid rulers.[39] It is therefore not only in the context of ch. 15 but, on the more general level, in the context of the book as a whole that the expression "the inheritance of our fathers" echoes Seleucid discourse.

This echo entails an ironic dimension since it aims at emphasizing that Antiochus behaves toward the Judeans in the very same way that his adversaries previously behaved toward him. The echo between Seleucid and Hasmonean discourses also has a strong political meaning, because it implies that the Seleucids and the Hasmoneans are from now on somehow on equal ground. Let us recall, following John Ma, that "power and empire are about language as much as about physical constraint."[40] The author of 1 Maccabees presents Simon as claiming a kind of reciprocity in his relationship with Antiochus. This can be explained by the fact that the Hasmoneans had gained the upper hand in Judea and had recovered autonomy to a large extent. Moreover, when 1 Maccabees was written, they had become fully independent of Seleucid rule.

IV. Hellenistic Discourse about Land Property Rights

Finally, let us assess Simon's answer to Antiochus by putting it in the context of Hellenistic discourse about land property rights. As aptly analyzed by Jean-Marie Bertrand, Angelos Chaniotis, and other historians of the Hellenistic and Roman world (who built on Elias Bickerman's pioneering work),[41] in

---

[38] Doran, "The First Book of Maccabees: Introduction, Commentary, and Reflections," *NIB* 4:172.

[39] See 1 Macc 7:2; 10:52, 55, 67; 11:9; 15:3, 10.

[40] Ma, *Antiochos III and the Cities of Western Asia Minor* (Oxford: Oxford University Press, 2000), 104.

[41] See Bickermann and Johannes Sykutris, "Speusipps Brief an König Philipp: Text,

the Hellenistic world there were four ways of arguing that one's possession of a territory was legitimate and that one had a legal right to a territory: inheritance, purchase, donation, and conquest. Conquest was legitimate if performed in a proper way, that is, against the legitimate owners and according to the rules of a just war—for instance, because one had been attacked first. The testimony of *IC* (*Inscriptiones Creticae*) III iv 9, an inscription pertaining to the arbitration by Magnesia on the Meander between the Cretan *poleis* of Hierapytna and Itanos in 112–111 B.C.E., proves illuminating. On lines 133–34, we read the following affirmation, only slightly reconstructed: "[... M]en have proprietary rights over land either because they have r[eceived] (the land) themselves from their ancestors, [or because they have] bought (it) [for] money, or because they have won it by the spear, or because [they have received it] from someone of the mightie[r]...."[42] Interestingly enough, the Seleucid discourse in 1 Maccabees uses similar expressions, speaking about κυριείαι ("lordships," proprietary rights) and about τόποι ("places"), for instance, in Antiochus's hostile missive to Simon (1 Macc 15:29–30).[43] Moreover, in the inscription the connection between property rights and inheritance or hereditary transmission is very strong. Both cities were arguing that they had an ancestral right to at least some part of the disputed land; however, in the end, the judges considered the claim of the citizens of Itanos, according to which the land was theirs through hereditary transmission (παρὰ προγόνων), to be more reliable.[44] The insistence on this argument corresponds to the Roman request to the Magnesians, when they made the latter responsible for the arbitration between the two cities, that the judges determine who had been in possession of the land

---

Übersetzung, Untersuchungen," in *Berichte über die Verhandlungen der Sächsischen Akademie der Wissenschaften zu Leipzig: Philologisch-historische Klasse*, vol. 80 (Leipzig: Teubner, 1928), 3:7–86, esp. 27–29, 40; Bickerman, "Bellum Antiochicum," *Hermes* 67 (1932): 47–76; idem, "Remarques sur le droit des gens dans la Grèce classique," *RIDA* 4, special issue, *Mélanges Fernand de Visscher*, vol. 3 (1950): 99–127, esp. 123–24; Andreas Mehl, "ΔΟΡΙΚΤΗΤΟΣ ΧΩΡΑ: Kritische Bemerkungen zum Speererwerb in Politik und Völkerrecht der hellenistischen Epoche," *Ancient Society* 11–12 (1980–81): 173–212; Bertrand, "Territoire donné, territoire attribué: Note sur la pratique de l'attribution dans le monde impérial de Rome," *Cahiers du Centre Gustave-Glotz* 2 (1991): 125–64; Chaniotis, "Justifying Territorial Claims in Classical and Hellenistic Greece," in *The Law and the Courts in Ancient Greece* (ed. Edward M. Harris and Lene Rubinstein; London: Duckworth, 2004), 185–213; idem, "Victory's Verdict: The Violent Occupation of Territory in Hellenistic Interstate Relations," in *La violence dans les mondes grec et romain: Actes du colloque international, Paris, 2–4 mai 2002* (ed. Jean-Marie Bertrand; Histoire ancienne et médiévale; Paris: Sorbonne, 2005), 455–64.

[42] 133 [... ἄν]θρωποι τὰς κατὰ τῶν τόπων ἔχουσι κυριείας ἢ παρὰ προγόνων π[αραλαβόν]τες αὐτοὶ [ἢ πριάμενοι] 134 [κατ'] ἀργυρίου δόσιν ἢ δόρατι κρατήσαντες ἢ παρά τινος τῶν κρεισσόν[ων σχόντες· ὧν] οὐθὲν [φανερόν]. See Sheila L. Ager, *Interstate Arbitrations in the Greek World, 337–90 B.C.* (Hellenistic Culture and Society 18; Berkeley: University of California Press, 1996), 442 (no. 158 II); and also F. Guizzi, "Conquista, occupazione del suolo e titoli che danno diritto alla proprietà: l'esemio di uno controversia interstatale cretese," *Athenaeum* 85 (1997): 35–52.

[43] Regarding these two terms, see Guizzi, "Conquista," 41–42.

[44] On the legitimizing role of references to the past, see, e.g., Ma, *Antiochus III*, 31–32.

prior to the war settled by Sulpicius around 141 B.C.E. However, the argumentation of the Cretan cities went further back in time and specified the principle according to which they considered themselves to be the legitimate owners. Finally, let us recall that the territory in dispute between Hierapytna and Itanos was located in the vicinity of a sanctuary to Zeus Diktaios; the people of Hierapytna claimed that the disputed piece of land was part of the sacred territory, which they controlled, whereas the Magnesian judges concluded that it was not. Noteworthy is the fact that, as in Simon's answer, no religious argument pertaining to the will of the deity to give sovereignty to one people in preference to the other is invoked in the inscription.[45]

There are also similarities between Simon's answer to Antiochus and Seleucid discourse as attested in Greek literary sources, for instance, in Polybius's account of Antiochus III's answer to Lucius Cornelius and the Roman emissaries in 196 B.C.E., when he was asked to withdraw from the territories that had previously been subject to Ptolemy IV, on the one hand, and to Philip V, on the other (*Hist.* 18.50.5–6). To this demand, Antiochus responded:

> … in the first place he was at a loss to know by what right they disputed his possession of the Asiatic towns; they were the last people who had any title to do so. 2. Next he requested them not to trouble themselves at all about Asiatic affairs; for he himself did not in the least go out of his way to concern himself with the affairs of Italy. 3. He said that he had crossed to Europe with his army for the purpose of recovering the Chersonese and the cities in Thrace, for he had a better title to the sovereignty of these places than anyone else [τὴν γὰρ τῶν τόπων τούτων ἀρχὴν μάλιστα πάντων αὐτῷ καθήκειν]. 4. They originally formed part of Lysimachus' kingdom, but when Seleucus went to war with that prince and conquered him in the war, the whole of Lysimachus' kingdom came to Seleucus by right of conquest [Σελεύκου δὲ πολεμήσαντος πρὸς αὐτὸν καὶ κρατήσαντος τῷ πολέμῳ πᾶσαν τὴν Λυσιμάχου βασιλείαν δορίκτητον γενέσθαι Σελεύκου]. 5. But during the years that followed, when his ancestors [τῶν αὐτοῦ προγόνων] had their attention deflected elsewhere, first of all Ptolemy and then Philip had robbed them of those places [τοὺς τόπους τούτους] and appropriated them. 6. At present he was not possessing himself of them by taking advantage of Philip's difficulties, but he was repossessing himself of them by his right as well as by his might [αὐτὸς δὲ νῦν οὐ κτᾶσθαι τοῖς Φιλίππου καιροῖς συνεπιτιθέμενος, ἀλλ' ἀνακτᾶσθαι τοῖς ἰδίοις δικαίοις συγχρώμενος]. (Polybius, *Hist.* 18.51.1–6)[46]

We are dealing here with a case of conquest, as the sentence κρατήσαντος τῷ πολέμῳ πᾶσαν τὴν Λυσιμάχου βασιλείαν <u>δορίκτητον</u> γενέσθαι Σελεύκου indicates. As rightly emphasized by Angelos Chaniotis, in the Hellenistic world conquest was a legitimate means to acquire a territory, provided that certain rules were followed. First,

---

[45] I thank Ashley Bacchi for drawing my attention to this aspect of the document.
[46] Translation according to Chaniotis, "Victory's Verdict," 459.

the real controversy was the determination of the *terminus a quo*.⁴⁷ As a matter of fact, a conquest was generally followed by another conquest, so that after a certain time, it would have been difficult to establish who had the right of property through conquest. The negotiation, therefore, was indeed about the *terminus a quo*. Now, in the case of Antiochus III, his argument was simply to affirm that the conquest of the Chersonese and the Thracian cities by his ancestor Seleucus I Nicanor in 281 B.C.E. was the real *terminus a quo*, and that the legitimate right of property belonged to the Seleucid dynasty, initially through conquest and then through hereditary transmission (thus combining two principles of legitimacy). Moreover, since one of the conditions for a legitimate proprietary right through conquest was that war had to be waged against the (at that time) legitimate owner of the territory, Antiochus argued that Ptolemy and Philip had no right to these territories, since neither of them waged war against the Seleucids but merely took advantage of the circumstances to seize these territories against the will of the Seleucids. Obviously, Antiochus's rhetoric is not to be taken at face value; as Ma emphasizes: "The Seleukids spoke about the past, in terms of ownership rights, not simply in reference to accepted legal principles, but in order to cover up or legitimize aggression against other kingdoms, the violent takeover of cities and the imposition of control in oppressive manifestations such as tribute or garrisons."⁴⁸ Nevertheless, Seleucid rhetoric proves illuminating in order to understand Simon's rhetoric in 1 Maccabees 15.

First, Simon uses the argument of heritage or hereditary transmission, just as Antiochus did; moreover, he also suggests that the Judean territory had been seized in an illegitimate way, stating that "the inheritance of our fathers" "had been unjustly conquered by our enemies using one opportunity or another" (ὑπὸ δὲ ἐχθρῶν ἡμῶν ἀκρίτως ἔν τινι καιρῷ κατεκρατήθη, v. 33). As in Polybius's account of Antiochus's argumentation, Simon argues that the Judeans have, therefore, the right to take over the territories again by conquest; since they have a legitimate right to the land, conquest becomes a legitimate means. However, in certain respects, Simon's argumentation is much less precise than that of Antiochus III. In particular, he does not refer to the initial conquest of the land, either by Joshua, by David, or by others, and, therefore, does not provide a *terminus a quo*. Maybe he can be seen as standing in line with the author of 1 Chronicles, who passes over the conquest of the land almost in complete silence and describes the occupation of the land from the patriarchs until the end of the monarchy as a quasi-linear phenomenon with nearly perfect continuity.⁴⁹ Alternatively, one could argue that, since the initial conquest of the land by Joshua was supposed to have occurred ten centuries before the period during which Simon ruled, the event was too distant for the

---

⁴⁷ See Chaniotis, "Victory's Verdict," 458–59.
⁴⁸ Ma, *Antiochus III*, 32.
⁴⁹ See Sarah Japhet, "Conquest and Settlement in Chronicles," *JBL* 98 (1979): 205–18, esp. 218; eadem, *The Ideology of the Book of Chronicles and Its Place in Biblical Thought* (BEATAJ 9; Bern: Lang, 1989), 374–79.

argument to be appropriate. However, this reasoning is not sound, because even the mythic past was sometimes used as an argument in Hellenistic debates about territories and peoples or about connections between peoples.[50] The works of historians and even poets were consulted by the judges who were in charge of interstate arbitrations in order to establish the veracity of historical claims.[51] So it is probably wrong to consider that the location of the biblical stories in a distant past would have prevented Simon from using biblical traditions as an argument, had he be willing to do so. In any case, it is highly significant for the correct interpretation of 1 Maccabees 15 and of 1 Maccabees as a whole, that, according to its author, Simon did *not* refer to the initial conquest of the land by Israel's ancestors but chose to argue solely on the basis of the right of inheritance. This again shows that interpreting 1 Maccabees 15:33–35 as a proof of Simon's intention to reconquer the "promised land" is clearly misleading.

V. Conclusion

In the history of scholarship, there has been, and still is, a general tendency to overinterpret 1 Macc 15:33–35 and to ground important conclusions concerning the history of the Hasmonean dynasty on this overinterpretation. Certainly, it must be acknowledged that there are multiple ways of reading the text as well as multiple layers of meaning, intertextuality, and context that are not necessarily exclusive. At least three contexts can be distinguished: (a) the context of ch. 15 and of the book as a whole, in which Simon's answer echoes Seleucid discourse; (b) the context of biblical and Jewish literature up to the second century B.C.E., which provides an important background for understanding the meaning of the expression "the inheritance of our fathers"; and (c) the context of Hellenistic diplomatic language and argumentation in cases of territorial disputes, which is also crucial in order to grasp the full significance of Simon's response to Antiochus. By taking all these contexts into account, one reaches several conclusions: First, a close analysis of Simon's answer to Antiochus reveals that the expression "the inheritance of our

---

[50] See, in particular, Martin P. Nilsson, *A History of Greek Religion* (trans. F. J. Fielden; 2nd ed.; Oxford: Clarendon, 1949), 236–40; Bickerman, "Remarques sur le droit des gens dans la Grèce classique," 123–24. *Syngeneiai* based on myths were particularly frequent, and one actually finds an example of such a mythic *syngeneia* in 1 Maccabees itself concerning Judeans and Spartans! See 1 Macc 12:21.

[51] On the use of historical arguments and historiographical works in arbitrations concerning territories, see Maurice Holleaux, "Notes sur la 'Chronique de Lindos,'" in *Études d'épigraphie et d'histoire grecques* (Paris: de Boccard, 1938), 1:401–7, esp. 404 n. 3; Olivier Curty, "L'historiographie hellénistique et l'inscription 'Inschriften von Priene' no. 37," in *Historia testis: Mélanges d'épigraphie, d'histoire ancienne et de philologie offerts à Tadeusz Zawadzki* (ed. Marcel Piérart and Olivier Curty; Seges n.F. 7; Fribourg: Éditions Universitaires, 1989), 21–35.

fathers" very probably refers to Judea, or a "greater Judah," but not to the "promised land," especially not according to its maximalist definition in some biblical texts. Second, Simon's argumentation and 1 Maccabees as a whole display a conspicuous lack of references to the original conquest of the land, to border issues, as well as to God's promise to Abraham or to the divine will to give the land to Israel. The expression "the inheritance of our fathers" may, however, allude to the biblical traditions concerning the lots of land attributed to the children of Israel according to their tribes and can be interpreted as emphasizing the legal right of the Judeans over Judea's territory. Simultaneously, the reference to a legal right acquired through inheritance perfectly fits Hellenistic modes of argumentation about territorial issues. As a matter of fact, Simon's discourse as formulated by the author of 1 Maccabees matches Seleucid and, more generally, Hellenistic diplomatic argumentation concerning property rights over a disputed territory to a surprisingly great extent. Except if one supposes that the translator freely modified the original Hebrew text to make it fit Hellenistic standards, one can conclude that, in spite of its being written in Hebrew, 1 Maccabees 15 reveals a thus far underestimated aspect of the Hasmoneans' integration into the Hellenistic world: their significant awareness and mastery of the diplomatic discourse used in interstate arbitrations in cases of territorial strife. It is somehow ironic that precisely this passage has been used to describe the Hasmoneans as religious zealots who planned to "reconquer the promised land."

Critical Studies

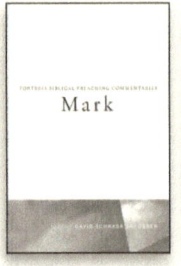   

Mark
Fortress Biblical Preaching Commentaries
DAVID SCHNASA JACOBSEN
9780800699239 224pp pbk $22

The Historical Character of Jesus
Canonical Insights from Outside the Gospels
DAVID M. ALLEN
9781451469370 224pp pbk $29

The Authors of the Deuteronomistic History
Locating a Tradition in Ancient Israel
BRIAN NEIL PETERSON
9781451469967 192pp pbk $34

Behind the Gospels
Understanding the Oral Tradition
ERIC EVE
9781451469400 224pp pbk $29

Encountering Jesus
Character Studies in the Gospel of John
Second Edition
CORNELIS BENNEMA
9781451470062 240pp pbk $39

Election of the Lesser Son
Paul's Lament-Midrash in Romans 9-11
DAVID R. WALLACE
9781451482959 192pp pbk $34

By Bread Alone
The Bible through the Eyes of the Hungry
SHEILA E. MCGINN,
LAI LING ELIZABETH NGAN,
AHIDA CALDERÓN PILARSKI, editors
9781451465501 224pp pbk $29

Available wherever books are sold or
800-328-4648
fortresspress.com

Matthew's *Titulus* and Psalm 2's King on Mount Zion

TUCKER S. FERDA
tferda@pts.edu
Pittsburgh Theological Seminary, Pittsburgh, PA 15206

Origen, Augustine, Aquinas, and others thought that the *titulus crucis* was an ironic divine decree that recalled Ps 2:6: "I have set my king on Zion, my holy hill." Although this reading is no longer mentioned in modern commentaries on Matthew, this article attempts to demonstrate that it is, in fact, quite plausible, given larger Matthean themes. The argument begins by suggesting that Matthew's passion narrative and crucifixion scene frequently recall the enthronement scenario in Ps 2:6–8—including the opposition to God and God's Messiah in vv. 1–3. Then it suggests that Matthew makes the crucifixion the climax of the opposition to Jesus as described in Psalm 2 and shapes the *titulus* into an ironic proclamation of the kingship of Jesus. The article thus concludes that Origen's proposed linkage between Psalm 2 and Matthew's inscription can be defended intratextually, if not intertextually.

It stands to reason that early Christian theology would be more apt to create the black sky, the rent temple veil, and the confession of faith than the insult on the *titulus crucis*: "This is Jesus, the King of the Jews" (Matt 27:37). And many historians have sensibly concluded that the *titulus* tradition preserves a reliable memory about the last moments of Jesus.[1] But one wonders if the exegesis of Matthew's crucifixion scene has been at all edified by this knowledge. Since the advent of historical criticism, many commentaries have adopted a striking shift of tone regarding Matt 27:37: some digress completely from the narrative to discuss the historical reasons for Jesus' death,[2] and others, interested only in the "theology" of

[1] For discussion and literature, see Ernst Bammel, "The *titulus*," in *Jesus and the Politics of His Day* (ed. Ernst Bammel and C. F. D. Moule; Cambridge: Cambridge University Press, 1984), 353–64.
[2] E.g., Edouard Reuss, *La Bible: Traduction nouvelle avec introductions et commentaires*, vol. 11, *Nouveau Testament*, part 1, *Histoire évangélique: Synopse des trois premiers évangiles* (Paris: Sandoz & Fischbacher, 1876), 689; Julius Wellhausen, *Das Evangelium Matthaei* (Berlin: G. Reimer, 1904; repr., Berlin: de Gruyter, 1987), 139; Alfred Loisy, *Les Évangiles synoptiques* (2 vols.;

the crucifixion scene, have not even deemed the title worthy of exegetical reflection.³ The problem here is patent: given the complex blend of memory and imagination in Matthew's Gospel, one should find it questionable, a priori, that the *titulus* is a bare spot on an otherwise colorful canvas.

There are, of course, many commentaries that claim that Matthew's *titulus* ironically communicates the truth about Jesus.⁴ But two problems remain. First,

---

Paris: Ceffonds, 1907–8), 2:667; Theodor Zahn, *Das Evangelium des Matthäus* (3rd ed.; Leipzig: Deichert, 1910), 711–12; Johannes Weiss and Wilhelm Bousset, *Die drei älteren Evangelien* (vol. 1 of *Die Schriften des neuen Testaments*; ed. Wilhelm Bousset and Otto Baumgarten; 4 vols.; Göttingen: Vandenhoeck & Ruprecht, 1917–20), 383–84; M.-J. Lagrange, *Évangile selon saint Matthieu* (EBib; Paris: Gabalda, 1948), 528; Adolf von Schlatter, *Der Evangelist Matthäus: Seine Sprache, seine Ziel, seine Selbstshändigkeit. Ein Kommentar zum ersten Evangelium* (6th ed.; Stuttgart: Calwer, 1963), 780; Paul Gaechter, *Das Matthäus Evangelium: Ein Kommentar* (Innsbruck: Tyrolia, 1963), 922–23; David Hill, *The Gospel of Matthew* (NCB 40; London: Oliphants, 1972), 353; Eduard Schweizer, *The Good News according to Matthew* (trans. David E. Green; Atlanta: John Knox, 1975), 512; Ben Witherington III, *Matthew* (Smyth & Helwys Bible Commentary; Macon, GA: Smyth & Helwys, 2006), 514–15.

³ E.g., Heinrich Holtzmann, *Die synoptischen Evangelien: Ihr Ursprung und geschichtlicher Charakter* (Leipzig: Wilhelm Engelmann, 1863), 205; Theodore H. Robinson, *The Gospel of Matthew* (MNTC; New York: Harper, 1927), 230–31; Josef Schmid, *Das Evangelium nach Mätthaus* (RNT 1; Regensburg: Pustet, 1965), 372–73; Daniel Patte, *The Gospel according to Matthew: A Structural Commentary on Matthew's Faith* (Philadelphia: Fortress, 1987), 384; Thomas G. Long, *Matthew* (Westminster Bible Companion; Louisville: Westminster John Knox, 1997), 316; Rudolf Schnackenburg, *The Gospel of Matthew* (trans. Robert R. Barr; Grand Rapids: Eerdmans, 2002), 287.

⁴ See William Gilpin, *An Exposition of the New Testament* (4th ed.; 2 vols.; London: Cadel & Davies, 1811), 1:117 ("fulfilling a prophecy undefignedly"); Alfred Durand, *Évangile selon saint Matthieu: Traduction et commentaire* (33rd ed.; Verbum salutis; Paris: Beauchesne, 1948), 518; John P. Meier, *Matthew* (New Testament Message 3; Wilmington, DE: Michael Glazier, 1980), 347; Donald A. Hagner, *Matthew 14–28* (WBC 33B; Waco: Word, 1982), 836; Joachim Gnilka, *Das Matthäusevangelium* (2 vols.; HTKNT 1; Freiburg: Herder, 1986–88), 2:472 ("Bei Mt wird der Schuldtitel zur Proklamation"); Robert H. Smith, *Matthew* (ACNT 1; Minneapolis: Augsburg, 1989), 324; Douglas R. A. Hare, *Matthew* (IBC; Louisville: John Knox, 1993), 320; Daniel J. Harrington, *The Gospel of Matthew* (SP 1; Collegeville, MN: Liturgical Press, 1991), 395; W. D. Davies and Dale C. Allison Jr., *A Critical and Exegetical Commentary on the Gospel according to Saint Matthew* (3 vols.; ICC; Edinburgh: T&T Clark, 1988–97), 3:615; Wolfgang Wiefel, *Das Evangelium nach Matthäus* (THKNT; Leipzig: Evangelische Verlagsanstalt, 1998), 479 ("paradoxes Bekenntnis"); Craig S. Keener, *A Commentary on the Gospel of Matthew* (Grand Rapids: Eerdmans, 1999), 690; Alberto Mello, *Évangile selon saint Matthieu: Commentaire midrashique et narratif* (trans. Aimée Chevillon; LD 179; Paris: Cerf, 1999), 481; Ulrich Luz, *Matthew: A Commentary*, vol. 3, *Matthew 21–28* (trans. James E. Crouch; Hermeneia; Minneapolis: Fortress, 2005), 534; Peter Fiedler, *Das Matthäusevangelium* (Theologischer Kommentar zum Neuen Testament 1; Stuttgart: Kohlhammer, 2006), 414; David L. Turner, *Matthew* (Baker Exegetical Commentary on the New Testament 1; Grand Rapids: Baker Academic, 2008), 661; Charles H. Talbert, *Matthew* (Paideia; Grand Rapids: Baker Academic, 2010), 303.

the observation that the message of Matthew's title is ironically true has largely been the extent of reflection on the matter. There have been no attempts to probe the ways in which the kingship proclaimed in the *titulus* relates to the rest of the Gospel. Second, it is not apparent that commentators have considered the history of interpretation of the *titulus*, which I believe has more to teach us on this point than do the historical critics.[5]

The particular interest of this article concerns an ancient reading of the *titulus* found in the works of Origen and many others. It says that, in spite of the soldiers' mocking intentions, the title recalls Ps 2:6 as a divine decree: "I have set my king on Zion, my holy hill."[6] In the pages that follow, I intend to show that there is much to commend this reading, given larger Matthean themes. I will first introduce the reading along with other preliminary exegetical issues, then turn to background context, and finally make five arguments that, taken together, support the hearing of a Psalm 2 subtext to Matthew's crucifixion scene.

I. Preliminary Exegetical Issues

The first question one must address is the disagreement in the history of interpretation concerning the significance of the *titulus* for the identity of Jesus. One can easily generalize here. Most have understood the title to communicate a truth deeper than Pilate or his soldiers intended, similar to the word of Caiaphas: "it is better that one man die for the people than to have the whole nation perish" (John 11:50).[7] But others have seen little positive concerning Jesus in the *titulus*.

---

[5] There is, to date, no thorough reception history of the *titulus*. Luz's brief history of interpretation mentions only a few ancient readers (*Matthew 21–28*, 532, 534). Hermann Fulda offers a two-page discussion (*Das Kreuz und die Kreuzigung: Eine antiquarische Untersuchung nebst Nachweis der vielen seit Lipsius verbreiteten Irrthümer, zugleich vier Excurse über verwandte Gegenstände* [Breslau: Koebner, 1878], 205–7), but all his material came from one source: Honorat Nicquet, *Titulus sanctae crucis* (Antwerp: Andrae Frisii, 1670).

[6] Translations from all sources are my own unless otherwise indicated. I provide references to English translations for selections from the history of interpretation if they were accessible to me.

[7] See, e.g., Clement of Alexandria, *Strom.* 2.5 (*ANF* 2:351); Gregory of Nyssa, *Comm. Cant.* 7 in *Commentary on the Song of Songs* (trans. Casimir McCambley; Archbishop Iakovos Library of Ecclesiastical and Historical Sources 12; Brookline, MA: Hellenic College Press, 1987), 142; Ephrem the Syrian, *Hymn. Pasc.* 4.6; 8.6, 7 (SC 502:220, 263–64); John Chrysostom, *Hom. Jo.* 85 (FC 41:429–30); Gregory of Nazianzus, *Or.* 20 (*NPNF*[2] 7:308–9); John of Damascus, *Frag. Matt.* (*PG* 96:1412); Rabanus Maurus, *Exp. Matt.* 8.335 (ed. B. Löfstedt; CCCM 174; Turnhout: Brepols, 2000), 748; Erasmus, *Paraphrase on Matthew* (trans. Dean Simpson; Collected Works of Erasmus 45; Toronto: University of Toronto Press, 2008), 369; Juan de Valdés, *Commentary upon the Gospel of St. Matthew* (trans. John T. Betts; London: Trübner, 1882), 484; John Calvin, *Commentary on a Harmony of the Evangelists, Matthew, Mark, and Luke* (trans. William Pringle; 3 vols.; Calvin's

Tertullian, for example, read the inscription alongside Heb 2:9 as an illustration of Christ's humiliation "a little lower than the angels."[8] A few more recent critics have suggested that the inscription becomes a proclamation only in John's Gospel, since the author presents it in three languages and claims that the Jews protested its wording.[9]

Matthew may not be as explicit as John, to be sure, but it is easy to demonstrate that his inscription tells the reader something true about Jesus. (i) The core of Matthew's *titulus*, taken from Mark 15:26, appears favorably in the infancy narrative as the magi seek "the one who is called the king of the Jews" (Matt 2:2).[10] (ii) Matthew celebrates Jesus' royal lineage (Matt 1:2–17) and has a preference for christological titles: Messiah/Christ, Son of David, Son of God, and King.[11] Matthew in general has a positive view of kingship: he emphasizes David "the king" in the genealogy (1:6), names Jesus "your king" in the triumphal entry (21:5), and makes Jesus use "king" self-referentially (25:34, 40). (iii) The irony of the *titulus* coheres with Matthew's theme, though less pronounced than Mark's, that many are blind to the truth of Jesus' identity and mission (11:25–27; 13:11; 16:17).[12] (iv) Matthew otherwise has Jesus questioned and mocked with theologically positive labels: Christ (26:63; 27:17, 22), Son of God (26:63 [cf. σὺ εἶ ὁ χριστὸς ὁ υἱὸς τοῦ θεοῦ τοῦ ζῶντος in 16:16]; 27:40, 43, 54), prophet (26:67–68).[13] (v) That Jesus responds with σὺ εἶπας or σὺ λέγεις to questions from Caiaphas and Pilate (26:64;

Commentaries 17; Grand Rapids: Baker, 2009), 3:302; Cornelius Lapide, *The Great Commentary* (trans. Thomas W. Mossman; 6 vols.; London: John Hodges, 1881), 3:294.

[8] See Tertullian, *Cor.* 14.4 (FC 40:266). Others who view the *titulus* as a shameful gesture include Melito of Sardis, *Hom. Pas.* 95–96, in *On Pascha and Fragments* (trans. Stuart George Hall; Oxford: Clarendon, 1979), 54–55; Gaius Juvencus, *Lib. Ev. IIII* 4.664 (ed. Carolus Marold; Leipzig: Teubner, 1886), 100; Asterius, *Comm. Ps.* 28.6 (ed. M. Richard; Oslo: Brogger, 1956), 226; Peter of Laodicea, *Comm. Matt.* ad loc. in *Des Petrus von Laodicea Erklärung des Matthäusevangeliums* (ed. C. F. Georg Heinrici; Leipzig: Durr, 1908), 329 ("And they did this in order that all who read it would find him prideful [ἀλαζόνα αὐτὸν σχῇ]").

[9] See Edouard Reuss, *Histoire évangelique*, 689 ("Le quatrième évangile donne un tout autre sens à cette inscription"); Raymond E. Brown, *The Gospel according to John: Introduction, Translation, and Notes*, vol. 2, *Chapters 13–21* (AB 29A; Garden City, NY: Doubleday, 1970), 919.

[10] See Jack Dean Kingsbury, "The Figure of Jesus in Matthew's Story: A Literary-Critical Probe," *JSNT* 21 (1984): 3–36, esp. 9.

[11] See the list of "positive labels" in Bruce J. Malina and Jerome H. Neyrey, *Calling Jesus Names: The Social Value of Labels in Matthew* (FF: Social Facets; Sonoma, CA: Polebridge, 1998), 155–57.

[12] See Stanley P. Saunders, "Matthew," in *Theological Bible Commentary* (ed. Gail R. O'Day and David L. Petersen; Louisville: Westminster John Knox, 2009), 308.

[13] For discussion, see A. Descamps, "Rédaction et christologie dans le récit matthéen de la passion," in *L'Évangile selon Matthieu: Rédaction et théologie* (ed. M. Didier; BETL 29; Gembloux: Duculot, 1972), 359–417, esp. 398. Note also Malina and Neyrey: "Labels of honor are ironically used to dishonor Jesus" (*Names*, 81–82).

27:11) demonstrates Matthew's ability to "underline the illocutionary force of (the words) ... independent of the mode of their enunciation."[14] (vi) It is otherwise clear that readers would see the insincere praises and genuflections of the soldiers (27:27-31) as unwitting acknowledgments of Jesus' dignity.[15] Thus, unless such narrative traits apply only to 1:1–27:36, we can be confident that Matthew's *titulus* is one of many experiments with dramatic irony: readers know that Jesus *is*, in some sense, "the king of the Jews."

The deeper and more perplexing question concerns the way in which the inscription confirms Matthew's presentation of Jesus as Israel's Messiah, the son of David. Given the density of scriptural echoes in the crucifixion scene as a whole, and in particular Matthew's prolific use of the Psalms in the immediate context (27:35, 38, 39, 43, 46), it should not surprise that many ancient exegetes thought that the *titulus* evokes a royal or enthronement psalm in upholding the messiahship of Jesus.[16] Many different psalms have been taken as prophecies of the title,[17] but the focus here is on Origen in his *Commentary on Matthew*:

> And for a crown, "over his head" is written "This is Jesus King of the Jews." And there is no other cause for his death (nor indeed was there) than that he was the King of the Jews. And concerning this it was spoken, "But I have been made King by him on Zion, his holy mountain."[18]

In this context, Origen cites Phil 1:18 ("whether in false motives or true, Christ is proclaimed") as commentary so that the inscription, written with "false motives," nevertheless proclaims the truth. For Origen, the messianic Psalm 2 highlights the sense in which the executioners inadvertently bring God's purposes to completion.

---

[14] O. T. Venard, "La parole comme enjeu narrative et théologique dans la passion selon saint Matthieu: Un commentaire littéraire de Mt 26–28," *RB* 115 (2008): 77. See a similar reading in Frank J. Matera, *Passion Narratives and Gospel Theologies: Interpreting the Synoptics through Their Passion Stories* (Theological Inquiries; New York: Paulist, 1986), 107.

[15] Hilary of Poitiers said it best: "Christ, being mocked, is adored" (*Comm. Matt.* 33.3 [SC 258:252–53]).

[16] While the *titulus* is not specified, it may be implied in the early Christian accusation that Jews omitted "from the wood" from LXX Ps 95:10: "The Lord reigned (from the wood)" (ὁ κύριος ἐβασίλευσεν ἀπὸ τοῦ ξύλου). See Justin Martyr, *1 Apol.* 41.1 (*ANF* 1:176); idem, *Dial.* 73.1 (*ANF* 1:235); Tertullian, *Marc.* 3.19 (*ANF* 3:337). Cf. Lapide, *Great Commentary*, 3:29.

[17] See, e.g., Augustine, *Enarrat. Ps.* 46.4 in *The Works of Saint Augustine: A Translation for the 21st Century*, part 3, *Sermons*, vol. 16, *Expositions of the Psalms 33–50* (ed. John E. Rotelle; trans. Maria Boulding; Hyde Park, NY: New City Press, 1990), 326–27; Cassiodorus, *Expl. Ps.* 15, 20, 46 (ACW 51:160–61, 209, 460). Also noteworthy are Byzantine icons of the crucifixion with *tituli* that read "the King of Glory" (cf. Ps 24:7–10). See Andreas Andreopoulos, *Metamorphosis: The Transfiguration in Byzantine Theology and Iconography* (Crestwood, NY: St. Vladimir's Seminary Press, 2005), 26.

[18] Origen, *Comm. Matt.* 130, in *Origenes Werke*, vol. 11, *Origenes Matthäuserklärung*, part 2 (ed. Erich Klostermann, Ernst Benz, and Ursula Treu; 2nd ed.; Berlin: Akademie, 1976), 267.

One finds a similar interpretation (though not necessarily of Matthew in particular) in the works of Pseudo-Cyprian, Augustine, Cassiodorus, Bede, the *Glossa ordinaria*, Albert the Great, and Thomas Aquinas.[19] Yet this reading has, for reasons I know not, dropped completely from Matthew commentaries. Even more surprising is that one rarely finds Psalm 2 mentioned in exegesis of the crucifixion scene as a whole.

To be sure, it may seem at first glance that a linkage between the title and Ps 2:6 would have to rely rather tenuously on a single word agreement ("king"). But the logic of this forgotten reading, I submit, is not limited to that alone. It can be argued that the First Gospel recalls Psalm 2 in multiple ways throughout the passion narrative to shape the crucifixion of Jesus into a key element of his enthronement as God's "king" and "son."[20] Thus, I suggest that Origen's reading can be defended if slightly restated to say that the title engages Psalm 2 as much intratextually as intertextually: the *titulus* is integral to the ironic nature of Matthew's Golgotha that consistently interacts with Psalm 2.

II. Background

Before we consider the narrative details, however, we can first say that Origen's reading coheres with what we know about the interpretation of Psalm 2 in the Second Temple period. Augustine's wording captures the point best: "a title ... showed that not even by killing him could they manage not to have him as king.... This is why we sing in the Psalm, *I, however, have been established by him as king on Zion his holy mountain.*"[21] Augustine here is aware of the original context of Ps 2:6, in which nations, peoples, kings, and rulers "take counsel together against the LORD and his anointed" (Ps 2:2). Augustine's "however" communicates the

---

[19] Pseudo-Cyprian, *De duobus montibus Sina et Sion* 9.1–2, in Anni Maria Laato, *Jews and Christians in De duobus montibus Sina et Sion: An Approach to Early Latin Adversus Iudaeos Literature* (Åbo: Åbo Akademi University Press, 1998), 177; Augustine, *Serm.* 218 5, in Rotelle, *Works of Saint Augustine,* part 3, *Sermons,* vol. 11, *Newly Discovered Sermons* (trans. Edmund Hill), 239; Cassiodorus, *Expl. Ps.* 2 (ACW 51:61); Bede, *Exp. Marc.* (ed. D. Hurst; CCSL 120; Turnhout: Brepols, 1960), 632; *Gloss. ord.* (on Mark 15:26) (*PL* 114:239c); Albert the Great, *Enarrat. Jo.,* in *Opera Omnia,* vol. 24 (ed. Auguste Borgnet; Paris: Ludovicum Vives, 1899), 657; Thomas Aquinas, *Super Evangelium S. Matthaei: Lectura* (ed. P. Raphaelis Cai; Turin: Marietti, 1951), 363.

[20] This would be similar to the way that the maze of Scriptures from Zechariah 13–14, Isaiah 53, and the Lament Psalms recurs in the passion narrative. See Barnabas Lindars, *New Testament Apologetic: The Doctrinal Significance of the Old Testament Quotations* (London: SCM, 1961), 75–137; Douglas J. Moo, *The Old Testament in the Gospel Passion Narratives* (Sheffield: Almond, 1983), 148–50, 154, 182–209, 264–74, 282.

[21] Augustine *Serm.* 218 5 (trans. Hill, 239 [italics Hill's]).

adversarial nature of the Ps 2:6 declaration: "however," or, "in spite of" enemy schemes, God has set up God's king in Zion. Both these notions—the opposition of God's enemies and the declaration of messiahship—are central to Second Temple readings of Psalm 2.

Of course, when composed, Psalm 2 probably referred to the historical opponents of Israel (vv. 1–2) and then to Israel's own national ruler (vv. 6–7).[22] But in later reception the oracle was often eschatologized: the "conspiring" of enemies described the final struggle of the wicked against God, and vv. 6–7's "king" and "son" were linked to a messianic-type figure. In 4Q174, the catena of messianic texts from 2 Samuel 7, Amos 9, and Psalm 89 probably refers to Psalm 2's "son" and "Zion," and is immediately followed by a citation of Ps 2:1–2 to describe opposition to God's people "in the last days."[23] *Psalms of Solomon* 17 also relies heavily on Psalm 2 in its description of the son of David, his victory over the Gentiles, and his purging of Zion. Aside from the thematic links of kingship and Jerusalem/Zion (*Pss. Sol.* 17:14, 22, 30; Ps 2:6), the imagery of smashing nations or sinners like a piece of pottery (*Pss. Sol.* 17:23; Ps 2:9), and the notion of Gentile nations serving under his yoke (*Pss. Sol.* 17:30; Ps 2:8, 10–11), the text further adopts LXX Psalm 2's ἄρχων/ἄρχοντες (*Pss. Sol.* 17:12, 20, 22, 36; Ps 2:2), χριστός (*Pss. Sol.* 17:32; Ps 2:2), and κληρονομία (*Pss. Sol.* 17:23; Ps 2:8). Here the text does not cite Psalm 2 explicitly but rather alludes to it via key words and expressions, all under the assumption that the Psalm speaks directly to its interest in the end-time battle of God's Messiah. Many other pseudepigraphic and rabbinic texts corroborate 4Q174 and *Psalms of Solomon* 17 in this regard (e.g., *1 En.* 46:5; 48:8–10; *4 Ezra* 13:32, 35–37; *Sib. Or.* 3:663; *Midr. Teh.* 2:2).[24]

Many early Christians read Psalm 2 in similar ways but with an expected twist: the end-time battle of God and God's Messiah referred to the passion and

---

[22] See Hermann Gunkel, *Die Psalmen* (1926; Göttingen: Vandenhoeck & Ruprecht, 1968), 5; Sigmund Mowinckel, *The Psalms in Israel's Worship* (1962; repr., Oxford: Blackwell, 1982), 61–65; P. C. Craigie, *Psalms 1–50* (WBC 19; Waco: Word, 1983), 64.

[23] See George J. Brooke, *Exegesis at Qumran: 4Q Florilegium in Its Jewish Context* (JSOTSup 29; Sheffield: JSOT Press, 1985), 209; Craig A. Evans, "Jesus and the Messianic Texts from Qumran: A Preliminary Assessment of the Recently Published Materials," in *Jesus and His Contemporaries: Comparative Studies* (AGJU 25; Leiden: Brill, 1995), 103–5.

[24] On rabbinic literature in particular, see J. J. Brierre-Narbonne, *Exégèse talmudique des prophéties messianiques* (Paris: P. Geuthner, 1934), esp. 34. Aquila H. I. Lee claims that "allusions to Ps 2 in rabbinic sources are usually associated with the idea of opposition, rebellion, and hostile attack upon God, the messiah, and Israel" (*From Messiah to Preexistent Son: Jesus' Self-Consciousness and Early Christian Exegesis of Messianic Psalms* [WUNT 192; Tübingen: Mohr Siebeck, 2005], 249). On different versions of Psalm 2, see Paul Maiberger, "Das Verständnis von Psalm 2 in der Septuaginta, im Targum, in Qumran, im frühen Judentum und im Neuen Testament," in *Beiträge zur Psalmenforschung: Psalm 2 und 22* (ed. Josef Schreiner; FB 60; Würzburg: Echter, 1988), 85–151.

resurrection of Jesus.²⁵ Wim Weren notes that the characters in Luke's passion narrative are tailor-made to fit Psalm 2 roles, as "leaders" (ἄρχοντες) and a "king" conspire against Jesus.²⁶ The same point is made explicit in Acts 4:25–26, which cites Ps 2:1–2. In Revelation, the challenge of "kings of the earth" to God and God's anointed appears presupposed in 11:15; 17:18; and 19:19. So too, many have heard Psalm 2 in Rom 1:4 ("declared to be Son of God in power … by resurrection from the dead"), and Psalm 2's description of struggle probably informs the adversarial sense of "declaration."²⁷ To be sure, scholars have typically discussed Psalm 2 when investigating the resurrection of Jesus, but the full picture is this: Psalm 2 had its important role in early christological development because it was taken to describe the Messiah's exaltation *and* his humiliation.²⁸ Psalm 2 was seen as a declaration of messiahship in the face of opposition.

It is clear, then, that Psalm 2 in the Second Temple period shares much with Matthew's passion narrative and crucifixion scene. For the evangelist too describes an eschatological showdown with opposing "nations/Gentiles" and "leaders," and confirms that, despite the opposition, his Jesus is God's "king" and "son" (27:37, 54). Five additional arguments suggest that these similarities may not be mere coincidence.

III. Five Arguments

Psalm 2 Elsewhere in Matthew's Gospel

One expects to find Psalm 2 in play in the crucifixion scene, given the ways that Matthew uses Psalm 2 to anticipate the death of Jesus. Most noteworthy here is the passion narrative itself.²⁹ Luke's Gospel has received the bulk of scholarly

---

²⁵ For a discussion of Mark, see Rikk E. Watts, "The Lord's House and David's Lord: The Psalms and Mark's Perspective on Jesus and the Temple," *BibInt* 15 (2007): 307–22.

²⁶ Weren, "Psalm 2 in Luke-Acts: An Intertextual Study," in *Intertextuality in Biblical Writings: Essays in Honour of Bas van Iersel* (ed. Sipke Draisma; Kampen: Kok, 1989), 189–204. Here following Martin Dibelius, "Herodes und Pilatus," *ZNW* 16 (1915): 113–26, esp. 25. Note also Joshua W. Jipp: "It is Psalm 2 that exerted the most influence on the early Christians in their conception of the Messiah, his relationship to God, and the opposition and persecution that Christians endured at the hands of Israel's leaders" ("Luke's Scriptural Suffering Messiah: A Search for Precedent, a Search for Identity," *CBQ* 72 [2010]: 272).

²⁷ See literature in James D. G. Dunn, *Romans 1–8* (WBC 38A; Waco: Word, 1988), 3–4.

²⁸ On Psalm 2 and the resurrection of Jesus, see Lindars, *New Testament Apologetic*, 140–43; James D. G. Dunn, *Christology in the Making: A New Testament Inquiry into the Origins of the Doctrine of the Incarnation* (London: SCM, 1989), 35–36.

²⁹ There are three other important examples that we do not have space to explore further: (i) οἱ βασιλεῖς τῆς γῆς in Matt 17:25 and Ps 2:2 (thanks to Michael Barber for bringing this to my attention); (ii) the well-known Matthean addition to the parable of the wedding banquet (22:7):

attention concerning Psalm 2, but Matthew also has shaped his passion narrative as a whole in ways that evoke the struggle against God's anointed in Psalm 2. This shaping is evident in Matthean redaction at the outset of the passion narrative (26:1–5), where others have noted that the evangelist foreshadows key things to come.[30] In Mark, the chief priests and scribes "were seeking" (ἐζήτουν) how they might put Jesus to death (Mark 14:1), but Matthew has the chief priests and elders of the people "gathered together" (συνήχθησαν) as they "conspired" (συνεβουλεύσαντο) to kill him.[31] Not only is the scenario evocative of Psalm 2's "scheming" (ἐφρύαξαν, רגשו) and "plotting" (ἐμελέτησαν, יהגו),[32] and thus is consistent with other early Christian uses of Psalm 2, but Matthew and LXX Psalm 2 share the key word συνήχθησαν (cf. Ps 2:2 יתיצבו).[33] In the remainder of the passion narrative, Matthew will again use (often redactionally) different inflections of συνάγω whenever describing organized opposition to Jesus (see 26:57; 27:1, 17, 27).[34] One of these examples displays further similarities with Psalm 2, including chief priests and elders "taking counsel" (συμβούλιον ἔλαβον; cf. Ps 2:2 נוסדו יחד)[35] with one

---

"And the king was enraged [ὠργίσθη] and after sending his troops he destroyed [ἀπώλεσεν] those murderers and burned their city," and ὀργισθῇ κύριος, ἀπολεῖσθε, and the image of God's wrath "being kindled" (ἐκκαυθῇ) in Ps 2:12; (iii) in Matt 22:34 the Pharisees and Sadducees συνήχθησαν ἐπὶ τὸ αὐτό, and in Ps 2:2 οἱ ἄρχοντες συνήχθησαν ἐπὶ τὸ αὐτό.

[30] See Descamps, "Rédaction et christologie," 375, 400.

[31] On the source-critical question about the origin of Matthew's non-Markan material, Nils Dahl is still correct that it "läßt sich sehr oft nicht entscheiden" ("Die Passionsgeschichte bei Mätthaus," NTS 2 [1955–56]: 20). The more important question is how Matthew integrates non-Markan details into his narrative, whether received or created by the evangelist himself. Cf. Mark Allan Powell, "Toward a Narrative-Critical Understanding of Matthew," Int 46 (1992): 341–46.

[32] Matthew may have been familiar with Psalm 2 in both Greek and Hebrew versions. On the question of Matthew's OT text tradition, see Robert H. Gundry, The Use of the Old Testament in St. Matthew's Gospel: With Special Reference to the Messianic Hope (NovTSup 18; Leiden: Brill, 1967), 151–88.

[33] Others put in mind of Psalm 2 here include Origen, Comm. Matt. 76 (ed. Klostermann et al.), 177; John Gill, An Exposition of the New Testament (London: William Hill, 1852–54; repr. in Gill's Commentary, vol. 5, Matthew to Acts [Grand Rapids: Baker, 1980], 260); Robert H. Gundry, Matthew: A Commentary on His Literary and Theological Art (Grand Rapids: Eerdmans, 1982), 518; Eugene M. Boring, "The Gospel of Matthew," NIB 8:464 n. 550. Matthew 26:1–5 glosses later opposition scenes with Psalm 2 as Matthew adds to Mark that the "gathering" occurred "in the palace [τὴν αὐλήν] of the high priest" (v. 3), that is, near where Jesus was later tried (cf. 26:58, 69). Here see Chrysostom, Hom. Matt. 36.3 (NPNF[1] 10:240).

[34] This point is noted also by Brian M. Nolan, who suggests that συνάγω "may echo" Psalm 2 throughout the passion narrative (The Royal Son of God: The Christology of Matthew 1–2 in the Setting of the Gospel [OBO 23; Göttingen: Vandenhoeck & Ruprecht, 1979], 88).

[35] Maarten J. J. Menken concludes that Matthew's quotations from the Psalms do not agree with any one version, though many have Septuagintalisms ("The Psalms in Matthew's Gospel," in The Psalms in the New Testament [ed. Steve Moyise and Maarten J. J. Menken; New Testament and the Scriptures of Israel; London: T&T Clark, 2004], 79).

another "against Jesus" (κατὰ τοῦ Ἰησοῦ; cf. LXX Ps 2:2 κατὰ τοῦ χριστοῦ) (27:1–2).[36] It is of little concern that Psalm 2's enemies were at first Gentile opponents of Israel, since in the Second Temple period (and especially in early Christian literature) "rulers" referred to any powerful group, Jewish or otherwise, that opposed God's cause.[37]

The attempt to align the experiences of Jesus with Psalm 2 is not a sudden concern in the passion narrative. In the infancy narrative, Herod the Great's conspiracy to kill "the Christ" (2:4; Ps 2:2) resembles the scenario of Psalm 2 in the same way that the opening of the passion narrative (Matt 26:1–5) does. Moreover, Matthew again uses συνάγω to describe Herod's "gathering" of the "chief priests and scribes" (2:4).[38] The connection to the end of the Gospel is transparent, as the "chief priests and scribes" do not reappear in narrative action until Jesus reaches Jerusalem during the final week.[39] The detail that Herod (and "all Jerusalem") "was terrified" (ἐταράχθη) also resembles the psalmist's claim that God "will terrify" (from ταράσσω) those "kings and rulers" who oppose God and God's "Christ." To be sure, not only do these Psalm 2 motifs foreshadow the passion and crucifixion of Jesus, they also relate directly to the interpretation of the *titulus*, since the phrase βασιλεὺς τῶν Ἰουδαίων (2:2)—identical to that of Matt 27:37 (as well as Pilate's query in 27:11)—here appears for the first time.[40] Thus, the narrative glosses the very

---

[36] The connection is not lacking precedent in the history of interpretation. Cf. Origen, *Hom. Ps.* ad loc. (*PG* 12:1102b); Theodoret, *Comm. Ps.* ad loc. (*PG* 80:874d). Also noteworthy here are illuminated manuscripts of the Psalms with marginal sketches of Jewish leaders "gathered" against Jesus at precisely Psalm 2. For the Stuttgart Psalter (ca. 820–830 C.E.), see the image reproduced in Gertrud Schiller, *Iconography of Christian Art* (trans. Janet Seligman; 2 vols.; Greenwich: New York Graphic Society, 1972), vol. 2, fig. 211. See also Psalm 2 in the Theodore Psalter (ca. 1066 C.E.) online: www.bl.uk/manuscripts/Viewer.aspx?ref=add_ms_19352_f001r.

[37] See Sam Janse, *"You Are My Son": The Reception History of Psalm 2 in Early Judaism and the Early Church* (CBET 51; Leuven: Peeters, 2009), 90–95. Psalm 2 is thus consistent with what Matera terms the focus of Matthew's passion narrative: "the rejection of the Messiah by Israel" (*Passion Narratives*, 81).

[38] Hilary of Poitiers recalls Matthew 2 in his *Tract. Ps.* II, 24 (CCSL 61:54), and Sedulius asks "Why do you rage, Herod?" (*Paschale Carmen* 2.83, in *Sedulius, The Paschal Song and Hymns* [ed. and trans. Carl P. E. Springer; Writings from the Greco-Roman World 35; Atlanta: Society of Biblical Literature, 2013], 50–51). See also Raymond E. Brown, *The Birth of the Messiah: A Commentary on the Infancy Narratives in the Gospels of Matthew and Luke* (1977; updated ed.; ABRL; New York: Doubleday, 1999), 173. Note that Schlatter entitles chapter 2 "The Battle of the King against the Christ" (*Matthäus*, 25).

[39] This is well known. See, e.g., Francis Wright Beare, *The Gospel According to Matthew: Translation, Introduction, and Commentary* (San Francisco: Harper & Row, 1981), 77; Davies and Allison, *Saint Matthew*, 1:239; David R. Bauer, "The Kingship of Jesus in the Matthean Infancy Narrative: A Literary Analysis," *CBQ* 57 (1995): 316 n. 29.

[40] Luz rightly says that the use of "king of the Jews" "gives a 'signal' about what is going to happen in the passion narrative" (*Matthew 1–7*, 113). On the contrast here between Jesus' true kingship and Herod's pseudo-kingship, see Dorothy Jean Weaver, "Power and Powerlessness:

wording of the *titulus* with the scenario of contestation and opposition to God's Messiah as described in Psalm 2.[41]

A clear conclusion, then, is that the messianic conflict of Psalm 2 surfaces at several points in Matthew's narrative with an eye toward the struggle's climax, the crucifixion.

Psalm 2's Enthronement Scenario and Matthew's Crucifixion Scene

As evident in Second Temple literature, Psalm 2 was often read as an enthronement or coronation psalm, and Matthew's Jesus undergoes a mock coronation in his trial and scourging that culminates in cruciform enthronement. To evoke Psalm 2 in this scenario especially befits Matthew's Gospel because the sense in Mark that the crucifixion is the enthronement of Jesus has been intensified.[42] In the trial scene, the addition of the phrase "from now on" (ἀπ' ἄρτι, 26:64) to the Markan dual citation from Psalm 110 and Daniel 7 suggests that the descriptions of earthly and cosmic enthronement in Psalm 110 and Daniel 7 begin to find fulfillment in the action that follows. Many have rightly noted that the resurrection of Jesus is clearly in view here, as Jesus will afterward declare "all authority on heaven and on earth has been given to me" (28:18).[43] But the passion of Jesus is also part of the enthronement. The one who said "whoever wishes to become great among you will be your servant" (20:26) is here true to his own philosophy. And the one who told the mother of James and John that it was not his prerogative to grant positions on his "right and left" "in his kingdom," is here crucified between two brigands on his "right and left" as a royal retinue (20:21; 27:38).[44]

Matthew further intensifies Mark's enthronement motif in the mockery of Jesus before the crucifixion (26:67–68; 27:27–31), and some of the editorializing

---

Matthew's Use of Irony in the Portrayal of Political Leaders," in *Treasures New and Old: Contributions to Matthean Studies* (ed. David R. Bauer and Mark Allan Powell; SBLSymS 1; Atlanta: Scholars Press, 1996), 179–96 esp. 182–87.

[41] Should the linkage here between the "king of the Jews" and "Jerusalem" assume the connection in Psalm 2 between kingship and "Zion," it would not be the first time. Cf. *4 Ezra* 13:32; *2 Bar.* 40:1–4. See Terrence L. Donaldson, *Jesus on the Mountain: A Study in Matthean Theology* (JSNTSup 8; Sheffield: JSOT Press, 1985), 37–38, 147–48, 199.

[42] On crucifixion and enthronement in the Gospels in general, see Joel Marcus, "Crucifixion as Parodic Exaltation," *JBL* 125 (2006): 73–87; Jipp, "Luke's Scriptural Suffering Messiah," 260.

[43] So T. de Kruijf, *Der Sohn des Lebendigen Gottes* (AnBib 16; Rome: Pontifical Biblical Institute, 1962), 98–99; Dale C. Allison Jr., *The End of the Ages Has Come: An Early Interpretation of the Passion and Resurrection of Jesus* (Philadelphia: Fortress, 1985), 48–49; Matera, *Passion Narratives*, 101.

[44] See Hare, *Matthew*, 320; Mello, *Évangile selon saint Matthieu*, 481; Dale C. Allison Jr., "Foreshadowing the Passion," in idem, *Studies in Matthew: Interpretation Past and Present* (Grand Rapids: Baker Academic, 2005), 230–32.

may evoke Psalm 2. In the two scenes where Jesus is beaten, Matthew includes three significant changes to Mark: (i) he adds the vocative χριστέ ("Messiah") to the imperative προφήτευσον ("prophesy")(26:68a); (ii) he says the soldiers "were gathering before Jesus" (συνήγαγον ἐπ' αὐτόν) in the praetorium (27:27); and (iii) he has the soldiers provide Jesus with a reed (κάλαμον 27:29) as a mock scepter, which they later use to strike him (27:30). Each of these additions to Mark is easily explained if the coronation scene from Psalm 2 is in the intertextual background: (i) God's "anointed" (משיח//χριστός) is there named (2:2), (ii) enemies "gather" in opposition (2:2), and (iii) the messianic appointee has as "rod of iron" (2:9),[45] which he uses either "to break" (MT: רעע) or "to lead/shepherd" (LXX: ποιμαίνω) the nations.[46]

Psalm 2's coronation theme is therefore consistent with Matthean redaction in context, and we may find Psalm 2 recalled in the mockery before the crucifixion of Jesus.

Psalm 2 and Matthew's Use of Scripture

Matthew's use of Scripture in the crucifixion scene suggests that Psalm 2 is near to hand. Even brief comparison with Mark shows that Matthew is more closely aligned with Scripture, especially the Psalms.[47] A few key examples are presented in the chart on the following page. Matthew not only strengthens Mark's echoes of Scripture, he subtly adds additional material to make the scene intertextually evocative.[48] Matthew's style at this point makes it probable that, as with nearly every other gesture, statement, or narrative description received from Mark in this context, he understood Mark's *titulus* in light of Israel's Scriptures.[49]

---

[45] Many Jewish and Christian texts adopt the rod of iron from Psalm 2 when describing a messianic figure; see *Pss. Sol.* 17:26; *Sib. Or.* 8:248; Rev 12:5. See John J. Collins, *The Scepter and the Star: The Messiahs of the Dead Sea Scrolls and Other Ancient Literature* (ABRL; New York: Doubleday, 1995), 54.

[46] Should Joel Willitts be correct that LXX Ps 2:9's ποιμανεῖς informs Matthew's "shepherd-king" motif, we have a further connection between Psalm 2 and the identity of Jesus (*Matthew's Messianic Shepherd-King: In Search of "the Lost Sheep of the House of Israel"* [BZNW 147; Berlin: de Gruyter, 2007], 67–70).

[47] So Holtzmann, *Die synoptischen Evangelien*, 205; Davies and Allison, *Saint Matthew*, 3:609 ("scriptural allusions have been added or strengthened").

[48] For comparison of Matthew's intertextual style with other texts, see Lawrence H. Schiffman, "Biblical Exegesis in the Passion Narratives and the Dead Sea Scrolls," in *Biblical Interpretation in Judaism and Christianity* (ed. Isaac Kalimi and Peter J. Haas; Library of Hebrew Bible/Old Testament Studies 439; New York: T&T Clark, 2006), 121; Craig Blomberg, "Matthew," in *Commentary on the New Testament Use of the Old Testament* (ed. G. K. Beale and D. A. Carson; Grand Rapids: Baker Academic, 2007), 97.

[49] I hesitate to agree with Frederick Bruner that Matthew's change of Mark's ἐπιγεγραμμένη to γεγραμμένην treats the inscription as a citation from Scripture, though this idea would support

Matt 27:33–54	OT citation(s)/ allusion(s)	Comment
Jesus offered "wine mixed with gall" (v. 34)	LXX Ps 68:22	Matthew changes Mark's ἐσμυρνισμένον οἶνον ("wine mixed with myrrh") to wine μετὰ χολῆς ("with gall") as in LXX Ps 68:22 (χολήν).
Second spoken insult: "he confided in God, let God save him now, if he desires" (vv. 41–43)	LXX Ps 21:9	Matthew adds this phrase to Mark, expanding the connection with LXX Psalm 21.
Darkness "over all the land" (v. 45)	Amos 8:9; Exod 10:22	Matthew changes Mark's ἐφ' ὅλην τὴν γῆν to ἐπὶ πᾶσαν τὴν γῆν, resembling Exod 10:22.[50]
Earthquake, resurrection of holy ones (vv. 51–53)	Ezek 37:12; Zech 14:4; Dan 12:2	Multiple texts are in play in this concatenation of eschatological signs.[51]

Even more significant than Matthew's general use of Scripture in context, however, is that some of Matthew's changes to Mark evoke Psalm 2 intratextually. This is particularly evident in the two words of insult from the passersby and the Jewish leaders. In the first insult, the mockers say, "Save yourself, if you are the Son of God [εἰ υἱὸς εἶ τοῦ θεοῦ], come down from the cross!" (v. 40). One recalls that the conditional phrase εἰ υἱὸς εἶ τοῦ θεοῦ, which does not appear in Mark, is taken directly from Matthew's temptation narrative (4:3, 6).[52] And there, Satan's taunt

---

the argument of this article (*Matthew: A Commentary*, vol. 2, *The Churchbook* [Grand Rapids: Eerdmans, 2004], 735). The change is more likely stylistic to avoid Mark's repetitive ἐπιγραφή … ἐπιγεγραμμένη. See Donald P. Senior, *The Passion Narrative according to Matthew: A Redactional Study* (BETL 39; Leuven: Leuven University Press, 1975), 281.

[50] See Dale C. Allison Jr., "Darkness at Noon (Matt. 27:45)," in *Studies in Matthew*, 79–106.

[51] See Dale C. Allison Jr., "The Scriptural Background of a Matthean Legend: Ezekiel 37, Zechariah 14, and Matthew 27," in *Life beyond Death in Matthew's Gospel: Religious Metaphor or Bodily Reality?* (ed. Wim Weren, Huub van de Sandt, and Joseph Verheyden; Biblical Tools and Studies 13; Leuven: Peeters, 2011), 153–88.

[52] So, e.g., A. H. M'Neile, *The Gospel according to St. Matthew: The Greek Text with Introduction, Notes, and Indices* (London: Macmillan, 1915), 419; J. C. Fenton, *Saint Matthew* (Westminster Pelican Commentaries; Philadelphia: Westminster, 1963), 441; Hagner, *Matthew 14–28*, 839; Luz, *Matthew 21–28*, 538.

follows and challenges the immediately preceding baptismal pronouncement from Ps 2:7: "this is my Son ..."[53] Thus, in the crucifixion scene, Matthew not only scores rhetorical points by having his mockers speak with Satan's tongue, he embraces, through their words, the reality of Jesus' Psalm 2 sonship.

There is more in the second insult. Here the chief priests, scribes, and elders mirror the first insult, but instead of saying "if you are the Son of God," they say "(if) he is the King of Israel, let him come down from the cross" (v. 42a). Here Matthew tightens the parallel between the first and second insults, suggesting they be read together. Mark has one imperative: "Let the Christ the King of Israel come down now from the cross!" (ὁ χριστὸς ὁ βασιλεὺς Ἰσραὴλ καταβάτω νῦν ἀπὸ τοῦ σταυροῦ), whereas Matthew maintains Mark's third person but makes it parallel v. 40:

Matt 27:40   εἰ υἱὸς εἶ τοῦ θεοῦ,   κατάβηθι   ἀπὸ τοῦ σταυροῦ
Matt 27:42   (εἰ) βασιλεὺς Ἰσραήλ ἐστιν,   καταβάτω νῦν ἀπὸ τοῦ σταυροῦ[54]

The result is two parallel insults that conjoin two titles, "Son" and "King."[55] The similar linkage of these titles in Ps 2:6–7[56] and the echo of the temptation scene suggest that Psalm 2 is near to hand.

It is also important to note that, in the material that immediately follows, Matthew makes one further addition to Mark that confirms the identification of Psalm 2 in this context. Matthew has the mockers accuse Jesus of saying, "I am God's Son" (v. 43). The phrase is conspicuous because, while Jesus never says exactly this in Matthew, the declaration of sonship in LXX Ps 2:7 is spoken by the messianic

---

[53] Noted as early as *1 Clem.* 36.4 (*The Apostolic Fathers in English* [trans. and ed. Michael W. Holmes; 3rd ed.; Grand Rapids: Baker, 2007], 92–93); Justin Martyr, *Dial.* 122.6 (*ANF* 1:261). Contra J. A. Gibbs, who prefers LXX Jer 38:20 over Psalm 2 ("Israel Standing with Israel: The Baptism of Jesus in Matthew's Gospel [Matt 3:13–17]," *CBQ* 64 [2002]: 511–26).

[54] Εἰ in v. 42 may well be original (A W Θ $f^{1.13}$ 𝔐 lat sy mae bo), though one's decision does not significantly affect the discussion here, as the conditional idea may be conveyed explicitly (with formal markers) or implicitly (without formal markers). See Daniel B. Wallace, *Greek Grammar beyond the Basics: An Exegetical Syntax of the New Testament* (Grand Rapids: Zondervan, 1996), 687–89. If secondary, the variant evidences an early attempt to read vv. 40 and 42 in parallel.

[55] See Meier, *Matthew*, 346 (Matthew "skillfully weaves together" these titles). On the relationship between titles in the passion narrative as a whole, see D. R. Bauer, "The Major Characters of Matthew's Story: Their Function and Significance," *Int* 46 (1992): 357–67, esp. 361.

[56] In fact, Psalm 2 is the only place in Scripture where "king" and "son" are conjoined in a manner of address such as this. This is a key reason why Nathaniel's confession in the Fourth Gospel (1:49: "Rabbi, you are the Son of God, you are the King of Israel!") has put numerous readers (including NA[28]) in mind of Psalm 2. See Janse, *"You are My Son,"* 127. See also D. Moody Smith, *John* (ANTC; Nashville; Abingdon, 1999), 77.

appointee himself: "the Lord said *to me*, you are my Son." So there is a clear parallel here in both content and form.[57]

In all these ways, then, Matthean redaction brings Psalm 2 into the heart of the crucifixion scene.

Psalm 2 in the Baptism, Transfiguration, and Titulus

On the surface, the *titulus* appears to be an impious charade staged by Roman soldiers, but Matthew has shaped the inscription to resemble the divine declarations of Psalm 2 at the baptism and transfiguration.[58] Narrative criticism provides two initial points of support here. The first is Jack Dean Kingsbury's observation that Matthew develops his Christology around the divine revelations of Jesus' identity (e.g., 1:21; 3:17; 17:5), thus equipping readers with knowledge to evaluate the statements and gestures of various characters.[59] Thus, as Peter's confession, and as the queries of Caiaphas and Pilate,[60] the identification of Jesus as "king of the Jews" invites comparison with God's own testimony. The second point concerns the otherwise well known linguistic and thematic parallels between the baptism, transfiguration (though less often recognized),[61] and crucifixion scenes.[62] It is clear that Matthew has interwoven these three climactic scenes at the beginning, middle, and end of Jesus' career, and so claims made about the identity of Jesus in the crucifixion scene are in formal parallel with God's announcements about the same elsewhere.

---

[57] It is clear that Matthew has Scripture in view, as the first part of this sentence, also redactional, is modeled on LXX Ps 21:9, and there are other similarities with Wisdom 2. See Donald Senior, *The Passion of Jesus in the Gospel of Matthew* (Passion Series 1; Wilmington, DE: Michael Glazier, 1985), 134.

[58] Brandon D. Crowe has recently questioned the common view that Matt 3:17 recalls Psalm 2 (*The Obedient Son: Deuteronomy and Christology in the Gospel of Matthew* [BZNW 188; Berlin: de Gruyter, 2012], 187–91). But the logic of his reading is not forthcoming. Since he admits that Mark 1:11 recalls Psalm 2, it is not at all clear why Matthew's redactional οὗτός ἐστιν would suggest a different intertext (on this redaction, see below). Moreover, if Psalm 2 is deficient on lexical grounds, certainly Exod 4:22–23 is no better.

[59] See Kingsbury, *Matthew as Story* (2nd ed.; Philadelphia: Fortress, 1988), 11–13; idem, "Figure of Jesus in Matthew's Story," 7. See a similar strategy in de Kruijf, *Der Sohn des Lebendigen Gottes*, esp. 83–84, 97, though he focuses more on Jesus' words.

[60] See Meier, *Matthew*, 332; Hare, *Matthew*, 308; Davies and Allison, *Saint Matthew*, 3:527. Note in particular Schlatter: "Der Hohepriester fragt nach dem königlichen Recht Jesu und nach seiner Begründung, die sich nach Ps. 2 in seiner Sohnschaft Gottes finden muß" (*Matthäus*, 759).

[61] For a convincing defense see Allison, "Foreshadowing the Passion," 226–30.

[62] See G. W. Derickson, "Matthew's Chiastic Structure and Its Dispensational Implications," *BSac* 163 (2006): 426–27. As examples, note that Jesus submits to baptism (3:15)//Jesus submits to die (27:35; cf. 26:53); the πνεῦμα of God descends (3:16)//Jesus expires τὸ πνεῦμα (27:50); and so on.

The linkage between the baptism, transfiguration, and *titulus* is all the more apparent given two important Matthean changes to Mark. The first concerns the title itself:

Mark 15:26   ὁ βασιλεὺς τῶν Ἰουδαίων
Matt 27:37   οὗτός ἐστιν Ἰησοῦς ὁ βασιλεὺς τῶν Ἰουδαίων

The demonstrative + copulative (οὗτός ἐστιν) is a Mattheanism that makes the *titulus*, in terms of form, similar to the divine revelations at the baptism and transfiguration, which also begin with οὗτός ἐστιν (3:17; 17:5). In the baptism scene, Matthew again adds "this is" to Mark:

Mark 1:11   σὺ εἶ   ὁ υἱός μου ὁ ἀγαπητός, ἐν σοὶ εὐδόκησα
Matt 3:17   οὗτός ἐστιν   ὁ υἱός μου ὁ ἀγαπητός, ἐν ᾧ εὐδόκησα

The addition functions to dramatize the heavenly word and assert that it was not heard by Jesus alone.[63] The similar redaction of Mark at both points (while retaining "this is" from Mark at 17:5) is unlikely to be coincidental.[64] One expects that the phrase on the *titulus* recalls the prior revelations about Jesus' identity[65] and functions to intensify the proclamatory sense of Jesus' announced kingship.[66]

---

[63] See John P. Meier, *A Marginal Jew: Rethinking the Historical Jesus*, vol. 2, *Mentor, Message, and Miracles* (ABRL; New York: Doubleday, 1994), 188 n. 25. Contra Jack Dean Kingsbury, "The Parable of the Wicked Husbandmen and the Secret of Jesus' Divine Sonship in Matthew: Some Literary-Critical Observations," *JBL* 195 (1986): 643–55, esp. 649.

[64] Bruner overstates the point when he says that οὗτός ἐστιν "turns the sign from an accusation into a proclamation, from a charge to a claim, from an indictment into a confession" (*Churchbook*, 735). The irony is present already in Mark, even if more cryptic, so οὗτός ἐστιν does not "turn" the *titulus* from an accusatory false claim into a theologically true one. See also Fenton, *Saint Matthew*, 440 (mentions Matt 3:17); Meier, *Matthew*, 347; Gundry, *Matthew*, 570 ("changes the accusation from an insulting joke to a Christian confession"); Boring, "Gospel of Matthew," 491 ("transform(s) the insult into a Christian confession"); John Nolland, *The Gospel of Matthew: A Commentary on the Greek Text* (NIGTC; Grand Rapids: Eerdmans, 2005), 1194. An antecedent to this reading may be found in the work of John Albert Bengel, who took the copulative to intensify the sense in which the *titulus* tells the truth about Jesus: for example, this *is* (truly), the king of the Jews (*Gnomon of the New Testament* [trans. James Bandinel; 5 vols.; Edinburgh: T&T Clark, 1860], 1:447).

[65] It is significant that other appearances of οὗτός ἐστιν in Matthew occur when a claim is made about Jesus' identity; see Matt 13:55 (carpenter's son); 14:2 (John the Baptist); 21:11 (the prophet from Nazareth); 21:38 (the heir), and these cases similarly generate meaning by either contrasting with or conforming to (see esp. 21:38) God's revelations about the identity of Jesus. See, e.g., Hagner, *Matthew 14–28*, 621; R. T. France, *The Gospel according to Matthew: An Introduction and Commentary* (TNTC; Leicester: InterVarsity, 1988), 813.

[66] Contra France (*Gospel according to Matthew*, 1068 n. 16), who accuses Gundry of putting "too much weight on a stylistic variation." Contra also Senior, *Passion Narrative*, 281 ("a more formal presentation"); Keener, *Commentary on the Gospel of Matthew*, 680. Contra also Bernhard Weiss, who claims that Matthew's "this is" makes the *titulus* "zu einer Verhöhnung des

A final detail concerns the seemingly minor notice, not included in Mark, that the *titulus* was posted "over the head" of Jesus (v. 37). When discussed by modern commentators at all, this small fact is taken to reconstruct the kind of cross on which Jesus was crucified.[67] Regardless of its historicity, however, the location of the *titulus* again recalls the divine proclamations at the baptism and transfiguration, where there appears "over/upon Jesus" some physical counterpart to the verbal or inscriptional testimony:

Matt 3:16   A dove ἐπ' αὐτόν (cf. Mark 1:10 εἰς αὐτόν)
Matt 17:5   A cloud ἐπεσκίασεν αὐτούς
Matt 27:37 A title ἐπάνω τῆς κεφαλῆς αὐτοῦ[68]

The placement may be less striking to those familiar with artistic portrayals of the cross, which normally have an inscription above Jesus. But, aside from the Gospels, there is no corroborating evidence that inscriptions were usually affixed to the top of crosses.[69] There is evidence that criminals were led to crucifixion with *tabula* around their necks.[70] But, as for inscriptions on crosses, we have nothing.[71] Matthew is not necessarily unhistorical in this regard, but emphasizing the placement of the

---

Gekreuzigten" (*Die vier Evangelien im berichtigten Text* [Leipzig: Hinrichs, 1900], 163). Contra also Wiefel: "Man kann den Wortlaut als beabsichtigte Distanzierung auffassen: der sogenannte" (*Das Evangelium nach Matthäus*, 479).

[67] See R. V. G. Tasker, *The Gospel according to St. Matthew: An Introduction and Commentary* (TNTC; Grand Rapids: Eerdmans, 1961), 265; France, *Gospel according to Matthew*, 1068; Nolland, *Gospel of Matthew*, 1193; Turner, *Matthew*, 661.

[68] The star of Bethlehem, which identified the Christ-child to the magi, shares the trope: a star ἐπάνω οὗ ἦν τὸ παιδίον (2:9). Augustine linked the *titulus* and the star of Bethlehem: "The magi were from the Gentiles. Pilate too was a Gentile. They saw a star in the sky; he wrote a title on the tree. Both, however, were looking for or acknowledging the king, not of the Gentiles but of the Jews" (*Serm. 201 2* in Rotelle, *Works of Saint Augustine*, part 3, *Sermons*, vol. 6, *184–229Z on the Liturgical Seasons*, 88).

[69] The total lack of evidence has not hindered commentators from claiming that it was "common" or "natural" to affix a title to the cross. See A. Carr, *The Gospel according to Matthew* (Cambridge Bible for Schools and Colleges 33; Cambridge: Cambridge University Press, 1887), 221 (a "Roman custom"); John Peter Lange, *A Commentary on the Holy Scriptures: Critical, Doctrinal, and Homiletical* (25 vols.; New York: Scribner's Sons, 1865–80), vol. 15, *Matthew* (trans. Philip Schaff; repr., Grand Rapids: Zondervan, 1950), 524; Hill, *Gospel of Matthew*, 353; Gundry, *Matthew*, 570; Hagner, *Matthew 14–28*, 835 ("apparently the custom"); D. A. Carson, *Matthew* (Expositor's Bible Commentary 8; Grand Rapids: Zondervan, 1984), 576; Smith, *Matthew*, 324; Mello, *Saint Matthieu*, 480–81; Witherington, *Matthew*, 514.

[70] Suetonius, *Cal.* 32.2; *Dom.* 10.1; Dio Cassius, *Hist. Rom.* 54.3.7; Eusebius, *Hist. eccl.* 5.1.44.

[71] The traditions about Helena finding the true cross may presuppose that *tituli* on crosses were uncommon. Helena identifies Jesus' cross with the help of its *titulus* and assumes that the robbers' crosses did not have them. See Socrates, *Hist. eccl.* 1.17 (NPNF² 2:21); Sozomenus, *Hist. eccl.* 2.1 (NPNF² 2:258); Ambrose, *Ob. Theo.* 45 (FC 22:236–37). Cf. Alfred O'Rahilly, "The Title of the Cross," *Irish Ecclesiastical Record* 65 (1945): 289–97.

title "over his head" may have surprised Matthew's readers and made the irony of the situation more palpable:[72] Jesus' executioners unwittingly evoke God's declaratory speech ("this is"), and they, like God, put the testimony "over his head."

It is thus clear that Matthew creatively shapes the *titulus* tradition atop the contours of his Gospel, making the once-inflammatory inscription a declaration of divine truth and a testimony to the Messiah's enthronement.

Psalm 2 in the Soldiers' Titulus (v. 37) and Confession (v. 54)

Matthew's crucifixion scene connects the soldiers' act of posting the *titulus* (27:37) with their confession (27:54), which is best explained by Ps 2:6–8. Indeed, to fail to recognize the connection between the posting and the confessing has been cause for confusion. On the one hand, Matthew is unique in making the soldiers responsible for posting the *titulus*. Neither Mark nor Luke tells the reader anything on this front. John names Pilate the author, and most harmonizers have either claimed that the soldiers posted a title that Pilate had written[73] or, unfortunately, have blatantly ignored the Gospels and blamed the Jews for writing it.[74] But even if John is right about Pilate, this is not information that Matthew knew or thought important to tell. On the other hand, the detail that the soldiers "sat down and watched him [Jesus] there" (27:36) before they affixed the inscription has been just as troublesome.[75] Why should the soldiers sit and watch before their work is completed? Would they not be more apt to watch after finishing their work on Jesus' cross? Some have even suggested that Matthew made a mistake and told the details in the wrong order.[76]

The fog lifts if we realize that both the soldiers' authorship and their sitting down "watching" (from τηρέω) connect the *titulus* to their confession in 27:54. For

---

[72] Note Luz, *Matthew 21–28*, 534.

[73] See Tatian, *Diat.* 51 (*ANF* 10:122–23); Rabanus, *Exp. Matt.* 8.335 (*Hrabani Mauri Expositio in Matthaeum* [ed. Bengt Löfstedt; 2 vols.; CCCM 174, 174A; Turnhout: Brepols, 2000], 2:748); Calvin, *Harmony*, 3:302; Sedulius Scottus, *Kommentar zum Evangelium nach Mätthaus* (11 vols.; Freiburg: Herder, 1991), 2:609; Johann Georg Rosenmüller, *Scholia in Novum Testamentum* (3 vols.; 6th ed.; Nuremburg: Felseckeriana, 1815), 1:549; Henry Alford, *The New Testament for English Readers* (2 vols.; London: Rivingtons, 1872–81), 1:206.

[74] See Ephrem the Syrian, *Hymn. Pasc* 4.6 (SC 502:219–20); Asterius, *Comm. Ps.* 28.6 (ed. M. Richard), 226 (Ἐγὼ αὐτοῖς τὰς πλάκας τοῦ νόμου κατέγραψα, καὶ αὐτοί μοι τὸν τίτλον τῷ σταυρῷ προσέπηξαν, "I wrote for them the tablets of the law, and they fasten for me the title on the cross").

[75] See Alexander Balmain Bruce, *The Expositor's Greek New Testament*, vol. 1, *The Synoptic Gospels* (1897; repr., Grand Rapids: Eerdmans, 1943), 329; William Hendricksen, *Exposition of the Gospel according to Matthew* (New Testament Commentary 1; Grand Rapids: Baker, 1973), 965; Nolland, *Gospel of Matthew*, 1194.

[76] See Holtzmann, *Die synoptischen Evangelien*, 205 (v. 36 creates "eine gewisse Varwirrung"); H. A. W. Meyer, *Das Matthäus-Evangelium* (ed. B. Weiss; Göttingen: Vandenhoeck & Ruprecht, 1890), 481 ("Die Darstellung erscheint nur ungenau"); R. C. H. Lenski, *The Interpretation of St. Matthew's Gospel* (Columbus: Wartburg, 1943), 1109.

at the end of the crucifixion scene Matthew has changed Mark again to make several soldiers (instead of Mark's sole centurion) confess Jesus as "Son of God."

	Matt 27:36–37	Matt 27:54
narrative activity:	ἐτήρουν αὐτὸν ἐκεῖ	τηροῦντες τὸν Ἰησοῦν
testimony:	Οὗτός ἐστιν Ἰησοῦς ὁ βασιλεὺς τῶν Ἰουδαίων	Ἀληθῶς θεοῦ υἱὸς ἦν οὗτος

Some exegetes have in fact claimed that in v. 36 Matthew anticipates the confession of v. 54 by introducing the same subject ("soldiers") and verb ("watching").[77] But the link is even closer in that both vv. 36–37 and v. 54 share a common order: the same soldiers "watch" Jesus, and then they make some claim about his identity.[78] The *titulus* and the confession are in clear parallel here.

What does Matthew achieve by linking the *titulus* and the confession? Two things. First, he shows that the eschatological inbreaking of Jesus' death has caused the soldiers to "uncover a second narrative."[79] The identity of Jesus has not changed in the interval between the posting of the title and the confession; the soldiers have just come to recognize the truth in light of the aftermath of his death. Readers do not see the soldiers' confession as "new" knowledge in context but rather as a reaffirmation of what was made evident during the crucifixion scene itself, just as the soldiers' prior actions of mixing wine with gall, dividing clothes, and casting lots actually fulfilled the scriptural narrative about Israel's Messiah (cf. 26:56). Thus, the identifications of the "king" (in mockery) and "son" (with sincerity) both confirm, for the reader, the same truth.[80]

Second, this change in the soldiers' perspective from the *titulus* to the confession serves to work out a tension that Psalm 2 brought to Matthew's Gospel early on: the relationship between sonship, obedience to God, and "the nations." For in the soldiers' confession we not only have the firstfruits of the Gentile mission (as many have noted),[81] we have the moment at which the Son of God, through

---

[77] See Krister Stendahl, "Matthew," in *Peake's Commentary on the Bible* (ed. Matthew Black and H. H. Rowley; London: Thomas Nelson, 1962), 797; Davies and Allison, *Saint Matthew*, 3:614; Matthias Konradt, *Israel, Kirche, und die Völker im Matthäusevangelium* (WUNT 215; Tübingen: Mohr Siebeck, 2007), 326.

[78] Long may be right to connect the soldiers "watching" with Jesus' command that his disciples "keep awake" in the garden (26:38) (*Matthew*, 316). See also Senior, *Passion Narrative*, 279–80. Does the notice that the soldiers were "sitting" and watching anticipate a call to discipleship, as Levi the tax collector (9:9) and the blind men at Jericho (20:30) were also "sitting" before Jesus called them?

[79] For this language, see David C. Steinmetz, "Uncovering a Second Narrative: Detective Fiction and the Construction of Historical Method," in *The Art of Reading Scripture* (ed. Ellen F. Davis and Richard B. Hays; Grand Rapids: Eerdmans, 2003), 54–65.

[80] This is also now the third time in the passion narrative that Matthew has juxtaposed "king" and "son" (cf. 26:63 and 27:11; 27:40, 42).

[81] See, e.g., Rolf Walker, *Die Heilsgeschichte im ersten Evangelium* (FRLANT 91; Göttingen:

obedience to death, begins to collect on God's promise: "Ask of me, and I will make the nations your heritage, the ends of the earth your possession" (Ps 2:8).[82] Matthew is clearly aware of the connection in Psalm 2 between kingship/sonship in vv. 6–7 and the possession of "the nations" and "the ends of the earth" that immediately follows in v. 8, as Satan's third temptation challenges the newly declared "Son of God" to seize that prerogative (4:8).[83] But throughout the Gospel, and particularly in the crucifixion scene, Matthew defines Psalm 2 messiahship via obedience to the will of God, whereby Jesus "saves his people from their sins" (1:21).[84] It is thus a fitting conclusion that, after his supreme act of obedience as "king of the Jews," the soldiers, speaking for "the nations," participate in the Psalm 2 drama and name him "God's Son."[85] Psalm 2 in the *titulus* and confession thus explains a great deal about the crucifixion scene and its relation to the rest of the Gospel.

IV. Conclusion

Irony can be fodder for imagination, as the history of interpretation of the *titulus* shows. But Origen's reading may, in fact, recover the imaginative effort of the first evangelist to retell the *titulus* tradition. Origen has the support of early Christian and Jewish reception of Psalm 2, the echoes of Psalm 2 elsewhere in Matthew's Gospel, the enthronement and coronation motifs of his crucifixion scene, the similar use of Scripture in context, redaction of Mark, and the convergence of three narrative themes at the crucifixion: Jesus' identity as God's "king"

Vandenhoeck & Ruprecht, 1967), 72–73; Jean Radermakers, *Au fil de l'évangile selon saint Matthieu* (2 vols.; Brussels: Institute of Theological Study, 1974), 2:344; Senior, *Passion Narrative*, 324–28.

[82] Matthias Konradt traces a similar thread (though without Psalm 2) in his excellent essay "Die Sendung zu Israel und zu den Völkern im Matthäusevangelium im Lichte seiner narrativen Christologie," *ZKT* 101 (2004): 397–425. He states, "Erst mit dem Kreuzesgeschehen ist Jesu Gottessohnschaft in ihrem Vollsinn erschlossen" (p. 421), noting both Jesus' obedience to God's will and the confession of the soldiers.

[83] So Gaechter, *Matthäus*, 114; Walter Grundmann, *Das Evangelium nach Matthäus* (Berlin: Evangelical Publishing House, 1968), 103; Schweizer, *Matthew*, 64; Donaldson, *Jesus on the Mountain*, 95. Note *b. Sukkah* 52a.

[84] See Tucker S. Ferda, "The Soldiers' Inscription and the Angel's Word: The Significance of 'Jesus' in Matthew's *Titulus*," *NovT* 55 (2013): 221–31. On the relationship between sonship and obedience see de Kruijf, *Der Sohn des Lebendiges Gottes*, 101–2; Meier, *Matthew*, 347; T. L. Donaldson, "The Mockers and the Son of God (Matthew 27.37–44): Two Characters in Matthew's Story of Jesus," *JSNT* 41 (1991): 11; Andrew R. Angel, "Crucifixus Vicens: The 'Son of God' as Divine Warrior in Matthew," *CBQ* 73 (2011): 303.

[85] See Justin Martyr, *Dial.* 122.6 (*ANF* 1:261); Eusebius, *Dem. ev.* 2.2 (*The Proof of the Gospel: Being the Demonstratio evangelica of Eusebius of Caesarea* [ed. and trans. W. J. Ferrar; 2 vols.; London: SPCK, 1920], 1:68) entitles Psalm 2: "Of the Plotting against Christ, and He that is called the Son of God, receiving His Portion and the Gentiles from the Father."

and "son," his mission of obedience to God's will, and God's promise to give him "the nations" as an inheritance. Origen's reading thus has the mark of any good argument: it takes the part and makes better sense of the whole.

I submit that these observations should not only cause future commentators to reconsider the relationship between Psalm 2 and Matthew's *titulus*, but, more broadly, the role of Psalm 2 in Matthew's crucifixion scene in general. After all, the reading of Origen, Augustine, Aquinas, and the others was never put to rest by argument. It was merely forgotten.

Evangelically Rooted. IVP Academic **Critically Engaged.**

CRITICAL AND COMPREHENSIVE

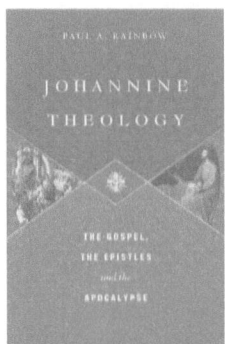

Johannine Theology
The Gospel, the Epistles and the Apocalypse

Paul A. Rainbow

This magisterial synthesis presents the most complete account of the theology of the Johannine corpus available today. Both critical and comprehensive, this volume includes all the books of the New Testament ascribed to John: the Gospel, the three epistles and the book of Revelation.

"Johannine Theology may well become an encyclopedia for Johannine studies for decades to come."

Scot McKnight, Northern Seminary

464 PAGES, HARDCOVER,
978-0-8308-4056-4, $40.00

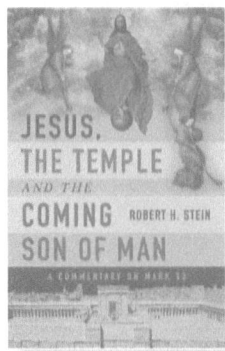

Jesus, the Temple and the Coming Son of Man
A Commentary on Mark 13

Robert H. Stein

Mark 13, the so-called Little Apocalypse, has puzzled readers for generations. Was Jesus speaking of the end-time return of the Son of Man or the coming destruction of Jerusalem or both? Robert Stein offers an in-depth and insightful commentary on an important and puzzling discourse of Jesus.

"Conversant with the best scholarship and unrelenting in his pursuit of the Evangelist's intended meaning, Stein has produced a helpful, sensible and persuasive interpretation of Mark 13."

Donald A. Hagner, Fuller Theological Seminary

160 PAGES, PAPERBACK,
978-0-8308-4058-8, $18.00

Visit *ivpacademic.com* to request an exam copy.

 Follow us on Twitter   Join us on Facebook   800.843.9487 | ivpacademic.com

Resisting Honor: The Markan Secrecy Motif and Roman Political Ideology

ADAM WINN
awinn@apu.edu
Azusa Pacific University, Azusa, CA 91702

This article builds on the work of David F. Watson, who has recently argued that major features of Mark's so-called messianic secret should not be understood in terms of "secrecy" at all, but rather should be understood in terms of intentional resistance to honor. While I agree with Watson's evaluation of the "secrecy motif" (as intentional resistance to honor), I find Watson's claim that the Markan evangelist inverts standard honor/shame conventions to be unsatisfactory. The article explores alternative explanations for the Markan Jesus' resistance to honor and proposes that a possible explanation might be found in Roman political ideology. While examples of resisting achieved and proscribed honor are few and far between in the ancient Mediterranean world, they are frequently found in the lives of first-century Roman emperors, particular emperors who were remembered favorably. I propose that this Roman political background might be a useful way forward in understanding Jesus' resistance to honor in Mark's Gospel. To support this argument, three spheres of evidence are considered: (1) the clear presentation in Mark's Gospel of Jesus as a world ruler; (2) the strong possibility of a Roman provenance for Mark; and (3) numerous features in Mark's Gospel suggesting that it is challenging Roman imperial power.

Just over a century ago, William Wrede left an indelible mark on the field of NT studies when he demonstrated the presence of a distinct secrecy motif in Mark's Gospel. Yet a century of scholarship has not produced a consensus regarding the motif's meaning and significance. In his recent monograph, *Honor among Christians: The Cultural Key to the Messianic Secret*, David F. Watson has taken a decisive step forward, a step I attempt to build on here.[1] While Watson rightfully reads the text in light of the first-century honor/shame value system, I believe his reading only partially resolves the conundrum of Mark's secrecy motif. This article complements Watson's work by adding a political dimension to his insights. In particular,

---

[1] Watson, *Honor among Christians: The Cultural Key to the Messianic Secret* (Minneapolis: Fortress, 2010).

Jesus' actions will be viewed through the lens of Roman political ideology and will be compared to the actions of Roman emperors. The results will be combined with Watson's insights on the Markan secrecy motif in an attempt to explain the motif's significance for Mark's first-century readers.

I. David F. Watson: Honor or Secrecy?

Watson uses the tools of social-scientific criticism to explore the meaning of secrecy in the ancient Mediterranean world as well as in the Markan pericopes that are so often associated with secrecy in modern scholarship. Regarding the former, he argues that the language and function of secrecy are virtually absent in Mark's Gospel. Words closely associated with secrecy (particularly in religious texts) such as κρύπτω, ἀποκρύπτω, λάθρᾳ, ἄρρητος, and μυστήριον are rare or absent in Mark.[2] In fact, Watson demonstrates that in the whole of Mark's Gospel, the language of secrecy occurs only four times, three of which come in two verses of ch. 4. Watson demonstrates that secrecy functioned in three primary ways in the ancient world: to protect from danger, to preserve community boundaries, and to defend an individual's or a group's reputation. According to Watson, none of these prominent functions of secrecy stands out in Mark's Gospel. Ultimately, Watson concludes that what is often described as a "secrecy" motif in Mark is misleading and that the intended readers of the Gospel would not have understood the pericopes that form such a motif in terms of secrecy.

But if Mark's readers would not understand these pericopes in terms of secrecy how would they understand them? Watson proposes that these pericopes must be understood in light of the honor/shame value system that dominated the ancient Mediterranean world.[3] He first considers pericopes in which Jesus performs a healing and commands the recipient not to report or speak of the healing (Mark 1:40–45; 5:21–24, 35–43; 7:31–37; 8:22–26). In these healing pericopes, Watson demonstrates that the dynamics of a client–patron relationship are present. Mark's readers would recognize Jesus as the patron and the sick person as the client. Once Jesus has healed the sick person, the client would be obligated to reciprocate by

---

[2] Note the following occurrences: κρύπτω (1x, 4:22), ἀποκρύπτω (1x, 4:22), λάθρᾳ (1x, 7:24), ἄρρητος (no occurrences), and μυστήριον (1x, 4:11).

[3] Both Bruce Malina and John Pilch have argued that Jesus' action of silencing those he healed should be understood in terms of honor and shame; see Malina, *The New Testament World: Insights from Cultural Anthropology* (3rd ed; Louisville: Westminster John Knox, 2001), 125; and Pilch, "Secrecy in the Gospel of Mark," *PACE: Professional Approaches for Christian Educators* 21 (1992): 150–53. Both argue that such silencing functions as a defense against envy, which would ultimately result in the removal of honor. Malina understands Jesus to be "concealing" or "hiding" honor rather than publicly rejecting it. Below I will consider whether rejecting public honor was used as a strategy in the ancient world for defense against envy.

showing Jesus, the patron, honor, which would involve public praise of the patron. Watson argues that Jesus' actions of silencing the healed person would be understood not as an attempt to keep the actions secret but as resistance to "achieved" honor.[4]

Similarly, Watson argues that, when demons declare Jesus to be "the Holy One of God" (1:24) or "Son of God," the value system of honor and shame is again at work. These are "honorific" titles being given to Jesus, and their proclamation by demons would lead to the spread of Jesus' honor. Watson also suggests that the giving of these titles might be a way for demons to draw Jesus into an obligation to reciprocate. Again, Jesus' actions would be understood not as attempts to keep his identity secret but as resistance to "ascribed" honor.[5]

Watson argues that Jesus' resistance to honor is only half the story. Jesus is not rejecting the honor/shame system *in toto*—a system too deeply ingrained in ancient Mediterranean culture—but rather he is offering a new vision of what is honorable and what is shameful. While Jesus resists the commonplace markers of honor and shame (e.g., acts of power, benefaction, honorific titles, etc.), he also establishes new markers (e.g., service, self-sacrifice, suffering, and crucifixion). Jesus establishes these new markers through his passion predictions (Mark 8:31; 9:31; 10:33) and teaching on discipleship (Mark 8:34–38; 9:33–36; 10:13–16, 29–31, 35–45). For Watson, the Markan Jesus ultimately inverts standard conventions by claiming that the least, the suffering, and the servants should be honored, while the great and the powerful should be ashamed.[6]

Such an explanation of Jesus' resistance to honor runs into trouble, however, when one considers the numerous places in Mark's Gospel where Jesus embraces rather than resists public honor. Watson actually addresses Markan pericopes in which the evangelist puts Jesus' honor on display and in which Jesus publicly embraces honor according to standard Mediterranean convention. He notes eighteen examples where Jesus' honor is on display before others and Jesus either does not resist/reject honor or actually embraces the honor he is due.[7] Unlike many interpreters, Watson rejects efforts to remove or mitigate the honor from these pericopes and claims that they are in fact as they appear, clear examples of Jesus playing by the standard conventions of honor and shame.[8]

Watson's explanation for these conflicting motifs is that they are used by the evangelist to advance different themes, themes that would be clearly recognized by Mark's readers. He argues that such inconsistent material was quite common in

---

[4] Watson, *Honor*, 37–56.
[5] Ibid., 56–62.
[6] Ibid., 63–85.
[7] See ibid., 89: Mark 1:21–28, 29–31, 32–34; 2:1–12, 28; 3:1–6, 7–12; 4:35–41; 5:1–20, 24b–34; 6:30–44, 45–52, 53–56; 7:24–30; 8:1–9; 9:14–28, 38–41; 10:46–52. These examples do not include the "triumphal entry" in Mark 11:10, a clear example of Jesus receiving public honor.
[8] For Watson's discussion of these pericopes, see *Honor*, 87–114.

ancient literature and that, therefore, Mark's readers would be untroubled by the juxtaposition of these conflicting motifs.⁹ But such a conclusion is unsatisfactory and seems to undermine Watson's explanation for the Markan Jesus' resistance to honor, that is, that Mark is seeking to invert/subvert conventional markers of honor and shame. It may be true that ancient readers were more comfortable with inconsistent literary motifs than modern readers are, but would or could they conclude that Jesus was inverting or subverting the conventions of honor and shame, when he frequently participates in such conventions throughout Mark's Gospel? This seems improbable. Ultimately, the pericopes in which the Markan Jesus displays and embraces public honor undermine Watson's conclusion that the evangelist is seeking to invert/subvert the honor-and-shame conventions of the Mediterranean world.

While Watson takes a decisive step forward in identifying Jesus' commands for silence as resistance to honor, he fails to explain adequately the purpose or significance of such resistance in Mark's Gospel. My purpose is to build on Watson's decisive step and provide an explanation for the Markan Jesus' frequent efforts to resist honor, an explanation that is not in conflict with the numerous pericopes in which Jesus publicly accepts honor. I seek to find an existing paradigm in the Greco-Roman world in which resistance to honor was both a normative and an expected paradigm that would have been easily recognized by the first readers of Mark's Gospel.

II. The Desire for Honor in the Greco-Roman World

Before I consider possible paradigms for understanding the behavior of the Markan Jesus, I will briefly consider the pride of place given to honor in the ancient Mediterranean world. Our primary sources make it quite clear that honor was one of the greatest and most prized virtues.¹⁰ In Thucydides' *History of the Peloponnesian War*, Pericles is reported to say, "For the love of honour alone is untouched by age, and when one comes to the ineffectual period of life it is not 'gain' as some say, that gives the greater satisfaction, but honour" (*Hist.* 2.44.4 [Smith, LCL]). In Xenophon, the poet Simonides states:

> For indeed it seems to me, Hiero, that in this man differs from other animals—I mean, in this craving for honour. In meat and drink and sleep and sex all creatures alike seem to take pleasure; but love of honour is rooted neither in the brute beasts nor in every human being. But they in whom is implanted a passion for

---

⁹ Watson, *Honor*, 115–37

¹⁰ For an excellent discussion on honor and shame in the primary literature, see Mark T. Finney, *Honor and Conflict in the Ancient World: 1 Corinthians in Its Greco-Roman Social Setting* (Library of New Testament Studies 460; London: T&T Clark, 2012). I am greatly indebted to this source.

honour and praise, these are they who differ most from the beasts of the field, these are accounted men and not mere human beings. (Xenophon, *Hier.* 7.3 [Marchant and Bowersock, LCL])

Aristotle emphasizes honor as the greatest external good:

> Now the greatest external good we should assume to be the thing which we offer as a tribute to the gods, and which is most coveted by men of high station, and is the prize awarded for the noblest deeds; and such a thing is honour, for honour is clearly the greatest of external goods. Therefore the great souled man is he who has the right disposition with regard to honours and disgraces. And even without argument it is evident that honour is the object with which the great-souled are concerned, since it is honour above all else which great men claim and deserve. (Aristotle, *Eth. nic.* 4.3.10 [Rackham, LCL])

Roman writers confirm the high opinion of honor found in the Greek world. Cicero writes, "Nature has made us, as I have said before—it must often be repeated—enthusiastic seekers after honour, and once we have caught, as it were, some glimpse of its radiance, there is nothing we are not prepared to bear and go through in order to secure it" (Cicero, *Tusc.* 2.24.58 [King, LCL]).[11]

In light of this testimony and the prominent place it gives honor in the ancient Mediterranean world, it is all the more striking that Jesus would reject the honor that he deserved. Certainly Mark's readers would be struck by such behavior and would seek a plausible explanation. We now turn our attention to paradigms that might give just such an explanation for Jesus' odd behavior.

III. Rejecting Honor: Possible Paradigms

I will consider three possible paradigms that might explain Jesus' rejection of public honor: (1) cynic philosophy and praxis, (2) envy avoidance strategies, and (3) Roman political ideology.

Cynic Philosophy and Praxis

Such love of honor certainly characterized the great majority in the Mediterranean world, but it did not characterize all. The Cynics are perhaps the most noteworthy example of the minority that did not embrace the virtue of φιλοτιμία, "the love of honor."[12] Cynics rejected material possessions, physical comfort, and

---

[11] See also Cicero, *Arch.* 28–29; *Fin.* 5.22.64; *Off.* 1.18.61.

[12] Here I am referring primarily to "Hard" Cynicism as opposed to "Soft" Cynicism. "Soft" Cynics were more likely to participate in societal and political institutions. On Cynics and the difference between "Hard" and "Soft" Cynics, see John R. Morgan, "Cynics," *OCD* (3rd ed.), 418–19. On "Hard" Cynics, see Diogenes Laertius, *Lives* 6.

societal convention. Such things were replaced with material poverty, ascetic practices, and shameful public behavior.[13] But, while Cynics are accurately described as people who resisted public honor, there are many reasons to reject Cynic philosophy and praxis as a paradigm for understanding the behavior of the Markan Jesus. Though the Markan Jesus does share some features with Cynics (e.g., itinerant, homeless, having few material possessions, teaching in bold aphorisms, etc.), many features of the Markan Jesus are radically inconsistent with Cynic practice (e.g., calling disciples, regularly participating in social feasts/meals, etc.). Mark also makes no explicit effort to link Jesus to the Cynics through his appearance or actions. Jesus is not described as wearing ragged or dirty garments, the attire of a Cynic, nor is Jesus presented as begging or partaking in shameful public activity. In fact, it seems that Jesus' instructions to his disciples not to take a bag on their mission may be an intentional attempt on the part of the Markan evangelist to distinguish Jesus and his disciples from Cynics, who customarily carried a beggar's bag. Perhaps more important is the difference between the Markan episodes in which Jesus resists honor, and such resistance by the Cynics. Jesus' resistance to honor is situation-specific and sporadic, differing from the philosophical and categorical rejection of honor exhibited by Cynics. In other words, Cynics largely avoided behavior or reputation that would merit honor, whereas Jesus rejected honor that his behavior and reputation merited. For these reasons, it seems unlikely that Mark's readers would recognize Cynic philosophy and praxis as a paradigm for understanding Jesus' occasional resistance to public honor.

Envy Avoidance Strategies

While honor was deeply desired in the ancient Mediterranean world, acquiring it was a double-edged sword. Honor was perceived as a limited good, meaning that one person's acquisition of honor meant another's loss.[14] The perception that honor was limited naturally led to the increase of envy (φθόνος), an emotion widely regarded as a dangerous and volatile vice that could result in hatred, harm, and

---

[13] For more discussion of Cynics, see Everett Ferguson, *Backgrounds of Early Christianity* (3rd ed.; Grand Rapids: Eerdmans, 2003), 348–53; Morgan, "Cynics," 418–19.

[14] This perception is clearly seen in the primary literature. Iamblicus states, "People do not find it pleasant to give honor to someone else, for they suppose that they themselves are being deprived of something" (*Anonymus Iamblici*, in Hermann Diels, *Die Fragmente der Vorsokratiker, griechische und deutsch* [ed. W. Kranz; 5th ed.; 3 vols.; Berlin: Weidmann, 1934–37], 2:400). And Plutarch states, "And whereas men attack other kinds of eminence and themselves lay claim to good character, good birth, and honour, as though they were depriving themselves of so much of these as they grant to others" (Plutarch, *An seni* 7 [Fowler, LCL]). For secondary literature on "honor" as a limited good, see Jerome H. Neyrey and Richard L. Rohrbaugh, "'He Must Increase and I Must Decrease' (John 3:30): A Cultural and Social Interpretation," *CBQ* 63 (2001): 468–69; and Malina, *New Testament World*, 81–107.

potentially the loss of honor.[15] Thus, the virtue of φιλοτιμία, "love of honor," requires a balancing act, one in which a person must find a way of obtaining and securing honor without incurring the dangerous envy of others.[16] Some interpreters have argued that Jesus' commands for silence in Mark's Gospel could be understood as means of preventing or curbing envy, a possibility I will consider here.[17] Greek and Roman authors provide a number of ways that one can avoid or mitigate the dangers of envy. These means include (1) using one's honors in order to benefit others rather than for purposes of self-interest or "vain-glory"; (2) adopting an attitude of humility toward one's honors; (3) downplaying or undervaluing one's honors; (4) demonstrating a life of great virtue; (5) giving praise and honor to others; (6) giving credit for honor and prosperity to divine fortune; and (7) practicing self-deprecation.[18] Relevant to our purposes is the absence of any instruction that one should reject bestowed honors as a means of avoiding envy.[19] No such instructions can be found. Therefore, while some of Jesus' behaviors in Mark's Gospel might be interpreted in terms of avoiding envy (e.g., his avoidance of crowds [4:36; 7:24], giving credit to God [5:19; 9:29], questioning the descriptor "good" [10:18], etc.), his rejection of deserved honors does not seem best understood in such terms.

Roman Political Ideology

We now turn our attention to Roman political ideology in order to find a paradigm to help explain Jesus' rejection of deserved honors. Roman political ideology was characterized by an unwavering commitment to self-rule and great disdain for monarchs and tyrants. As a result, this ideology necessitated certain limitations to an individual's acquisition of public honors, particularly either

---

[15] See Cicero, *Or.* 2.209–10. Also note that envy and hatred are not the same, though the former is often closely related to the latter; see Plutarch, *De invidia et odio.*

[16] According to Plutarch, the moderate person is able to enjoy honors and prosperity without exciting the envy of others (*Lib. ed.* 10).

[17] See Malina, *New Testament World*, 125; and Pilch, "Secrecy in the Gospel of Mark," 150–53.

[18] On these strategies for avoiding and/or minimizing envy, see Cicero, *Or.* 2.209–11; and Plutarch, *Ivn. od.* 6; *De laude* 4, 6, 9, 11, 12,

[19] Malina's assessment of Jesus' commands for silence, namely, that Jesus is concealing his actions to avoid envy, is largely dependent on envy-avoidance behaviors outlined in George Foster's article "The Anatomy of Envy: A Study of Symbolic Behavior," *Current Anthropology* 13 (1972): 165–202. Foster lists four types of behavior used for avoiding or mitigating envy: concealment, denial, symbolic sharing (Malina uses the term "conciliatory bribe"), and true sharing. Clearly, these four categories overlap with the behaviors we have noted above, and Foster's work is indeed helpful for analyzing envy and responses to envy in the NT. But the rejection of honor does not seem to fit into the categories provided by Foster. Because Malina understands Jesus' behavior as concealing honor rather than rejecting honor, he finds support in Foster's work. But if Jesus' actions are understood as rejecting honor, Foster's work does not prove as useful for understanding this behavior.

honors that in some way undermined the republican government (e.g., excessive appointments as consul, abuse of the dictatorship, etc.) or honors that were closely associated with monarchy (e.g., building temples in one's honor, receiving divine worship, accepting monarchical titles, etc). On the whole, this political ideology prevented the granting of such public honors to individual Romans during the republican era, and thus there are few examples of such honors being rejected.[20] But with the establishment of the Augustan principate, the situation regarding the granting of public honors changed drastically. Absolute power over the Roman Empire rested with Augustus. That absolute power engendered the desire to grant unprecedented (at least by Roman standards) public honors, honors that clearly violated republican sensibilities. Augustus found himself in a tenuous situation, as he was, for all intents and purposes, an autocrat governing a people who deeply despised autocrats. To negotiate these two diametrically opposed realities, Augustus adopted the strategy of *recusatio*, a strategy in which Augustus rejected the outward appearance of absolute power but not the power itself.[21] This strategy was extremely successful and became the standard for those who held the principate.

Central to this strategy of *recusatio* was the rejection of public honors that were deemed excessive, honors that violated republican sensibilities. Augustus strenuously refused to be addressed as "Lord" and once issued an edict that sharply censured a crowd that had innocently applied the title to him (Suetonius, *Aug.* 53.1; cf. Philo, *Embassy* 23.254). When the Senate and people conferred on Augustus the office of dictator, he refused the position and begged the people not to insist on it (Suetonius, *Aug.* 52.2; cf. Tacitus, *Ann.*1.9). Augustus refused attempts by the people and the Senate to honor him with the title "Father of his Country" and only accepted after great persistence (Suetonius, *Aug.* 52.1; *Res gest. divi Aug.* 5.1). Likewise he rejected the attempts of the Senate and the people to honor him with a lifelong consulship (*Res gest. divi Aug.* 5.3). He emphatically refused attempts to build or dedicate, within the city, temples in his honor (Suetonius, *Aug.* 52.1; Cassius Dio, *Roman History* 52.35).[22] He also melted down all silver statues in the

---

[20] Non-republican honors were offered to Julius Caesar, who, though he refused some, accepted many that violated republican sensibilities (e.g., the dictatorship for life, temples and priests in his honor, etc); see Suetonius, *Jul.* 76.1; Cassius Dio, *Roman History* 44.4–6. The acceptance of such honors was significant motivation for those who conspired to assassinate Caesar. In contrast to the behavior of Caesar is that of Cato, a Roman senator remembered for his unwavering dedication to republican ideology. When traveling throughout the Roman Empire, Cato frequently rejected honors that he felt violated republican sensibilities; see Plutarch, *Cat. Min.* 8.2; 13.1–3; 15.1–3.

[21] On Augustus's strategy of *recusatio*, see Andrew Wallace-Hadrill, "Civilis Princeps: Between Citizen and King," *JRS* 72 (1982): 32–48; and Jean Béranger, "Le refus du pouvoir," *MH* 5 (1948): 178–96.

[22] Tacitus seems to contradict Suetonius's testimony here, claiming, "He had left small room for the worship of heaven, when he claimed to be himself adored in temples and in the image of godhead by flamens and by priests!" (*Ann.* 1.10 [Jackson, LCL]). Because Tacitus's testimony is so

city of Rome that had been erected in his honor (Suetonius, *Aug.* 52.1; *Res. gest. divi Aug.* 24.2; cf Cassius Dio, *Roman History* 52.35). Augustus himself notes that he participated in only three triumphs and that he declined all other triumphs voted to him by the Senate (*Res. gest. divi Aug.* 4.1).

For the Roman memory of Augustus's general attitude toward public honors, the words of Cassius Dio are noteworthy. He uses the fictional advice of Maecenas to Augustus to describe the first emperor's attitude toward public honor:

> As regards your subjects, then, you should so conduct yourself, in my opinion. So far as you yourself are concerned, permit no exceptional or prodigal distinction to be given you, through word or deed, either by the senate or by anyone else. For whereas the honor which you confer upon others lends glory to them, yet nothing can be given to you that is greater than what you already possess, and, besides, no little suspicion of insincerity would attach to its giving. No subject, you see, is ever supposed to vote any such distinction to his ruler of his free will, and since all such honors as a ruler receives he must receive from himself, he not only wins no commendation for the honor but becomes a laughing-stock besides. You must therefore depend upon your good deeds to provide for you any additional splendor. And you should never permit gold or silver images of yourself to be made, for they are not only costly but also invite destruction and last only a brief time; but rather by your benefactions fashion other images in the hearts of your people, images which will never tarnish or perish. Neither should you ever permit the raising of a temple to you. (Cassius Dio, *Roman History* 52.35 [Cary, LCL])

Likely, these words not only reflect the way in which Augustus's attitude toward public honor was remembered in the mid-second century C.E. but also a political ideal that Roman citizens held for their rulers.

Like Augustus, Tiberius frequently resisted public honor. While Tiberius immediately succeeded Augustus by taking up imperial authority, he refused the formal title for a significant period of time, accepting it only after the Senate expressed great frustration at his reluctance (Suetonius, *Tib.* 24.1; Cassius Dio, *Roman History* 57.2.1).[23] He also refused to take the title "Augustus" for himself (Cassius Dio, *Roman History* 57.2.1; 57.8.1). Like Augustus, Tiberius refused the voting of temples, flamens, or priests in his honor (Suetonius, *Tib.* 26.1; Cassius

---

inconsistent with all other historians on this point, many historians have rejected Tacitus's claims as inaccurate, perhaps reflecting the historian's bias against the Augustan principate (see, e.g., F. R. D. Goodyear, *The Annals of Tacitus: Books 1–6* [2 vols.; Cambridge Classical Texts and Commentaries 15, 23; Cambridge: Cambridge University Press, 1972], 2:166). However, Ittai Gradel has argued that Tacitus is referring to Augustus's desire (and perhaps instruction) to be deified posthumously by the Roman Senate (*Emperor Worship and Roman Religion* [Oxford Classical Monographs; Oxford: Oxford University Press, 2002], 276–77).

[23] Suetonius views Tiberius's actions as hypocritical and a sign of false modesty. It seems that Tiberius was trying to follow the example of the reluctant ruler set by Augustus but that he was not as adept at the strategy as his predecessor.

Dio, *Roman History* 57.9.1). He refused the honorific titles "Imperator" and "Father of his Country," and he refused efforts to name the month of September after himself (Suetonius, *Tib.* 26.2; Cassius Dio, *Roman History* 57.8.1). He regularly refused to have statues made in his honor within the city, and any statue he allowed could not be set among the statues of the gods (Suetonius, *Tib.* 26.1; Cassius Dio, *Roman History* 57.9.1). He also refused the honor of the civic crown being placed at his door, an honor granted to Augustus identifying him as savior of the Roman citizenry (Suetonius, *Tib.* 26.2).

The resistance to public honor is again seen in the careers of Claudius and Vespasian, though less specific examples are found in our sources. By all accounts, Claudius refused excessive honors and acclamations (Suetonius, *Claud.* 12.1; Cassius Dio, *Roman History* 60.5.4). According to Suetonius, Claudius refused the title "Imperator" (Suetonius, *Claud.* 12.1). Cassius Dio claims that Claudius initially refused the title of "Father of his Country," though he eventually accepted it (Cassius Dio, *Roman History*, 60.3.2). Claudius also did not allow himself to be worshiped as a god or be offered any sacrifice (Cassius Dio, *Roman History*, 60.5.4). With few exceptions, he rejected honorific statues that were voted to him (Cassius Dio, *Roman History*, 60.5.4). Suetonius also claims that Vespasian was reluctant to accept his tribunician powers as well as the title "Father of his Country" (Suetonius, *Vesp.* 12).[24] It seems that Vespasian ended the practice of Romans worshiping the "genius" of the living emperor, a practice instituted by Gaius Caligula.[25]

Again, I must stress that such imperial acts of resisting public honor should not be understood as examples of true humility, but rather should be understood in terms of Roman political ideology. Honors such as monarchical or divine titles, direct worship, temples, priesthoods, and excessive triumphs were, in the Roman mind, all associated with tyrannical kings of the East, and therefore Augustus and many of his successors rejected such honors. It must be noted that Roman emperors did indeed receive and embrace great public honors, but these honors were distinctly Roman honors, that is, honors that were grounded in Roman tradition and consistent with Roman political sensibilities. Yet even such Roman honors were not to be enjoyed in excess, lest one Roman be elevated too high above his peers. The successful Roman emperor who took seriously (at least publicly) Roman political ideology and his identity as *princeps* or "first citizen" would avoid the appearance of being a monarch and thus would resist any public honor that would be associated with such a figure. Ultimately, resisting these excessive honors led to greater honor for the Roman emperor in the eyes of the Roman citizenry.

It is no coincidence that Suetonius's *Lives of the Caesars* and Cassius Dio's *Roman History* address every emperor's attitude toward the bestowal of public

---

[24] Vespasian's tribunician powers were reckoned from July 1 of 69. It is possible that Suetonius is referring to his official use of these powers rather than their official reckoning. For this solution, see Barbara Levick, *Vespasian* (London: Routledge, 1999), 67.

[25] For this conclusion, see Gradel, *Emperor Worship*, 189–90.

honors. While positive examples of resisting public honor have been noted above, negative examples can be given. Julius Caesar and Gaius Caligula were both censured for embracing such excessive honors. Julius Caesar accepted the title and position of dictator for life, placed a statue of himself among the statues both of Rome's former kings and of Rome's gods, and accepted temples, altars, and priests in his honor (Suetonius, *Jul.* 76.1; Cassius Dio, *Roman History* 44.4–6). Caligula presented himself as an absolute monarch, accepted worship as a divine figure, and established temples and priests for such worship (Suetonius, *Cal.* 22.1–3). Such honors evidence the departure of Julius Caesar and Gaius Caligula from Roman political ideals and are closely associated with their failure as Roman rulers.

It should be noted that such an attitude toward excessive honors was distinctly Roman, characterizing the city of Rome and perhaps Roman colonies, but this view would have been absent in the larger Mediterranean world (e.g., in Greece, Asia Minor, Egypt, Syria, and elsewhere).[26] In fact, in the larger empire, Rome's emperors accepted honors that they would never have embraced in Rome itself.[27] It seems, however, that accepting such honors elsewhere was largely not problematic for these emperors in the capital city. While some opponents might criticize them for embracing the trappings of monarchy in the East, Romans for the most part seemed to care little if a single Roman was elevated above non-Romans (e.g., Greeks, Gauls, Egyptians, and others). It was exalting one Roman too high over other Romans that was regarded as problematic. Therefore, it is only from a distinctly Roman perspective that resisting public honor was regarded as a virtue of an ideal ruler; that is, such actions would be foreign to much of the Mediterranean world.

IV. The Markan Jesus and Roman Political Ideology: Three Supporting Factors

Here we ask whether such a background might provide the paradigm that would explain for Mark's readers Jesus' resistance to public honor in the Gospel. Jesus rejects recognition for his powerful healings (1:44–45; 5:43; 7:36; 8:26) as well as honorific titles/identification (1:25, 34; 3:12; 8:30; 9:9). Is it possible that through such actions Mark's Gospel is presenting Jesus in terms of Roman political ideology, that is, Jesus as an ideal ruler? I suggest that there are three factors that, taken together, strongly indicate that this is in fact what Mark's Gospel is up to, and that

---

[26] See Wallace-Hadrill, "Civilis Princeps," 41–48; and A. Jakobson and H. Cotton, "Caligula's Recusatio Imperii," *Historia Zeitschrift für alte Geschichte* 34 (1985): 503.

[27] For numerous examples of honors that Roman emperors received in the Roman East, see S. R. F. Price, *Rituals and Power: The Roman Imperial Cult in Asia Minor* (Cambridge: Cambridge University Press, 1985), 133–233; note especially the catalogue of imperial shrines and temples, 249–73.

the so-called secrecy motif of the Gospel is best understood in terms of Roman political ideology.

Factor 1: A Roman Audience

Traditionally, the Gospel of Mark was believed to have been written in Rome, for Roman Christians. While the twentieth century saw proposals for both a Galilean and a Syrian provenance for Mark, there remain both strong evidence and strong scholarly support for the traditional position. Since this topic has been thoroughly addressed in a number of recent studies, I will only briefly discuss the relevant evidence for a Roman provenance here.[28] The external evidence from early church witnesses is virtually unanimous in its testimony that Mark's Gospel was written in Rome.[29] Such early and consistent traditions are not easily dismissed, and recent efforts to this end have fallen short.[30] Additionally, significant internal evidence exists that supports a Roman provenance for Mark. The Greek transcription of Latin words (*caesar, census, denarius, flagellare, grabatus, legio, modius, praetorium, sextarius, quadrans*, et al.) as well as Latin idioms that are translated into unnatural Greek word combinations (ὁδὸν ποιεῖν = *viam facere*, 2:23; ἐσχάτως ἔχει = *ultimum habere*, 5:23; κατακρινοῦσιν θανάτῳ = *capite damnare* 10:33).[31] Mark

---

[28] I leave aside for now the evidence for and against both a Galilean and a Syrian provenance. A thorough argument for a Galilean provenance is provide by Hendrika N. Roskam, *The Purpose of the Gospel of Mark in Its Historical and Social Context* (NovTSup 114; Leiden: Brill, 2004). Arguments for a Syrian provenance can be found in Joel Marcus, *Mark 1–8: A New Translation with Introduction and Commentary* (AB 27; New York: Doubleday, 2000); and Gerd Theissen, *The Gospels in Context: Social and Political History in the Synoptic Tradition* (Minneapolis: Fortress, 1991), 236–45. For arguments against both a Galilean and a Syrian provenance, see Adam Winn, *The Purpose of Mark's Gospel: An Early Christian Response to Roman Imperial Propaganda* (WUNT 2/245; Tübingen: Mohr Siebeck, 2008), 83–91.

[29] The first link between Mark and Rome can be found in Irenaeus, who claims that Mark wrote his Gospel after Peter's and Paul's deaths in Rome, the city where Mark served as Peter's interpreter (*Haer.* 3.1.1). While Irenaeus does not explicitly claim that Mark wrote his Gospel in Rome, this conclusion seems implicit. The "anti-Marcionite" prologue places the composition of Mark's Gospel in Italy, while Clement of Alexandria (late second/early third century) specifically places Mark's composition in Rome. Additionally, Origen, Eusebius, the Monarchian Gospel prologues, Epiphanius, and Jerome all affirm a Roman provenance for Mark's Gospel. The only deviation from this tradition, is John Chrysostom's fourth-century claim that Mark's Gospel was written in Alexandria, a claim that likely grows out of the tradition that John Mark, at some point after Peter's death, became the bishop of Alexandria.

[30] For attempts to mitigate the significance and merit of this external evidence, see C. Clifton Black, *Mark: Images of an Apostolic Interpreter* (1994; Studies on Personalities of the New Testament; repr., Minneapolis: Fortress, 2001), 224–25. For a response to Black, see Winn, *Purpose*, 78–80.

[31] For discussion of these loanwords and idioms, see Winn, *Purpose*, 81; Bas van Iersel, *Mark: A Reader Response Commentary* (trans. W. H. Bisscheroux; JSNTSup 164; Sheffield:

also uses grecized Latin expressions to explain Greek words. For example, the Greek word λεπτά (a small copper coin) is explained with the phrase ὅ ἐστιν κοδράντης ("which is a quadrans," 12:42) and the Greek word αὐλή (courtyard/palace) is explained or clarified with the phrase ὅ ἐστιν πραιτώριον ("which is the praetorium," 15:16). Perhaps most noteworthy are the distinct elements of both common Latin sentence structure and Latin word usage that are embedded in Mark's Gospel, elements that betray the influence of a "Latin-speaking milieu on speakers whose mother-tongue was not Latin."[32] This internal evidence strongly corroborates the external evidence that claims Mark's Gospel was written in Rome. Additionally, a Roman provenance makes sense of the motif of suffering discipleship found in Mark's Gospel, as Rome was the location of the most significant and historically documented persecution of first-century Christians.[33] It must be noted that there is no evidence, internal or external, that precludes or even significantly undermines a Roman provenance for Mark.

Such a Roman provenance (and presumably audience) for Mark's Gospel has significant implications for our present interest in how Mark's first readers would understand Jesus' rejection of both achieved and ascribed honor. While most Mediterranean readers would have no paradigm for understanding Jesus' behavior, distinctly Roman readers would have such a paradigm, namely, Roman rulers resisting and rejecting public honor. It seems highly probable that, when presented with this confusing behavior of Jesus, Mark's Roman readers would naturally use the one paradigm they had to understand it. Thus, that Mark's Roman readers would identify Jesus' behavior with the ideal behavior of their own rulers seems highly plausible. But does Mark's Gospel give the reader additional signals that might lead them to such a conclusion?

Sheffield Academic Press, 1998), 31–35; idem, "De thuishaven van Marcus," *TvT* 32 (1992): 125–42.

[32] See van Iersel, *Mark: A Reader Response Commentary*, 34. The first noteworthy example of Latinisms embedded in the language of Mark's Gospel is the word order of verbs and direct objects. In Greek, the direct object generally follows the verb that governs it, while in Latin, the reverse is normative. The Latin word order occurs thirty-seven times in Mark's Gospel, while in Luke and Matthew, this Latinism only occurs twice independently of Mark. The second example involves a rather unnatural use of the word ἵνα after verbs of asking, commanding, speaking, or persuading, a usage that parallels the function of the Latin word *ut*. This presumably Latin-influenced use of ἵνα is found thirty-one times in Mark's Gospel, while in Luke and Matthew, this Latinism only occurs twice independently of Mark. A number of Lukan and Matthean texts maintain a Markan parallel, but both often correct Mark's use of ἵνα with a more natural Greek word. For further discussion, see van Iersel, *Mark*, 34–35; and Winn, *Purpose*, 81–82.

[33] On the motif of suffering discipleship in Mark's Gospel, see John. R. Donahue, *The Theology and Setting of Discipleship in the Gospel of Mark* (Milwaukee, WI: Marquette University Press, 1983); Ernest Best, *Disciples and Discipleship: Studies in the Gospel according to Mark* (Edinburgh: T&T Clark, 1986); Theissen, *Gospels in Context*; Brian Incigneri, *The Gospel to the Romans: The Setting and Rhetoric of Mark's Gospel* (Biblical Interpretation Series 65; Leiden: Brill, 2003), 105–8; Roskam, *Purpose*.

Factor 2: Mark's Presentation of Jesus as a World Ruler

It is widely recognized that Mark's Gospel presents Jesus as God's appointed ruler. From the outset, the Markan Jesus is identified as God's Messiah (1:1), and this identity is confirmed throughout the rest of the Gospel (8:29; 14:61). There is significant evidence that Mark understands "Messiah" as one who rules on God's behalf. God twice identifies Jesus as his Son (1:11 and 9:7), clearly echoing the royal coronation of Psalm 2 and thus establishing Jesus as God's appointed ruler, that is, one to whom God will give the nations and the ends of the earth as an inheritance. Jesus' triumphal entry also identifies him as God's appointed ruler, as the people identify him with the kingdom of David (11:7–10). The universal nature of Jesus' rule is evidenced by his identification as "Son of Man," an identification that is explicitly linked with the Danielic "Son of Man" in 13:26 and 14:62. In this way, Mark presents Jesus as one who is granted an everlasting dominion over all "peoples, nations, and languages" (cf. Dan 7:14).[34] Therefore, as God's messianic ruler, the Markan Jesus reigns over the entire world.[35]

Jesus' identity as a world ruler increases the likelihood that Mark's Roman readers would understand Jesus' resistance to public honor in terms of such resistance exercised by their own rulers, that is, in terms of Roman political ideology. It is noteworthy that out of five instances in which Jesus either resists or rejects honorific identification (what Watson identifies as ascribed honor), three are clearly associated with his identity as God's appointed ruler. In Mark 3:12, Jesus silences the demons that identify him as "Son of God," a title associated with both Jewish and Greco-Roman rulers.[36] Again, in 8:28–30, Jesus orders his disciples not to make known his identity as God's Messiah, an identity that in Mark's Gospel and much of Second Temple Judaism is associated with God-appointed ruler. Finally, in 9:9, Jesus prohibits his disciples from making known his transfigured identity, namely, his identity as God's Son. In all of these instances, Jesus resists honor that was associated with his role as God's appointed ruler of the world. It seems highly likely that Roman readers would connect the world ruler Jesus who resists such honorific identifications with the similar behavior of their own rulers.

---

[34] On the title "Son of Man" in Mark's Gospel, see Winn, *Purpose*, 102–7; Martin Hengel, *Studies in Early Christology* (Edinburgh: T&T Clark, 1995), 104–8; Jack Dean Kingsbury, *The Christology of Mark's Gospel* (Philadelphia: Fortress, 1983), 157–76; D. R. A. Hare, *The Son of Man Tradition* (Minneapolis: Fortress, 1990), 183–211.

[35] For a more thorough discussion of the christological identity of the Markan Jesus, see, e.g., Winn, *Purpose*, 99–107; Kingsbury, *Christology*. See also Elizabeth Struthers Malbon (*Mark's Jesus: Characterizaton as Narrative Christology* [Waco: Baylor University Press, 2009]), who, contra Kingsbury, rejects the idea that Mark presents Jesus as a kingly messiah.

[36] See Adela Yarbro Collins, "Mark and His Readers: The Son of God among Jews," *HTR* 92 (1999): 393–408; eadem, "Mark and His Readers: The Son of God among Greeks and Romans," *HTR* 93 (2000): 85–100.

Excursus: Jesus as βασιλεύς?

While royal imagery is frequently attributed to Jesus in Mark's Gospel, the title βασιλεύς, "king", is surprisingly not. Elizabeth Struthers Malbon has noted that Jesus is identified as βασιλεύς only by those who are clearly his opponents—for example, Pilate (15:2, 9, 12, 26 [Pilate's inscription above the cross]), the Roman soldiers (15:18), and the chief priests and scribes (15:32)—characters that are certainly untrustworthy to the reader.[37] She argues further that all referenced "kings" in Mark's Gospel are portrayed in a negative light, for example, Herod Antipas (6:14, 22, 25, 26, 27) and those before whom Jesus' disciples will stand (13:9).[38] Even God is not identified as a king in Mark's Gospel. The apparent unimportance (or perhaps negative connotation) of this title in Mark is all the more striking when Mark is compared with Matthew. The title is much more frequent in Matthew's Gospel and is often used in a positive way. In four different non-Markan parallels, Jesus is identified, either by himself or by the narrator, as a king (Matt 2:2; 21:5; 25:34; 25:40).[39] Matthew even indirectly identifies God as a king in the parable of the wedding feast (Matt 22:2–14). Why is Mark willing to attribute royal imagery to Jesus but, unlike Matthew, apparently reluctant to identify Jesus as βασιλεύς?

The vast majority of interpreters see no reluctance on the evangelist's part to identify Jesus as king. Most point to the kingly identifications made by Pilate, the Roman soldiers, and the chief priests and scribes and conclude that, while these identifications are clearly derisive, they are steeped in irony—that is, the mocking identification of Jesus as king is in fact true! But in light of the evidence noted above, the astute reader knows that no trustworthy character in the story (e.g., Jesus, the narrator, God, the disciples, or any of the insightful minor characters) has identified Jesus as βασιλεύς. Therefore, it might be more accurate to interpret the derisive identifications of Jesus as king not only as derisive but also as wrong! Thus, for the author and the audience, identifying Jesus as βασιλεύς is just one more false charge among many others (e.g., general false charges [14:56]; the charge of destroying the temple [14:58]; the charge of blasphemy [14:64]; general accusations before Pilate [15:3]; etc.). Malbon suggests that this "anti-kingship" element of Mark's Gospel is similar to the "anti-monarchical" strand of tradition that can be found in the Hebrew Bible, particular in the David stories—an apt comparison indeed.[40] But in light of Mark's Roman audience, this "anti-king" motif might be best explained in

---

[37] Malbon, *Mark's Jesus*, 119–20. Contra the present argument, Malbon concludes that neither the title βασιλεύς nor royal imagery is viewed favorably in Mark's Gospel. In her view, "reign" and "ruling" in Mark belong to God and not to Jesus. Instead, Jesus is God's ambassador who announces God's reign.

[38] Ibid.

[39] This number could actually be five, if the reference to the "great king" in Matt 5:35 is understood as a reference to God's Messiah—a conclusion that seems highly likely.

[40] Malbon, *Mark's Jesus*, 121.

light of Roman disdain for kings and tyrants. The Markan evangelist does not identify Jesus as a king because Roman readers abhor such a title. Such a reading would be complemented by Jesus' resistance to public honor, an act that was associated with the Roman rulers distancing themselves from identity as a βασιλεύς.

Factor 3: Challenges to Roman Imperial Claims in Mark's Gospel

Recent studies have argued that Mark's Gospel contains a thoroughgoing response to the claims and propaganda of Roman emperors.[41] This response begins with Mark's incipit, "The beginning of the good news of Jesus Christ, Son of God" (1:1), a title that is rife with imperial language and imagery. With these opening words, Mark challenges the gospel of Rome and the claims of Rome's emperors.[42] The true gospel begins with Jesus rather than Caesar; and it is Jesus, not Caesar, who is true Son of God. Throughout the Gospel, Jesus' identity as Son of God is confirmed both by God (1:11; 9:7) and by supernatural demons (3:11; 5:7). The challenge to Roman imperial claims is clearly evident in the actions of the Markan Jesus. Jesus' healings both imitate and surpass the propagandistic healings performed by the Roman emperor Vespasian.[43] Like Roman emperors, the Markan Jesus commands "legions," though legions of supernatural demons rather than legions of Roman soldiers (5:1–20).[44] Reminiscent of poetic descriptions of Augustus calming storms and bringing peace to the seas (e.g., *Res gest. divi Aug.* 4.25; Philo, *Embassy* 145–46), Jesus demonstrates the ability to calm storms literally and

---

[41] See Winn, *Purpose*; Craig A. Evans, "Mark's Incipit and the Priene Calendar Inscription: From Jewish Gospel to Greco-Roman Gospel," *Journal of Greco-Roman Christianity and Judaism* 1 (2000): 67–81; idem, "The Beginning of the Good News and the Fulfillment of Scripture in Mark's Gospel," in *Hearing the Old Testament in the New Testament* (ed. Stanley E. Porter; Grand Rapids: Eerdmans, 2006), 83–103. Note that neither Winn nor Evans denies the Isaianic influence on this passage, but both argue that Roman imperial language and imagery have been brought together with Isaianic language and imagery.

[42] For more thorough discussion of this topic, see Winn, *Purpose*, 92–99, 178–80; and Evans, "Incipit."

[43] After his ascension to power, Emperor Vespasian healed two people in Alexandria. He healed a man's withered hand by touching it with his foot and cured a man's blindness by touching his eyes with his own spittle (see Suetonius, *Vesp.* 7.2; Tacitus, *Hist.* 4.81.1–3; compare strikingly similar miracles performed by Jesus in Mark 3:1–6 and 8:22–26. For arguments that these Markan miracles are intentionally paralleling those of Vespasian, see Winn, *Purpose*, 184–85; and Incigneri, *Gospel to the Romans*, 170–71.

[44] For anti-Roman readings of Mark 5:1–20, see Richard A. Horsley, *Hearing the Whole Story: The Politics of Plot in Mark's Gospel* (Louisville: Westminster John Knox, 2001), 140–41; Ched Myers, *Binding the Strong Man: A Political Reading of Mark's Story of Jesus* (Maryknoll, NY: Orbis, 1992), 190–92; John Dominic Crossan, *The Historical Jesus: The Life of a Mediterranean Jewish Peasant* (San Francisco: HarperSanFrancisco, 1991), 314; Winn, *Purpose*, 184–85.

bring peace to the seas (4:35–41).⁴⁵ Like Roman emperors who provided grain to the hungry Roman populace (*Res gest. divi Aug.* 15.1–4; Suetonius, *Aug.* 41.2), the Markan Jesus twice provides an abundance of bread for people in need (6:30–44; 8:1–10).⁴⁶ Even Mark's passion narrative contributes to the Gospel's response to imperial claims, as Jesus' crucifixion is cleverly presented as a Roman triumph.⁴⁷ Through what is intended to be Jesus' moment of defeat and humiliation, the Romans unwittingly grant him the triumph he deserves, one in which a Roman centurion recognizes Jesus as Son of God (15:39)!

I propose that the significance of Jesus' resistance to public honor comes into sharper focus for Mark's readers when it is placed alongside these Markan responses to Roman imperial claims. From the opening words of Mark's Gospel, the Roman readers are presented with a blatant challenge to the claims of Rome's rulers. Such readers would thus be attentive to ways that this challenge is advanced by the following narrative. With this Roman imperial background firmly planted in the minds of Mark's readers, it seems difficult to deny that they would understand Jesus' resistance to public honor in light of such resistance exhibited by their own rulers.

Taken together, these three factors strongly suggest that the Markan Jesus' resistance to public honor is best understood in light of similar resistance exhibited by Rome's emperors. Thus, I conclude that the Markan evangelist is presenting Jesus as one who, at least in this one regard, is consistent with Roman political ideology.

V. What Is Mark Up To? Summarizing Thoughts

But why would Mark be presenting Jesus as one who is consistent with Roman political ideology? I propose that such a presentation is a part of Mark's thoroughgoing challenge to the propagandistic claims of Roman emperors. In an effort to demonstrate that Jesus is the true "Son of God" and true ruler of the world, Mark co-opts language, imagery, and other realities from the world of the Roman emperors and incorporates them into his story of Jesus. Through co-opting the imperial motif of resisting public honor, Mark offers a contextualization of Jesus' identity as world ruler that resonates with Roman readers. Unlike recent Roman rulers such

---

⁴⁵ For arguments that Mark's readers would read the sea narratives in light of Roman imperial power, see Wendy Cotter, *Miracles in Greco-Roman Antiquity: A Sourcebook* (London: Routledge, 1999), 131–48; Winn, *Purpose*, 185–86. For the citations of the *Res gestae*, see the new critical translation and commentary by Alison E. Cooley, *Res gestae divi Augusti: Text, Translation, and Commentary* (Cambridge: Cambridge University Press, 2009).

⁴⁶ On Vespasian giving out grain, see Levick, *Vespasian*, 124–25, esp. n. 2, which references *CIL* 6:3747.

⁴⁷ For the parallels between Mark's passion narrative and a Roman triumph, see T. E. Schmidt, "Mark 15:16–32: The Crucifixion Narrative and the Roman Triumphal Procession," *NTS* 41 (1995): 1–18; and Winn, *Purpose*, 127–32.

as Caligula and Nero, Jesus embodies what is truly good and virtuous from Roman political ideology, namely, the rejection of tyrannical behavior—rejection that is symbolized by resistance to public honor. If, as has been argued elsewhere, Mark's Gospel is a response to the propaganda of Vespasian, Jesus' resistance to public honor may be an attempt to counter similar behavior exhibited by the new Flavian emperor. In essence, the Markan Jesus beats the Roman emperors at their own game by easily embodying the ideology they must work so hard to appease. In other words, through resisting public honor, the Markan Jesus out-Caesars the Caesars.

VI. An Advantageous Solution

The issue of consistency is a notorious problem for interpretations of Mark's "secrecy motif." While Jesus at times silences those who proclaim his identity, he does not always do so (see 5:7; 10:47–48). And while Jesus commands some recipients of healings to be silent, he does not command all. Such inconsistencies forced Wrede to conclude that the "messianic secret" was not the creation of the evangelist but simply the remnants of earlier efforts within the Jesus tradition to explain why Jesus was not recognized as the Messiah. Later solutions that attributed the "secrecy motif" to the evangelist have difficulty explaining the inconsistent application of the motif. If the motif serves to advance a theology of the cross—namely, that Jesus cannot be truly identified as Son of God/Messiah before his crucifixion—then why is the secret broken before Jesus' crucifixion (5:7; 10:47–48; 14:62)?[48] If the motif is an apologetic device to explain why Jesus' contemporaries did not recognize him as the Messiah, how are the proclamations of Jesus' messianic identity in Mark accounted for (5:7; 10:47–48)?[49] If the secrecy motif serves to highlight Jesus' identity through the intentional and frequent breaking of the secret, why is the secret not broken at certain points (1:25, 34; 3:12; 8:30; 9:9)?[50] If the secrecy motif is not about secrecy at all, but rather an attempt to invert societal understandings of honor and shame, then why are traditional understandings of honor and shame affirmed throughout Mark's Gospel? The inconsistency of the Markan secrecy

---

[48] For those who support this reading of the Markan secrecy motif, see e.g., Kingsbury, *Christology*; Francis J. Moloney, *The Gospel of Mark: A Commentary* (Peabody, MA: Hendrickson, 2002), 59–60; M. Eugene Boring, *Mark: A Commentary* (NTL; Louisville: Westminster John Knox, 2006), 270. Among current Markan interpreters, this is the most widespread interpretation of the Markan secrecy motif.

[49] For those who propose an apologetic reading, see Martin Dibelius, *From Tradition to Gospel* (trans. Bertram Lee Woolf; Library of Theological Translations; London: James Clarke, 1971), 230–31; and T. Alec Burkill, *Mysterious Revelation: An Examination of the Philosophy of St. Mark's Gospel* (Ithaca, NY: Cornell University Press, 1963).

[50] For such a solution, see Hans Jürgen Ebeling, *Das Messiasgeheimnis und die Botschaft des Marcus-Evangelisten* (BZNW 19; Berlin: Töpelmann, 1939), esp. 167–70.

motif is a sandbar on which numerous explanations of the motif have run aground. But the issue of the motif's inconsistency poses no problem for my proposed solution. While resisting public honor was an expression of Roman political ideology, absolute resistance to public honor was not. Roman emperors were both allowed and expected to receive public honor to a point. Resistance to public honor was a means by which the emperor drew a line between appropriate and excessive honor, a way in which the emperor could outwardly affirm his identity as first citizen and his commitment to Roman political ideology. Thus, the fact that Jesus receives public honor at numerous points throughout Mark's Gospel is not problematic for my proposed solution. As God's appointed ruler, Jesus is both allowed and expected to accept honor. But his occasional resistance to honor demonstrates his consistency with Roman political ideology and thus contributes to Mark's response to Roman imperial claims.

Evangelically Rooted. *Critically Engaged.*

NEW FROM IVP ACADEMIC

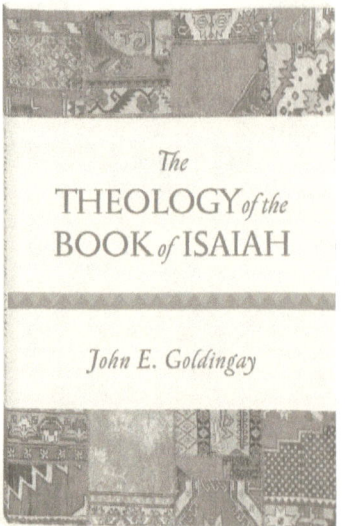

160 pages, paperback, 978-0-8308-4039-7, $18.00

The Theology of the Book of Isaiah
John E. Goldingay

What should we make of the sprawling and puzzling book of Isaiah—so layered and complex in its composition? John Goldingay helps us see, hear and understand the grandeur of this prophetic masterpiece among the Prophets as both separate parts and as a whole, clearly tied together with unifying themes.

"The strength of this work is its sensitivity to the thematic emphases of the major sections of Isaiah as well as the book as a whole. It is a helpful guide for those seeking to discover order in the midst of the creative intricacies of the book of Isaiah, whether before they tackle a detailed study . . . or at the end of a patient exegesis."

—**Mark J. Boda,** McMaster Divinity College, McMaster University

Follow us on Twitter Join us on Facebook 800.843.9487 | ivpacademic.com

Μόνον or μονῶν?
Reading 1 John 2:2c from the
Editio Critica Maior

TOAN DO
tojosephdo@gmail.com
Australian Catholic University, Fitzroy Victoria 3065, Australia

For 1 John 2:2 the eighth corrected printing of Nestle-Aland[27] (1994) lists three variants of μονῶν in place of μόνον. Since then more manuscripts have been added to the list. The 2003 *Novum Testamentum Graecum Editio Critica Maior* (ECM and NA[28]) provides nineteen variants, plus lacunae, for μονῶν. Moreover, the presence of δέ and καί occurs in some manuscripts but not in others. The difference between these variants has the potential to affect their theological interpretation: it questions the authorship or editorship of the text; it alters the syntax and/or grammar of (v. 2c) οὐ περὶ τῶν ἡμετέρων δὲ μόνον (v. 2d) ἀλλὰ καὶ περὶ ὅλου τοῦ κόσμου. The variants suggest a plurality of grammatical and theological interpretations of 1 John 2:2. Applying the criteria in the Coherence-Based Genealogical Method (CBGM) in the ECM, this paper evaluates the different readings of v. 2c in the textual tradition to see whether μόνον or μονῶν (with or without δέ–καί) is likely to be the initial text.

One of the objectives of textual criticism is to reconstruct,[1] as far as possible, the initial text[2] and to arrive at the appropriate interpretation along with its

A shorter version of this article was presented at the annual meeting of the Society of Biblical Literature in 2012. I am grateful to the anonymous reviewers for *JBL*.

[1] See *Introductory Presentation* by Gerd Mink in http://egora.uni-muenster.de/intf/service/downloads_en.shtml, 9-39. Also Holger Strutwolf states, "The most important task of textual criticism is to reconstruct the original text, or to be more modest: to establish a sound and well-argued hypothesis about the initial text of the transmission of a certain piece of literature that was handed down to posterity via manuscripts" ("Scribal Practices and the Transmission of Biblical Texts: New Insights from the Coherence-Based Genealogical Method," in *Editing the Bible: Assessing the Task Past and Present* [ed. John S. Kloppenborg and Judith H. Newman; SBLRBS 69; Atlanta: Society of Biblical Literature, 2012], 139).

[2] Paul Maas declares that since "we have no autograph manuscripts of the Greek ... and no copies which have been collated with the originals ... the business of textual criticism is to produce a text as close as possible to the original (*constitutio textus*)" (*Textual Criticism* [1927; trans.

theological meaning.³ For 1 John 2:2 the eighth revised printing of Nestle-Aland²⁷ (1994) lists three variants of μονῶν in place of μόνον. Since then more manuscripts have been added to the list. The 2003 *Editio Critica Maior* (ECM) provides nineteen variants, plus lacunae, for μονῶν.⁴ Moreover, the presence of δέ and καί occurs in some manuscripts but not in others. The differences among these variants have the potential of affecting the theological interpretation:⁵ the differences question the editorship of the text; they alter the syntax and/or grammar of (2c) οὐ περὶ τῶν ἡμετέρων δὲ μόνον (2d) ἀλλὰ καὶ περὶ ὅλου τοῦ κόσμου.⁶ Accordingly, various readings are possible: (i) μόνον with δέ–καί; (ii) μόνον without δέ–καί; (iii) μονῶν with δέ–καί; and (iv) μονῶν without δέ–καί. The variants thus suggest a plurality of grammatical and theological interpretations of v. 2.

Applying the criteria of the Coherence-Based Genealogical Method (CBGM)

Barbara Flower; Oxford: Clarendon, 1967], 1). Recent studies on NT textual criticism no longer employ the traditional term "original text." Klaus Wachtel and Michael W. Holmes state in their introduction to *The Textual History of the Greek New Testament: Changing Views in Contemporary Research* (SBL Text-critical Studies 8; Atlanta: Society of Biblical Literature, 2011), "The concept of editing or reconstructing the original is no longer a matter of course" (p. 2). Instead the term "initial text" is used. Gerd Mink defines "initial text" as follows: "The initial text is a hypothetical, reconstructed text, as it presumably existed, according to the hypothesis, before the beginning of its copying" ("Problems of a Highly Contaminated Tradition, the New Testament: Stemmata of Variants as a Source of a Genealogy for Witnesses," in *Studies in Stemmatology II* [ed. Pieter van Reenen, August den Hollander, and Margot van Mulken; Amsterdam: John Benjamins, 2004], 25). According to Mink, "The simplest working hypothesis must be that there are no differences between the original [i.e., authorial] and the initial text" (p. 26). Further, the term "living text" is used by David C. Parker, *The Living Text of the Gospels* (Cambridge: Cambridge University Press, 1997), 203–13. Cf. Bart D. Ehrman, "The Text as Window: New Testament Manuscripts and the Social History of Early Christianity," in *The Text of the New Testament in Contemporary Research: Essays on the 'Status Quaestionis.' A Volume in Honor of Bruce M. Metzger* (ed. Bart D. Ehrman and Michael W. Holmes; SD 46; Grand Rapids: Eerdmans, 1995), 361; and Bart D. Ehrman, "A Problem of Textual Manuscripts," *Bib* 70 (1989): 377–88.

³ Eldon Jay Epp proposes the following: "New Testament textual criticism, employing aspects of both science and art, studies the transmission of the New Testament text and the manuscripts that facilitate its transmission, with the unitary goal of establishing the earliest attainable text (which serves as a baseline) and, at the same time, of assessing the textual variants that emerge from the baseline text so as to hear the narratives of early Christian thought and life that inhere in the array of meaning variants" ("Traditional 'Canons' of New Testament Textual Criticism: Their Value, Validity, and Viability – Or Lack Thereof," in Wachtel and Holmes, *Textual History of the Greek New Testament*, 127).

⁴ The Nestle-Aland 28th edition (2012) compiles the manuscripts for the Catholic Epistles based largely on the ECM.

⁵ Holger Strutwolf, "Original Text and Textual History," in Wachtel and Holmes, *Textual History of the Greek New Testament*, 23–25.

⁶ For convenience, the text of 1 John 2:2 is offered as follows: (a) καὶ αὐτὸς ἱλασμός ἐστιν (b) περὶ τῶν ἁμαρτιῶν ἡμῶν, (c) οὐ περὶ τῶν ἡμετέρων δὲ μόνον (d) ἀλλὰ καὶ περὶ ὅλου τοῦ κόσμου.

compiled from the ECM (tables 6ab in the appendix),[7] this article evaluates the readings of v. 2c in the textual tradition to discover whether μόνον or μονῶν is likely to be the initial text. The use of μόνον or μονῶν stems from the three-ending adjective μόνος, -η, -ον. The absence or presence of δέ and/or καί also affects the readings of the text. Two findings will be presented. First, the variant μόνον cannot be taken as an adjective since it does not modify τῶν ἡμετέρων but functions as an adverb in οὐ περὶ τῶν ἡμετέρων δὲ μόνον ἀλλὰ καὶ περὶ ὅλου τοῦ κόσμου. Second, the variant μονῶν must be taken as an adjective since it agrees in case, number, and gender with τῶν ἡμετέρων.

A text-critical analysis, backed by the CBGM, suggests that δὲ μόνον ἀλλὰ καί is the preferred reading in accordance with the textual tradition for v. 2c. Thus, the variant μονῶν (in B 1 *rell*) is probably due to scribal error.[8]

I. External Criticism

It is important to evaluate the external evidence of μόνον and μονῶν according to the ECM and CBGM.[9] Gerd Mink indicates that "the study of coherence and contamination requires full collation of relevant witnesses."[10] Using the "Text Categories,"[11] the inventories in tables 1abc below are drawn to facilitate the lists

---

[7] See http://www.uni-muenster.de/INTF/Genealogical_method.html for explanation about the CBGM in the ECM; Klaus Wachtel, "The Coherence-Based Genealogical Method: A New Way to Reconstruct the Text of the Greek New Testament," in Kloppenborg and Newman, *Editing the Bible*, 123–38; and D. C. Parker, *An Introduction to the New Testament Manuscripts and Their Texts* (Cambridge: Cambridge University Press, 2008), 169–71. Cf. E. C. Colwell, "Genealogical Method: Its Achievements and Its Limitations," *JBL* 66 (1947): 109–33. At the annual meeting of the SBL in 2012, Bart Ehrman and Michael Holmes verified the growing acceptance of the CBGM as an inevitable method in NT textual criticism (see Ehrman and Holmes, *Text of the New Testament in Contemporary Research*).

[8] Here the specification of manuscripts follows the Gregory-Aland numbers. For explanation, see Kurt Aland and Barbara Aland, *Der Text des Neuen Testaments: Einführung in die wissenschaftlichen Ausgaben sowie in Theorie und Praxis der modernen Textkritik* (Stuttgart: Deutsche Bibelgesellschaft, 1982), 82–190, esp. 83–84; Eng. trans., *The Text of the New Testament: An Introduction to the Critical Editions and to the Theory and Practice of Modern Textual Criticism* (trans. Erroll F. Rhodes; 2nd rev. and enl. ed.; Grand Rapids: Eerdmans, 1995), 72–184, esp. 73–75. Page references throughout the article are to the English translation.

[9] The significance of considering external and internal evidence to reconstruct and recover the initial text is discussed by Michael Holmes, "The Case for Reasoned Eclecticism," in *Rethinking New Testament Textual Criticism* (ed. David Alan Black; Grand Rapid: Baker Academic, 2002), 77–100.

[10] Gerd Mink, "Contamination, Coherence, and Coincidence in Textual Transmission: The Coherence-Based Genealogical Method (CBGM) as a Complement and Corrective to Existing Approaches," in Wachtel and Holmes, *Textual History of the Greek New Testament*, 146.

[11] The expression "Text Categories" is used by Aland and Aland, *Text*, 159–63, 317, 332.

of manuscripts that either support each variant or indicate doubt about each (with or without the omission of καί), respectively.

Table 1a. Variants for μόνον and μονῶν in v. 2c with More Clearly Attested MSS[12]

Readings[13]	Category I Alexandrian	Category II Egyptian	Category III Independent Text	Category IV D (Western) Text	Category V Byzantine Text
μόνον[14]	ℵ(01) A(02) 33C 614[15] 1241 1739 **1832**	C(04) Ψ* 35 81 876 1175 1292 1409 1735 2464	5 6 61 **93** 94 104 180 181 206 218 **252** 254 307 **321** 323 365 378 398 **400** 424Z[16] 429 431 436 442 453 459	720 Clem Cyr Did Or PsOec L:VT K:SB^ptV S:PH A G:A1	K^ap L^ap P^apr 049 0142 18 319 467 607 **665 1729** 1874 2423 L60 **L596** **L921 L938** L1281 L1442

---

[12] Raymond E. Brown indicates that scholars (up until his time of 1982) classified the Johannine Epistles into three main groups: Alexandrian (with three subgroups), Byzantine (seven subgroups), and mixed (three subgroups), covering only eighty-one manuscripts of the Johannine Epistles (*The Epistles of John: Translated, with Introduction, Notes, and Commentary* [AB 30; Garden City, NY: Doubleday, 1982], 129). Since Brown's time, the number of Greek manuscripts has increased to over 5,500, and the ECM 4:3 (2003) lists some 112 manuscripts for 1 John alone and some 540 manuscripts for the Catholic Epistles. In this inventory I use five categories to describe the complexity of different readings of v. 2c. This "Text Categories" is also reflected in the analysis of the Alands' method in the Greek NT by William Larry Richards, "An Analysis of Aland's *Teststellen* in 1 John," *NTS* 44 (1998): 26–44, esp. 40. Richards defines the methodological approach and application of each category. His evaluation of the manuscripts points to some nuances and differences regarding the "Text Categories" in comparison with those of the Alands. Note that Richards's analysis must be checked against what is discussed in Aland and Aland, *Text*, 155–59. Since Richards's study, more manuscripts have been collated in the ECM 4:3.

[13] Compiled on the basis of Kurt Aland, Matthew Black, Carlo M. Martini, Bruce M. Metzger, and Allen Wikgren, eds., *The Greek New Testament* (3rd ed.; Stuttgart: United Bible Societies, 1983), xi–liii; Aland and Aland, *Text*, 73–180, esp. 152–53; and ECM 4:3 in the *Text* and *Supplement Material*; NA²⁷, 684–718; Bruce M. Metzger and Bart D. Ehrman, *The Text of the New Testament: Its Transmission, Corruption, and Restoration* (4th ed.; New York: Oxford University Press, 2005), 52–92, 217.

[14] Boldface numbers indicate manuscripts that have not been cited in the Greek NT prior to the 1984 edition. In the ECM 4:3 they have been collated in the manuscripts for 1 John.

[15] Manuscript 614 is classified as category I by Aland and Aland (*Text*, 330), because it is of significant value for all the Catholic Epistles. Metzger and Ehrman (*Text of the New Testament: Its Transmission*, 310) classify MS 614 as one of the important Western witnesses. Similarly, MS 1832 is classified as "significant" in ECM 4:3.

[16] The double underlining (=) of numbers (33 424 2412) shows the overlapping of the manuscripts that support μόνον and μονῶν.

Table 1a (cont.)

Readings	Category I Alexandrian	Category II Egyptian	Category III Independent Text	Category IV D (Western) Text	Category V Byzantine Text
			522 **617** 621C 623 629 630 642 808(?) 915 918 945 **996** 1067 **1127** **1270 1297** 1359 1448 **1490 1501** 1505* 1523 1524 1563 **1609** 1611* **1661** 1678 1751 1799 **1827 1831** 1836 1842 1844 1845(?) 1852 1874 1875 1881 **1890** 2138 2147 2200 **2243** 2298 2344 2374 2412Z 2492 2541 2652 2744 **2805** **2818**		
μονῶν	B(03) 33*V		1 326 330 424T 621* 1243 1837 2412T 2544	Cyr Or **K**:B^pt **Sl**:ChMSiS	43 468 1595 L1141

Table 1b. Variants for μόνον and μονῶν in v. 2c with Lacunae and Defects

Reading	Category I	Category II	Category III	Category IV	Category V
Both μόνον and μονῶν cannot be determined in MSS	p⁹ p⁷⁴	048* 0245* 0296*(?)	1718 1838 1846 **2186**	Pr	L156 L590 L1126

Table 1c. Variant μόνον with or without καί in v. 2c[17]

Readings	Category I	Category II	Category III	Category IV	Category V
Reading 1 (without καί): οὐ περὶ τῶν ἡμετέρων δὲ μόνον ἀλλὰ περὶ ὅλου τοῦ κόσμου			442 1067	Cyr K:S	
Reading 2 (with καί): οὐ περὶ τῶν ἡμετέρων δὲ μόνον ἀλλὰ καὶ περὶ ὅλου τοῦ κόσμου	Same as in table 1a	Same as in table 1a	Majority text	Not cited by: Clem Cyr Did Eus HesH Or PsOec L:VT K:BV S:PH	
Reading 3 (with lacunae): cannot be determined whether καί is omitted or inserted	p⁹ p⁷⁴	048* 0245* 0296*(?)	1838 1846 **2186**	Pr	L156 L590 L1126

The evaluation of these manuscripts is presupposed as follows by Kurt and Barbara Aland:[18] (a) "None of the methods, however well suited for particular purposes, has offered a reliable and verifiable way of examining the *total* range of known manuscripts [ca. 5,500[19]] and identifying *all* the ones pertinent to a given investigation [ca. 112 MSS for 1 John]."[20] (b) Manuscripts that are important for the Gospels may not, however, be of the same level of significance for the Catholic Epistles.[21] (c) Some "manuscripts are mere copies, repeating the same text with

---

[17] The readings (1 and 2) of μόνον with/without καί in table 1c are produced based on a deductive process in examining the manuscripts for their own variants and the manuscripts (e.g., 442, 1067) and witnesses (e.g., Clem Cyr Did Or PsOes L:VT K:SB^PtV S:PH **A** G:A1) in table 1a. These noted manuscripts support μόνον.

[18] Aland and Aland, *Text*, 317–37.

[19] Cf. "Ein Teil rund 5000 griechischen Manuskripte aus der Zeit vom 2. Jahrhundert nach Christus bis zum Beginn der Neuzeit könnte dank der Evolutionsforscher endlich in einem Familienstammbaum geordnet werden" (*Der Spiegel* 53 [1998] 151).

[20] Aland and Aland, *Text*, 317–18. Also Maas, *Textual Criticism*, 16–21. Aland and Aland's observation echoes the thought of Alfred Edward Housman, "The Application of Thought to Textual Criticism," in idem, *Selected Prose* (ed. John Waynflete Carter; Cambridge: Cambridge University Press, 1961), 131–50.

[21] Aland and Aland, *Text*, 133, 330. So Metzger and Ehrman show that among the so-called Western witnesses, Codex ℵ is one of the most important witnesses for the Gospel (*Text of the*

only minor variation, irrelevant to the reconstruction of the original text, and properly to be eliminated."[22] Accordingly, there is every reason to presume that a number of manuscripts supporting μονῶν are mere copies of those earlier ones (e.g., B and 33*V). If B made a transcriptional mistake from its archetype text, it is likely that its successive manuscripts would repeat the same error.

According to table 1a, the quantitative witnesses indicate that μόνον is more attested than μονῶν.[23] Among the Greek manuscripts shown in categories I, II, III, and V, the earliest ones can be dated back only to the fourth century (e.g., ℵ, A, and B). Many of these contain reliable readings of the NT texts.[24] In this case, the text of v. 2c is included.

Leaving aside the simple issue of the number of witnesses,[25] the overall results for μόνον and μονῶν appear practically equal in quality and weight.[26] While μόνον receives more support from the witnesses in the first, second, and third categories (e.g., ℵ, A, and 614), μονῶν is attested by the so-called primary authority from Codex B (see table 1a).[27] The closeness in quality can be further demonstrated by

---

New Testament: Its Transmission, 310–13). But for Acts MS 614 is considered the more important one.

[22] Aland and Aland, *Text*, 321.

[23] See Aland et al., *Greek New Testament*, xi–liii; also Metzger and Ehrman, *Text of the New Testament: Its Transmission*, 216–18.

[24] See Bart D. Ehrman, "The Use and Significance of Patristic Evidence for NT Textual Criticism," in *New Testament Textual Criticism, Exegesis, and Church History: A Discussion of Methods* (ed. Barbara Aland and Joël Delobel; CBET 7; Kampen: Kok Pharos, 1994), 118–35.

[25] See the discussion on the "Quantitative Method" by E. C. Colwell and E. W. Tune, "The Quantitative Relationships between MS Text-types," in *Biblical and Patristic Studies in Memory of Robert Pierce Casey* (ed. J. Neville Birdsall and Robert W. Thomson; Freiburg: Herder, 1963), 25–32; reprinted as "Method in Establishing Quantitative Relationships between Text-types of New Testament Manuscripts," in Ernest Cadman Colwell, *Studies in Methodology in Textual Criticism in the New Testament* (NTTS 9; Grand Rapids: Eerdmans 1969), 56–62. See also E. C. Colwell, "The Significance of Grouping of New Testament Manuscripts," *NTS* 4 (1958): 73–92; and a response to Colwell by Klaus Wachtel, "Colwell Revisited: Grouping New Testament Manuscripts," in *The New Testament Text in Early Christianity: Proceedings of the Lille Colloquium, July 2000* (ed. Christian-B. Amphoux and J. Keith Elliott; Histoire du texte biblique 6; Lausanne: Zèbre, 2003), 31–43.

[26] With regard to 1 John we find the following observations: Metzger and Ehrman judge that the "primary" authorities of the manuscripts are Codex B and the Syriac versions; that the secondary authorities include ℵ, early Greek lectionaries, the Coptic witnesses, and some Syriac versions; and that the tertiary authority consists of Codex C and 33 (*Text of the New Testament: Its Transmission*, 217). Aland and Aland suggest that category I (cf. Metzger's "primary" authority) contains the manuscripts of a "very" special quality, which should always be considered in establishing the initial text; that category II (Metzger's secondary authority) shows the manuscripts of a "special" quality for evaluating the initial text; and that category III indicates the manuscripts of a "distinctive" character also for evaluating the initial text (*Text*, 155–56).

[27] Caution should be the guiding principle. One has to take into consideration the criteria suggested by Metzger and Aland/Aland that the intended directions of these criteria are fixed

the fact that lacunae from their respective readings are found in papyri and manuscripts of all five categories, especially in the first, second, and third (see table 1b). The equal footing and condition of the two variants suggest that preference for the initial text can hardly be established based on the examination of the external evidence.

However, the matter seems to resolve itself when we examine the possible omission of καί presented in table 1c. In this sense, it is necessary to test each variant in table 1a in parallel with the omission of καί in table 1c, always keeping in mind the lacunae and defects shown in table 1b and reading 3 in table 1c.

Manuscripts Supporting μονῶν

Μονῶν is attested by Codex B (a fourth-century majuscule), which Bruce Metzger, Kurt Aland, and Barbara Aland consider the "primary" authority among manuscripts.[28] Based on the CBGM, Codex B results in an imperfect coherence in the textual flow for v. 2c (see table 6b). Beside this single most important witness, some reservations accompany μονῶν (table 1a). First, the ninth-century MS 33, which reads μονῶν and has been considered by Metzger[29] as the "tertiary" authority, but by Aland and Aland[30] as the first category, is listed with two symbols "*" and "V."[31] The symbol "*" indicates that the reading has suffered from "successive" corrections. The text may have been erased, defaced, or marked for deletion in the initial text. The symbol "V" indicates that μονῶν in MS 33 has been recorded by a church father. Second, the eleventh-century MS 424 is accompanied by the symbol "T"; thus, the critical apparatus in ECM presents μονῶν as an "alternative" reading for μόνον. Third, the same symbol "T" accompanies the twelfth-century MS 2412, which supports μονῶν.

Based on these symbols, therefore, the variant μονῶν in table 1a suggests multiple layers of redaction in the textual transmission before its final form in some

---

much more on the evaluation of the Gospels and some of the undisputed Pauline letters than on the Catholic Epistles. This is especially the case when attention to 1 John by Christian writers did not come about until the first part of the second century, while attention to the Gospels was much earlier. Thus, for example, Metzger and Ehrman warn, "Not all of these criteria are applicable in every case. The critic must know when it is appropriate to give primary consideration to one type of evidence and not to another" (*Text of the New Testament: Its Transmission*, 304). In this regard, the point of the entire process of evaluating the initial text is to avoid at all cost the one-sided and/or oversimplified attention to any one manuscript over and against the other(s). This ancillary discipline is endorsed by Epp, who says, "In the final analysis, therefore, the exegete is the arbiter in textual-critical decisions" ("Traditional 'Canons,'" 125).

[28] Metzger and Ehrman, *Text of the New Testament: Its Transmission*, 217. In addition, Aland and Aland judge that, among the important manuscripts such as B ℵ A C, "B is by far the most significant of the uncials" (*Text*, 106–7).

[29] Metzger and Ehrman, *Text of the New Testament: Its Transmission*, 217.

[30] Aland and Aland, *Text*, 107, 129, 155.

[31] See the loose-leaf insert in ECM 4:3 for abbreviations and symbols.

manuscripts (33 424 2412). Moreover, these same manuscripts support μόνον (see the underlining [=] of witnesses in table 1a). We now turn to the external evidence of μόνον in v. 2c.

Manuscripts Supporting μόνον

Μόνον is supported not by the "primary" but by the "secondary" authority (e.g., ℵ A).[32] According to the CBGM, the parent manuscript for μόνον is 617 (see table 6a). Μόνον receives strong support from those manuscripts of the first and second categories by Aland and Aland[33] and tertiary authority by Metzger[34] (C Ψ* 35 81 2464). This is not the case for μονῶν. For Aland and Aland, the manuscripts of the first and second categories are of "very special" or "special" quality in establishing the initial text. For Metzger, the authority of manuscripts has to do with the traceable geographical distribution of ancient local texts. Moreover, Mink shows that in the CBGM "a *hypothetical witness 'A'* was assigned to the hypothetical initial text."[35] This means that the lost archetype witness "*A*" is the parent manuscript for 617. From here the genealogy of 617 continues to 1799, yielding a perfect coherence in the textual flow for v. 2c (see table 6a).[36]

From these criteria, it is likely that μόνον gains priority of better readings. Moreover, we notice three manuscripts (33 424 2412) that overlap in the reading between μονῶν and μόνον. These deserve attention. First, in its support of μόνον, MS 33 is accompanied by the symbol "C." In the ECM, "C" indicates that the text has undergone corrections but not serious ones. The other two manuscripts, 424 and 2412, have the symbol "Z." While "Z" is coordinated with "T" in the case of μονῶν, the former displays a reading that has neither undergone corrections nor is an alternative reading. This implies that the text has received some redaction in its transmission. In comparison with μονῶν, one can say that the redaction for μόνον is relatively minor.

A careful examination of manuscripts hitherto suggests that the external evidence favors μόνον. Yet this evaluation cannot be securely grounded because μονῶν is attested by Codex B. Thus, a firmer answer requires us to go a step beyond μονῶν and/or μόνον. In what follows, therefore, I consider the variant usage of the conjunction καί in v. 2d.

Manuscripts Reading καί

In table 1c, the manuscripts in the first and second categories witness καί. This attestation may imply that the scribes found significant difference in the presence

---

[32] Metzger and Ehrman, *Text of the New Testament: Its Transmission*, 217.
[33] Aland and Aland, *Text*, 106–7, 116, 129, 155.
[34] Metzger and Ehrman, *Text of the New Testament: Its Transmission*, 217.
[35] See http://intf.uni-muenster.de/cbgm/guide_en.html.
[36] See Wachtel, "Coherence-Based Genealogical Method," 123–38.

(not omission) of καί. Moreover, upon further examination of the witnesses in table 1c, μόνον receives considerable support. Two factors stand out.

First, while reading 1 omits καί in table 1c, 442 and 1067 in category III appear among the manuscripts in table 1a. Yet, in table 1a, both 442 and 1067 advocate μόνον. Such is not the case for μονῶν in table 1c in conjunction with table 1a. This calls to mind the position of Aland and Aland that, in case of the absence of the manuscripts in categories I and II, those in category III are "of a distinctive character with an independent text, usually important for establishing the initial text, but particularly important for the history of the text."[37] In tables 1a and 1c, both 442 and 1067 support μόνον over against μονῶν.

Second, reading 2 in table 1c, while citing καί, is supported by a number of ancient versions in category IV (e.g., Clem Cyr Did). All of these adduced from table 1a support μόνον. Again, μονῶν does not receive this attestation in table 1c in comparison with table 1a. The manuscripts reading καί thus confirm μόνον to be the preferred reading.

In short, the external evidence suggests that μόνον is a better reading than μονῶν. This conclusion is based on two assessments. First, μόνον receives stronger support than μονῶν based on categories I, II, and III. Second, while the "level" of authority shows cautions in comparing the two variants, μόνον is further strengthened by the manuscripts reading καί. We may now turn to the internal evidence.

II. Internal Criticism

Which reading is likely to have been the initial text and which is likely to have been produced by the scribes? I will use two broad criteria to evaluate μόνον and μονῶν, namely, transcriptional probability and intrinsic probability.[38] Thus, the following will address the issue surrounding the transmission of the text, the style, the syntax, and the intention of the author.[39]

---

[37] Aland and Aland, *Text*, 155; cf. Metzger and Ehrman, *Text of the New Testament: Its Transmission*, 217.

[38] See Joël Delobel, "Textual Criticism and Exegesis: Siamese Twins?" in Aland and Delobel, *New Testament Textual Criticism, Exegesis, and Church History*, 97–117. I have elsewhere applied Delobel's hypothesis; see my "'That You May Not Sin': On the Reading of 1 John 2,1b," *ZNW* 102 (2011): 77–95.

[39] This observation is related to the fact that $\mathfrak{p}^9$, $\mathfrak{p}^{74}$, and 048* did not contain the text in question or had it in a defective form. The process of transmission of the text and the syntax of the initial word may have caused such a change between μόνον and μονῶν.

Transcriptional Probability

Transcriptional probability primarily concerns the likelihood that the scribe changed μόνον to μονῶν.[40] Changes made to the initial text can be intentional or unintentional and can be introduced for various reasons.[41] Joël Delobel notes, "Whenever an explanation of a particular reading on the level of transcriptional probability presupposes a deliberate change by the scribe, there is a great deal of hypothetical construction involved, because the textual critic has to imagine what the scribe's intention might have been."[42] The statistics of μόνον and μονῶν in the NT facilitate our analysis.

Tables 2a and 2b show minor difference if we closely compare the occurrences of μόνον (66x) and μονῶν (52x) in the NT. In 1 John μόνον is used more frequently than μονῶν for two reasons. First, the three-ending adjective μόνος, -η, -ον, ον never occurs in the genitive plural μονῶν. In fact, the NT does not employ the genitive case, masculine, feminine, or neuter.[43] In the Johannine writings, the absence of μονῶν suggests a high probability against the scribe's changing the more frequent usage of μόνον to the rare occurrence of the feminine genitive plural μονῶν. Second, the genitive plural μονῶν does not occur, while the adverb μόνον occurs five times in John. The usage of the adjective μόνος, -η, -ον in John corresponds to less than one percent (ca. 0.33 percent) of the NT occurrences (52x), while the adverb μόνον is more frequent (5 percent). At this point, then, the uses of μόνον and μονῶν specifically in 1 John require our close attention.

---

[40] Caution is required in the examination of transcriptional probability. Thus, Strutwolf advises that "we have to distinguish between the behavior of individual scribes and the overall tendencies of the textual history in general" ("Scribal Practices," 147). So also Parker says, "One has to distinguish between the habits of individual manuscripts and the habits of textual histories" (*New Testament Manuscripts*, 296).

[41] For different reasons for transcriptional changes, see Metzger and Ehrman, *Text of the New Testament: Its Transmission*, 250–57.

[42] Delobel, "Textual Criticism," 111.

[43] Grammatically there are ten cases (five in singular and five in plural) and three genders (masculine, feminine, and neuter) for the three-ending adjective μόνος, -η, -ον. The number of cases further multiplies itself by virtue of the cases in each gender respectively (thus 30). If one divides the fifty-two occurrences of this adjective into its various cases and genders (30) and compares them with the sixty-six occurrences of μόνον (one single adverb form), then the chance for the genitive masculine plural μονῶν to be employed in v. 2c is very small (1.7 percent). This percentage for μονῶν is relatively low compared to the chances for the adverb μόνον to occur in v. 2c (66 percent).

Table 2a. List of μόνος (as Adjective) and μόνον (as Adverb) in the NT[44]

μόνος, -η, -ον (52 Adjectival Uses)								μόνον (66 Adverbial Uses)								
Gospels (30x)				Acts	Paul	Heb/Rev	Catholic Letters (5x)			Gospels (15x)				Acts	Paul	Heb	Catholic Letters (5x)		
Mt	Mk	Lk	Jn	1	14	2	1 Jn	2 Jn	Jud	Mt	Mk	Lk	Jn	8	36	2	Ja	1 Pe	1 Jn
7	4	9	10				2(?)	1	2	7	2	1	5				2	1	2(?)

Table 2b. List of μόνος (as Adjective) and μόνον (as Adverb) in the Johannine Writings

Readings	Gospel	1 John	2 John
μόνος, -η, -ον (as adjective)	10 different cases (5:44; 6:15, 22; 8:9, 16, 29; 12:24; 16:32 [2x]; 17:3), but never with μονῶν as genitive plural	With μονῶν 2:2c (?) With μόνῳ in 5:6, but also disputed with μόνον (?)	V. 1: καὶ οὐκ ἐγὼ μόνος
μόνον (adverb)	5 times (5:18; 11:52; 12:9; 13:9; 17:20)	2:2c (?) 5:6 (?)	None
μονῶν (as genitive plural) in the NT	None, except the disputed case in 1 John 2:2c (?)		

Transcription from μονῶν to μόνον

The μον- stem occurs only twice in 1 John (2:2; 5:6) and has textual variants in both cases.

Table 3. External Evidence for μονῶν and μόνον in 2:2; 5:6[45]

Readings	Category I	Category II	Category III	Category IV	Category V
μονῶν	B	81^vid	**1837** 1844	None	None
μόνον	ℵ A 33	C Ψ* **35** 2464	**617** and Majority text	Except: PsOec Cry **L**:KVT S:H	None

---

[44] Statistics are taken from W. F. Moulton and A. S. Geden, *Concordance to the Greek New Testament* (6th ed.; ed. I. H. Marshall; London: T&T Clark, 2002), 707–9.

[45] Compiled from NA[28] and ECM 4:3. See the explanation in the critical apparatus of ECM for signs, symbols, and abbreviations regarding the variants in 1 John 5:6.

When we evaluate the transcriptional probability in table 3, it is rather difficult to make a strong argument for either usage; there are not enough examples of the μον- stem in 1 John. To discover a possible solution we must expand our search to neighboring words surrounding 2:2.

Table 4. Different Readings with/without δέ in v. 2cd

Readings	Supporting Manuscripts	
r 1: οὐ περὶ τῶν ἡμετέρων δὲ μόνον	Majority text, except the following: 43f1 330f1 630f2 Clem Cyr Did Eus Or PsOec S:H A G:A1 S:ChMSiS	All with μόνον
r 2: οὐ περὶ δὲ τῶν ἡμετέρων μόνον	2138	
r 3: οὐ περὶ τῶν ἡμετέρων δή μόνον	1241	
r 4: οὐ περὶ τῶν ἡμετέρων μόνον	614 2412f K:S^msV	

Let us examine δέ in table 4. We notice four readings: two place δέ in different positions: one has a postpositive particle δή instead of δέ, and one has none of these. In reading 1, supported by important manuscripts, δέ seems to stand in an odd position with μονῶν. While δέ is a postpositive conjunction, its place in the clause or sentence usually does not interrupt the attributive positions of an adjective modifying a noun (e.g., here ἡμετέρων δὲ μονῶν).[46] Blass and Debrunner argue that, unless δέ precedes an adverb "partly because of necessity, as in 1 John 2:2 οὐ περὶ τῶν ἡμετέρων δὲ μόνον,"[47] it often takes the first position in a subordinate clause.[48] This is indeed the case in reading 2, where δέ precedes τῶν ἡμετέρων. Furthermore, reading 2 is supported by MS 2138 (a category III manuscript of the eleventh century),[49] which also supports μόνον (see table 1a). When we juxtapose readings 1 and 2, the placement of words implies that μονῶν would be rather an odd reading as compared to μόνον.

Reading 3 with δή is attested by only 1241.[50] Here δή means "in fact" or "of course" with a sense of exhortation or an imperative.[51] Since only a twelfth-century manuscript (1241[52]) reads v. 2cd with δή, it is safe to say that this reading is weak

---

[46] Hardy Hansen and Gerald M. Quinn, *Greek: An Intensive Course* (2nd rev. ed.; New York: Fordham University Press, 1992), 92–93, 103, 147, 213, 217. Cf. A. T. Robertson, *A Grammar of the Greek New Testament in the Light of Historical Research* (4th ed.; Nashville: Broadman, 1934), 424, 1185.

[47] BDF, §475; cf. also §§442, 443(1), 447, 462(1).

[48] Explanation and usage of δέ in classical Greek are found in Raphael Kühner and Bernhard Gerth, *Ausführliche Grammatik der griechischen Sprache*, vol. 2, *Satzlehre* (1898; Darmstadt: Wissenschaftliche Buchgesellschaft, 1966), 267–68.

[49] Aland and Aland, *Text*, 134.

[50] Hansen and Quinn, *Greek*, 71.

[51] BDAG, s.v., δή.

[52] Aland and Aland, *Text*, 132.

and probably a transcriptional error. This finds support in the CBGM (table 6a below), where it is clear that 1241 has no further genealogy. Note that, while this reading may be due to a scribal mistake, it also supports μόνον.

Finally, reading 4, which has neither δέ nor δή, is supported by 614 2412f and Coptic versions (K:S^msV). A careful evaluation however shows that reading 4 still favors μόνον over μονῶν for three reasons. First, while 2412 omits δέ and δή, the reading suffers a symbol indicating a defect (symbol "f").[53] Moreover, 2412 through the external criticism demonstrates no support for either μονῶν (symbol "T") or μόνον (symbol "Z"). The absence of δέ or δή here suggests no significant changes in meaning. Second, 614 supports μόνον (table 1a).[54] Combining reading 4 in table 4 and μόνον in table 1a, the supposed text for v. 2c should thus be τῶν ἡμετέρων μόνον. In this reading, μόνον is clearly rendered as an adverb, not an adjective. Third, Coptic versions (K:S^msV) also read μόνον (table 1a). Together with reading 4 in table 4, the Coptic versions likewise attest to τῶν ἡμετέρων μόνον.

Overall, it is quite unlikely that a transcription occurs from μονῶν to μόνον. Indeed, the probability for μονῶν to have been the initial reading becomes increasingly difficult. The evidence shows strong support for μόνον. The following diagram demonstrates the transcriptional error by the scribe.[55] Graph 1 concerns whether a certain scribe committed an intentional or unintentional error between Ο and Ω.[56]

Graph 1. Transcriptional Error by One Letter *omicron* (Ο) or *omega* (Ω)

This mistake is possibly the result of a questionable reading. "In some cases," Delobel argues, "the scribe wanted to eliminate a 'lectio difficilior'.... He may have corrected an apparent *inconsistency* in the text."[57] In v. 2c the phrase οὐ περὶ τῶν

---

[53] See the critical apparatus and explanation of the symbols in ECM 4:3 and NA[28].

[54] See my "'That You May Not Sin,'" 80–82, for reasons why 614 is considered a "control manuscript" for 1 John.

[55] According to Metzger and Ehrman, the transcriptional probabilities depend on the considerations of paleographical details and the habits of scribes (*Text of the New Testament: Its Transmission*, 302–3). See also Bruce M. Metzger, *A Textual Commentary on the Greek New Testament: A Companion Volume to the United Bible Societies' Greek New Testament (Fourth ed.)* (2nd ed.; Stuttgart: Deutsche Bibelgesellschaft, 1994), 12–14*.

[56] Delobel observes, "Whenever an explanation of a particular reading on the level of transcriptional probability presupposes a deliberate change by the scribe, there is a great deal of hypothetical construction involved, because the textual critic has to imagine what the scribe's intention might have been. However ... these deliberate changes by scribes are to be distinguished from passages that they 'corrected' by guess-work" ("Textual Criticism," 111).

[57] Ibid., 108.

ἡμετέρων μόνον (without δέ; see reading 4 in table 4 and the supporting MSS 614 2412f **K**:S^msV) displays an inconsistency between τῶν ἡμετέρων and μόνον. Note the following graphs:

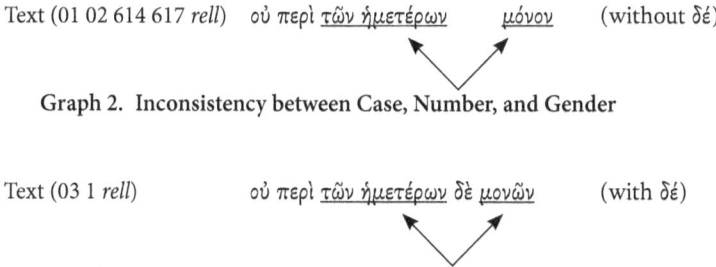

Graph 2. Inconsistency between Case, Number, and Gender

Graph 3. Consistency between Case, Number, and Gender

If we suppose that μόνον is the initial reading, some observations can be made with regard to μονῶν in the cited manuscripts. First, there seems to be an assimilation of one letter at the end of the μον- stem. In the uncials, the difference between an unaccented MONON and MONΩN is easily overlooked, and so could easily result in a mistake in the transcription. There might have been a lacuna in the parent manuscript (i.e., 03 1 *rell*), in which case the scribe would have to make his own decision in filling the lacuna.[58] Second, errors may well be the result of faulty hearing of words that are phonetically similar to one another. The shift from *omicron* (μόνο̲ν) to *omega* (μονῶ̲ν) could easily result from such scribal confusion, thus supporting μονῶν.

This having been said, we must consider the opposite transcription: from μόνον to μονῶν.

Transcription from μόνον to μονῶν

If the initial text was μόνον and was changed to μονῶν by the scribe (03 and *rell*) (see table 1a), he must have changed μόνον to μονῶν out of carelessness.[59] There are some grammatical issues related to μόνον. 1 John 2:2c is not a full sentence but

---

[58] Delobel indicates that "*transcriptional* probability takes into account the possibility of an intentional change as a result of the scribe's own 'exegesis'" ("Textual Criticism," 105).

[59] According to David Trobisch, one can hardly establish any so-called final edition of the NT, because "the evidence provided by the extant manuscripts indicates that the history of the New Testament is the history of an edition.... The term *final redaction* [or final edition used with regard to anthology] ... designates editorial elements that serve to combine individual writings into a larger literary unit and are not original components of the collected traditional material" (*The First Edition of the New Testament* [Oxford: Oxford University Press, 2000], 8–9). Similarly Mink notes, "Philological plausibility is the criterion in instances in which the question of the origin of a variant is definitely left open" ("Contamination, Coherence, and Coincidence," 204). Cf. Maas's comment in n. 2 above.

only a prepositional phrase introduced by περί. As such, the word order is vital, especially in some attributive positions.[60] While word order in Greek enjoys more freedom than in some modern languages, "there are, nevertheless, certain tendencies and habits in the NT especially in narrative which have created something like *a normal word order*."[61] In addition, the presence of δέ is necessary in this particular instance, not only to strengthen the meaning of the phrase but also to follow successively the structure of v. 2a.[62] In v. 2a the author speaks of Jesus as ἱλασμός for (περί) sins. In the construction οὐ μόνον, ἀλλὰ καί, the presence of δέ as a supporting word to connect the thoughts in v. 2abc catches our attention. The Greek sentence can be introduced in English by the structure "not only, but also." An example occurs in John 17:20, in which Jesus prays not only for his own, but also for those who believe through his words.[63]

The question is where δέ should stand. As the variants of v. 2c indicate (see readings 1 and 2 in table 4), δέ stands in pre- or postposition to τῶν ἡμετέρων. The interchanges of δέ neither affect the grammatical features nor suggest a new meaning in οὐ περὶ τῶν ἡμετέρων δὲ μόνον.[64] However, if the variant is for μονῶν, then the postposition of δέ to τῶν ἡμετέρων will affect its syntax and imply certain theological nuances.[65] This variant interferes with the attributive positions of τῶν ἡμετέρων and μονῶν. The fact that Codex B (and *rell*) reads μονῶν and has δέ as a postposition to τῶν ἡμετέρων and an antecedent to μονῶν (see table 1a and reading 1 in table 4) indicates that the scribe was possibly confused in placing δέ in that position (see graph 3). In so doing, however, he seems to have been mistaken about the intervention of δέ in the attributive positions between τῶν ἡμετέρων and μονῶν. Such an error could also be due to confusion of the adjective μονῶν with the adverb μόνον.

---

[60] See the discussion on word order in Greek in C. F. D. Moule, *An Idiom-Book of New Testament Greek* (2nd ed.; Cambridge: Cambridge University Press, 1977), 166–70; James Hope Moulton, *A Grammar of New Testament Greek*, vol. 3, *Syntax*, by Nigel Turner (Edinburgh: T&T Clark, 1963), 344–50; and Maximilian Zerwick, *Biblical Greek* (8th ed.; trans. Joseph Smith; Scripta Pontificii Instituti Biblici 114; Rome: Biblical Institute Press, 2005), §467. See also the discussion by Robertson, *Grammar*, 424; and Hansen and Quinn, *Greek*, 92–93, 103, 147, 213, 217.

[61] BDF, §472 (emphasis added); see also §§473–78.

[62] Ibid., §475; and Turner, *Syntax*, 331–33.

[63] John 17:20 reads, Οὐ περὶ τούτων δὲ ἐρωτῶ μόνον, ἀλλὰ καὶ περὶ τῶν πιστευόντων διὰ τοῦ λόγου αὐτῶν εἰς ἐμέ. Cf. 2 John 1, which reads, καὶ οὐκ ἐγὼ μόνος ἀλλὰ καὶ πάντες οἱ ἐγνωκότες τὴν ἀλήθειαν. In all of the Johannine writings, John 17:20 comes closest to 1 John 2:2c in structural use of οὐ μόνον ἀλλὰ καί. For examples of this construction in the NT, see BDAG, 659 (2); and Klaus Beyer, *Semitische Syntax im Neuen Testament* (SUNT 1; Göttingen: Vandenhoeck & Ruprecht, 1962), 126–29. See also J. Ramsey Michaels, *The Gospel of John* (NICNT; Grand Rapids: Eerdmans, 2010), 874–76.

[64] Robertson notes that "these words [ἄν, γάρ, γε, δέ, μέν, μέντοι, οὖν, and τε] vary in position according to the point to be made in relation to other words" (*Grammar*, 424).

[65] See the section below on "Intrinsic Probability."

There are two factors that support this argument. First, Turner has defended the possibility that "there is therefore not surprisingly some confusion of μόνος with the adverb μόνον."[66] This observation is reasonable. The three-ending adjective μόνος, -η, -ον, occasionally has identical case endings in the singular and plural. They occur not only in the masculine accusative but also in the neuter nominative, accusative, and vocative cases (μόνον). Further, the adverb μόνον is derived from, and is identical with, the neuter singular.[67] The second possibility is simply that the scribe was not well versed in Greek grammar and thus was unable to see the syntactical difference between μόνον and μονῶν. He could have plausibly committed a transcriptional mistake by changing the adverb μόνον to the adjective μονῶν (graphs 1–3).

In short, the transcriptional probabilities suggest that μονῶν is unlikely to have been the initial reading. The interchanges of δέ make more probable the case that μόνον was the actual reading. The attestation of μονῶν in some manuscripts is a transcriptional error resulting from faulty hearing by a scribe. Having thus discussed the transcriptional probability, in what follows I consider the intrinsic probability.

Intrinsic Probability

Which variant might originate with the author?[68] Here we assume that 2:1–2 is a textual unit within 1 John.[69] This having been said, I now turn to discussion of the theological issues concerning μονῶν and μόνον with δέ.

Reading Using μονῶν together with δέ

The particle δέ appears 2,768 times in the NT and nine times in 1 John. By frequency of times per 1,000 words, δέ occurs only 4.2 times in 1 John compared

---

[66] Turner, *Syntax*, 225–26.

[67] A particular example occurs in 1 John 5:6 (cf. 2:2c). The same manuscripts (e.g., Codex B) support μονῶν, while the majority of the manuscripts read μόνον. BDAG (659 [2]) notes that it is very common in the NT that as "a marker of limitation, *only*, *alone*, the neuter μόνον [is] being used as an adverb ... limiting the action or state to the one designated by the verb." Cf. Robertson, *Grammar*, 294–95.

[68] Delobel says, "In an evenly balanced text-critical method, the examination on the level of intrinsic probability, i.e., exegesis, has to play an essential role.... Which of the readings fits best within the style, the vocabulary, the theology of the author? Content and context are examined" ("Textual Criticism," 98, 102, respectively). In "'That You May Not Sin,'" I argue that "the impetus of examining the intrinsic probability rests on the author of, and his intention for, the text" (p. 87). See also Metzger and Ehrman, *Text of the New Testament: Its Transmission*, 302–4.

[69] The reason for this assumption is that Rudolf Bultmann argues in his source hypothesis that 1 John 2:1–2 was not composed by the author. See his "Analyse des ersten Johannesbriefes," in *Festgabe für Adolf Jülicher zum 70. Geburtstag, 26. Januar 1927* (Tübingen: Mohr, 1927), 141.

with 20.2 times in the overall NT.⁷⁰ In coping with the possibility that John may or may not have composed μονῶν together with δέ, it is helpful to list the instances of δέ.

Table 5. Occurrences of δέ in 1 John

1:3 καὶ ἡ κοινωνία <u>δὲ</u> ἡ ἡμετέρα	3:12 τὰ <u>δὲ</u> τοῦ ἀδελφοῦ αὐτοῦ δίκαια
1:7 ἐὰν <u>δὲ</u> ἐν τῷ φωτὶ περιπατῶμεν	4:18 ὁ <u>δὲ</u> φοβούμενος οὐ τετελείωται
2:2c οὐ περὶ τῶν ἡμετέρων <u>δὲ</u> <u>μόνον</u> or <u>μονῶν</u> (?)	5:5 τίς [<u>δέ</u>] ἐστιν ὁ νικῶν τὸν κόσμον
2:11 ὁ <u>δὲ</u> μισῶν τὸν ἀδελφὸν αὐτοῦ	5:20 οἴδαμεν <u>δὲ</u> ὅτι
2:17 ὁ <u>δὲ</u> ποιῶν τὸ θέλημα τοῦ θεοῦ	

As table 5 suggests, in 1 John δέ never interrupts an attributive construction; moreover, it never occurs immediately preceding or following an adjective without a definite article.⁷¹ Only in 1:3 does δέ stand between a noun and an adjective.⁷² However, this reading obviously follows the tendencies of the normal word order; namely, the article ἡ is used to make clear that ἡ ἡμετέρα stands in one of the normal attributive positions with ἡ κοινωνία.⁷³

The question, therefore, becomes how one renders δέ and μονῶν in the phrase οὐ περὶ τῶν ἡμετέρων δὲ μονῶν.⁷⁴ Two points stand out. First, in comparison with 1:3 above, the correct grammar would require τῶν in 2:2c, so that τῶν μονῶν could

---

⁷⁰ Statistics come from Robert Morgenthaler, *Statistik des neutestamentlichen Wortschatzes* (Zurich: Gotthelf, 1958), 164.

⁷¹ BDF, §472; also §§473–78.

⁷² The critical apparatus in the ECM 4:3 indicates that there is some textual problem regarding ἡ κοινωνία δὲ ἡ ἡμετέρα in 1 John 1:3. Only one manuscript, 378 (twelfth century), shows the omission of ἡ. In fact, some manuscripts support the omission of δέ. With or without δέ, therefore, the reading in 1 John 1:3 neither affects the structure of the phrase nor suggests significant theological implications. See the different readings with/without δέ and/or ἡ in 1 John 1:3 below:

Readings	Supporting Manuscripts
r 1: ἡ κοινωνία <u>δὲ</u> ἡ ἡμετέρα μετὰ τοῦ πατρὸς	Majority text, including 01 02 03
r 2: ἡ κοινωνία ἡ ἡμετέρα μετὰ τοῦ πατρὸς	04 1241
r 3: ἡ κοινωνία <u>δὲ</u> ἡμετέρα μετὰ τοῦ πατρὸς	378

In r 1, Codex B (03) is the same manuscript that supports δὲ μονῶν in v. 2c. In r 2, MS 1241 is the same witness that attests to δή in v. 2c. Certainly there is error resulting in faulty hearing between δέ and δή committed by the scribe of MS 1241. In r 3, an argument can be made based on haplography, that is, the omission of ἡ because of the postposition of δέ in this context (ΔΕΗΜΕΤΕΡΑ for δὲ ἡμετέρα).

⁷³ See Hansen and Quinn, *Greek*, 92–93, 103, 147, 213, 217; BDF, §§269–72; and Turner, *Syntax*, 185, 217.

⁷⁴ BDAG, 659 (2), s.v. μόνος as adverb, provides various uses of δὲ μόνον in the NT.

be seen as parallel with τῶν ἡμετέρων.⁷⁵ In this regard, the position of δέ, whether it precedes or succeeds τῶν ἡμετέρων, would not be considered grammatically unusual. Second, the reading οὐ περὶ τῶν ἡμετέρων δὲ <u>τῶν</u> μονῶν does not occur elsewhere in the NT. Also at stake is how one translates μονῶν as a modifying adjective to τῶν ἡμετέρων in οὐ μόνον ἀλλὰ καί.⁷⁶ In the Johannine writings, the closest parallel to 1 John 2:2c in this construction occurs in John 17:20.⁷⁷ There are, however, differences in these places. In John 17:20, οὐ μόνον ἀλλὰ καί is used to introduce a complete sentence. Certainly one must read μόνον in John 17:20 as an adverb. Yet, in 1 John 2:2c, this usage occurs in a prepositional phrase; its meaning can only be completed in relation to the main clause in v. 2ab.

Moreover, elsewhere in NT, μονῶν is not employed as an alternative for the adverb μόνον in οὐ μόνον ἀλλὰ καί. Thus, if the variant in v. 2c is μονῶν, the reading of v. 2abcd faces difficulty. Verse 2 cannot be rendered smoothly without some modifications: "and he [Jesus] is the expiation for our sins, but/and [δέ] not for ours alone [μονῶν/adjective], but also for the whole world."⁷⁸ The adjective here would render the construction of v. 2cd irregular; the use of μονῶν does not fit well in οὐ μόνον ἀλλὰ καί.⁷⁹ We need to admit that μονῶν in postposition to an adjective is possible, as in 2 John 1. However, μόνος in 2 John 1 is in a nominal sentence, accommodating a nominative adjective as its predicate.⁸⁰

If μονῶν is the intended text, its presence in οὐ μόνον ἀλλὰ καί would be grammatically unusual. In this sense the literal translation would have to be modified in order for the text to flow well with the rest of v. 2. This makes μονῶν together with δέ quite unlikely to have been the initial text.

Reading Using μόνον together with δέ

According to NA²⁸, v. 2 reads: (a) καὶ αὐτὸς ἱλασμός ἐστιν (b) περὶ τῶν ἁμαρτιῶν ἡμῶν, (c) οὐ περὶ τῶν ἡμετέρων δὲ μόνον (d) ἀλλὰ καὶ περὶ ὅλου τοῦ κόσμου. Scholars have indicated the irregular use of δέ in this instance. For example, I. Howard Marshall notices that the oddity of δέ at the end of v. 2c causes an "ultimately inadequate" expression of the paradox of the advocacy and efficacy of Jesus.⁸¹ Similarly for J. L. Houlden, "It comes then as something of a surprise when we read that Christ is the offering not only for the sins of the Christians, but for the whole

---

⁷⁵ Of all the 112 manuscripts collated and compiled by the ECM 4:3, there has not yet been any textual variant indicating the presence of τῶν preceding μονῶν.

⁷⁶ For further discussion of this translation, see my article, "Does περὶ ὅλου τοῦ κόσμου Imply 'the sins of the whole world' in 1 John 2:2?" *Bib* 94 (2013): 415–35.

⁷⁷ See Brown, *Epistles of John*, 222. See n. 63 above.

⁷⁸ I am stressing the modifying quality of the adjective μονῶν for τῶν ἡμετέρων.

⁷⁹ Brown notes, "If there is a grammatical irregularity in these two *peri* phrases of 2:2, it is that the object of the first is 'our sins,' while the object of the second is 'the whole world'—a seeming mixture of things and people" (*Epistles of John*, 222).

⁸⁰ 2 John 1 reads καὶ οὐκ ἐγὼ μόνος ἀλλὰ καὶ πάντες οἱ ἐγνωκότες τὴν ἀλήθειαν.

⁸¹ Marshall, *The Epistles of John* (NICNT; Grand Rapids: Eerdmans, 1978), 119 n. 30.

world."[82] The odd position of δέ finds its way into some modern translations, assuming an ellipsis of τῶν ἁμαρτιῶν with an insertion of "the sins" in v. 2d.[83]

The issue, as it seems, is how one interprets v. 2c in the context of the Johannine view of the sin expiation for the world (cf. 4:14). Raymond Brown suggests that one should not overtranslate the conjunction δέ, but rather place more emphasis on the idea of expiation (ἱλασμός) in v. 2a.[84] If we follow Brown, we gain a twofold advantage. First, this approach softens somewhat the subtlety in the grammatical distinctions and lessens the sharp nuance in the theological implications that John seems to have intended in the context of 2:2, and in the entire epistle (1 John 4:14; cf. John 3:16–18; 4:42; 12:47; 17:20). Second, the suggestion also resolves the complaints raised by Marshall and Houlden regarding δέ. While Brown's proposal may answer some of the theological questions among the scholarly attempts to cope with this text, it does not, in my opinion, do justice to the author's intent. Indeed, we are left with an improper interpretation. Recalling our analysis of v. 2c, which favored δέ and μόνον, it is viable to stress the author's intended text as far as possible.

While the grammatical irregularity in the two περί clauses in v. 2cd may be caused by δέ, John seems aware of it. In 1 John (esp. 1:3 in table 5) δέ is employed in a manner that Blass and Debrunner classify as normal word order. They defend the idea that the presence of δέ in v. 2c is necessary in this somewhat irregular construction.[85] We should also observe that δέ is present in John 17:20 (i.e., οὐ περὶ τούτων δὲ ἐρωτῶ μόνον, ἀλλὰ καὶ περὶ τῶν πιστευόντων διὰ τοῦ λόγου αὐτῶν εἰς ἐμέ). Whether one translates δέ as "but" or "and," the force it places on v. 2cd (cf. John 17:20) lies in the sin expiation, including the Johannine members and the world.[86]

---

[82] Houlden, *A Commentary on the Johannine Epistles* (HNTC; New York: Harper & Row, 1973), 62–63.

[83] See NIV, RSV, and NRSV. Attic Greek allows a certain level of ellipses in expressions (cf. John 5:36; Heb 9:7). However, when such an ellipsis or elision occurs, the contexts are often clear. Certainly the renderings of the modern translations noted above, for example, pertain to the making of a smooth reading of the text. They do not represent the literal reading of v. 2cd.

[84] Brown states, "In my judgment any attack on secessionist error here is in the very idea of atonement rather than in the extent of the forgiveness" (*Epistles of John*, 222).

[85] BDF, §475.

[86] Compare the following construction οὐ μόνον ἀλλὰ καί in the Johannine writings (compiled based on ECM 4:3 and NA[28]):

1 John 2:2c	οὐ περὶ τῶν ἡμετέρων δὲ μόνον ἀλλὰ καὶ περὶ ὅλου τοῦ κόσμου
1 John 5:6	οὐκ ἐν τῷ ὕδατι [δὲ] μόνον ἀλλ' [καὶ] ἐν τῷ ὕδατι καὶ ἐν τῷ αἵματι
2 John 1	καὶ οὐκ ἐγὼ μόνος ἀλλὰ καὶ πάντες οἱ ἐγνωκότες τὴν ἀλήθειαν
John 8:16	ὅτι μόνος οὐκ εἰμί, ἀλλ' ἐγὼ καὶ ὁ πέμψας με πατήρ
John 11:52	καὶ οὐχ ὑπὲρ τοῦ ἔθνους [δὲ] μόνον ἀλλ' ἵνα καὶ τὰ τέκνα τοῦ θεοῦ
John 12:9	οὐ διὰ τὸν Ἰησοῦν μόνον ἀλλ' ἵνα καὶ τὸν Λάζαρον ἴδωσιν
John 13:9	Κύριε, μὴ τοὺς πόδας μου μόνον ἀλλὰ καὶ τὰς χεῖρας καὶ τὴν κεφαλήν
John 17:20	Οὐ περὶ τούτων δὲ ἐρωτῶ μόνον, ἀλλὰ καὶ περὶ τῶν πιστευόντων

While properly called an adversative conjunction, δέ can also introduce "an explanation or an intensification."[87] This inclusiveness is expressed through the advocacy and efficacy of Jesus as the expiation for sins (2:1–2; 4:10).

In evaluating the theological issues of μόνον with δέ, we note that the result is less surprising than it is for the case of μονῶν with δέ. Grammatically the construction οὐ μόνον ἀλλὰ καί favors the use of μόνον over against μονῶν. The combination of δέ and μόνον here expresses well the author's theology that the sin expiation concerning the Johannine Christians and the whole world is safeguarded by the advocacy and efficacy of Jesus' death.[88]

The intrinsic probabilities suggest that the variant μόνον (with δέ) is most likely the initial text. While the reading with μονῶν is possible,[89] it does not carry out the best grammatical and theological interpretations for v. 2. Thus, it seems that the variant μονῶν, attested by some manuscripts (e.g., B 1 033 *rell*), was cited out of an error arising from the scribe's faulty hearing or intentional mistake.

The probabilities (transcriptional and intrinsic) have unanimously demonstrated that μόνον is most likely identical with the initial text.

III. Conclusion

This study examined two criteria in the so-called reasoned eclecticism (external and internal evidence) and evaluated the variants for μόνον and μονῶν in 1 John 2:2c. It also examined δέ and καί. In Johannine studies, little attention is paid to the

---

In 1 John 5:6, it should be noticed that MS 1735, which supports the reading with δέ in 1 John 5:6, is the same manuscript that supports the reading μόνον both in 1 John 2:2c and 5:6. In John 11:52, the textual transmission has variants with regard to the presence of δέ. This is supported by ℵ² Ψ 073 33 579 *pc*, the same manuscripts supporting the reading of δὲ μόνον in 1 John 2:2c. In John 12:9, the textual transmission shows a possibility of an omission of μόνον, which is supported by D *pc* b e sy^s. In John 13:9, the textual transmission also indicates omission or replacement of τοὺς πόδας μου μόνον, which is supported by 1 2 4, $\mathfrak{P}^{66}$ et al.

[87] BDF, §447.8; see also Edwin Mayser, *Grammatik der griechischen Papyri aus der Ptolemäerzeit*, vol. 2.3 (Berlin: de Gruyter, 1934), 125–30.

[88] BDF, §475, states, "Some co-ordinating conjunctions take first position, e.g., καί, ἤ, ἀλλά, others second; the latter sometimes come third, fourth or fifth in the clause ..., partly because of necessity, as in 1 John 2:2 οὐ περὶ τῶν ἡμετέρων δὲ μόνον, John 8:16 καὶ ἐὰν κρίνω δὲ ἐγώ ('Even if I however'), and partly by the choice of the author." Thus, in v. 2 the lack of the coordinating conjunction δέ in οὐ μόνον ἀλλὰ καί would lose the force of the sin expiation that seems to have been intended by the author. The theology of John's universal salvation based on Jesus' death is explained in Joseph T. Do, "Jesus' Death as *hilasmos* according to 1 John," in *The Death of Jesus in the Fourth Gospel* (ed. Gilbert Van Belle; BETL 200; Leuven: Leuven University Press, 2007), 537–65.

[89] Different cases of the three-ending adjective μόνος, -η, -ον occur elsewhere in the Johannine writings. See John 6:15, 22; 8:9, 16, 29; 12:24; 16:32ab; 17:3; 2 John 1. Nowhere does the plural μονῶν occur.

textual variants μόνον and μονῶν with the presence of δέ and καί. This study, however, has demonstrated that, in 1 John 2:2, the presence of δέ and καί presents noticeable differences in the grammatical and theological interpretation. Considering these criteria, I propose that in v. 2c μόνον is the preferred reading over its alternative μονῶν.[90]

This conclusion is displayed by the CBGM in tables 6a and 6b below. (For reasons of space, tables 6a and 6b are presented in reverse order.)

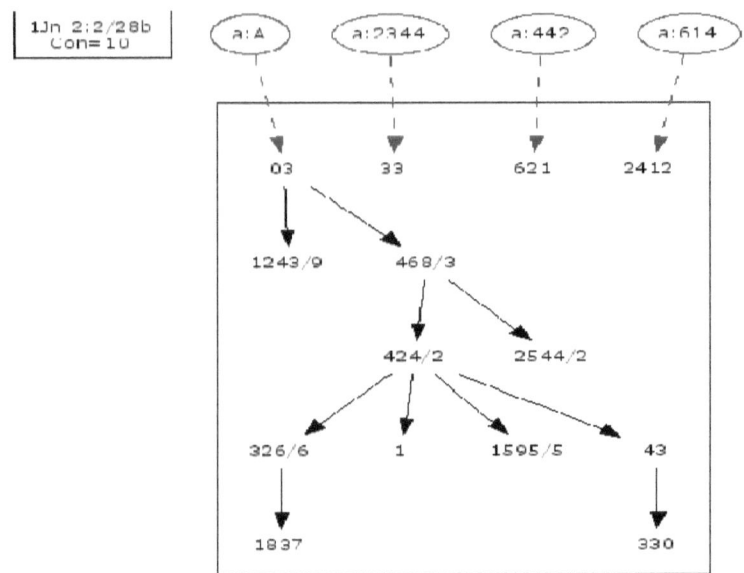

Table 6b. Imperfect coherence in the textual flow diagram for 2:2/28b showing multiple origins, one of which is Codex B (03), regarded as initial text[91]

---

[90] I wish to express my deep appreciation to Dr. Gerd Mink, who is one of the editors of the ECM 4:3, for his valuable time and insightful information as well as recommendations. In the spring of 2010 I had a personal meeting with him at the Institute for New Testament Textual Research INTF in Münster, Germany. We discussed at length the pros and cons of the criteria for evaluating and judging the initial readings of the text in v. 2. Given the information and evidence submitted, Mink concluded that most of the time it is difficult, based exclusively on evidence, to decide clearly which reading is the initial text. Reading any initial text is rather "a matter of interpretation" [his own words]. Thus, my conclusion in this textual problem regarding the variants for μόνον and μονῶν in v. 2c is partly influenced by my conversation with Mink, and largely based on the critical analysis of the text. I also wish to thank Dr. Charles Brown for his proofreading of this manuscript; any errors found herein remain mine.

[91] http://intf.uni-muenster.de/cbgm/Coh1_4.html (accessed June 13, 2013).

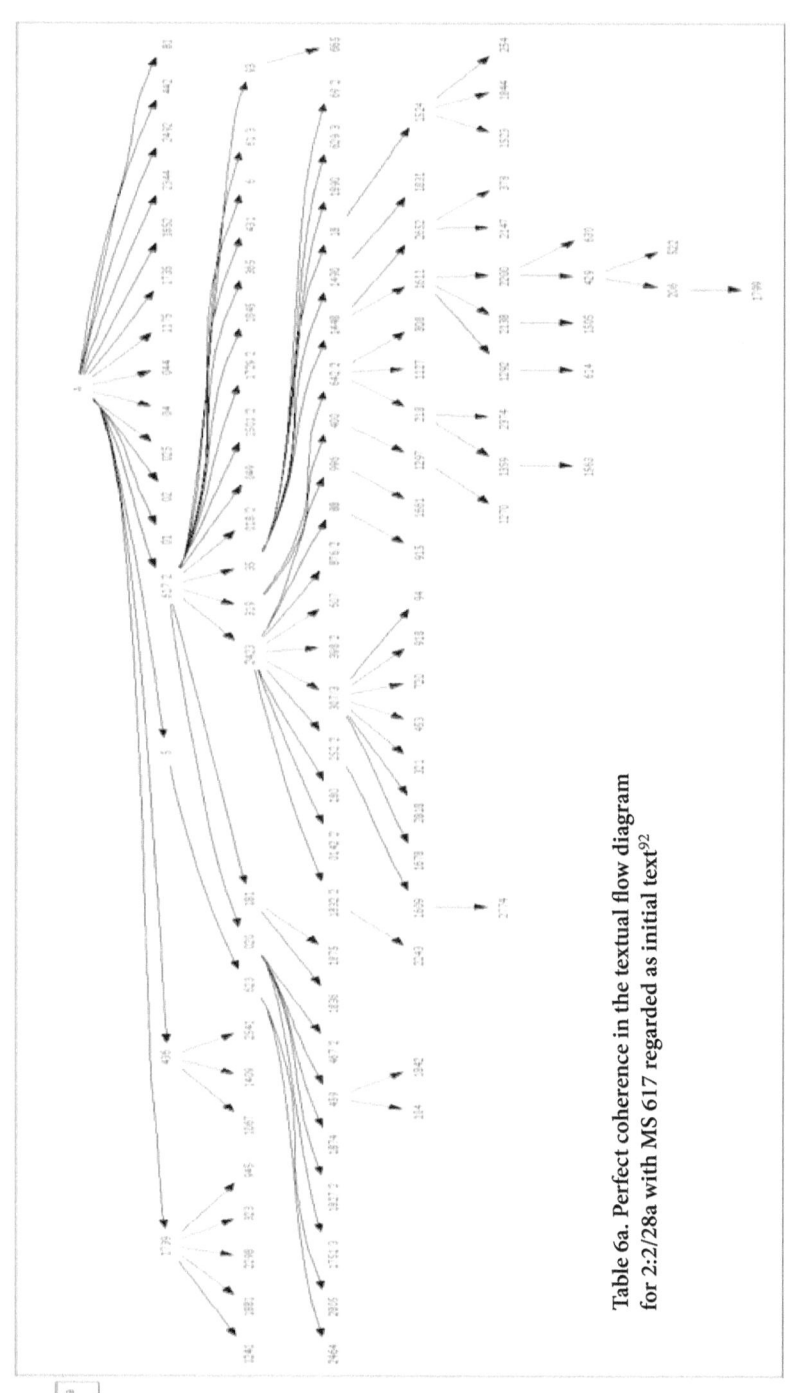

Table 6a. Perfect coherence in the textual flow diagram for 2:2/28a with MS 617 regarded as initial text[92]

[92]http://intf.uni-muenster.de/cbgm/Coh1_4.html (accessed June 13, 2013).

New Titles

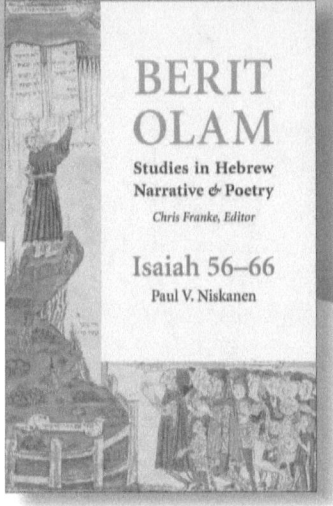

How Human Is God?
Seven Questions about God and Humanity in the Bible
Mark S. Smith

"Smith not only asks questions that we all have about God, . . . he also offers answers with theological and pastoral sensitivity and depth. All kinds of readers will find themselves enriched by Smith's clarity and his sensible, yet learned, reflections."

Jacqueline E. Lapsley
Associate Professor of Old Testament
Princeton Theological Seminary

978-0-8146-3759-3
Paperback, 216 pp., 5 ³⁄₈ x 8 ¹⁄₄, $19.95
978-0-8146-3784-5 eBook, $17.99
B3759 Paperback & eBook Bundle, $24.49

Available October 2014
Isaiah 56–66
Paul V. Niskanen
Berit Olam Series
Chris Franke, Editor

The last chapters of the book of Isaiah offer a vision of new hope at the dawn of the postexilic period. The dense and complex imagery of light, espousal, and victory gives expression to the joyful reality of a return to Jerusalem and to the as-yet-unrealized dreams of rebuilding and repopulating what has been laid to waste.

978-0-8146-5068-4
Hardcover, 128 pp., 6 x 9, $29.95
978-0-8146-8256-2 eBook, $26.99
B5068 Hardcover & eBook Bundle, $37.49

LITURGICAL PRESS
www.litpress.org | 1-800-858-5450

"Fishers of Humans," the Contemporary Theory of Metaphor, and Conceptual Blending Theory

BLAKE E. WASSELL
blakewassell@gmail.com
Macquarie University, Sydney, NSW, Australia 2109

STEPHEN R. LLEWELYN
stephen.llewelyn@mq.edu.au
Macquarie University, Sydney, NSW, Australia 2109

The present study argues for a new interpretation of the expression "fishers of humans" that is sensitive to current understandings of intertextuality, narrative, and metaphor. "Fishers of humans" is treated as a metaphorical expression, being viewed through the apposite lenses of the Contemporary Theory of Metaphor (CTM) and Conceptual Blending Theory (CBT). Both theories emphasize the role of a metaphorical expression's immediate context, and thus the Markan narrative is analyzed closely; intratextuality is valued over intertextuality. Metaphor is seen to enhance not just the Markan characterization of the Twelve but also a historical construction that takes into consideration their emergence in Jesus' public career. By way of CTM, the expression's underlying conceptual metaphor is deduced as A PROCLAIMER OF THE KINGDOM IS A FISHER. Further, the evocation of transformed social identity is affirmed by an application of CBT.

καὶ εἶπεν αὐτοῖς ὁ Ἰησοῦς· Δεῦτε ὀπίσω μου, καὶ ποιήσω ὑμᾶς γενέσθαι ἁλιεῖς ἀνθρώπων.

And Jesus said to them: "Come after me, and I will make you to become fishers of humans." (Mark 1:17)

Although "fishers of humans" (ἁλιεῖς ἀνθρώπων) is a patently metaphorical expression, the cognitive linguistic view of metaphor is conspicuously absent from its modern interpretations. It is largely for this reason that divergence, incoherence, and speculation abound in scholarly views on its sense and objective.[1] The present

---

[1] This phenomenon is described and analyzed in the conclusion of this study.

study endeavors not only to redress this but also to reinvigorate investigation into the historical origin of the Twelve. E. P. Sanders suggests,

> apart from what we learn from the symbolic nature of the number twelve, we do not know Jesus' purpose in calling [the disciples].... The call of the early disciples ... gives us no knowledge about how Jesus gathered about himself a small group of followers.[2]

His concerns seem to be widespread, although John P. Meier presents an exception.[3] We will offer a cautious historical construction only after close consideration of the expression "fishers of humans" alongside the Contemporary Theory of Metaphor (CTM) and Conceptual Blending Theory (CBT).[4] The first section of the article will outline CTM and the multivalent usage of the source domain FISHING in antiquity. The second will establish the conceptual metaphor by way of analysis of the Markan narrative. The third will discuss "fishers of humans" in light of CBT, and the final section will review the relevant secondary literature and suggest a historical construction sensitive to the issues of narrative and memory. By expounding on the compatibility of the strange metaphor with both the Markan narrative and the hypothetical pragmatic concerns of a forward-thinking, Galilean charismatic, we intend to show up the scholarly predisposition to reach at whispers of intertextuality.

I. CTM AND A MULTIVALENT METAPHOR

Metaphors seek to understand one thing in terms of another. Thus, sin, a somewhat abstract concept, can be understood either in terms of dirt, a more

---

[2] Sanders, *Jesus and Judaism* (Philadelphia: Fortress, 1985), 103. By silence, Sanders assumes the same view in his *The Historical Figure of Jesus* (London: Penguin, 1995).

[3] Meier, *A Marginal Jew: Rethinking the Historical Jesus*, vol. 3, *Companions and Competitors* (ABRL; New York: Doubleday, 2001), 159–63.

[4] CTM was originally expounded as Conceptual Metaphor Theory in George Lakoff and Mark Johnson, *Metaphors We Live By* (Chicago: University of Chicago Press, 1980). Its development over the last few decades into a prominent theory of metaphor makes it a useful choice in the present study. Recent treatments of CTM include Zoltán Kövecses, *Metaphor: A Practical Introduction* (2nd ed.; Oxford: Oxford University Press, 2010) and Francisco José Ruiz de Mendoza Ibáñez and Lorena Pérez Hernández, "The Contemporary Theory of Metaphor: Myths, Developments and Challenges," *Metaphor and Symbol* 26 (2011): 161–85. But this choice, as well that of CBT, is made primarily to narrow and simplify the focus of the present study as much as possible. We do not intend to downplay the efficacy of other theories of metaphor and thus need not argue for any sort of superiority on the parts of CTM and CBT. Categorization Theory, for example, might also prove useful; see Boaz Keysar and Sam Glucksberg, "Metaphor and Communication," *Poetics Today* 13 (1992): 633–58, esp. 647–56. Further, in a cogent study that critiques all of the above theories of metaphor, L. David Ritchie propounds his Context-Limited Simulators Theory (*Context and Connection in Metaphor* [Basingstoke: Palgrave Macmillan, 2006]).

tangible and embodied reality, or again in terms of a dangerous animal that is ready to devour the unprepared, or again in terms of a weight to be carried. In the jargon, SIN is the target domain and DIRT, DANGEROUS ANIMAL, or WEIGHT are the source domains.[5] Invariably the lesser known (more abstract) is explained in terms of the better known (more tangible). We structure SIN in terms of DIRT when we wish to speak of its removal, in terms of a DANGEROUS ANIMAL or even SNARE when we seek to understand human vulnerability, or a WEIGHT when we seek to understand the consequences of sin for the sinner. In other words, different source domains are used to structure the target domain depending on what aspect of the target domain is being considered. By "structuring" we mean the mapping of constituent elements from the source domain to the target domain. Thus, in the conceptual metaphor of SIN IS A WEIGHT, the thing weighed down by an object is mapped to the person who acts wrongly; the object is mapped to the wrongful act; the weight of the object is mapped to the nature of the wrongful act; and so on. It can be said that sins are burdens; they weigh one down, and they can be too heavy to bear. Our "rich" knowledge of lifting or carrying weights can lead to metaphorical entailments, that is, the mapping of nonconstituent elements of the source domain onto the target domain.[6] For example, as we know from experience that others can help in carrying a heavy object, in the Christian tradition Jesus can be seen as carrying the believers' sins; for example, "He himself bore our sins in his body on the cross" (1 Pet 2:24). Some metaphorical expressions (and their underlying conceptual metaphors) are so familiar that we do not even have to think about what they mean. The meaning is already given, being mediated through language and culture. Instances here are:

> And if you do not do well, sin is lurking at the door;
> its desire is for you, but you must master it. (Gen 4:7)
>
> Wash me thoroughly from my iniquity, and cleanse me from my sin. (Ps 51:2)

Such metaphors have become lexicalized, part of our everyday vocabulary. They have entered into our cognitive conception of the abstract term.

The meaning of some metaphors is not mediated to us through our cultural traditions; some are ambiguous and can be variously construed. Such metaphors require a context against which to interpret or understand how the source domain structures the target domain. To understand how this occurs, CTM avails itself of the spatial metaphor of mapping. As noted above, the constituent elements of the source domain are said to be mapped onto elements of the target domain. In nonlexicalized metaphors it is the role of context to determine what elements are highlighted in the mapping process. In other words, the mapping process is

---

[5] Source and target domains will be represented in SMALL CAPS.
[6] It should be noted that the distinction between constituent (basic) and nonconstituent (additional) elements is somewhat problematic, as it is dependent on the perspective of the speaker.

indeterminate without context, and it is the context that provides the clues to which elements in the target domain are to be foregrounded (or highlighted) and which are to be backgrounded (or hidden).[7] Novel and multivalent (ambiguous) metaphors fall within this consideration, and it is here that linguistic context must be viewed in the broadest sense, that is, the clause, the sentence, the paragraph, the whole literary work, the tradition (i.e., in terms of intertextuality), and so on. But of equal importance is consideration of pragmatics, that is, to whom the metaphor was expressed, on what occasion, and at what time and place, and so on. The pragmatic context, however, is complicated by the complex web of voices that underlie narrative texts. Is it (a) the author (real or implied) who addresses his/her reader (real or implied), (b) the narrator who addresses his/her narratee, or again (c) one character in the narrative addressing another? All three levels of address can be redactionally constructed, though (c) permits the possibility of the recording of an actual address, that is, an *ipsissimum verbum*. The last of the levels is especially important for this study, as it asks whether the metaphor is to be understood against the memory of a past utterance that has been redactionally used by Mark to construct his understanding of the Twelve. But to return to our general description of CTM and how it works, all linguistic and pragmatic factors can enter into the process of highlighting and backgrounding elements of the target domain.

The usage of FISHING through antiquity is amorphous. It has various target domains (principally TEACHING, MISSION, JUDGMENT, and WARFARE), and it can be construed negatively or positively even within the same target domain.[8] All this has been underappreciated in modern interpretations of the expression "fishers of humans" (see conclusion below). We will briefly illustrate the disharmony between significant uses of FISHING in the Hebrew Bible, the Dead Sea Scrolls, and early Christianity. The subsequent discussion indicates that the use of FISHING does not necessarily evoke a lexicalized metaphor.

The conceptual metaphor JUDGMENT IS CATCHING PREY might seem to be quasi-standard across the Hebrew Bible, Dead Sea Scrolls, and early Christian literature, but a careful analysis shows that this is not the case.[9] Consider Eccl 9:12:

> For no one can anticipate the time of disaster. Like fish taken in a cruel net, and like birds caught in a snare, so mortals are snared at a time of calamity, when it suddenly falls upon them.[10]

---

[7] A complementary process occurs in the source domain with elements either utilized or not.

[8] See Wilhelm H. Wuellner, *The Meaning of "Fishers of Men"* (NTL; Philadelphia: Westminster, 1967). Meier has rightly shown the many methodological problems in Wuellner's study (*Marginal Jew*, 3:193 n. 119).

[9] HUNTING and FISHING are subsource domains or instantiations of the conceptual metaphor.

[10] This and other quotations are derived from the NRSV.

Simile makes the comparison apparent in this text. The immediate context of the expression "fish taken in a cruel net" indicates that (a) the constituent elements mapped are 'fish' and 'net' and (b) the entailments mapped are 'suddenness,' 'inevitability,' and 'trapping.' Humans experience disaster just as fish are trapped in the net. Note that DISASTER, not JUDGMENT, is provided as the target. JUDGMENT is not evoked in any explicit terms.

Examples from prophetic literature, however, illustrate how context can explicitly identify the target domain JUDGMENT. Regarding those fished for in Jer 16:16, "[YHWH] will doubly repay their iniquity and their sin" (16:18). In Ezek 29:4–6 and 32:3 the prophet uses FISHING to juxtapose the autonomy of YHWH with Pharaoh's vulnerability. The entailment of 'violent capture' is highlighted by the impassioned use of FISHING in both the former two examples and Amos 4:2. In Hab 1:14–17 the susceptibility of humankind at the hands of the enemy is conveyed with FISHING. In addition, those caught are eaten in Hab 1:14–17; Ezek 29:4–5; and 32:3. JUDGMENT is not a timid or meticulous undertaking but a violent assertion of dominance. Thus, the target domain that is understood in terms of FISHING is ascertained by the context of the metaphorical expressions, in which a selection of the source domain's constituent elements and entailments are foregrounded or highlighted. Two entailments are generally discernible among the examples given above, namely, the helplessness of those fished, and the abrupt violence of catching (by the images of fishing tools such as various nets and hooks, all constituent elements). JUDGMENT is the violent and emphatic means of capturing people; or, more evocatively, it is FISHING.

The conceptual metaphor JUDGMENT IS CATCHING PREY is, to some extent, sustained throughout the Dead Sea Scrolls, especially in the *Hodayot*. Juxtaposed with the above metaphorical expressions from the Hebrew Bible, the instances in the Dead Sea Scrolls evidence similar contexts yet the mapping processes look rather different: eating is not indicated at all; helplessness is overcome and often turned back onto the enemy setting the nets; and hooks are not used, thereby somewhat lessening the graphically violent sense of the source domain. The speaker in 1QH^a XIII, 5–9 gives thanks that he is not one of the judged but one of the judging, a fisher and not a fish:

> (7) You made my (8) lodging with many fishermen, those who spread the net upon the surface of the water, those who go hunting the sons of injustice. And there you established me for the judgment.

These words would seem to be inspired by Jer 16:16.[11] Elsewhere, the constituent element 'nets' is used to portray the traps set by Belial.[12] But these can be avoided

---

[11] This passage is also indicative of the sectarians' belief that they are the sons of light who fight in the company of angelic beings and exact God's judgment against the company of Belial.

[12] 1QH^a X, 29–30; XI, 26–30; XII, 10–14; CD IV, 12–19; XIV, 1–2; 4Q427 1–4; 4Q437 I, 1–3; 11Q11 VI, 3–6.

and overcome, according to the hymns. The examples from the Hebrew Bible are prophetic proclamations, while those in the Dead Sea Scrolls are communal hymns of thanksgiving. Therefore, the metaphor is nuanced differently in the two corpora.

Matthew 13:47–50, the parable of the dragnet, is an apocalyptic parable in which FISHING is used in an eschatological context. The mapping of 'gathering in with nets' connotes a measured action; both the unjust and the just are caught in God's dragnet. Whereas the action of fishing itself is not erratic and violent, the entailment of 'sorting the fish' indicates the target JUDGMENT. The linguistic expression of JUDGMENT IS CATCHING PREY here is strikingly different from any in the Hebrew Bible or the Dead Sea Scrolls. And in another parable, *Gos. Thom.* 8, human beings are likened to intelligent fishers who, after drawing up their net, kept the big fish and returned the little fish to the sea. F. F. Bruce suggests that the big fish is used to understand either THE TRUE GNOSTIC or TRUE KNOWLEDGE.[13] Negative and violent entailments are largely absent in these two metaphors. Therefore, both Matthew and the *Gospel of Thomas* attest that the Hebrew Bible and the Dead Sea Scrolls did not necessarily influence the metaphorical use of FISHING in early Christianity. It is a further consideration that the usage of FISHING across these discussed corpora is also subject to respective genres and conventional themes. We have discussed examples from poetry, psalms, narrative, and prophecy, from the communal thanksgiving hymns of the Dead Sea Scrolls, and from early Christian parables. No uniform application of FISHING across the Hebrew Bible, Dead Sea Scrolls, and early Christianity can be gleaned from the above evidence; and, indeed, it should not be expected or sought after.

II. Mark and the Conceptual Metaphor

Naturally we proceed to the point that Mark provides the primary linguistic context for the conceptual metaphor underlying the expression "fishers of humans." The previous section showed the simple amorphous quality of the source domain FISHING. But some brief narratological considerations really press how untenable an invocation of intertextuality is vis-à-vis our metaphor. In narratology the notion of intertextuality has two important premises: (a) texts are (inevitably) constructed from other texts; and (b) these relationships are not limited to allusions but rather give rise to great intertextual complexes. The latter is especially germane here. Whereas the scene of Mark 1:16–20 is explicable in these terms, seemingly evoking the Elijah and Elisha narrative, the metaphor itself is not.[14] If the metaphor were

---

[13] Bruce, *Jesus and Christian Origins outside the New Testament* (Grand Rapids: Eerdmans, 1974), 115–16.

[14] Mark 1:16–20 alludes to 1 Kgs 19:19–21 in several ways: (1) the teacher chooses the disciple(s) and not they him (rabbinic mode); (2) the disciple(s) is/are engaged in their occupation and leave it as a result of the teacher; (3) the use of ὀπίσω. However, Mark also makes notable

explicable in terms of intertextuality, it would need to be but one strand in a visible intertextual complex.¹⁵ Moreover, the Markan narrative elucidates the metaphor with sufficiently rich color (as will be explicated below). Intertextuality is an unnecessary and restrictive assumption in the case of the expression "fishers of humans." Another important preliminary point is that the Lukan formulation, ἀνθρώπους ἔσῃ ζωγρῶν ("you will be catching humans," 5:10), is derived from Mark.¹⁶ The redactional efforts of the former are clearly discernible.¹⁷ Mark's imperative "come after me" is dropped in preference for the traditional imperative of the epiphany scene, "fear not" (cf. Judg 6:23; Dan 10:12, 19; Luke 1:13, 30; 2:10; etc.); and "I will make you to become fishers of humans" becomes "from now you will be catching humans." Further, the plurals in Mark are changed to the singular in Luke as only Simon is addressed. The change in wording from "fishers" (ἁλιεῖς) to "catcher" (ζωγρῶν) is deliberate, as it softens the traditional image evoked by CATCHING PREY discussed above.¹⁸ The pronouncement now speaks of Simon Peter's catching of

---

departures from 1 Kings: (1) the use of δεῦτε not ἀκολουθήσω; (2) the initiative to follow is shown by Elisha (note the double use of the cohortative in the absence of an explicit call from Elijah); (3) the fishermen follow immediately. Further, this scene is but one among several allusions to Elijah in Mark. See, e.g., Christine E. Joynes, "The Returned Elijah? John the Baptist's Angelic Identity in the Gospel of Mark," *SJT* 58 (2005): 455–67.

¹⁵ For example, Richard Hicks shows sufficient precedent within the Markan narrative for intertextuality with Malachi; only subsequently does he analyze Mark 10:17–22 as a part of the intertextual complex ("Markan Discipleship according to Malachi: The Significance of μὴ ἀποστερήσῃς in the Story of the Rich Man [Mark 10:17–22]," *JBL* 132 [2013]: 179–99, esp. 183–88).

¹⁶ Contra W. D. Davies and Dale C. Allison Jr., *A Critical and Exegetical Commentary on the Gospel according to Saint Matthew* (3 vols.; ICC; Edinburgh: T&T Clark, 1988–97), 1:394; Craig S. Keener, *The Gospel of Matthew: A Socio-Rhetorical Commentary* (Grand Rapids: Eerdmans, 2009), 148; idem, *The Historical Jesus of the Gospels* (Grand Rapids: Eerdmans, 2009), 183–84, 203; and Ben Witherington III, *The Christology of Jesus* (Minneapolis: Fortress, 1990), 129–31.

¹⁷ See Rudolf Pesch, *Der reiche Fischfang, Lk 5, 1–11/Jo 21, 1–14: Wundergeschichte, Berufserzählung, Erscheinungsbericht* (KBANT; Düsseldorf: Patmos, 1969), 134–35. Pesch sees Luke 5:1–4a and 5:10–11 as redactional adaptations of Mark 2:13; 3:7, 9; 4:1–2, 35; and 1:16–20, respectively. With the framework of a traditional miracle/epiphany story (Luke 5:4b–9 par. John 21:2–4a, 6, 11), the evangelist fabricates his call narrative. For Pesch, this explains a number of problematic features in Luke's version of the call: for example, (a) the omission of Andrew, who did not feature in the miracle story; (b) the ambiguity of Jesus' location either in the boat or on the shore; (c) the change of Mark's "come after me" to "fear not" (Luke 5:10a), which reflects the epiphany of Jesus as holy Lord in the miraculous catch of fish (Luke 5:8). In addition, Pesch suggests that the future mission of Peter the apostle is underlined by (a) Luke's emphasis on Jesus' preaching of the "word of God" to the crowds (Luke 5:1–3); (b) the prospective use of "from now on" (Luke 5:10), which marks a decisive change in salvation history; and (c) the symbolic nature of the catch of fish.

¹⁸ Pesch does not give due attention to the softening present in Luke's choice of term (*Der reiche Fischfang*, 74–75). For him, the choice of word is conditioned by (a) LXX usage; (b) the use of ἄγρα in vv. 4 and 9; (c) its tone, which is more conducive to Christian mission; and (d) that, given the elevation of and focus on Peter in the miracle/epiphany story of Luke 5:1–11, the plural

humans alive (ζωγρῶν) with the associations that this term had among Greek speakers of sparing the lives of those conquered in conflict and war.[19] It is further underlined that the change presumes a Greek-speaking context in the preparation for the pronouncement in the wording of the miracle story (Luke 5:4: εἰς ἄγραν; 5:10: ἐπὶ τῇ ἄγρᾳ). The play is deliberate and precludes the possibility of translational variance, as suggested by Martin Hengel.[20] Therefore, other texts cannot elucidate the sense and objective of the metaphor under investigation. We must view the Markan narrative as its primary linguistic context. It is to Mark that we now turn.

In Mark 1:17 Jesus expresses a conditional promise to some fishermen. He gives the command "come after me" (δεῦτε ὀπίσω μου) with the assurance of being

---

reference to "the fishers" in v. 2 can no longer provide sufficient context for his adoption of the Markan expression "fishers of men."

[19] The following examples illustrate the meaning of ζωγρέω: Thucydides, *Hist.* 2.92.3; 7.41.4; Appian, *Bell. civ.* 4.7.55; Philo, *Virt.* 43; Josephus, *Ant.* 14.85; Num 31:17–18.

[20] Hengel supplies an Aramaic translation of Mark 1:17 to argue for a possible Palestinian origin of the saying (*The Charismatic Leader and His Followers* [trans. J. C. G. Greig; Studies of the New Testament and Its World; Edinburgh: T&T Clark, 1981], 76–77). He stresses, however, that this is not an argument for its being an *ipsissimum verbum Jesu*, but only for its provenance. The strength of the argument does not rest so much on being able to translate it back into the tongue of first-century Galilee, as there is nothing particularly Semitic about the expression, nor does it render some difficulty in the Greek explicable. Its strength lies in its apparent power to explain Luke's use of ζωγρῶν (Luke 5:10) instead of ἁλιεύς (Mark 1:17); it does this by postulating an underlying Aramaic word (ציד) that carried both senses. However, one may need to show a little caution here. As is obvious, the two sayings are quite different, and it is not as if they are different only in this term. There is also a second problem with the postulated Semitic reconstructions. One can understand where the idea for the reconstruction came from, for Jer 16:16 parallels the terms fishermen (דיגים) and hunters (צידים). However, a closer look at the terminology indicates that ζωγρέω does not offer an appropriate translation for the postulated צוד and its cognates. Indeed, the Septuagint never translates this term by ζωγρέω, preferring to use instead θηρεύω (see Gen 27:3, 5, 33; Lev 17:13; Jer 16:16; Hos 9:13 with cognate; Ps 140:12 = LXX 139:12; Job 38:39; and Lam 3:52; 4:18) or some other term (ἀγρεύω in Job 10:16 and Prov 6:26; ἐκθλίβω in Mic 7:2; and various compounds of στρέφω in Ezek 13:18 and 20). The translation of צוד/ציד is problematic, as we are dealing with conceptual categories that differ between Hebrew/Aramaic and English. In other words, ציד is a generic term that encompasses hunter, fowler, and fisherman. This is clearly seen in the usage of the Mishnah when it speaks of hunters (ציידים) of animals, birds, and fish (*m. Šeb.* 7:4), or of those hunting (צדים) fish, animals, and birds (*m. Beṣah* 3:1; cf. *b. ʿAbod. Zar.* 19a, which speaks of the man who hunts birds [אדם שצד צפרין], and *b. Šabb.* 106b, which lists liability for hunting sorts of animals in relation to the Sabbath), or of the nets for animals, birds, and fish (*m. Šabb.* 1:6, *m. Beṣah* 3:2, which also speaks of the animals as caught [נצודו] in the nets). See Jastrow, 1276, s.v. ציד, wherein a reference is given to the character of Adda and his advice on the eating of fish. He is introduced as אדא ציידא (*b. Moʿed Qaṭ.* 11a). The epithet may more properly be translated as "one who uses the net"; cf. מצודת הדג in *b. B. Bat.* 21b. Another usage in relation to fishing is found in *b. B. Meṣiʿa* 23b, which considers the right of a finder of fish dried on string and speaks of the fisherman's knot (קטרא דצײדא) as a possible determining factor. Intriguing is חרם ("dragnet") with its homophone for the ban in holy war.

made "to become fishers of humans" (γενέσθαι ἁλιεῖς ἀνθρώπων). A nominal sense is highlighted with the infinitive γενέσθαι. Whereas their being fishers was oriented toward fish, it will now be oriented toward humans. The expression indicates an emphasis on being made something that is both familiar and unfamiliar, normal and abnormal, old and new. Thus, we will label the source domain A FISHER. It is the makeup of A FISHER that will structure conceptually (and experientially) the fishers' 'coming after' Jesus.

Both constituent elements and metaphorical entailments of A FISHER are mapped in the Markan narrative in order to structure a unique target domain. Mark 1:16–20 is a narrative unit that has been ascribed several labels. Rudolf Bultmann uses "biographical apophthegm" or "ideal scene."[21] He favors the view that the scene is a unitary composition; in other words, the saying never circulated independently of the scene.[22] As an apophthegm, it lacks psychological interest in those who are called and supplies only minimal historical detail regarding time and place.[23] It selectively provides such details as make the saying, especially its central metaphorical expression, comprehensible. In terms of CTM, these various pieces of information in the narrated situation are relevant primarily insofar as they contextualize the expression's underlying conceptual metaphor, highlighting (and backgrounding) aspects of its source and target domains. In the first part of the scene, Simon and Andrew are "casting about into the sea" (ἀμφιβάλλοντας ἐν τῇ θαλάσσῃ; 1:16) and leave behind "their nets" (1:18). The phrase "for they were fishers" (ἦσαν γὰρ ἁλιεῖς; 1:16) emphasizes that they are commercial fishermen.[24] Thus, skill, method, and locale are the elements of A FISHER highlighted. In the second part, James and John are "in their boat mending their nets" (ἐν τῷ πλοίῳ καταρτίζοντας τὰ δίκτυα; 1:19) and leave "their father Zebedee in the boat with the hired men" (1:20).[25] These verses foreground the maintenance of work tools and relationships, both familial and business, in A FISHER. The scene denotes actions

---

[21] Bultmann, *The History of the Synoptic Tradition* (trans. J. Marsh; Oxford: Blackwell, 1963), 11–69. However, only Mark 1:16–17 properly adheres to the structure, that is, narrative situation that leads up to a saying. Martin Dibelius sees it as a chria (*From Tradition to Gospel* [trans. Bertram Lee Woolf and M. Dibelius; Library of Theological Translations; Cambridge: James Clarke, 1971], 152–64), and Vincent Taylor, a pronouncement saying (*The Formation of the Gospel Tradition: Eight Lectures* [London: Macmillan, 1933], 63–87).

[22] On Bultmann's discussion of his terms "ideal" and "unitary composition," see *History of the Synoptic Tradition*, 56–61. See Davies and Allison, *Matthew*, 1:393–94; Hengel, *Charismatic Leader*, 76–78, esp. 77 n. 149; Meier, *Marginal Jew*, 3:161.

[23] Bultmann, *History of the Synoptic Tradition*, 28.

[24] See M. Eugene Boring, *Mark: A Commentary* (NTL; Lousville: Westminster John Knox, 2006), 58. Mark 5:42 gives a similar explanatory phrase: ἦν γὰρ ἐτῶν δώδεκα ("for she was twelve years old").

[25] Contra Meier (*Marginal Jew*, 3:161), it seems clear to us that the call of the second pair of fishers (which parallels the first call) is intended to contribute to an understanding of the metaphorical expression "fishers of humans."

and relationships typical of commercial fishermen in first-century Galilee and conveys the metaphorical entailment of 'family-based vocation.' A broad idea of the source domain is impressed upon the audience, as if to portray Jesus reassuringly motioning around to the fishers' familiar surroundings while at the same time calling them to do something different.[26]

K. C. Hanson sees fishing in first-century Galilee as part of an "embedded economy" that was "conceptualized, controlled, and sustained either by the political hierarchy or kin-groups."[27] Individuals do not "go to work" in a capitalist free-market system, so to speak. Rather they are embedded in relationships, as is underlined in Mark. While much of Hanson's evidence is necessarily directed at the political aspect of this economy, the kin-group aspect and the relationships that it entailed are here relevant. Indeed, it is this that is most apparent in the scene. Fishing is a vital part of the economy of many Galilean villages. Fishing is a kin-based profession: sons work with fathers; sons undertake every aspect of the work and, like their fathers, make only a subsistence living from it.[28] Thus, the selection of elements highlighted in the scene indicates that the target is related to the entailment of social identity, of which family connections and occupation are among some of the primary determinants. The target itself is indicated throughout the Markan narrative and is tied to the characterization of the Twelve.

At the moment when the fishers follow the command and "come after" Jesus, anticipation of the promise materializing is evoked. The transformation of the fishers into "fishers of humans" is colored through the plot in the context of the total characterization of the disciples in Mark. Narrative critics recognize that they are not 'flat' but 'round' characters: they display both positive and negative attributes.[29] The metaphor is not simply a positive or a negative image, yet it factors into this 'round' mode of characterization. First, a positive thread visibly traverses 1:16–20; 3:13–19; and 6:7–13: the disciples are (i) commanded to "come after" with an ambiguous promise; they are then (ii) appointed for a more tangible task; and finally (iii) they are sent to fulfill their function as coworkers in Jesus' Galilean mission. But, second, this positive thread is problematized for the audience by

---

[26] Similarly, Meier, *Marginal Jew*, 3:160: "Far from being a generic image applicable to many people in varied circumstances, 'fishers of men' makes sense only at the moment when Jesus encounters some fishermen at their ordinary task, calls them away from their old task, and promises them a new but corresponding task." See also Seán Freyne, *Jesus, a Jewish Galilean: A New Reading of the Jesus Story* (London: T&T Clark, 2004), 52: "There is no condemnation of fishing or the fish industry, only the call to view their association with him in terms that would be understandable to those familiar with such an enterprise."

[27] Hanson, "The Galilean Fishing Economy and the Jesus Tradition," *BTB* 27 (1997): 100.

[28] Ibid., 108–9.

[29] See David Rhoads, Joanna Dewey, and Donald Michie, *Mark as Story: An Introduction to the Narrative of a Gospel* (2nd ed.; Minneapolis: Fortress, 1999), 102, 122–28; Elizabeth Struthers Malbon, *In the Company of Jesus: Characters in Mark's Gospel* (Louisville: Westminster John Knox Press, 2000), 11, 41–69.

intervening instances of the disciples' fallibility. In 4:13 and 6:52 they are among those who do not understand; in 4:40–41 they show not faith but fear; and in 5:31 and 6:35–37 their apparent foiling efforts are tinged with sarcasm. Thus, it is with great dramatic irony that, in the intercalation of 6:6b–30, "the disciples serve as the best Christological analog."[30] The strange title "fishers of humans" shares in this irony. It heralds the conceptual framework in which the portrayal of the disciples is constructed throughout the narrative of Mark. Several other elements of the characterization of the Twelve through the narrative should be noted.

The usage of κηρύσσω and cognates ("proclaiming") throughout the first several chapters of Mark constitutes a pertinent verbal thread. Verbal threads are intratextual devices comprising the repetition of "certain key words and phrases" that can both "occur within episodes" and "connect adjacent episodes."[31] Through repetition, verbal threads "echo for the reader the earlier occurrences and at the same time accumulate meaning and associations that fill out the reader's understanding."[32] John is the subject of "proclaiming" in 1:4 (κηρύσσων) and 1:7 (ἐκήρυσσεν). It is only after John is "handed over" in 1:14 that Jesus becomes the subject (1:14, 39: κηρύσσων; 1:38: κηρύξω). The only other subject to take the verb more than once is the Twelve.[33] Jesus appoints the Twelve "so that they would be with him and so that he could send them out to preach and to have authority to expel demons" (3:14: κηρύσσειν). Later, after Jesus sent them out two by two, they "proclaimed that people should repent" (6:12: ἐκήρυξαν).[34] Three conceptual threads also factor in the characterization of the Twelve. First, just as the fishermen were called in pairs (1:16–20), the Twelve were sent out in pairs (6:7). This parallel hints that this particular missionary journey is the fulfillment of the promise made in Mark 1:17. Second, the phrasing of the condition in 1:17 parallels John's words in 1:7.[35] Here John speaks of the one "coming after me" (ἔρχεται ... ὀπίσω μου), and the notion is emphasized in 1:14 as Jesus comes (ἦλθεν) into Galilee only after John's arrest. Similarly, Jesus commands the fishermen to "come after" him (δεῦτε ὀπίσω μου). This is not simply in the sense of following; Jesus does not give the imperative "follow me" (ἀκολούθει μοι) as he does to Levi in 2:14.[36] The nuance in 1:17 differentiates

---

[30] Geoffrey David Miller, "An Intercalation Revisited: Christology, Discipleship, and Dramatic Irony in Mark 6:6b–30," *JSNT* 35 (2012): 191.

[31] Rhoads et al., *Mark as Story*, 47, 48.

[32] Ibid., 48.

[33] Other subjects include the healed leper, Legion (1:45; 5:20: κηρύσσειν) and a crowd (7:36: ἐκήρυσσον). The verb is used in the passive twice (13:10: κηρυχθῆναι; 14:9: κηρυχθῇ).

[34] A closely related thread is that of exorcism: proclaiming and exorcising are linked in Jesus' ministry (1:39) just as they are in the Twelve's (3:15; 6:7, 13).

[35] Brian J. Incigneri suggests that the formulation of the call in Mark 1:17 might be an allusion to 2 Kgs 6:20–21, but an intratextual thread is more likely (*The Gospel to the Romans: The Setting and Rhetoric of Mark's Gospel* [Biblical Interpretation Series 65; Leiden: Brill, 2003], 329).

[36] Incigneri notes that ἀκολουθέω and cognates are used eighteen times throughout Mark (*Gospel to the Romans*, 329). Cf. Boring, *Mark: A Commentary*, 58.

the fishers from just any other follower. As Jesus superseded John, so the narrative devices suggest that the fishermen would at least in some senses supersede Jesus. It should not be disregarded as a simple coincidence that the Twelve went out and "proclaimed" without Jesus in 6:12 just as Jesus did without John in 1:14. Third, another thread may be inferred by the juxtaposition of Jesus' special title for himself, "Son of Man," and the title ascribed to the fishers, "fishers of humans." Both names use genitival forms of ἄνθρωπος (although one is in the plural and the other singular), are (at least partially) ambiguous in Greek, and are distinctive. The verbal and conceptual threads noted above indicate an inherently ironic juxtaposition between Jesus and the disciples.

The metaphor assures that the fishermen would retain their sense of social identity through a new livelihood that is mobile, profoundly relational, requiring unwavering skill and patience, and based on the Sea of Galilee and its environs. "Fishers of humans" thus conveys a vocation provided by Jesus. It has become clear that such a vocation is doing as Jesus does, namely, proclaiming the good news throughout Galilee. They are made a significant promise at the start of the story; and as the narrative develops, the promise does not disappear, but its fulfillment looks ever more distant and unlikely. At the point when they finally become agents and proclaimers of the kingdom, the sense of irony is unmistakable (6:6b–30). Yet this is the answer to the metaphor aired at the outset of the story. The transition from fishers to "fishers of humans" is ironic yet realistic, unnerving but reassuring. Thus, the target domain of the underlying conceptual metaphor is A PROCLAIMER OF THE KINGDOM. The Markan Jesus creates and expresses the metaphor A PROCLAIMER OF THE KINGDOM IS A FISHER in an effort to make the fishermen feel the same way about human-oriented vocation as he does.[37] He structures a new vocational identity as both a cognitive and experiential blueprint. It denotes what constitutes not the actions of, but the nature of, A PROCLAIMER OF THE KINGDOM. To come after him, Jesus says, is not an abstract, theological enterprise, but it is necessarily tangible and socioeconomic. The metaphor puts the onus on Simon and Andrew as everyday Galilean fishermen: they were subsumed within familial and broader socioeconomic responsibilities, so they will be as Jesus' agents. Just as the fishers' identity was informed by the source domain, so it is now by the target domain. The metaphor cannot be dispensed with because it has no literal equivalent.[38] The target is essentially a conglomerate abstract concept that cannot be expressed in any singular literal sense. The one metaphor can encompass new notions of vocation, identification, practical work, discipleship, and devotion; no

---

[37] Ted Cohen, "Metaphor, Feeling, and Narrative," *Philosophy and Literature* 21 (1997): 233: "When I offer you a metaphor I invite your attempt to join a community with me, an intimate community whose bond is our common feeling about something"; 236: "It is the feeling that anchors the metaphor and signals its success"; 239: "One motive to metaphor is the desire to communicate how one feels and why one feels that way."

[38] Ibid., 234.

one literal sense can. Jesus evokes in the fishermen a feeling that all that makes them
A FISHER makes them A PROCLAIMER OF THE KINGDOM. They may be effective and
identifiable not just in a socioeconomic domain but in a sociotheological domain.

III. CBT and "Fishers of Humans"

It is clear from the above discussion that one cannot speak of metaphor without metaphor (e.g., source, target, and mapping). A different way of thinking about metaphor (equally dependent on metaphor to enunciate itself) was developed by Gilles Fauconnier and Mark Turner.[39] They see metaphor as being a special case of how we think as we compress and integrate concepts. Here distinct mental spaces (input spaces) are blended to create a new mental space (the blend) where conceptual integration (a) selectively projects and compresses elements and relations from the input spaces and then (b) develops the emergent structure of the blend through composition, completion, and elaboration.[40] Metaphor occurs under this model in cases where there is single- and double-scope blending, that is, where either one or both input spaces provide the frame that organizes the blend.[41] To return to our discussion of sin, we consider the conceptual metaphor SIN IS A DANGEROUS ANIMAL.

> Is it not (the case) if you do right [תיטיב],
> (there is) dignity [שאת],
> but if you do not do right,
> sin is crouching at the door
> and its craving is for you,
> and you must master it! (Gen 4:7)

Here we have two input spaces, the first consisting of the predator and its prey. This input space is structured by the frame *being hunted*. The second input space consists

---

[39] Fauconnier and Turner, *The Way We Think: Conceptual Blending and the Mind's Hidden Complexities* (New York: Basic Books, 2002).

[40] Mental spaces are "small conceptual packets constructed as we think and talk, for purposes of local understanding and action" (Fauconnier and Turner, *Way We Think*, 40). Mental spaces consist of elements and relations that are organized by frames. Fauconnier and Turner speak of vital relations, especially cause–effect, change, time, identity, intentionality, part–whole, and so on, that are compressed in the blend (ibid., 89). An input space may have its own internal vital relation(s) and organizing frame, called "topology." Frames can be organized hierarchically from specific to abstract with the latter including the former.

[41] A frame is defined as "long-term schematic knowledge" that is connected to mental spaces and which helps to organize or structure that mental space (Fauconnier and Turner, *Way We Think*, 40, 102–3). Such organizing frames specify "the nature of the relevant activity, its events and participants" (ibid., 104). But the definition is recursive in that the frames are themselves mental spaces that have become culturally or experientially entrenched.

of the agent and his actions (i.e., sin)⁴² and is structured by the theological frame *effect of actions on agent*.⁴³ The elements of the two input spaces match each other (i.e., cross-space map), the predator to sin and prey to the agent. In other words, for the elements in one input space there is a corresponding element in the other. These elements are projected to the blend, which is then structured by the frame *being hunted*, the frame of the first input space. The result is that the agent now mapped to prey has lost his agency—indeed, it is for this reason that שאת is best translated by "dignity"—and is now the potential victim of his actions. The blend is allowed to run and develops its own emergent structure and, by composition and elaboration, creates the safety of the house symbolized by the door. However, the blend does not stop at this point with the agent just told to stay safe indoors. As he must venture outside, by further elaboration the agent is told to 'master' the dangerous animal, that is, to reclaim his agency. So interpreted, Gen 4:7 is a single-scope blend, as the frame of only one input space, that is, *being hunted*, structures the blend. The advantage of blending in the study of metaphor is that it drives one back to a careful study of the syntax and context of the utterance, or saying itself, and to consider the expression in which the metaphor is located as a totality.⁴⁴

Fauconnier and Turner argue that syntax and words are prompts that tell one how to construct a blend and that meaning arises in the blended space.⁴⁵ To support their view they provide a discussion of expressions in the form 'X to be Y of Z,' for example, 'Newton is the father of physics.' It will be observed that this syntactic form lies at the heart of Mark 1:17 with x being 'you' (i.e., a deictic pointing to Simon and Andrew), y 'fishers,' and z 'humans.' It is argued that this syntactic structure entails two input spaces, one consisting of x and z, that is, 'you' and 'humans,' and the second of the relational frame (or second input space) containing y ('fishers') and an unstated w. The expression 'X to be Y of Z' by the use of the copula 'is' reads x and y as counterparts, and the syntactic form prompts one to

---

[42] The second input space is informed by the preceeding lines, where the effect on the agent of doing right is dignity.

[43] Fauconnier and Turner, in their model, designate a further mental space that is produced in the matching (cross-space mapping) of elements in the input spaces and results in a more schematic or generalized structure that is shared by the input spaces. This, they call "generic space." In the case of Gen 4:7 the generic space is the schematic situation of the exercise of agency. It is derived from the shared elements of the two input spaces, namely, the agency of the predator over its prey and of the one who does not do right (note the *hiphil* תיטיב) over his action.

[44] Despite its strengths, CBT is not without problems. For example, Ritchie highlights the unnecessary complexity of the model, citing in particular the number of distinct spaces that must be generated and the often long sequences by which they are integrated ("Lost in Space: Metaphors in Conceptual Integration Theory," *Metaphor and Symbol* 19 [2004]: 31–50). For Ritchie, the problems arise from the model's conceptualization—that is, in terms of spatial, container, and blending metaphors and their entailments—and its use to represent neural processes.

[45] Fauconnier and Turner, *Way We Think*, 139–68.

look for a w in the relational frame to act as the counterpart of z in the other input space. In constructing the blend, the relationship between y and w is used as a frame to structure the relationship between x and z in the blend. One example that Fauconnier and Turner give is 'vanity (x) is the quicksand (y) of reason (z).' The hearer is given one input space consisting of 'vanity' and 'reason,' and the syntax prompts one to form the other input space 'quicksand' (y) and 'traveler' (w) with the relationship between these two elements used as a frame to structure the blend. The resultant meaning that arises can be stated: just as quicksand is a trap to a traveler, so is vanity to reason. We think of the relationship of vanity and reason in terms of quicksand and traveler. But here again context is very important, as it provides the frame against which the y–w relationship is understood. For example, if one were instead to see quicksand as stopping the traveler from straying from the safe path, in the blend vanity would play a positive role, stopping reason from taking shortcuts and falling into danger. In addition, context may prompt us to postulate a different w and thus change the relational frame consisting of y. Fauconnier and Turner give the example where the w of the relational frame (or input space) containing 'quicksand' is completed by 'bacteria.' There is, of course, no immediate frame against which to structure this mental space in and of itself, and an external frame is needed to achieve this. In their example, the citation 'vanity is the quicksand of reason' is given a frame by an introductory observation that certain bacteria can live only in quicksand. With this relational frame provided to the 'quicksand' input space, 'vanity' and 'reason' are projected to the blended space and structured by the relationship between 'bacteria' and 'quicksand.' In the blend, we perceive that vanity is essential to reason, that reason cannot exist without it. Of course, one feels that these interpretations of the expression are somewhat forced, but this is due to optimalization; that is, when the context does not provide a different frame, the default frame (based on entrenchment or experience) is activated.

Returning to the instance of Mark 1:17, 'you' points out Simon and Andrew, and these persons occupy the same input space as 'humans.' The relational frame containing 'fishers' needs to be completed, and the most obvious element to complete this is 'fish.' The scene as it is described by Mark entails this. Jesus is walking by the Sea of Galilee and sees Simon and Andrew casting their nets into the water (Mark 1:16). Luke's reconfiguration of the account and wording of the saying further underlines that he understood 'fish' to be the unstated element of the relational frame.[46] This being the case, the question arises as to how the relational frame containing 'fishers' is structured and if there is an external frame in operation, for if this is the case, it is that frame that is projected to the blend structuring the relationship between 'you' (Simon and Andrew) and 'humans.' This is where context again comes into play.

---

[46] The word 'fish' occurs in Luke 5:6 and 10. It will be noted that Luke, however, does not give the saying in the form 'X is a Y of Z', but this little affects how he read Mark.

Many approaches to Mark 1:17 in the past have sought to evoke other metaphorical uses of 'fish,' 'nets,' 'hooks,' and so on, drawn from the Hebrew Bible or the Dead Sea Scrolls. They have understood the metaphor to be lexicalized, or, in the words of Fauconnier and Turner, the relational frame to be entrenched. But one must question whether this is the case here. Is there another frame in operation here that structures the relationship between 'fishers' and 'fish'? Consider the example of quicksand again and how the relational frame is restructured if one assumes that it keeps the traveler from taking shortcuts and falling into danger. Is there a similar external frame that can structure the relationship between 'fishers' and 'fish'? Or do we even need an external frame? It will be noted that when Mark introduces Simon and Andrew casting their nets into the sea, he offers an explanation, "for they were fishers" (Mark 1:16). The word "fisher" indicates their livelihood and identity, and it is the same word that is picked up in the following verse. If this is correct, then the relational frames of livelihood and identity are projected to the blended space and structure it. One should also note that the blended space created by the syntax 'X to be Y of Z' is itself an input space in a second blend 'A will make B,' which evokes through the use of the future tense the disciples' present vocation as fishermen and underlines the role of A in effecting the change. In other words, the agency of the second blend (or megablend) resides in A, that is, Jesus, the "I" of Mark 1:17, who will change Simon and Andrew from fishers of fish to fishers of humans. This being the case, both deictic pronouns "I" and "you" fix the saying in a concrete situation where the "I" will make something different of the "you" and the context of this direct address (first to second person) provides the frame against which to understand the megablend itself. The clue to this is in the imperative that precedes the blend ("come after me") and the immediate context of the fishers making their living on the shores of the Sea of Galilee. They are commanded to leave their present livelihood, and therefore identity, and come after Jesus. They will no longer live or be identified as fishers of fish.[47] Their senses of livelihood and identity are now dependent not on a familiar socioeconomic domain but on a new sociotheological domain.

IV. CONCLUSION

The primary linguistic context of the expression "fishers of humans" is the Markan narrative. Modern scholarship has long shown a tendency, however, to look elsewhere for the basis of the metaphor. Lurking beneath the façade of intertextuality has been mere guesswork, unbounded by methodological controls such

---

[47] A note of warning is worth sounding at this point. Fauconnier and Turner observe that, in most expressions, there is much that still remains unspecified (*Way We Think*, 147). In turn this gives rise to a multiplicity of blends and resultant meanings, as hearers variously supply the missing details.

as CTM and CBT. The assumption that Mark cannot sufficiently illuminate the metaphor is both pervasive and incorrect.

Jindřich Mánek postulates that Jer 16:16 and cosmological myths involving the sea elucidate a sense of rescue in the expression.[48] Charles W. F. Smith argues that the dark motif of judgment in the Hebrew prophets and Qumran literature supplies the expression with an ominous ring.[49] Wilhelm Wuellner suggests that the multivalent usage of FISHING in antiquity informs the call of disciples as one denoting partnership in Jesus' eschatological mission.[50] And J. Duncan M. Derrett posits that the expression is derived from Ezekiel 47.[51] More recently, Joel Marcus has synthesized much of the relevant scholarship:

> There may not be any need to choose among these different interpretations; the disciples' fishing for people is probably a multivalent image that includes their future missionary preaching, their future teaching, and their future exorcisms (cf. 3:14–15; 6:7, 12–13, 30; 13:9–10), all of which are understood as a participation in God's eschatological war against demonic forces; this war, moreover, recapitulates God's redemption of Israel from Egyptian bondage.[52]

On the other hand, several scholars suggest that the metaphorical expression is formulated so as to match the first disciples' original profession.[53] Unfortunately,

---

[48] Mánek, "Fishers of Men," *NovT* 2 (1957): 138–41. Contra Mánek, the fishing image in Jeremiah 16 does not have salvific implications at all. Interestingly, Ben Witherington III cites Mánek's view as authoritative (*The Gospel of Mark: A Socio-Rhetorical Commentary* [Grand Rapids: Eerdmans, 2001], 86).

[49] Smith, "Fishers of Men," *HTR* 52 (1959): 187–203. He gives the assertion underlying his case on p. 187: "It is insufficient to observe that, since the four men are depicted as fishermen, the summons is appropriately phrased." See also p. 194 for similar statements.

[50] Wuellner, *Meaning of "Fishers of Men."* In much the same vein as Smith and Wuellner, William L. Lane posits that the eschatological sense of FISHING given in the Hebrew Bible and the Dead Sea Scrolls should be transferred to the expression "fishers of men" (*The Gospel According to Mark: The English Text with Introduction, Exposition, and Notes* [2nd ed.; NICNT; Grand Rapids: Eerdmans, 1974], 66–70). See also Scot McKnight, *Jesus and His Death: Historiography, the Historical Jesus, and Atonement Theory* (Waco: Baylor University Press, 2005), 146; Davies and Allison, *Matthew*, 1:398.

[51] Derrett, "Jesus's Fishermen and the Parable of the Net," *NovT* 22 (1980): 108. Two assumptions direct Derrett's case: (a) that the relevant haggadic information (found in the popular midrashic material on Ezekiel 47, Genesis 49, and Deuteronomy 33) was contemporary with *and* known to the historical Jesus, and (b) that therein lies the primary rationale underpinning his movements toward Capernaum, where he would find his first emissaries, fishermen. Moreover, even if these were not assumptions, the proposed bearing of the texts on the historical Jesus is unclear. "That Ezek. xlvii lies in the background to the Calling of the Apostles is recognized in some places in early Christian literature" is extrapolated not with an argument but by a few irrelevant references that are relegated to a brief footnote (p. 120).

[52] Marcus, *Mark 1–8: A New Translation with Introduction and Commentary* (AB 27; New York: Doubleday, 2000), 185. Similarly, Boring, *Mark: A Commentary*, 59: "The imagery and connotations [of the metaphor] are multilayered."

[53] Keener, *Gospel of Matthew*, 151 n. 223; Joy Palachuvattil, *"He Saw": The Significance of*

such promising comments are not accompanied by substantial analysis of the metaphor. Joy Palachuvattil, for example, cites William L. Lane's conclusion as authoritative, one that, by her own argument, is methodologically flawed.[54] In addition, S. O. Abogunrin does not argue for the sense of the metaphor but speculates, "The task to which he called them was to fish for men, to save and bring people into the Kingdom through the preaching of the Good News."[55]

Further, some interpretations exhibit either sensible methodology or conclusions comparable to ours while not arriving at a persuasive marriage of the two. Brian J. Incigneri laudably treats the expression within his reading of the Markan narrative. The unfortunate result is that, in the end, he concludes, "[Jesus'] alluring promise to be 'fishers of men' now seems as if it was deliberately ambiguous."[56] It might well have been so at the beginning of the narrative, but, as we have demonstrated above, this ambiguity is not sustained in Mark. James D. G. Dunn realizes that Mark uses the expression "fishers of humans" as a part of its representation of Jesus' plan to have disciples "assisting or sharing in his own mission" but does not argue or pursue the point.[57] Similarly, N. T. Wright astutely comments, "Jesus commanded [the disciples], imperiously, to leave their present commitment and to follow him, to embrace his way of life and support the needs of his programme and mission."[58] The general sense conveyed by Wright coheres with ours, but it lacks extension vis-à-vis the tangibility of the metaphor itself (which he does not actually treat specifically).

Meier concludes that the expression "fishers of humans" was used by the historical Jesus in calling Simon and Andrew with an eye to the Galilean mission they would embark on.[59] The present study departs from Meier in two respects. First,

---

Jesus' Seeing Denoted by the Verb εἶδεν *in the Gospel of Mark* (Tesi Gregoriana, Serie Teologia 84; Rome: Gregorian University Press, 2002), 109; S. O. Abogunrin, "The Three Variant Accounts of Peter's Call: A Critical and Theological Examination of the Texts," *NTS* 31 (1985): 590; Vincent Taylor, *The Gospel according to St. Mark: The Greek Text with Introduction, Notes, and Indexes* (2nd ed.; London: Macmillan, 1966), 169. Although no footnotes mark this explicitly, it seems as though Abogunrin is following Taylor's comments here. Taylor first states that the "fishers of men" expression surfaces in various OT passages and then suggests that the metaphor "can quite naturally have been suggested by the daily occupation of the brothers." Abogunrin departs from Taylor in emphasizing "quite naturally must" rather than "can quite naturally."

[54] Palachuvattil, *"He Saw,"* 109.

[55] Abogunrin, "Three Variant Accounts," 589. We might also note a similar example from Richard Bauckham: Jesus' promise "probably does envisage the disciples' future missionary role after the resurrection" (*Jesus and the Eyewitnesses: The Gospels as Eyewitness Testimony* [Grand Rapids: Eerdmans, 2006], 171).

[56] Incigneri, *Gospel to the Romans*, 331.

[57] Dunn, *Christianity in the Making*, vol. 1, *Jesus Remembered* (Grand Rapids: Eerdmans, 2003), 557–58; quotation from 558.

[58] Wright, *Christian Origins and the Question of God*, vol. 2, *Jesus and the Victory of God* (Minneapolis: Fortress, 1996), 298.

[59] Meier, *Marginal Jew*, 3:159–63.

Meier does not appreciate the metaphorical nature of the expression and the consequent implications for its sense. The full structuring of the source and target domains through the mapping of the entailment social identity is missed for the sake of a simple transference of 'fishing action' to 'mission action.'[60] Second, while we are perhaps more cautious than Meier with regard to the notion of historicity, we suggest that the Markan narrative indicates one occasion that encompasses the calling, appointing, and sending of the fishers. Such an image might reflect the historical circumstances of Jesus' initial efforts to enroll fellow proclaimers.

"All history involves imaginative reconstruction."[61] An assessment of historicity is inevitably problematic, but it is worth considering how the Markan representation of the metaphor might be compatible with the public career of the historical Jesus.[62] Such a context sufficiently facilitates the creation and efficacy of the metaphor. The same cannot be said of the Markan narrative, even though the metaphor is indeed a coherent aspect of the ironic depiction of the Twelve. The source domain of an effective metaphor must be tangible, because it is chosen specifically in order to elucidate a less familiar concept in a certain way. Familiarity and relevance are basic criteria in the selection. More than simply decorating language, the metaphor structures a new idea(s) and experience(s). Without intuitive, and even intimate, knowledge of the source domain, the intended structure of the target domain is elusive and the metaphor can be unsuccessful. In the case of LIFE IS A JOURNEY, for example, the timeless and universal elements of the source ensure the metaphor's efficacy in structuring LIFE not only linguistically but also cognitively and experientially.[63] A FISHER as depicted in Mark, however, is specifically Galilean and first-century in appearance. It is clear that the historical context in which the source domain A FISHER is most evocative and tangible is in Jesus' first-century Galilean career. In Galilee, and especially on the sea, it is not at all surprising that Jesus would encounter fishermen.[64] And in all likelihood Jesus chose to partner with fishermen because their lifestyle could be adapted to suit his itinerant movement (as opposed to that of peasant farmers, for example).[65] It is indeed natural to construe the creation of the metaphor as instrumental in Jesus' effort to persuade fishers to join him. The metaphor might have been created spontaneously or over a period of time. Jesus may have formulated it in significantly different ways. He may have

---

[60] For example, ibid., 3:161: "[the fishers] who once caught fish before Jesus called them to be disciples, will in the future fish for and catch human beings."

[61] Wright, *Jesus and the Victory of God*, 8.

[62] On the problems associated with the traditional authenticity criteria, see especially Chris Keith and Anthony Le Donne, eds., *Jesus, Criteria, and the Demise of Authenticity* (London: T&T Clark, 2012). Several scholars have argued for the authenticity of the "fishers of humans" logion and/or its surrounding scene with the traditional criteria (see n. 16 above).

[63] Lakoff and Johnson, *Metaphors We Live By*, 5, 61–65.

[64] Consider Josephus, *J.W.* 3.506–8; Strabo, *Geogr.* 16.2.45; Pliny, *Nat.* 5.15.71.

[65] Freyne, *Jesus, a Jewish Galilean*, 52. Consider, too, the frequent use of boats in Mark (3:7, 9; 4:1, 35; etc.). Fishermen afforded Jesus easy mobility.

aimed it at a large number of fishermen without much success. The way in which it has been remembered in Mark might simply be a distortion of a relatively long and complex recruitment campaign in a bustling public space. Or it may simply be the most memorable and successful element of such a campaign. In any case, pragmatic concerns conceivably gave impetus to the metaphor. Persuasive and evocative, it may well have proved the most effective means of drawing individuals away from their families and socioeconomic responsibilities. The metaphor is remembered as the ultimate assurance offered by Jesus to the fishermen. If they embark on preaching and exorcising missions as Jesus does, they will still be accountable to a family, and they will still have an influential social role. "Metaphors may create realities for us, especially social realities. A metaphor may thus be a guide for future action."[66] Thus, we conclude with the proposal that the event of calling, appointing, and sending of the fishermen to proclaim, exorcise, and heal is both the linguistic and the historical context of the metaphor. Mark illustrates the structural metaphor A PROCLAIMER OF THE KINGDOM IS A FISHER in such a way as to suggest, and even reflect, a metaphor that the historical Jesus created and used in his effort to convince some Galilean fishers of their potential efficacy as his agents.

[66] Lakoff and Johnson, *Metaphors We Live By*, 156.

The *JBL* Forum,
an Occasional Exchange

The second *JBL* Forum does not concern a new—or newish—theoretical approach but one of the foundations of "higher criticism" of the Hebrew Bible: source criticism. The main article, by Serge Frolov, is a thoughtful reflection on an earlier article by Philip Yoo, "The Four Moses Death Accounts," which appeared in *JBL* 131 (2012): 423–41. Frolov's article raises serious questions about the epistemological validity of source criticism. Philip Yoo and two other biblical scholars, Shawna Dolansky and David Carr, were invited to respond to Frolov's analysis. I hope you will enjoy the debate, which demonstrates, once more, that while there is nothing new under the sun, all things old can become new again.

We welcome you to join in the conversation by logging onto the Society of Biblical Literature website with your SBL member number. See http://www.sbl-site.org/publications/Journals_JBL_Login.aspx

Adele Reinhartz
General Editor, *Journal of Biblical Literature*

The Death of Moses and the Fate of Source Criticism

SERGE FROLOV
sfrolov@smu.edu
Southern Methodist University, Dallas, TX 75275

The inductive reading of Deuteronomy 34 offered in the present article suggests that the chapter is an entirely coherent, integral composition that fits well in its context on multiple levels and plays an important compositional and conceptual role in this context. By contrast, Philip Y. Yoo ("The Four Moses Death Accounts," *JBL* 131 [2012]: 423–41) argues, deductively building on preceding source-critical scholarship, that the text in question displays traces of all four classical pentateuchal sources that were brought together by a redactor. The sharply divergent results of the two studies expose the source-critical approach as self-contradictory and therefore raise serious doubts about its epistemological validity.

A recent article in *JBL* by Philip Yoo offers a detailed source-critical analysis of Deuteronomy 34.[1] Despite his focus on a specific and relatively short fragment of the Pentateuch, one that has never been pivotal to the source-critical project, Yoo's conclusions raise serious questions about the project's overall epistemological validity. In order to demonstrate this, I will briefly examine Deuteronomy 34 in a strictly inductive manner—in other words, without presupposing any findings of preceding source-critical scholarship or, for that matter, any other diachronic research. The results of this examination will be then juxtaposed with those of Yoo's predominantly deductive study.[2]

---

[1] Philip Y. Yoo, "The Four Moses Death Accounts," *JBL* 131 (2012): 423–41.
[2] I am grateful to two anonymous *JBL* reviewers for their helpful comments on this article and to Dr. Reinhartz for suggesting *JBL* Forum as a venue for it. I would also like to thank the Forum's participants for their thoughtful contributions and to express hope that the discussion of the issues raised will continue in a productive and collegial manner.

I. Deuteronomy 34: An Inductive Reading

Deuteronomy 34:1a

Governed by the *wayyiqtōl* verb ויעל, the sentence has Moses finally comply with YHWH's order to ascend a mountain. Since both Moses (Deut 3:27) and the narrator (Num 27:12; Deut 32:49) quote the order, uniformly using עלה as the predicate, Deut 34:1a is consistent with both the reported speech of Moses and the narratorial discourse. Moreover, in the text's narrative master sequence, formed by *wayyiqtōl*s, the action recounted by the sentence immediately follows the deity's speech cited in Deut 32:49–52.[3] Chapter 33, which separates the two texts, is in essence an enormous nominal clause, with Moses' discourse in vv. 2–29 subordinated to וזאת הברכה אשר ברך משה איש האלהים את־בני ישראל, "and this is the blessing with which Moses, the man of God, blessed the children of Israel" in 33:1. The chapter presents itself therefore as a narrator's digression and thus leaves open the question whether Moses ascended the mountain immediately upon receiving the divine command or lingered to offer blessings to the tribes of Israel.[4] But, even with the latter assumed to be true, it would be difficult to deny that what takes place in Deut 34:1a is thoroughly prepared for by the preceding text. In particular, the area from which Moses begins his ascent, ערבת מואב ("steppes of Moab"), corresponds to that presupposed by Deuteronomy 1, which places the Israelite camp in both the ערבה ("steppe," 1:1b) and ארץ מואב ("the land of Moab," 1:5a), and especially by Num 26:3, 63; 31:12; 33:48–50; 35:1; 36:13; and Josh 13:32.

Following several earlier studies and commentaries, Yoo perceives a tension between Deut 3:27, where YHWH tells Moses (or, more precisely, Moses quotes YHWH as telling him) to ascend ראש הפסגה, and Num 27:12 and Deut 32:49, where his destination is referred to as הר העברים (in the latter case, with the addition הר־נבו). In his opinion, this means that Deut 34:1a conflates two different locations or

---

[3] On *wayyiqtōl* as the basic narrative form of Biblical Hebrew, see, e.g., Wolfgang Schneider, *Grammatik des biblischen Hebräisch: Ein Lehrbuch* (1974; Munich: Claudius, 1993), 182–87, 207–8; Alviero Niccacci, *The Syntax of the Verb in Classical Hebrew Prose* (JSOTSup 86; Sheffield: JSOT Press, 1990); Galia Hatav, *The Semantics of Aspect and Modality: Evidence from English and Biblical Hebrew* (Studies in Language Companion Series 34; Amsterdam: John Benjamins, 1997); Tal Goldfajn, *Word Order and Time in Biblical Hebrew Narrative* (Oxford Theological Monographs; Oxford: Clarendon, 1998), 105–15, 123–35, 143–48; Roy L. Heller, *Narrative Structure and Discourse Constellations: An Analysis of Clause Function in Biblical Hebrew Prose* (HSS 55; Winona Lake, IN: Eisenbrauns, 2004), esp. 430–32.

[4] Further complicating the matter is the *wayyiqtōl verbum dicendi* ויאמר in Deut 33:2. In this respect, the framework syntactic pattern of Moses' final blessing follows that of Deuteronomy as a whole, which begins with an asyndetic nominal clause (1:1–2) but introduces the individual discourses of Moses that constitute almost the entire book with syndetic *wayyiqtōl verba dicendi*.

two different designations of the same location.⁵ Yet the purported tension would exist only if both Abarim/Nebo and Pisgah are individual mountains; this is definitely the case with the former but not necessarily with the latter. Despite most dictionaries (including BDB) and modern translations (the Artscroll Tanach is one rare exception), it is not even obvious that פסגה is a proper noun. Indeed, the fact that it occurs only with a definite article and only in constructs (ראש הפסגה [Num 21:20; 23:14; Deut 3:27; 34:1] and אשדות הפסגה [Deut 3:17; 4:49; Josh 12:3; 13:20]) strongly suggests otherwise.⁶ It is possible therefore that the lexeme should be translated, in accordance with Modern Hebrew usage, as generic "summit" or "ridge."⁷ Even if פסגה is indeed a proper noun, unlike Nebo it does not have to refer to a punctual orographic feature. In Deut 3:16–17; 4:49; and Josh 12:3, אשדות הפסגה ("slopes of the פסגה") serve as tribal boundaries together with such linear markers as the Jabbok, the Arnon, and the shores of the Dead Sea and the Kinnereth; this indicates that the lexeme may refer to the entire massif towering over the Dead Sea and the southern part of the Jordan Valley. In both cases, the divine command quoted by the narrator in Num 27:12 and Deut 32:49 would direct Moses to a specific mountaintop whose very name (עברים, "Crossings") foreshadows the Israelites' upcoming crossing (עבר) of the Jordan and thus suggests a location next to their current encampment.⁸ Moses, however, would disclose to the people in Deut 3:27 only that the deity sent him to the top of the ridge of which this mountain is a part—perhaps to keep the place of his burial secret (as it indeed has been according to the narrator in Deut 34:6b) or maybe because the poignant irony of his having to look at the promised land from the Mountain of Crossings because the divine decree (Deut 3:27; cf. 34:4) forbids him to cross the Jordan was too bitter for him to spell out. As to Deut 34:1a, by bringing the two toponyms together, it would forge a link between the words of Yhwh quoted by Moses and

---

⁵ Yoo, "Four Moses Death Accounts," 425–27. Cf., e.g., S. R. Driver, *A Critical and Exegetical Commentary on Deuteronomy* (ICC; New York: Scribner's Sons, 1895), 418; Martin Noth, *Überlieferungsgeschichtliche Studien: Die sammelnden und bearbeitenden Geschichtswerke im Alten Testament* (Tübingen: Max Niemeyer, 1957), 213 n. 2; Philipp Stoellger, "Deuteronomium 34 ohne Priesterschrift," *ZAW* 105 (1993): 27–28; Lothar Perlitt, "Priesterschrift im Deuteronomium?" in idem, *Deuteronomium-Studien* (FAT 8; Tübingen: Mohr Siebeck, 1994), 139–41; John Van Seters, *The Life of Moses: The Yahwist as Historian in Exodus–Numbers* (Kampen: Kok Pharos, 1994), 452.

⁶ As noted by Joüon-Muraoka, 473, Hebrew proper names usually do not take the definite article. The only exception is the toponyms with an apparently obvious etymology. However, it would be rather unusual for one summit out of many to be called The Summit; note that as proper names הגבעה and הרמה always denote towns rather than elevations as such.

⁷ See Peter C. Craigie, *The Book of Deuteronomy* (NICOT; Grand Rapids: Eerdmans, 1976), 123, 404.

⁸ Eckart Otto sees עברים as a "Kunstname" derived from "Motiv des Jordanüberganges" (*Das Deuteronomium im Pentateuch und Hexateuch: Studien zur Literaturgeschichte von Pentateuch und Hexateuch im Lichte des Deuteronomiumrahmens* [FAT 30; Tübingen: Mohr Siebeck, 2000], 225).

those quoted by the narrator. The significance of such a link in Deuteronomy, whose collection of commandments is the only one in the Pentateuch to be enunciated by Moses (without the deity's explicit command) rather than by Yhwh, is difficult to overestimate.

Deuteronomy 34:1b–3

These two and a half verses constitute a single sentence, governed by *wayyiqtōl* ויראהו and mostly consisting of a long series of direct objects. What transpires here predictably stems from v. 1a: once Moses is on the mountaintop, Yhwh can show him the promised land. Yoo contends that, with the deity quoted in 32:49 as telling Moses to *see* (וראה) the promised land (similarly Deut 3:27), one might expect 34:1b to have Moses *seeing* it (וירא) rather than Yhwh *showing* it to him (ויראהו).[9] That, however, would leave the audience perplexed, for the simple reason that under normal circumstances it is impossible to see the entire promised land (34:1b) all the way to the Mediterranean (הים האחרון, 34:2b), including such far-flung areas as Negeb, Dan, and Naphtali, from any point in the Transjordan.[10] Indeed, under a variety of relatively common weather conditions Moses would not be able even to discern the opposite bank of the Jordan. By bringing Yhwh into the picture and switching, accordingly, to the *hiphil* of ראה, the narrator provided what within the biblical framework qualifies as a satisfactory explanation: the deity vastly extended Moses' horizons by using its supernatural powers. This, in turn, rendered redundant any mention of Moses actually accepting the deity's invitation to "lift [his] eyes westward, northward, southward, and eastward" (3:27) in order to "see the land of Canaan" (32:49): since this is what he pleads for Yhwh to let him do in 3:25, why would he suddenly refuse to look? It is also possible that, by keeping the deity from explaining what exactly Moses is going to see and how exactly he will be able to see it, the text deliberately tricks the audience into fretting that the promised land may have now—after Israel's repeated disaffection and disobedience in the desert—shrunk to what can be normally glimpsed from Nebo. Given the subject's sensitivity, the suspense generated by this maneuver was guaranteed to keep the intended listeners or readers on the edge of their seats through most of Deuteronomy.[11]

---

[9] Yoo, "Four Moses Death Accounts," 429.

[10] As acknowledged by multiple commentators, e.g., Driver, *Deuteronomy*, 419–21; Gerhard von Rad, *Deuteronomy: A Commentary* (OTL; Philadelphia: Westminster, 1966), 210; Jeffrey H. Tigay, *Deuteronomy* דברים: *The Traditional Hebrew Text with the New JPS Translation* (JPS Torah Commentary; Philadelphia: Jewish Publication Society, 1996), 336; Mark E. Biddle, *Deuteronomy* (Smyth & Helwys Bible Commentary; Macon, GA: Smyth & Helwys, 2003), 506.

[11] A similar strategy may be operative in the postponement of Moses' death on the threshold of the promised land, which, as noted by Patrick D. Miller, is foreshadowed already in Numbers 20 and repeatedly mentioned thereafter but actually takes place only in Deuteronomy 34 (*Deuteronomy* [IBC; Louisville: John Knox, 1990], 243). Additionally, Sven Tengström points

The list of the areas that Moses saw neither fully corresponds to other pentateuchal outlines of the promised land nor contradicts any of them. This is precisely what can be expected, given that elsewhere the Pentateuch draws the land's *boundaries* (comprehensive in Num 34:2b–12, much less so in Gen 15:18; Exod 23:31; Deut 11:24; note the word גבול in all these texts except Gen 15:18), while Deut 34:1b–3 lists some of its *components*—future tribal allotments (Dan, Naphtali, Ephraim, Manasseh, and Judah) and geographical regions (Gilead, Negeb, and the Jordan/Dead Sea depression).[12] In this, Deut 34:1b–3 not only makes a contextual adjustment (Moses' wish was to see *the land*, not its boundaries) but also foreshadows the emphasis of Joshua and other books of the Former Prophets on the internal divisions, tribal and otherwise, within the land.[13] If so, the idiosyncratic character of the fragment under discussion contributes to the text's coherence on both the micro-scale of Deuteronomy 34 and the macro-scale of the Enneateuch.

Deuteronomy 34:4

In the next link of the text's master sequence, the deity, having shown Moses the land, appropriately, if somewhat pedantically, confirms that this is indeed what it has sworn to give to Israel's ancestors and that Moses will not cross there. With regard to the land, the verse closely resembles Exod 33:1; Deut 1:8b; and especially Gen 12:7 and follows the substance but not the language of Deut 3:28b; 32:49b, 52b. With regard to Moses, it echoes Deut 3:27b; 31:2b, and, somewhat more remotely, Num 20:12 and Deut 32:52b.[14] Since in Exod 33:1; Num 20:12; Deut 32:49b, 52b

---

out that the *hiphil* of ראה forges a link to Abraham's call in Gen 12:1—in other words, to the very beginning of the quest for the promised land, which Abraham's descendants are now poised to enter, in no small part due to Moses' indefatigable efforts (*Die Hexateucherzählung: Eine literaturgeschichtliche Studie* [ConBOT 7; Lund: Gleerup, 1976], 146).

[12] Such a shift makes good sense in the wake of ch. 33, with its first complete enumeration of Israel's tribes in Deuteronomy; see J. G. McConville, *Deuteronomy* (Apollos Old Testament Commentary 5; Leicester: Apollos, 2002), 476–77. Although the narrator insists that Yhwh showed Moses כל־הארץ ("all the land"), the fact that the list includes allotments of only five tribes clearly indicates that it is not meant to be comprehensive. Interestingly, all the tribes listed here are those represented by major characters of Joshua and Judges: Dan by Samson, Naphtali by Barak, Ephraim by Joshua and Deborah, Manasseh by Gideon, Abimelech, and Jephthah (with the latter also representing Gilead), and Judah by Caleb and Othniel; conversely, only Benjamin, Ehud's tribe, is not included.

[13] By contrast, boundary references in Joshua–Kings are all cursory and desultory, e.g., Josh 1:4; 12:7; 1 Kgs 5:1, 4. See Richard D. Nelson, *Deuteronomy: A Commentary* (OTL; Louisville: Westminster John Knox, 2002), 395.

[14] With regard to the connection between Deut 34:4a and Gen 12:7, see, e.g., Thomas Römer, *Israels Väter: Untersuchungen zur Väterthematik im Deuteronomium und in der deuteronomistischen Tradition* (OBO 99; Freiburg: Universitätsverlag; Göttingen: Vandenhoeck & Ruprecht, 1990), 254–55; Félix García López, "Deut 34, Dtr History and the Pentateuch," in *Studies in Deuteronomy:*

the deity is quoted by the narrator and in Deut 1:8b; 3:27b, 28b; 31:2b by Moses, the sentence once again has the narrator obliquely certify the authenticity of the divine speech in Moses' rendition.

Deuteronomy 34:5

In another move adequately prepared for by the preceding biblical texts (Num 27:12–13; Deut 32:49–50, the most likely referent of על־פי יהוה, "by Yhwh's word"), Moses dies, in narrative terms, immediately upon seeing the promised land. Yoo correctly notes that the sequence עבד־יהוה ("Yhwh's servant") does not occur in the Pentateuch, but he also concedes that, with the deity calling Moses its עבד in Num 12:7, this does not constitute even a minor difficulty.[15] Even more importantly, there are as many as fourteen references to משה עבד־יהוה ("Moses, Yhwh's servant") in Joshua, including two in the first chapter of the book. While to some extent setting Deuteronomy 34 apart from what precedes it, the expression in question (which occurs elsewhere only in 2 Kgs 18:12; 2 Chr 1:3; 24:6) closely connects the chapter to what follows—and, on a broader plane, forges a memorable link between the enneateuchal accounts of Mosaic and post-Mosaic times.

Deuteronomy 34:6a

Burial logically follows Moses' death. By taking care of it and thus preventing desecration of the body by animals or humans, Yhwh—the only suitable antecedent of the sentence's masculine singular predicate—acts as Moses' loving relative (Genesis 23; 2 Sam 21:1–14) or loyal ally (1 Sam 31:8–13). By placing the grave "in the land of Moab" (cf. Deut 1:5; 28:69) and "opposite Beth Peor" (cf. 3:29; 4:46), the narrator further confirms that Moses died not far from the Israelite encampment on the left bank of the Jordan (see above).[16] Yoo astutely observes that the two toponyms never appear together in Deuteronomy.[17] Yet, given the association of both locations with the Jordan and Moses' exposition of the Torah (1:5; 4:44–46), it would not take an exceptionally perspicacious reader or listener to draw a connection between them; all that the narrator does in 34:6a is spell it out.

In Honour of C. J. Labuschagne on the Occasion of His 65th Birthday (ed. F. García Martínez et al.; VTSup 53; Leiden: Brill, 1994), 55; Otto, *Das Deuteronomium*, 217–18; Nelson, *Deuteronomy: A Commentary*, 395.

[15] Yoo, "Four Moses Death Accounts," 432.

[16] Jean-Pierre Sonnet (*The Book within the Book: Writing in Deuteronomy* [Biblical Interpretation Series 14; Leiden: Brill, 1997], 194) and Nelson (*Deuteronomy: A Commentary*, 396) point out that, by echoing the reference to "the land of Moab" in Deut 1:5, the discussed clause completes an *inclusio* around Moses' discourses in Deuteronomy. Moses dies in the general area of his farewell addresses to the people.

[17] Yoo, "Four Moses Death Accounts," 433. Cf. Stoellger, "Deuteronomium 34," 32–33.

Deuteronomy 34:6b–7

The text's narrative master sequence is now interrupted by a series of four non-*wayyiqtōl* clauses, one nominal (v. 7a) and three governed by *qatal* verbs (vv. 6b, 7bα, 7bβ). Both the syntax of the piece and its content (it supplies additional information associated with Moses' death and burial) identify it as a narrator's digression. The digression's placement and its structure are anything but haphazard. First, although the comments concerning Moses' age and physical condition at death might seem more suitable right after v. 5, having them there would spoil the impression of Yhwh interring Moses without delay; at the same time, after v. 6a they would awkwardly intrude between two mutually connected clauses dealing with Moses' burial and therefore prominently featuring the root קבר. Second, by momentarily arresting the narrative's flow, the digression as a whole facilitates the switch from what transpires between Yhwh and Moses on the mountaintop (vv. 1–6a) to the developments in the Israelite camp in the valley below (vv. 8–9) while at the same time preparing for the (likewise digressive) paean to Moses in vv. 10–12 (see below).

Concerning Moses' age, the digression echoes his words in Deut 31:2, but his admission of his concomitant inability "to go out and come in," that is, to direct the conquest of the promised land discussed in the verses that follow, possibly contradicts the narrator's upbeat assessment of his fitness at death (34:7b).[18] Even if, in the narrator's mind, keen vision and overall suppleness (cf. the adjective לֵחַ, apparently a close cognate of לַח, in Gen 30:37; Num 6:3; Judg 16:7–8; Ezek 17:24; 21:3) were not sufficient for military leadership, the fact remains that in Deut 31:2 Moses emphasizes the deterioration of his physical condition while in 34:7b the narrator insists that it did not change.[19]

In assessing this contradiction, it is important to keep in mind the differences between the communicative situations of the two speakers and, accordingly, their widely divergent rhetorical objectives. The narrator in Deut 34:7 is preparing the ground for the proclamation of Moses' unique stature in vv. 10–12 and therefore

---

[18] For "going out and coming in" as military activity, see, e.g., Josh 14:11; 1 Sam 18:13; 29:6; 2 Sam 5:2. Note also that in Num 27:17 Moses specifically requests a successor "to take [the people] out and to bring them in" and that in Num 27:21 the deity obliquely endorses this job description while reserving for itself the prerogative to authorize these moves through the high priest.

[19] See Otto, *Das Deuteronomium*, 211; A. D. H. Mayes, *Deuteronomy* (NCB Commentary; Grand Rapids: Eerdmans, 1979), 413; Van Seters, *Life of Moses*, 454; Thomas C. Römer and Marc Z. Brettler, "Deuteronomy 34 and the Case for a Persian Hexateuch," *JBL* 119 (2000): 403; Nelson, *Deuteronomy: A Commentary*, 395; Yoo, "Four Moses Death Accounts," 434. Tigay suggests, following traditional Jewish commentaries, that "Moses' *vigor* had, in fact, abated … but despite his years he did not look aged" (*Deuteronomy*, 338). For a somewhat different understanding of the term לֵחַ, see W. F. Albright, "The 'Natural Force' of Moses in the Light of Ugaritic," *BASOR* 94 (1944): 32–35.

trying to counterbalance the negative impression caused by the character's forced demise in punishment for the alleged lack of faith (Num 20:1-12). For that purpose, v. 7b claims that Moses managed not only to reach the limit of human life established by YHWH already in Gen 6:3 (an achievement rivaled, apart from the ancestors of all Israel, only by Aaron [Num 33:39]) but also to escape the ravages of advanced age, something that no other biblical character is credited with.[20] Moses, by contrast, seeks in Deut 31:1-6 to reassure his listeners with regard to the impending invasion of the promised land—a prominent motif that Deuteronomy shares with both Numbers and, on a massive scale, with the opening chapter of Joshua (note the imperative חזק ואמץ, "be strong and take courage," in Deut 31:6-7, 23; Josh 1:6-7, 9, 18). Therefore, he has to address the people's inevitable concerns about the deity taking away the only leader they have ever known (in terms of Num 14:20-38, all of them, except Caleb and Joshua, must have been born in the desert). In an elegant maneuver, Moses confirms that YHWH has indeed prohibited him from crossing the Jordan (Deut 31:2b) but plays down the potential effect of the divine decree by proclaiming himself unfit to go to war (v. 2a) and then stressing that Joshua and the deity will be more than adequate replacements (vv. 3-6).[21]

Deuteronomy 34:8a

As already mentioned, after the break in vv. 6b-7 the text's narrative thread resumes in v. 8 at new spatial and probably temporal coordinates (although the Israelites are likely aware that Moses went away to die, they have no way of knowing when exactly it will happen).[22] Nevertheless, the events follow the order of a typical funeral: in the last *wayyiqtōl* clause before the digression (v. 6a) Moses is buried, and in the first *wayyiqtōl* clause after it (v. 8a) the people mourn his death.

---

[20] See George W. Coats, "Legendary Motifs in the Moses Death Reports," *CBQ* 39 (1977): 35-36.

[21] Dennis T. Olson sees here a dialectic of Moses being "heroic and legendary and at the same time subject to the limits and weaknesses of all human beings" (*Deuteronomy and the Death of Moses: A Theological Reading* [OBT; Minneapolis: Fortress, 1994], 168). According to Sonnet, in ch. 31 "Moses was ... trying to impress the audience, evading the real issue that his forthcoming death is at God's order" (*Book within the Book*, 194).

[22] For this reason, it is difficult to sustain the contention of Olson (*Deuteronomy and the Death of Moses*, 166), García López ("Deut 34," 52-53), and Römer and Brettler ("Deuteronomy 34," 402) that Deuteronomy 34 falls into three main parts, vv. 1-6, 7-9, and 10-12. The same is true of the five-part structure (vv. 1-3, 4, 5-8, 9, 10-12) suggested, without substantiation, by McConville (*Deuteronomy*, 476). Thematically, there are two major components in the piece, one dealing with Moses' death proper (vv. 1-7) and the other with Israel in this death's aftermath (vv. 8-12, including the statement of vv. 10-12 that Moses' stature forever remained unmatched). Syntactically, each part begins with a piece of the narrative master sequence (vv. 1-6a, 8-9) and ends with a narrator's digression (vv. 6b-7, 10-12).

Thirty-day mourning for Moses precisely matches that for Aaron (Num 20:29), and the location where it takes place, ערבת מואב, precisely matches Deut 34:1a.

Deuteronomy 34:8b–9

Joshua tactfully picks up the reins of leadership (v. 9a) only when the mourning period is over (v. 8b). The hiatus is indicated also by the use of *qatal* מלא in v. 9a despite the nondigressive character of the clause. The reference to Moses laying hands upon Joshua reminds the audience about Num 27:12–23, and the mentions in Deut 34:9b of the people obeying (וישמעו) Joshua and doing as Yhwh had commanded (צוה) Moses allude to the same piece (cf. Num 27:19b, 20b, 22–23).[23] As demonstrated by Jean-Pierre Sonnet, both roots also forge multiple, and possibly meaningful, links to several Deuteronomic texts.[24]

Deuteronomy 34:10–12

Governed by the *qatal* verb קם and dominated by the enormous subordinated clause in vv. 10b–12, the piece unambiguously presents itself as a narrator's digression meant to draw a line under Moses' life and the period of his leadership, both spanning four of five books of the Pentateuch. By no means accidentally, when the text's narrative master sequence resumes in Josh 1:1, the narrator immediately identifies everything reported thereafter as taking place "after the death of Moses"—even though technically the mourning for him in Deut 34:8 and Joshua's assumption of power in v. 9 also fall in this category. With regard to Yhwh knowing Moses "face to face," the text echoes Exod 33:11 and, of course, distills the gist of the long relationship between the two.[25] The rest of the digression most closely resembles

---

[23] Yoo contends that the statement of Deut 34:9 that Moses transferred his authority to Joshua by laying hands upon him agrees with Num 27:18–23 but not with Deut 31:7–8, 14–23, where first Moses and then the deity give Joshua instructions ("Four Moses Death Accounts," 435–36). It is by no means clear why the two scenes cannot be seen as complementary: Joshua is appointed Moses' successor in Numbers 27 and installed as such in Deuteronomy 31. By mentioning only the former act, Deuteronomy 34 singles it out as crucial.

[24] Sonnet, "Redefining the Plot of Deuteronomy—From End to Beginning: The Import of Deut 34:9," in *Deuteronomium: Tora für eine neue Generation* (ed. Georg Fischer, Dominik Markl, and Simone Paganini; Beihefte zur Zeitschrift für altorientalische und biblische Rechtsgeschichte 17; Wiesbaden: Harrassowitz, 2011), 37–49.

[25] Römer and Brettler maintain that this statement "fundamentally contradicts" Deut 4:15 ("Deuteronomy 34," 406). Even apart from the fact that Moses' "you have seen no image" in the latter verse does not necessarily mean "I have seen no image," Hebrew פנים אל־פנים does not have to be understood literally, no more so than French *tête-à-tête*. Nothing demonstrates this more clearly than Moses' words in Deut 5:4, addressed to the people: "Face to face [פנים בפנים] did Yhwh speak to you on the mountain, out of the midst of fire." Finally, the subject of Deut 34:10b is the

Deut 4:34; 26:8: both pieces mention אתת ומופתים ("signs and wonders"), יד חזקה ("strong hand"), and מורה גדול ("great terror"), with minor variations.[26] Strikingly, all of these, attributed elsewhere to Yhwh, are associated here with Moses; the only difference is that there is no command to acknowledge Moses' feats liturgically (contrast Deut 26:1–11). By essentially erasing the boundary between the deity and its human agent, the narrator obliquely indicates that no distinction should be made between the Deuteronomic instruction, ascribed to Moses, and that of Exodus–Numbers, coming directly from Yhwh.[27] The concluding verses of the chapter under discussion thus give a powerful boost to its tendency to affirm the ultimately numinous origin of Moses' discourses cited in Deuteronomy (see on vv. 1a, 4 above).

It has almost become a truism of (diachronic) scholarship that, by singling out Moses as the greatest prophet of all times, the text contradicts—or, perhaps, corrects—his promise in Deut 18:15, 18 that Yhwh will raise up "a prophet like [him]."[28] However, "like me" does not necessarily mean "of the same stature"; it may refer to functions, responsibilities, authority, and the like. Indeed, in the context of Deut 18:15–22, which discusses the proper role of the prophet in the community, it would be highly incongruous—not to mention grossly immodest—for Moses to utter something along the lines of "there will never be another prophet like me." Conversely, such a statement is both contextually and conceptually appropriate in the narrator's mouth, as a part of what essentially constitutes Moses' epitaph, whose ultimate purpose is to bolster the authority of the instruction that, according to Deuteronomy, he first delivered orally (most of the book) and then wrote down

---

deity, not Moses; even if Moses never actually saw Yhwh, the latter, at the very least, had to see Moses at close quarters while burying him (see above on Deut 34:6a).

[26] For a list of other occurrences of these expressions, see Römer and Brettler, "Deuteronomy 34," 406–7.

[27] The disappearance of the boundary between Yhwh and Moses also explains why the former had to keep the burial place of the latter in secret by singlehandedly interring him (see above on Deut 34:6a), while no such precautions were taken with regard to Abraham, Isaac, Jacob, Joseph, Aaron, Joshua, Samuel, or David. In Moses' case, the risk of posthumous deification was substantially higher.

[28] E.g., Noth, *Studien*, 209 n. 3; Mayes, *Deuteronomy*, 413–14; Otto, *Das Deuteronomium*, 229; Nelson, *Deuteronomy: A Commentary*, 395, 397; Bernard M. Levinson, "Deuteronomy," in *The Jewish Study Bible: Jewish Publication Society Tanakh Translation* (ed. Adele Berlin, Marc Zvi Brettler, and Michael Fishbane; Oxford: Oxford University Press, 2004), 450; Karin Finsterbusch, *Deuteronomium: Eine Einführung* (Uni-Taschenbücher 3626; Göttingen: Vandenhoeck & Ruprecht, 2012), 195; Yoo, "Four Moses Death Accounts," 436–37. Relatively rare exceptions include Georg Braulik, *Deuteronomium* (2 vols.; NEchtB 15, 28; Würzburg: Echter, 1986, 1992), 2:246; Christa Schäfer-Lichtenberger, *Josua und Salomo: Eine Studie zu Autorität und Legitimität des Nachfolgers im Alten Testament* (VTSup 58; Leiden: Brill, 1995), 188 n. 399; and Sonnet, *Book within the Book*, 197.

(31:9). If there has never been a prophet of his caliber, all past, present, and future challenges to his Torah can be dismissed out of hand.[29]

II. Summary and Reflection

The inductive reading of Deuteronomy 34 undertaken above shows that the chapter in question (1) does not display any internal inconsistencies; (2) fits well into its context on multiple levels, from that of Moses' farewell in Deut 32:48–33:29 to that of the Enneateuch as a whole;[30] (3) contains multiple intertextual links to several biblical books, especially to the balance of Deuteronomy, but also (in the descending order of density) to Numbers, Joshua, Genesis, and Exodus; (4) stands in any degree of tension to only one other biblical text, Deut 31:2aβ. If so, inductively there is no warrant whatsoever to ascribe Deuteronomy 34 to multiple hands and very little to ascribe it to a hand different from that of any other part of the Enneateuch. In the latter respect, the tension between Deut 31:2aβ and Deut 34:7b with regard to Moses' physical condition at death may be an exception, but, as explained above, even here multiple authorship is not the only available solution.[31]

By contrast, Yoo's deductive analysis "reveals that the contents of [Deuteronomy 34] can be satisfactorily traced back to *each of the four classical pentateuchal documents.*"[32] Among other things, he demonstrates that within the source-critical framework, ראש הפסגה in Deut 34:1 and the entire v. 4 should be assigned to J, the honorary title משה עבד־יהוה in v. 5 and the entire paean to Moses as the greatest

---

[29] On the competing norms that the Deuteronomic narrator could have in mind, see Tigay, "The Significance of the End of Deuteronomy (Deuteronomy 34:10–12)," in *Texts, Temples, and Traditions: A Tribute to Menahem Haran* (ed. Michael V. Fox et al.; Winona Lake, IN: Eisenbrauns, 1996), 137–43.

[30] Concerning the latter level, see esp. Hans-Christoph Schmitt, "Dtn 34 als Verbindungsstück zwischen Tetrateuch und Deuteronomistischem Geschichtswerk," in *Das Deuteronomium zwischen Pentateuch und Deuteronomistischem Geschichtswerk* (ed. Eckart Otto and Reinhard Achenbach; FRLANT 206; Göttingen: Vandenhoeck & Ruprecht, 2004), 181–92; and, in the same volume, Konrad Schmid, "Das Deuteronomium innerhalb der 'deuteronomistischen Geschichtswerke' in Gen – 2 Kön," 193–211.

[31] I have argued elsewhere that it is methodologically sound to follow the Bible's default framework as long as it is possible (Serge Frolov, *The Turn of the Cycle: 1 Samuel 1–8 in Synchronic and Diachronic Perspectives* [BZAW 342; Berlin: de Gruyter, 2004], 30–34). From this standpoint, in the absence of explicit attributions of Deut 31:2aβ and Deut 34:7b to different hands, it is redundant to postulate them if the tension between the two verses can be chalked up to the divergent rhetorical goals of the speakers. But even in a strictly diachronic perspective, the tension in question might at most indicate that Deuteronomy 31 and 34 belong to different sources, not that there are four sources behind the latter.

[32] Yoo, "Four Moses Death Accounts," 440 (emphasis added).

prophet of all time in vv. 10–12 to E, the geographical reference גי מול בית פעור and the comment that Moses' grave remains unknown in v. 6 to D, and the mention of הר נבו in v. 1a and the entire list of locations in vv. 1b–3 to P.[33] Yoo concludes, accordingly, that what we know today as Deuteronomy 34 is a pastiche put together by a redactor.[34]

This, in turn, raises a serious epistemological concern. One of the most basic premises of source criticism is that the individual or individuals responsible for the canonical shape of the Pentateuch were unable or unwilling to get rid of all the factual discrepancies, conceptual disagreements, rough transitions, and the like between the four documents they used, thereby making it possible to isolate these documents. Yet, as far as Deuteronomy 34 is concerned, by deductively building on existing source-critical scholarship, Yoo comes to the conclusion that the putative redactor(s) *were*, after all, able and willing to create out of all four putative pentateuchal documents a text that reads inductively—if the present article is any indication—as perfectly coherent and perfectly or almost perfectly integrated in its immediate and larger contexts. To put it more bluntly, Deuteronomy 34 exposes source criticism as it stands today as self-contradictory.

It is possible to argue, of course, that in certain cases the redactor may have had reasons, rhetorical or otherwise, deliberately to leave the text rough. However, this line of reasoning runs into what is commonly known as the paradox of the vanishing redactor: the same argument applies to an author, making it unnecessary to postulate multiple sources underlying the text. Neither is it possible to identify any considerations that might have caused the redactor to handle Deuteronomy 34 with greater care than other parts of the Pentateuch. Yoo does seem to make a step in this direction when he postulates that "in an uninterrupted narrative, Moses can die only once."[35] This is by no means certain, given that in the received biblical text Joshua dies twice (Josh 24:29; Judg 2:8), as does Samuel (1 Sam 25:1; 28:3).

To be sure, any reading of the Bible is just that: a reading open to contestation.[36] However, given the sharp discrepancy between the findings of Yoo's study and those of the present article, demonstrating that one or both of them are way off the mark would not be sufficient to address the epistemological concern formulated above. Deuteronomy 34 may be just a tip of the iceberg, and to determine whether this is

---

[33] See especially the painstaking reconstruction of the texts allegedly underlying Deuteronomy 34 in Yoo, "Four Moses Death Accounts," 441.

[34] See esp. Yoo, "Four Moses Death Accounts," 439–40.

[35] Yoo, "Four Moses Death Accounts," 424.

[36] Although virtually all diachronically minded exegetes have identified multiple sources or redactional layers behind Deuteronomy 34, many, if not most, of them might disagree with Yoo's thesis that the chapter displays traces of all four classical pentateuchal sources (note, however, the claim of Driver [*Deuteronomy*, 417] that it is a combination of JE, D, and P). The only detailed synchronic study of Deuteronomy 34 that I am aware of, that of García López ("Deut 34," 52–56), brings him to the conclusion that it "can be read as *one single narrative*" (emphasis his).

indeed the case it is necessary to check in a systematic manner whether the existing source-critical hypotheses self-contradictorily presuppose multiple documents behind comparably coherent pieces. In other words, these hypotheses not only need to untangle texts that are problematic but also need to avoid problematizing those that are not.[37] And if that proves impossible, they might have to take a cue from Moses and head to Mount Nebo.[38]

---

[37] Characteristically, the stated purpose of Yoo's article is to find "a plausible solution that untangles the complexities of [Deuteronomy 34]" ("Four Moses Death Accounts," 424). As pointed out above, from the inductive standpoint, these "complexities" are almost or completely nonexistent.

[38] Redaction criticism avoids the epistemological problem discussed here because it postulates that each successive redactor purposefully revised the received text in accordance with a certain agenda. Source criticism (which, perhaps not accidentally, has been much less popular among scholars in recent decades) views the redactor as mainly an antiquarian whose primary purpose was to combine several texts created independently of each other in a satisfactory way. Yoo's conclusion that in Deuteronomy 34, "nowhere does the redactor offer a significant contribution to the content" ("Four Moses Death Accounts," 440) is a good example of the latter approach.

The Place of Deuteronomy 34 and Source Criticism: A Response to Serge Frolov

PHILIP Y. YOO
philip.yoo@theology.ox.ac.uk
University of Oxford, Oxford OX1 3LD, United Kingdom

In his discussion on source criticism, Professor Frolov frequently refers to my essay "The Four Moses Death Accounts," and I welcome the opportunity to respond to his conclusions.[1] Verse by verse and section by section, Frolov follows my analysis of Deuteronomy 34 and offers an alternative explanation for what I identify as the literary difficulties that led to my conclusion that this chapter is composed from four originally independent documents. Opposing the approach that I have undertaken, Frolov argues that an inductive reading of Deuteronomy 34 reveals neither any internal contradictions within this chapter nor external contradictions with other biblical materials outside of this chapter (with the possible exception of Deut 34:7b with 31:2b). Furthermore, Frolov argues that the incompatibility of my deductive reading with his inductive reading of Deuteronomy 34 reveals that source criticism is contradictory; he ultimately questions source criticism's epistemological validity and joins the calls for its final marching orders. My purpose here is not to respond directly to these calls, as other critics have done so elsewhere.[2] Instead, my comments will focus on the utility of some of the current expressions of source criticism toward interpreting Deuteronomy 34 and its application in the wider biblical corpus.

The abbreviations employed in this essay are as follows: D (Deuteornomy); E (Elohist); J (Yahwist); P (Priestly); P^G (Priestly *Grundschrift*); H (Holiness).

[1] Serge Frolov, "The Death of Moses and the Fate of Source Criticism," *JBL* 133 (2014): 648–60; Philip Y. Yoo, "The Four Moses Death Accounts," *JBL* 131 (2012): 423–41.

[2] From the perspective of the so-called Neo-Documentary Hypothesis, see responses in Baruch J. Schwartz, "Does Recent Scholarship's Critique of the Documentary Hypothesis Constitute Grounds for Its Rejection?" in *The Pentateuch: International Perspectives on Current Research* (ed. Thomas B. Dozeman, Konrad Schmid, and Baruch J. Schwartz; FAT 78; Tübingen: Mohr Siebeck, 2011), 1–16; Joel S. Baden, *The Composition of the Pentateuch: Renewing the Documentary Hypothesis* (AYBRL; New Haven: Yale University Press, 2012).

As presented in Frolov's essay, an inductive reading of Deuteronomy 34 demonstrates that this text can be read and understood without significant internal or external inconsistencies. Similar readings of other pentateuchal texts are also likely to conclude that these texts are a coherent whole, fit quite well within their surrounding corpus, and support the opinion that the Pentateuch actually contains few contradictions. However, the fact that a single chapter of the Pentateuch or the entire corpus can be read both inductively and deductively does not undermine source criticism but covers its basic tenets: specifically, the preservation and collation of the documents and the reasonable success of this enterprise undertaken by the redactor(s). Readings of the biblical text are open to contestation, and this certainly applies to the identification of literary problems—contradictions included—that are to some degree a value judgment exercised by each exegete. I agree that the Pentateuch reads reasonably well as a whole, but I consider the discrepancies in the laws and the disagreements in narrative claims to be the main indications that signify that the Pentateuch is an eclectic text shaped from originally independent sources. Accordingly, contradictions in the Pentateuch are unavoidable due to the preservation of the literary and ideological differences among the source documents. Occasionally, the precision of certain details is lost to a redactor because of his temporal distance from the source materials.[3] Compared to other units of the Pentateuch, the contradictions are subtle in Deuteronomy 34. Some of the original claims of the sources are preserved, such as Moses' ability to see the entire land (vv. 1b–3) because his vision had not dimmed (v. 7);[4] however, the unique juxtaposition of Pisgah with Nebo in v. 1a reflects a geographical understanding that is lost to the redactor.[5]

For early critical readers, Deut 34:1–12 raised a question: How could Moses write all of this chapter if he dies in 34:5? In an oblique reference to the final verses of Deuteronomy 34, R. Nehemiah opines that Joshua, not Moses, wrote "eight verses of the *torah*" (*b. B. Bat.* 14b). The rabbis of the Talmud anticipate the view

---

[3] Here I also have in mind the loss of precision of Priestly terminology as demonstrated by H's supplementation of P. See examples in Jacob Milgrom, *Leviticus 17–22: A New Translation with Introduction and Commentary* (AB 3A; New York: Doubleday, 2000), 1327–28.

[4] This is a detail that surfaces not only in the final form of Deuteronomy 34 but also in one of the source documents; specifically P. See Yoo, "Four Moses Death Accounts," 434.

[5] I maintain that הפסגה is a proper noun in Deut 34:1a and elsewhere (see Frolov, "Death of Moses," 649–51). It is unusual for a Hebrew proper name to take on the definite article, but here is an exception to the rule. In another exception, ירדן ("Jordan") is frequently attested as an arthrous noun. The explanation may lie in that ירדן and פסגה were originally common nouns that became proper nouns to refer to a specific geographical location. The conflation of originally different names to refer to a single geographic place can be found in later commemorations of events. According to 1 Kgs 19:18, Elijah fasts on Horeb (with Sinai absent in Kings), but in his praise of Elijah, Ben Sira follows the final form of the Pentateuch and equates Horeb and Sinai as the same place (48:7) (see Patrick W. Skehan and Alexander A. Di Lella, *The Wisdom of Ben Sira: A New Translation with Notes* [AB 39; New York: Doubleday, 1987], 533).

that the final verses of Deuteronomy were composed from multiple hands. Félix García López opines that Deuteronomy 34 "can be read as *one single narrative*," but he also presents this chapter as a multilayered composition that consists of Deuteronomistic, Priestly (KP), and pre-Priestly Deuteronomic (KD) materials.[6] In response to the classical view that Deuteronomy 34 contains P, Lothar Perlitt raises the question, "Priesterschrift im Deuteronomium?"[7] In short, his answer is no. The impact of Perlitt's separation of Deuteronomy 34 from the original Priestly materials is most evident in contemporary Continental European pentateuchal criticism. Combined with the quick demise of E and eventually J in Continental European and European-influenced scholarship, questions on the existence of Priestly materials in Deuteronomy 34 have resulted in robust discussion on two separate but related fronts: the stratification of the Priestly materials (as I shall discuss below, with a growing number of proposals for the end of P^G in Exodus and less so in Numbers) and the composition of the book of Numbers, with an ascending view that Numbers does not contain Priestly materials but rather, post-Priestly hexateuchal and pentateuchal redactions, which are, in turn, the last layer(s) of the Pentateuch.[8]

The solution that I propose for Deuteronomy 34 follows a line of inquiries into the composition of this chapter. Not all practitioners of source criticism would

---

[6] García López, "Deut 34, Dtr History and the Pentateuch," in *Studies in Deuteronomy: In Honour of C. J. Labuschagne on the Occasion of His 65th Birthday* (ed. F. García Martínez et al.; VTSup 53; Leiden: Brill, 1994), 61 (emphasis original). García López adapts the insights in Erhard Blum, *Studien zur Komposition des Pentateuch* (BZAW 189; Berlin: de Gruyter, 1990), esp. 76–88.

[7] Perlitt, "Priesterschrift im Deuteronomium?" *ZAW* 100 Supplement (1988): 65–88; reprinted in *Deuteronomium-Studien* (FAT 8; Tübingen: Mohr, 1994), 123–43.

[8] See Thomas Römer, "Das Buch Numeri und das Ende des Jahwisten: Anfragen zur 'Quellenscheidung' im vierten Buch des Pentateuch," in *Abschied vom Jahwisten: Die Komposition des Hexateuch in der jüngsten Diskussion* (ed. Jan Christian Gertz, Konrad Schmid, and Markus Witte; BZAW 315; Berlin: de Gruyter, 2002), 215–31; idem, "Israel's Sojourn in the Wilderness and the Construction of the Book of Numbers," in *Reflection and Refraction: Studies in Biblical Historiography in Honour of A. Graeme Auld* (ed. Robert Rezetko, Timothy H. Lim, and W. Brian Aucker; VTSup 113; Leiden: Brill, 2007), 419–45; idem, "Zwischen Urkunden, Fragmenten und Ergänzungen: Zum Stand der Pentateuchforschung," *ZAW* 125 (2013): esp. 19–20; Reinhard Achenbach, *Die Vollendung der Tora: Studien zur Redaktionsgeschichte des Numeribuches im Kontext von Hexateuch und Pentateuch* (Beihefte zur Zeitschrift für altorientalische und biblische Rechtsgeschichte 3; Wiesbaden: Harrassowitz, 2003); idem, "Die Erzählung von der gescheiterten Landnahme von Kadesch Barnea (Numeri 13–14) als Schlüsseltext der Redaktionsgeschichte des Pentateuchs," *ZABR* 9 (2003): 56–123; Rainer Albertz, "Das Buch Numeri jenseits der Quellentheorie: Eine Redaktionsgeschichte von Num 20–24," *ZAW* 123 (2011): 171–83, 336–47; idem, "A Pentateuchal Redaction in the Book of Numbers? The Late Priestly Layers of Num 25–36," *ZAW* 125 (2013): 220–33. See, however, arguments for the continuation of $P^{(G)}$ in Numbers in Ludwig Schmidt, "Die Priesterschrift—kein Ende am Sinai!" *ZAW* 120 (2008): 481–500; Suzanne Boorer, "The Place of Numbers 13–14* and Numbers 20:2–12* in the Priestly Narrative (Pg)," *JBL* 131 (2012): 45–63; Jean-Louis Ska, "Old and New in the Book of Numbers," *Bib* 95 (2014): 102–16.

share my conclusions concerning the division of Deuteronomy 34, and there exist other solutions.[9] However, the observation that multiple practitioners of the same method can arrive at different results does not invalidate the method itself.[10] Rather, divergent results invite further discussion toward refining the method. I anticipate that more diachronically minded solutions to Deuteronomy 34 will follow due to the importance of the relationship of this chapter with its surrounding texts.[11] How one views the composition of Deuteronomy 34 influences one's views on the composition of the book of Deuteronomy, the formation of the Pentateuch, the extent of the Priestly source, and to a lesser extent the shape of the pentateuchal materials that are neither Priestly nor Deuteronomic.

Near the end of his article, Frolov absolves redaction criticism of the problems he associates with source criticism by remarking that it "avoids the epistemological problem discussed here because it postulates that each successive redactor purposefully revised the received text in accordance with a certain agenda."[12] It is my understanding that redactors (however their roles are defined) do not operate uniformly throughout the biblical corpus, and my intent here is not to turn this discussion into a critique of another method. It is my estimation, however, that redaction criticism and source criticism share similar methodological problems. Returning to the discussion of the end of the original Priestly materials before Deuteronomy 34, some critics perceive a sharp break in the depictions of the Israelites in Numbers and, placing these materials as later strata, argue that the base layer of P portrays an Israelite mission that is successfully completed after the establishment of the tabernacle cult. There is, however, a lack of consensus on the extent of Israel's success and, in turn, of P^G's precise end.[13] Placing P^G's last verse in Exod 40:34b, Albert

---

[9] For example: J, P, and the first additional layer to D (Dtn1) in Richard Elliot Friedman, *The Bible with Sources Revealed: A New View into the Five Books of Moses* (San Francisco: HarperSanFrancisco, 2003), 367–68; E, P, and D in Menahem Haran, *The Biblical Collection: Its Consolidation to the End of the Second Temple Times and Changes of Form to the End of the Middle Ages* (in Hebrew; 3 vols.; Jerusalem: Bialik and Magnes, 1996–2008), 2:193 n. 8; and the three non-Deuteronomic sources in Baden, *Composition of the Pentateuch*, 147–48.

[10] On this point, see Schwartz, "Documentary Hypothesis," 5.

[11] Since the publication of my article, see Angela Erisman Roskop, "Transjordan in Deuteronomy: The Promised Land and the Formation of the Pentateuch," *JBL* 132 (2013): 779–88. Roskop detects a series of revisions that give Deuteronomy 34 its final shape.

[12] Frolov, "Death of Moses," 660 n. 38.

[13] Among the proposals are the following: Exod 29:42–46 (Eckart Otto, "Forschungen zur Priesterschrift," *TRu* 62 [1997]: 1–50); 40:33b (Thomas Pola, *Die ursprüngliche Priesterschrift: Beobachtungen zur Literarkritik und Traditionsgeschichte von Pg* [WMANT 70; Neukirchen-Vluyn: Neukirchener Verlag, 1995], 291–97); v. 34 (Reinhard G. Kratz, *Die Komposition der erzählenden Bücher des Alten Testaments: Grundwissen der Bibelkritik* [UTB 2157; Göttingen: Vandenhoeck & Ruprecht, 2000], 104–5; Eng., *The Composition of the Narrative Books of the Old Testament* [trans. John Bowden; New York: T&T Clark, 2005], 105–6); Lev 16:34 (Christoph Nihan, *From Priestly Torah to Pentateuch: A Study in the Composition of the Book of Leviticus* [FAT

de Pury writes, "Within Elohim's nations of the earth, Israel has one mission only: to establish and keep the dwelling that will allow Yhwh (i.e. Elohim in his ultimate identity) to reside among humanity in the midst of the Israelites."[14] I agree to a certain extent. The Israelites, as was the case with any respectable ancient Near Eastern people, were under the obligation to maintain the earthly abode of their deity and to appease Yhwh with proper sacrifice. However, the claim that P must end with the successful establishment of the tabernacle cult and that subsequent redactors reshaped P to suit another agenda is, I submit, akin to a hypothetical proposal that a basic layer of Mark exists with its original end in the climactic transfiguration of Jesus on a mountain in Mark 9:8, from which the first edition of Mark was supplemented with additional pericopes that align the evangelist's testimony with the other Gospels. Critics can reasonably postulate that an addition to Mark indeed exists after 9:8 but not until 16:9–20 and there is solid support for upholding 16:9–20 as an addition to the original Gospel: Mark's original conclusion in Mark 16:8 was deemed to be theologically deficient after the other Gospels, namely, Matthew, Luke, and John, were widely circulated.[15] Returning to the issue of the stratification of the Priestly materials, the question as to whether $P^{(G)}$ actually conceived that the Israelites were successful in establishing and properly maintaining Yhwh's earthly abode remains an open one in the absence of recovered evidence from the Israelite priesthood.

The problem of a secure methodological identification of a theological or ideological agenda of a redactor exists in another form for source criticism. In support for the continuation of the Priestly source beyond the establishment of the tabernacle, it is my opinion that the Priestly writers believed that the Israelites could not meet the high standards of care for Yhwh's earthly abode after its construction and even after Yhwh issues the sacrificial and procedural laws. However, until a parchment of an actual pentateuchal source or fragment is securely recovered, the investigation of a literary unit continues to be determined by the exegete's academic (and to a certain degree, nonacademic) environment but seeks balance through scholarly debate and discussion. Accordingly, how a biblical literary unit is defined is subject to examination and, when necessary, revision. In a historical review on the state of scholarship on J, Jean-Louis Ska remarks on the nature of the dialogue that has shaped the discussion of a biblical "source" throughout modern biblical criticism:

2/25; Tübingen: Mohr Siebeck, 2007], 20–68); and, Num 27:12–13 (Ed Noort, "Bis zur Grenze des Landes? Num 27,12-13 und das Ende der Priesterschrift," in *The Books of Leviticus and Numbers* [ed. Thomas Römer; BETL 215; Leuven: Peeters, 2008], 99–119).

[14] De Pury, "P^G as the Absolute Beginning," in *Les dernières rédactions du Pentateuque, de l'Hexateuque et de l'Ennéateuque* (ed. Thomas Römer and Konrad Schmid; BETL 203; Leuven: Peeters, 2007), 111.

[15] See Adela Yarbro Collins, *Mark: A Commentary* (Hermeneia; Minneapolis: Fortress, 2007), 801–18.

> As long as the discussion remains ideological, very little progress can be made and J will continue to travel from century to century, and to change face according to new exegetical "fashions." The basic problem, which is not always discussed with the required accuracy, is that of the literary nature of J, since this "source" is not exactly a "theological treatise." The future of J depends mostly on our ability to discover J's "plot," to define J's style, to list his compositional devises and patterns, to identify his particular way of unfolding a complete and structured narrative about Israel's origins and of integrating Israel's fundamental legislation into this narrative.[16]

"J" could be replaced by the name of any other source, fragment, or redactional layer, and, with any appropriate yet minor changes, the above statement would perceptively continue to describe any other biblical literary unit. For source criticism, the challenge to define a source on the basis of its own unique ideological and historiographical frame is applicable not only for J but also for D, E, and P. In this regard, I maintain that Deuteronomy 34 may be viewed as a microcosm of the Pentateuch: the four source documents agree on the basic event of Moses' death in the Transjordan, but, when read on their own, the source documents disagree among themselves as they recount the same event through their own perspectives. On a grander scale, the overarching narrative of each of the source documents depicts the origins of Israel's cult and confederacy but through the ideology of the individual source. The recognition that the source documents are unique in their own right and promote their own underlying *Weltanschauung* remains a challenging, but crucial, step toward addressing the incoherence of the final form of the Pentateuch.

Critics have observed the resonances between Deuteronomy 34 and other biblical texts, most notably in Genesis, Exodus, Numbers, the rest of Deuteronomy, and Joshua. Frolov and I follow these critics, but I relate Deuteronomy 34 to the Pentateuch (specifically, the source documents) and Frolov places Deuteronomy 34 within the Enneateuch. Here a question is raised: What are the parameters for determining the coherence and, if desirable, the literary units for Deuteronomy 34 or any other pentateuchal text? With the shifting views on the viability of a Tetrateuch, Pentateuch, Hexateuch, or Enneateuch, there are new questions on the relationship between the books and units in Genesis–Kings. However, source criticism does not address the composition of most of the Former Prophets, and its focus is mainly on the Pentateuch.[17] To take an example from another part of the Pentateuch and one commonly found in introductions to the Hebrew Bible, I have yet to be convinced of explanations for Genesis 6–9 as derived from (for the most part) a single hand as a suitable alternative to the source-critical solution of two

---

[16] Ska, "The Yahwist, a Hero with a Thousand Faces: A Chapter in the History of Modern Exegesis," in Gertz et al., *Abschied vom Jahwisten*, 23.

[17] An exception is Richard Elliot Friedman, *The Hidden Book in the Bible* (San Francisco: HarperSanFrancisco, 1998).

originally independent accounts in Genesis–Deuteronomy.[18] As is the case with Genesis 6–9, any source-critical solutions to Deuteronomy 34, or for that matter any unit in the Pentateuch, should take into account the surrounding text. Some clarity, however, is required in defining the exact parameters of the surrounding text. I believe that a positive direction for future investigation of Deuteronomy 34—and for that matter the Pentateuch—lies in a renewed examination of the composition of Joshua. Compared to Genesis–Deuteronomy, Joshua poses a different set of compositional challenges, as it contains textual complications on a greater scale than those detected in Genesis–Deuteronomy. While I am not fully advocating for a complete return to an older expression of the Documentary Hypothesis, within the discussion on the place of Deuteronomy in its surrounding corpus, there exist reasons to re-examine the classical source-critical view of the continuation of D, E, J, and P into Joshua and to raise the possibility of any *hexateuchal* source documents.[19]

There are indeed questions that source criticism cannot and should not address. Source criticism would have little, if any, relevance for questions surrounding the shape of the book of Deuteronomy that was read in the early Christian period.[20] Likewise, few (if any) practitioners of source criticism would propose documents in order to untangle any existing literary problems in the Latter Prophets or biblical wisdom literature. The biblical corpus reflects the production of different types of literature (prose, poetry, legal texts, dirges, aphorisms, etc.) in ancient Israel. Specifically with regard to the laws and narratives that form the Pentateuch (and perhaps in Joshua), source criticism provides a "literary solution to a literary

---

[18] See the spirited argument for the coherence and later reworking of Genesis 6–9 in Gordon J. Wenham, "The Coherence of the Flood Narrative," *VT* 28 (1978): 336–48; idem, *Genesis 1–15* (WBC 1; Waco: Word, 1987), 163–64.

[19] For the classical view of the source documents continuing into Joshua, see Julius Wellhausen, *Die Composition des Hexateuchs und der historischen Bücher des Alten Testaments* (1899; 4th repr.; Berlin: de Gruyter, 1963), 116–34; William E. Addis, *The Documents of the Hexateuch: Translated and Arranged in Chronological Order* (2 vols.; New York: Putnam, 1893); J. Estlin Carpenter and George Harford-Battersby, *The Hexateuch according to the Revised Version* (2 vols.; London: Longmans, Green, 1900), esp. 2:303–59. For portions of Joshua 18–19 as P, see Jacob Milgrom, *Leviticus 1–16: A New Translation with Introduction and Commentary* (AB 3; New York: Doubleday, 1991), 30–31; Philippe Guillaume, *Land and Calendar: The Priestly Document from Genesis 1 to Joshua 18* (Library of Hebrew Bible/Old Testament Studies 391; London: T&T Clark, 2009), 157–63. Against the existence of Priestly materials in Joshua, see Rainer Albertz, "The Canonical Alignment of the Book of Joshua," in *Judah and the Judeans in the Fourth Century B.C.E.* (ed. Oded Lipschits, Gary N. Knoppers, and Rainer Albertz; Winona Lake, IN: Eisenbrauns, 2007), 287–303. I speculate that the composition of Joshua lies in a complex accretion of sources, fragments, and redactions.

[20] For the use of the entire book of Deuteronomy among early Christian exegetes, see David Lincicum, *Paul and the Early Jewish Encounter with Deuteronomy* (WUNT 2/284; Tübingen: Mohr Siebeck, 2010), 64–192.

problem."²¹ The idea of four originally independent source documents, once identified on the basis of their ideological and historical claims about deity, cult, and Israel's past, not only fits well into the diversity of literature from ancient Israel but also offers solutions to the complexities detected in the Pentateuch. Despite our differences on the validity of source criticism in reading biblical texts, I thank Professor Frolov for his responses to my essay and for raising points that challenge the tenets of source criticism. In my view, some of the current expressions of source criticism have benefited from engaging with and responding to similar challenges.

[21] Baden, *Composition of the Pentateuch*, 249.

# Deuteronomy 34: The Death of Moses, Not of Source Criticism

SHAWNA DOLANSKY
shawna.dolansky@carleton.ca
Carleton University, Ottawa, ON K1S 5B6, Canada

Serge Frolov's article is formulated as a response to Philip Yoo's argument that all four pentateuchal sources can be found in the final chapter of the book of Deuteronomy.[1] Yoo's argument is based on the Documentary Hypothesis; using his knowledge of each of the separate sources within the Pentateuch up to that point, Yoo is able to separate the works of the J, E, P, and D sources in the culminating chapter of Deuteronomy. Frolov refers to Yoo's method as exemplary of deductive reasoning, as indeed it is. In contrast, Frolov seeks to demonstrate that inductive reasoning would lead to the opposite conclusion: that, in fact, Deuteronomy 34 is a unified "master narrative."[2] Frolov concludes that, if he can read the text as coherent and unified and yet Yoo finds four sources behind this unified document, then "Deuteronomy 34 exposes source criticism as it stands today as self-contradictory."[3]

But finding a unified passage—especially in Deuteronomy—where others see multiple sources hardly seems cause enough to characterize the entire source-critical enterprise as self-contradictory. Frolov's emphasis on method is to be commended, as a basic understanding of methodology in source-critical study is sorely lacking in our field. Unfortunately, Frolov's method of reading the text inductively and the conclusions he derives only serve to further muddy the waters concerning what the Documentary Hypothesis is, and what source critics do.

First, in terms of his discussion of Yoo's arguments, Frolov's postulation of a

[1] Philip Yoo, "The Four Moses Death Accounts," JBL 131 (2012): 423–41; Serge Frolov, "The Death of Moses and the Fate of Source Criticism," JBL 133 (2014): 648–60.
[2] By this Frolov means that the text can be read inductively as a coherent whole (both in itself and in terms of its "perfect" integration within the larger contexts of both Deuteronomy and the Pentateuch).
[3] Frolov, "Death of Moses," 659.

669

unified "master narrative" behind Deuteronomy 34 is not so much argued for as stated repeatedly in contrast to Yoo's evidence to the contrary. For example, Yoo argues that 34:1a conflates Deut 3:27, in which Moses quotes Yhwh as having told him to ascend ראש הפסגה, with Num 27:12 and Deut 32:49, where his destination is referred to as הר העברים (with the addition הר־נבו in Deut 32:49). Frolov claims that Pisgah is not necessarily the name of a mountain and may mean simply "summit" or "ridge," or even the whole set of mountains over the Dead Sea and southern Jordan Valley. In any case, rather than the different terms being in tension or contradiction, Frolov asserts that "by bringing the two toponyms together, it would forge a link between the words of Yhwh quoted by Moses and those quoted by the narrator. The significance of such a link in Deuteronomy, whose collection of commandments is the only one in the Pentateuch to be enunciated by Moses (without the deity's explicit command) rather than by Yhwh, is difficult to overestimate."[4]

Similarly, in 34:6a, Yhwh buries Moses "in the land of Moab" and "opposite Beth Peor." Yoo notes that these two toponyms are never found together elsewhere; Frolov states that this does not mean anything, asserting that it is logical to link the site of Moses' last speech with the area of the Israelite encampment on the left bank of the Jordan.

I fail to see an argument in either case. Frolov posits that it might make sense to bring together distinct terms into one comprehensive designation. I cannot speak for Yoo, but I do not see how he would disagree with that. Yoo's point—and the point of source criticism—is not to dispute that separate, contradictory sources have been brought together into one unified text here. Frolov's demonstration of the ways in which these verses in their present form constitute a coherent whole does not undermine the argument for originally separate sources underlying that whole.

Further, while in 34:6b-7 Yoo posits separate sources,[5] Frolov maintains that the break in flow constitutes a "narrator's digression" rather than a seam between sources, explaining that "the digression's placement and its structure are anything but haphazard."[6] But justification or rationalization of the placement of this piece is not an argument for a "master narrative." At most it is again an argument that a "master narrative" may have been forged very deliberately and carefully from originally separate sources.

---

[4] Frolov, "Death of Moses," 650–51.

[5] Many others have noted the existence of separate sources in Deut 34:6–7. See, e.g., S. R. Driver, *A Critical and Exegetical Commentary on Deuteronomy* (ICC; New York: Scribner's Sons, 1909), 424; Richard E. Friedman, *The Bible with Sources Revealed: A New View into the Five Books of Moses* (San Francisco: HarperSanFrancisco, 2003), 368; Richard D. Nelson, *Deuteronomy: A Commentary* (OTL; Louisville: Westminster John Knox, 2002), 395; Thomas C. Römer and Marc Z. Brettler, "Deuteronomy 34 and the Case for a Persian Hexateuch," *JBL* 119 (2000): 403.

[6] Frolov, "Death of Moses," 654.

In dealing with the disparity between Moses' physical condition in Deut 34:7b (which Yoo attributes to P) and 31:2 (which Yoo attributes to D), Yoo argues for a stark contrast between the reasons for Moses' not crossing the Jordan in each source.[7] Frolov compares the "widely divergent rhetorical objectives" between the discrepant accounts and explains how they both form part of the same master narrative with no need for source divisions.[8]

Once again, Frolov has dismissed Yoo's argument without actually engaging it. Yoo's point is not that the narrative does not make sense or cannot be read as a coherent whole in its present form if one explains away seeming contradictions; rather, it is that the text contains contradictions that can be directly traced back to two separate sources in the larger Pentateuch. Frolov does this again in 34:8a, where the "digression" gives way to a new temporal and spatial setting, and similarly when he explains 34:10–12 as "a narrator's digression meant to draw a line under Moses' life and the period of his leadership, both spanning four of five books of the Pentateuch."[9] Looking outside of Deuteronomy 34 (which would seem contrary to his inductive method of isolating ch. 34 to demonstrate its inherent unity), Frolov similarly dismisses the tension between 34:10b and Deut 4:15 pointed out by Thomas Römer and Marc Zvi Brettler,[10] and that between 34:12 and Deuteronomy 18:15 (for which Yoo presents alternative source-critical solutions, and then argues for his own). Once again, Frolov simply explains the contradictions away. It is unclear here how this demonstrates the underlying unity of Deuteronomy 34 as a "master narrative," but it does clarify a larger agenda: Frolov is ultimately seeking to debunk any source-critical reading of any Pentateuchal text.

Frolov explains his "inductive" method by reference to its use in his earlier work on 1 Samuel,[11] in which he proceeds from the assumption that "as long as there is no weighty rationale not to read the text on its own terms, a reasonably unbiased interpretation tends toward the default frame of reference, integrating the pieces of evidence that do not readily fit in with it or pronouncing them

---

[7] Further, he sees congruence between Deut 34:8 and P's account of Aaron's burial in Num 20:29 (Yoo, "Four Moses Death Accounts," 434–35). Yoo concludes with the proposition that "similarities (the age of Moses' death) and differences (Moses' physical condition) exist in the P and D death reports" (p. 434 n. 45).

[8] Frolov, "Death of Moses," 654–55: "In assessing this contradiction, it is important to keep in mind the differences between the communicative situations of the two speakers and, accordingly, their widely divergent rhetorical objectives.... In an elegant maneuver, Moses confirms that Yhwh has indeed prohibited him from crossing the Jordan (Deut 31:2b) but plays down the potential effect of the divine decree by proclaiming himself unfit to go to war (v. 2a) and then stressing that Joshua and the deity will be more than adequate replacements (vv. 3–6)."

[9] Frolov, "Death of Moses," 656.

[10] Römer and Brettler, "Deuteronomy 34 and the Case for a Persian Hexateuch," 406.

[11] Frolov, "Death of Moses," 658 n. 31: "I have argued elsewhere that it is methodologically sound to follow the Bible's default framework as long as it is possible."

inconsequential."¹² Source criticism proceeds from the same premise, only offered as a means of resolution when a given passage cannot be read coherently without positing more than one hand at work.¹³ Where Frolov and source criticism part ways is in his choice to either force contradictory evidence to fit a predetermined framework or ignore it altogether. (This is also where Frolov's method parts ways with good scientific inquiry.) Critical reading of the text since the eighteenth century has acknowledged that the Pentateuch is not a unified composition, and ignoring the contradictions, doublets, and discontinuities in the narrative,¹⁴ as Frolov proposes, still does not make it so.

Further, it is not self-evident that reading the text in its "default frame of reference," that is, in its received canonical form, necessarily forms the basis for a "reasonably unbiased interpretation." Conservative theologians regularly read the text this way, from firmly entrenched biases; in fact, the canonical form represents a set of theological biases that scholars, through source criticism and other critical means, have sought for the past 250 years to uncover, sift through, and make sense of from a more secular and scholarly position. It seems to me that in good literary analysis—as in proper scientific analysis—if data do not all conform to one's initial hypothesis, then that hypothesis needs to be corrected to accommodate the data. In his treatment of 1 Samuel, Frolov seems to be proposing the opposite state of affairs; that one could equally "integrat[e] the pieces of evidence that do not readily fit in with [the hypothesis] or pronounc[e] them inconsequential." Frolov continues his elucidation of method with an explanation that if the contradictions do lead one to reject the initial hypothesis in favor of a different one, "Each choice [i.e., rejection of contradictory data, or rejection of initial hypothesis] would be essentially arbitrary, or, rather, logical only in terms of the exegete's ideological and/or aesthetic preferences having nothing to do with the text as such. Moreover, both

---

¹² Serge Frolov, *The Turn of the Cycle: 1 Samuel 1–8 in Synchronic and Diachronic Perspectives* (BZAW 342; Berlin: de Gruyter, 2004), 33.

¹³ For an excellent and up-to-date overview of source criticism and the Documentary Hypothesis, see the first chapter of Joel Baden's *The Composition of the Pentateuch: Renewing the Documentary Hypothesis* (AYBRL; New Haven: Yale University Press, 2012), which begins "The critical study of the composition of the Pentateuch begins, in practical terms, and began, in terms of the history of scholarship, with the attempt to read the pentateuchal narrative from beginning to end as a unified whole."

¹⁴ Baden highlights these three overlapping groups of problems as demonstrative of the lack of unification of the text. "The hallmark of a unified composition, one created by a single author, is internal consistency: consistency of language and style, consistency of theme and thought, and above all, consistency of story. Every narrative makes certain claims about the way events transpired—who, what, when, where, how, and why. When these elements are uniform throughout a text, there is no pressing need to inquire as to its unity. In the Pentateuch, however, historical claims made in one passage are undermined or contradicted outright in another. The problems identified by the Reformation scholars are the same as those we struggle with today and can be classified in three major overlapping groups: contradictions, doublets, and discontinuities" (*Composition of the Pentateuch*, 16).

interpretations would be equally true no matter how divergent and even incompatible they might prove."[15]

Perhaps I misunderstand, or perhaps I have a different definition of what it might mean for interpretations to be "equally true." Perhaps my own ideological and/or aesthetic preferences tend too much toward the logical. To be sure, the goals of the interpreter are central in choosing, say, between a theological interpretation and a literary or historical one, but if, for example, the text at hand contains internal contradictions, and if those contradictions, when separated, line up exactly with previous texts in terms of theme and content, then it would be incumbent upon the "reasonably unbiased" exegete to consider a source-critical analysis of the text in question. This basic premise of the Documentary Hypothesis is missed by Frolov in his discussion of Yoo. It is further missed (or misunderstood) in Frolov's attempt to undermine the validity of the source-critical method or of the hypothesis, based only on a reading of Deuteronomy 34, that concludes (and also begins with the assumption) that this chapter can be read as a coherent whole. This is simply not a valid test of either the hypothesis or the source-critical method.

Like Frolov, source critics begin with an attempt to read the text as it has been received. However, when problems with the text's internal consistency (of language, style, theme, thought, and general story line) are perceived by the reader, a solution to those problems in the form of a documentary hypothesis—a theory that several originally distinct documents underlie the received unified text—is posited. Source criticism is an attempt to discern those underlying documents in cases where the text does not seem internally consistent. In other words, the Documentary Hypothesis is not an a priori assumption imposed on the Pentateuch, as Frolov seems to understand it. It is rather a solution to problems dictated by the text itself.

Frolov's misunderstanding of both the nature of the Documentary Hypothesis and the source-critical method used to investigate it is demonstrated by his conclusion: that if the "putative redactor(s) *were*, after all, able and willing to create out of all four putative pentateuchal documents a text that reads inductively ... as perfectly coherent and perfectly or almost perfectly integrated in its immediate and larger contexts ... [then] Deuteronomy 34 exposes source criticism as it stands today as self-contradictory."[16] But even assuming that Frolov is able to persuade anyone that Deuteronomy 34 is "perfectly coherent," Frolov mischaracterizes the nature of pentateuchal redaction. Contradictions between sources are found throughout the Pentateuch—even if Frolov explains each one away—which is why the Documentary Hypothesis was proposed in the first place. But this does not mean that where there are no contradictions there are no sources.

As Joel Baden has argued, and as Frolov has inadvertently demonstrated:

> the compiler did not simply preserve his sources: if this had been the sole aim, he could have simply set them down one after the other. The sources have been

---

[15] Frolov, *Turn of the Cycle*, 33.
[16] Frolov, "Death of Moses," 659.

combined into a single story, and in this the compiler reveals himself as a master of narrative logic.... The manner in which the compiler has interwoven his sources is deceptively simple: he set them down in the only logical, chronological order possible.... If something could logically happen twice, even if it seems literarily infelicitous to the modern reader, the compiler left it twice ... contradictions are not the issue: the creation of a single chronologically coherent story is apparently what drove the compiler's method.[17]

And, as Baden has further noted, throughout the Pentateuch, the compiler intervenes to harmonize birth, death, and marriage notices—precisely those events that cannot logically have happened more than once—so that "none is told more than once, though it is almost certain that J, E, and P all told them."[18]

Both inductive reasoning and deductive reasoning are employed in scientific investigations, and both have a place in literary criticism of the Bible. Inductive reasoning makes broad generalizations from specific observations. For example, one could read Genesis 1–3 or 6–9 inductively and come to the conclusion that there is clearly more than one source represented in each of these sections of Genesis. This would warrant the proposal of a hypothesis to be generalized across the entire book of Genesis, or the Pentateuch, or the Tanakh, that there is more than one documentary source behind the received form of the text. The next stage of investigation, however, would be to see how such a documentary hypothesis holds up for other segments of text. The method by which this investigation would be conducted is source criticism, and it builds on the aggregate of accumulated evidence for separate sources that are often in tension with each other but are each internally consistent across the larger body of received text.[19] In other words, after inductive reasoning proposes a hypothesis, deductive reasoning is required to test that hypothesis. Source criticism represents the type of deductive reasoning used to explore, expand, and refine the Documentary Hypothesis in biblical study.

Equally, one could start with an inductive reading of Deuteronomy 34 in isolation from the rest of the Pentateuch and conclude that, since it reads fairly coherently as a unified narrative, therefore the rest of the Pentateuch must as well. If Deuteronomy 34 does not require a division among sources in order to make sense of it, then no chapter, pericope, or section of the Pentateuch requires dividing among sources in order to make sense. However, once the exegete attempted to test this unified hypothesis deductively against other portions of the received text, it would become apparent that a unified hypothesis cannot account for the variety of discrepancies *within* other segments of text that also happened to line up

---

[17] Baden, *Composition of the Pentateuch*, 225–26.
[18] Ibid., 226.
[19] For an important and concise discussion of the Documentary Hypothesis relying on an aggregate of converging lines of evidence, see Richard E. Friedman, *The Hidden Book in the Bible* (San Francisco: HarperSanFrancisco, 1998), 350–78; idem, *Bible with Sources Revealed*, 27–31; see also Baden, *Composition of the Pentateuch*, esp. ch. 1.

consistently with discrepancies *across* texts. Eventually, the exegete would notice that, although Deuteronomy 34 *could* be read as a unified whole, in light of the aggregate of evidence from the rest of the Pentateuch, Deuteronomy 34 in fact manages to tie up loose ends from at least three, if not all four[20] of the other documentary sources into one seemingly unified account of Moses' death.[21]

A deductive reading to investigate the hypothesis (which is the method by which hypotheses are tested in scientific investigation) also eliminates Frolov's "paradox of the vanishing redactor,"[22] by which he means "if the received version of the text makes sense as it stands, why see it as a redactional compilation rather than an integral authorial creation? And if it does not, perhaps there was no redactor at all?"[23] The redactor is necessarily posited as part of the Documentary Hypothesis once it is observed that (a) there are several, often contradictory, perspectives contained within a given text; (b) these differing perspectives line up with (and often continue, or refer back to) themes, ideas, and historical points of view contained in preceding strands of text in other passages; and (c) these perspectives have been combined into a single narrative. If the text does not make sense as it stands, and if an exegete posits from this that there are multiple sources behind its current form, it is not therefore logical to conclude there was no redactor (someone clearly had to put it all together), but rather it is incumbent on the exegete to try to understand the redactor's reasoning and method in putting these sources together. If, however, one reads the text inductively and sees it as a coherent "master narrative," there is no need to posit a redactor, as there are no sources to redact: hence, the redactor vanishes, along with the sources that require redaction.[24]

---

[20] Baden maintains that the D source is absent from this chapter (*Composition of the Pentateuch*, 146–48). Yoo posits possible connections to D in the phrase "the land of Moab" and in aspects of vv. 10–12 ("Four Moses Death Accounts," 432 n. 37).

[21] See Baden, *Composition of the Pentateuch*, 147–48, in which he argues that the J source can be found in the location of Pisgah, which picks up where J's wilderness itinerary left off in Num 21:16–20, as well as in the repetition of J's patriarchal promise word for word from Exod 33:1 (and these are hypothesized to be J texts based on exegetical analysis of each of these passages in light of their affinity and continuity with other passages assigned to J). The location referred to as "the steppes of Moab" harks back to other passages assigned to P, as do the phrase "Mount Nebo, opposite Jericho" as the place of Moses' death, the clause "at the command of Yhwh" in reference to Moses' dying, and the note of Moses' age of 120 years and his physical state in Deut 34:7–9. The notion of Moses as Yhwh's servant repeats the phrase from the E text of Num 12:7, as does the concept of Yhwh's exclusive "face-to-face" relationship with Moses.

[22] Frolov, "Death of Moses," 659.

[23] Frolov, *Turn of the Cycle*, 26. One wonders if, by the same logic, Frolov's analysis of the *Diatessaron* would cause Tatian to vanish. Or would the four Gospel writers vanish instead?

[24] As William H. C. Propp notes, only the redactor's work has survived: *it* is the received version of the text with which we are all working, regardless of method. The hypothetical source constituents are exactly that—hypothetical. But they require a hypothetical redactor to have put them together (*Exodus 19–40: A New Translation with Introduction and Commentary* [AB 2A; New York: Doubleday, 2006], 734). Further, as Propp points out here (p. 734) and as Friedman

It is true that historically source critics have tended to be overconfident, methodologically inconsistent, and often at odds with each other. The lack of a clear and consistent source-critical method applied universally has led, on the one hand, to a proliferation of unwieldy and ultimately untenable arguments for overly complicating and fragmenting the Documentary Hypothesis.[25] On the other hand, the lack of method has led to the facile dismissal of the hypothesis as "dead" by those who deny the validity or purpose of source criticism and yet are unable or unwilling either to propose a better solution to the problems of the text than the Documentary Hypothesis or to engage in the exegetical work required by the Documentary Hypothesis—"deductive" methodical source criticism across the entire Pentateuch—in order to refine our understanding of the means by which the received text was composed, compiled, and canonized.

Yoo's method of investigating each of the contradictions and breaks in narrative flow that he finds in Deuteronomy 34 and correlating them with earlier Pentateuchal texts is precisely what source critics do. The Documentary Hypothesis proposes the consistency of each contradiction in a redacted passage with aspects of identified source texts by the same authors outside that particular piece. This is why it is unclear to what end an exegete would conduct an inductive reading of an isolated chapter (when the chapter divisions themselves are *post factum* and often arbitrary) in the context of a discussion of source criticism. If the purpose were to examine the form, tradition, theological, or rhetorical strategies of that piece, an inductive reading would make sense. What is self-contradictory is to impose an inductive reading on a piece of text for the purpose of refuting the hypothesis that there are several sources represented in it. If an inductive reading is conducted in order to develop a different hypothesis for the origin of the text, proper scientific investigation should proceed by testing that hypothesis against deductive readings across other related texts. Frolov's hypothesis that Deuteronomy 34 is coherent and unified makes sense only if he ignores or eschews scientific investigation of preceding pentateuchal texts to test such a "unified hypothesis" against the evidence for a documentary hypothesis. Asserting a unified hypothesis based on an inductive reading of one chapter of the Pentateuch does not (and cannot) call into question the validity of a source-critical method for testing a documentary hypothesis across the entire Pentateuch.

---

exemplifies in his work (e.g., from his 1987 *Who Wrote the Bible?* and following works on source criticism in 1998 and 2005 to his *Commentary on the Torah* in 2001), reading and appreciating the received text, on the one hand, and speculating about its original antecedents, on the other, need not be mutually exclusive enterprises.

[25] Friedman discusses the dearth of method in literary criticism in more detail in *Hidden Book in the Bible*, 361–78. For an overview of problems with the classical formulation of the Documentary Hypothesis and approaches to (and reasons for) renewing the Hypothesis, see the concluding chapter in Baden, *Composition of the Pentateuch*.

Unified until Proven Disunified? Assumptions and Standards in Assessing the Literary Complexity of Ancient Biblical Texts

DAVID M. CARR
carrdavid@gmail.com
Union Theological Seminary, New York, NY 10027

Serge Frolov's response to Philip Yoo's article on Deuteronomy 34 purports to "expose [the] source-critical approach as self-contradictory" and to raise "serious doubts about its [source criticism's] epistemological validity." I argue here that Frolov's article does nothing of the sort. Instead, both Yoo's and Frolov's articles show how a researcher's specific assumptions—whether those of Yoo or of Frolov himself—can limit that researcher's analysis. Yoo stratifies Deuteronomy 34, a text that Frolov rightly states "has never been pivotal to the source-critical project," based on a set of assumptions that derive from his specifically *Neo*-Documentarian approach. Frolov's response discards all source-critical assumptions and presents a somewhat harmonizing, "inductive" reading of Deuteronomy 34 that smooths over some mild problems within the chapter itself and also its contrasts with some other biblical traditions.[1]

Yoo begins with an unstated assumption that the Pentateuch was created out of four source documents, and he moves on to state that three of the sources—J, E, and P—"included an account of Moses' death," and he is "open to the probability that D includes a death account of Moses."[2] This is his sole reason for assigning the two words reporting Moses' death, וימת משה ("and Moses died"; 34:5*), to all four

---

[1] Philip J. Yoo, "The Four Moses Death Accounts," *JBL* 131 (2012): 423–41; Serge Frolov, "The Death of Moses and the Fate of Source Criticism," *JBL* 133 (2014): 648–60.

[2] Yoo, "Four Moses Death Accounts," 424.

sources.³ In most other cases (including the rest of 34:5), Yoo assigns parts of Deuteronomy 34 to J, E, D, and P by comparing these parts of Deuteronomy 34 to other pentateuchal passages assigned by him to these four sources as they are contained in a database of assignments of pentateuchal texts to J, E, D and P that he does not give in his article. For example, Yoo (following others) assigns Moses' ascent of Mount Nebo in the plains of Moab in 34:1a to P based on its connections to Deut 32:49, a verse Yoo assigns to P but which many other contemporary source critics would not.⁴ Sometimes he adds additional arguments. For example, he presupposes a complete source analysis of the Pentateuch (not given or referred to in the article itself) in arguing that the description of Joshua's succession to Moses in Deut 34:9 cannot be assigned to J because of "the lack of mention [in J] of a character named Joshua up to this point."⁵ Furthermore, he notes connections of 34:9 to P materials anticipating this "laying on of hands" in Num 27:18, 23, while arguing that 34:9 is *not* compatible with the description of Moses' commissioning of Joshua in 31:7 (assigned by Yoo to D) and Yhwh's commissioning of Joshua in 31:14, 23 (assigned by Yoo to E). Finally, a major assumption for Yoo is "that R, whenever possible, fully preserves and uses his sources,"⁶ and this leads him to make sure that his source assignments connect with each other as much as possible and produce maximally readable texts.

In sum, Yoo presupposes that Deuteronomy 34 is a conflation by a redactor ("R") of four sources found across the rest of the Pentateuch—J, E, D, and P—each of which is preserved virtually completely across the Pentateuch, whose parts can be recognized primarily through similarity to other parts of the same source (as analyzed by Yoo), along with occasional conflicts of parts of Deuteronomy 34 with other pentateuchal source materials (as assigned by Yoo). Since Yoo neither gives nor cites an overview of the pentateuchal source texts that are the basis of his analysis, it is ultimately impossible for any reader of his article (without access to his source database) to verify crucial parts of his argument (the distribution of criteria, the plausibility of the source attributions used to derive them, the absence of certain features from a source) or his general claim that the Pentateuch is created out of the four sources by a redactor who preserved them almost completely.⁷

---

³ Ibid., 432: "I assume that each document must include Moses' death and contain the phrase וימת משה (or a close variant)."

⁴ Ibid., 425–26. For brief discussion of recent disintegration of consensus on P in Deuteronomy, see below, pp 680–81 and n. 15.

⁵ Ibid., 435.

⁶ Ibid., 438.

⁷ Clarity on the shape of Yoo's postulated pentateuchal sources is less a problem for P and D, since it seems clear that Yoo generally presupposes a consensus on identification of D and P texts that is a few decades out of date (on this see below, pp. 680–81 and n. 15), but it is a more substantial problem for E and J. Past source analyses substantially diverged from each other on assignment of pentateuchal texts to J and E, and the Neo-Documentarian approach, of which Yoo

Frolov is not as explicit about his assumptions as Yoo, but his article appears guided by one major premise, briefly stated in a footnote, "that it is methodologically sound to follow the Bible's default framework as long as it is possible."[8] By this statement he seems to mean that one should read a biblical text as literally unified unless it is clearly shown to be otherwise, not having recourse at any point to results from analyses of other, potentially related texts. Put another way: a text is unified for Frolov unless proven disunified. Sometimes this principle leads Frolov to relatively persuasive alternative readings to those offered by Yoo. Where Yoo, for example, argues that Yʜᴡʜ showing Moses the land in 34:1b is not compatible with Moses' report of Yʜᴡʜ's command for Moses to ascend the top of Pisgah and see the land (3:27),[9] Frolov plausibly suggests (building on other commentators) that Yʜᴡʜ plays an extra role in helping Moses see the land from Pisgah (34:1b), because seeing the whole land from Pisgah could be regarded as something unachievable with unaided human sight.

In other cases, Frolov's reading is less successful. For example, he suggests that Moses himself downplays his abilities to lead the people "to go out and come in" in Deut 31:2 in order to comfort them about their impending loss of his leadership, while the apparently contrary proclamation that Moses died at the ripe age of 120 years "with his vigor intact" (ולא נס לחה) is meant to counter potential negative impressions of him implied by his forced death. Yet even Frolov himself seems to lack faith in this harmonizing reading, noting in his conclusion that Deuteronomy 34 "stands in tension" with Deut 31:2.[10]

Some other readings by Frolov similarly strain against the evidence of the text itself. For example, some interpreters have struggled with the apparent incompatibility between the statement in 34:1 that Moses "ascended from the plains of Moab to Mount Nebo" (מערבת מואב אל־הר נבו) and the continuation in 34:1 that Moses ascended "the head of the Pisgah which is opposite Jericho" (ראש הפסגה אשר על־פני ירחו). These designations could refer to a similar place, but if so, Deut 34:1 provides a double description of the location where Moses ascended and died, with "from the plains of Moab to the mountain of Nebo" using expressions seen elsewhere in P layers (Num 22:1; 26:3, 63; 31:12; etc.; and 32:3, 38; 33:28, 47) and "the head of Pisgah" linking to Deut 3:27 and otherwise characteristic of non-Priestly texts (Num 21:20; 23:14). Frolov's "purely inductive reading" offers two ways to harmonize these geographical designations: (1) using Modern Hebrew (not usually

---

is a part (Yoo's article started as a student paper for Joel Baden), diverges significantly from past analyses of the contents of J and E. On the relationship of the Neo-Documentarian approach to prior source-critical approaches, see, for now, Joel S. Baden, *The Composition of the Pentateuch: Renewing the Documentary Hypothesis* (AYBRL; New Haven: Yale University Press, 2012).

[8] Frolov, "Death of Moses," 658 n. 31.
[9] Yoo, "Four Moses Death Accounts," 429.
[10] Frolov, "Death of Moses," 658.

a good source for philological analysis of ancient Hebrew) to reinterpret "the Pisgah" as designating "generic 'summit' or 'ridge,'" or (2) suggesting that the term הפסגה "may refer to the entire massif towering over the Dead Sea and the southern part of the Jordan valley."[11]

So also, Deut 34:9 conspicuously refers back only to the (Priestly) account of Moses laying his hands on Joshua, his successor, in Num 27:18-23 and not to subsequent accounts in Deuteronomy of Moses (Deut 31:7) and Yhwh (31:14, 23) verbally commissioning Joshua. In relation to this issue, Frolov inconclusively states in a footnote, "It is by no means clear why the two scenes cannot be seen as complementary," and suggests that Deut 34:9 mentions the scene in Numbers 27 only to single it out as crucial.[12] Frolov does not clarify why a "purely inductive" reader would see such a reading as necessary, nor does he offer a possible reason why 34:9 would single out Numbers 27 and not the competing scenes in Deuteronomy 31 of verbal commissioning.

Finally, numerous scholars have been struck by the contrast between Moses' proclamation in the core of Deuteronomy (18:15; see also 18:18) that "Yhwh will raise up a prophet like me" and the statement in Deut 34:10 that "no prophet like Moses has arisen again in Israel." Frolov reinterprets Deuteronomy 18 as referring only to a limited similarity of later prophets to Moses.[13] Deuteronomy 18 itself, however, lacks any specific wording to support Frolov's understanding. His proposal seems to be the product not of "purely inductive reading," but of an attempt to harmonize otherwise incompatible texts.

Frolov—and any other reader—certainly has a right to explore how one might read Deuteronomy 34 in its present form as if it did not conflict with any other pentateuchal tradition. Nevertheless, he is incorrect when he asserts that his reading is what results when one approaches the text without any assumptions and reads it in a purely inductive way. Moreover, he overreaches when he states that, according to his reading, "Deuteronomy 34 exposes source criticism as it stands today as self-contradictory."[14] Instead, Frolov illustrates the results of a reading of a pentateuchal text that (a) does not presuppose any results of literary-critical analysis of the rest of the Pentateuch and (b) reinterprets the text in question and related ones so that all can be read as a unified whole, the latter reinterpretation requiring the addition of new information and/or development of new philological analyses of words so that they do not contradict each other.

Meanwhile, Yoo's particular analysis of Deuteronomy 34 does not represent "source criticism as it stands today," but a particular type of (Neo-Documentarian) source criticism built on its own set of premises (outlined above). Furthermore, many contemporary advocates of source criticism have given up on source-critical

---

[11] Ibid., 650.
[12] Ibid., 656 n. 23.
[13] Ibid., 657.
[14] Ibid., 659.

analysis of Deuteronomy 34, largely in the wake of an influential article—remarkably not cited by Yoo—published over twenty-five years ago by Lothar Perlitt.[15] In this article, Perlitt maintained that no part of Deuteronomy originated in a Priestly document, and he specifically argued that the few clear echoes of P in Deuteronomy 34, such as the mention of the "plains of Moab" in 34:1, were the result of late, post-Priestly revision rather than the conflation of sources. His article has led to a widespread movement in recent European pentateuchal scholarship, already disinclined to find J or E in the Pentateuch, to deny the existence of P in Deuteronomy 34 as well. And this—not Martin Noth's hypothesis of a Deuteronomistic History (cf. Yoo, 423–24)—then led to the widespread tendency, noted by Yoo at the outset of his article, of scholars to see the chapter as basically Deuteronomistic. Yoo does not show in his article an awareness of the widespread questioning of the presence of P in Deuteronomy, and at points he assigns parts of Deuteronomy 34 to P based on similarities to other passages in Deuteronomy, such as Deut 32:48–52, without noting substantial questions raised by prior scholars about their Priestly (P^G) status.

In sum, Yoo's analysis has problems, but it cannot be taken as a measure of the "epistomological validity" of a source-critical approach in general. It relies on a prior Neo-Documentarian source-critical analysis of the Pentateuch as a whole which—at the time of writing this response—has not been published, and it fails to engage crucial alternative source-critical treatments of Deuteronomy 34 and other texts on which he depends. The question of the validity of the source-critical approach would be better explored by examining a text such as the flood narrative in Genesis 6–9, which has been and remains foundational for past and present source criticism of the Pentateuch. The crucial test, one not accomplished to date, would be to read Genesis 6–9 and other foundational chapters for pentateuchal source criticism as literary unities without creative philological analyses and/or the addition of harmonizing details that are not actually present in the biblical texts being interpreted.

---

[15] Perlitt, "Priesterschrift im Deuteronomium," *ZAW* 100 Supplement (1988): 123–43. An accessible, relatively recent, English-language summary of the discussion of this question is Christophe Nihan, *From Priestly Torah to Pentateuch: A Study in the Composition of the Book of Leviticus* (FAT 25; Tübingen: Mohr Siebeck, 2007), 20–58, esp. 20–30.

SBL PRESS — New and Recent Titles

QUMRAN HEBREW
An Overview of Orthography, Phonology, and Morphology
Eric D. Reymond
Paper $37.95, 978-1-58983-931-1   328 pages, 2013   Code: 060376
Hardcover $52.95, 978-1-58983-933-5   E-book $37.95, 978-1-58983-932-8
Resources for Biblical Study 76

EVIDENCE OF EDITING
Growth and Change of Texts in the Hebrew Bible
Reinhard Müller, Juha Pakkala, and Bas ter Haar Romeny
Paper $32.95, 978-1-58983-747-8   266 pages, 2013   Code: 060375
Hardcover $47.95, 978-1-58983-883-3   E-book $32.95, 978-1-58983-748-5
Resources for Biblical Study 75

WARFARE, RITUAL, AND SYMBOL IN BIBLICAL AND MODERN CONTEXTS
Brad E. Kelle, Frank Ritchel Ames, and Jacob L. Wright, editors
Paper $38.95, 978-1-58983-958-8   322 pages, 2014   Code: 062618
Hardcover $53.95, 978-1-58983-960-1   E-book $38.95, 978-1-58983-959-5
Ancient Israel and Its Literature 28

SOURCEBOOK FOR ANCIENT MESOPOTAMIAN MEDICINE
JoAnn Scurlock
Paper $84.95, 978-1-58983-969-4   786 pages, 2014   Code: 061536
Hardcover $104.95, 978-1-58983-970-0   E-book $84.95, 978-1-58983-971-7
Writings from the Ancient World 36

ARISTAENETUS, *EROTIC LETTERS*
Translated with an Introduction and Notes by
Peter Bing and Regina Höschele
Paper $24.95, 978-1-58983-741-6   184 pages, 2014   Code: 061632P
Hardcover $39.95, 978-1-58983-882-6   E-book $24.95, 978-1-58983-742-3
Writings from the Greco-Roman World 32

SBL Press • P.O. Box 2243 • Williston, VT 05495-2243
Phone: 877-725-3334 (toll-free) or 802-864-6185 • Fax: 802-864-7626
Order online at www.sbl-site.org

SBL PRESS New and Recent Titles

THE BIBLE IN THE PUBLIC SQUARE
Its Enduring Influence in American Life
Mark A. Chancey, Carol Meyers, and
Eric M. Meyers, editors
Paper $29.95, 978-1-58983-981-6   230 pages, 2014   Code: 061127
Hardcover $44.95, 978-1-58983-982-3   E-book $29.95, 978-1-58983-983-0
Biblical Scholarship in North America 27

FEMINIST BIBLICAL STUDIES IN THE
TWENTIETH CENTURY
Scholarship and Movement
Elisabeth Schüssler Fiorenza, editor
Paper $56.95, 978-1-58983-583-2   464 pages, 2014   Code: 066002
Hardcover $76.95, 978-1-58983-922-9   E-book $56.95, 978-1-58983-921-2
Bible and Women 2

THE BIBLE AND POSTHUMANISM
Jennifer L. Koosed, editor
Paper $43.95, 978-1-58983-751-5   356 pages, 2014   Code: 060674
Hardcover $58.95, 978-1-58983-939-7   E-book $43.95, 978-1-58983-752-2
Semeia Studies 74

READING 1–2 PETER AND JUDE
A Resource for Students
Eric F. Mason and Troy W. Martin, editors
Paper $35.95, 978-1-58983-737-9   294 pages, 2014   Code: 060377
Hardcover $50.95, 978-1-58983-940-3   E-book $35.95, 978-1-58983-738-6
Resources for Biblical Study 77

MYTH AND SCRIPTURE
Contemporary Perspectives on Religion, Language,
and Imagination
Dexter E. Callender Jr., editor
Paper $36.95, 978-1-58983-961-8   322 pages, 2014   Code: 060378
Hardcover $51.95, 978-1-58983-963-2   E-book $36.95, 978-1-58983-962-5
Resources for Biblical Study 78

SBL Press • P.O. Box 2243 • Williston, VT 05495-2243
Phone: 877-725-3334 (toll-free) or 802-864-6185 • Fax: 802-864-7626
Order online at www.sbl-site.org

New from Mohr Siebeck

Tobias Nicklas
Jews and Christians?
Second-Century ›Christian‹ Perspectives on the »Parting of the Ways« (Annual Deichmann Lectures 2013)

When exactly did the »Parting of the Ways« between Jews and Christians take place? Was it already Jesus who separated himself and his followers from »the Jews«? Or did Paul with his mission of pagans make the decisive step? Or do we have to wait longer – until after 70 CE, when the Jerusalem Temple was destroyed? In his new book, which goes back to the 2013 Deichmann lectures at Ben Gurion University, Beersheva, Tobias Nicklas shows that the above question is formulated inadequately. Instead, one has to distinguish between the situations of different groups (and even individuals) in different historical circumstances. To show this, Nicklas discusses images of »Jews« in early Christian writings, concepts of Israel's God and his Covenant with Israel, »Christological« and »Ecclesiological« hermeneutics of the Scriptures, and matters of Halakha for believers in Christ.

2014. IX, 233 pages.
ISBN 978-3-16-153268-9
sewn paper

Takayoshi Oshima
Babylonian Poems of Pious Sufferers
Ludlul Bēl Nēmeqi and the *Babylonian Theodicy*

Takayoshi Oshima analyses two key Babylonian Wisdom texts: *Ludlul Bēl Nēmeqi* and the *Babylonian Theodicy*. He offers new critical text editions based on published and hitherto unpublished cuneiform manuscripts and also discusses the cultural and historical background of these poems.

2014. 590 pages (est.) + 65 plates. (ORA). ISBN 978-3-16-153389-1
cloth (October)

Knut Backhaus
Religion als Reise
Intertextuelle Lektüren in Antike und Christentum

Reise und Religion überschreiten Grenzen. In diesen intertextuellen Lektüren verfolgt Knut Backhaus die Welt-Wanderer der klassischen Epen, Jesus und die urchristlichen Wanderradikalen, die paganen Helden (Apollonios von Tyana, Herakles, Orpheus, Dionysos), die Seeabenteuer des Paulus und die antiken Jenseitsfahrten. Dabei tritt eine gemeinsame Erzähl- und Hoffnungskultur zutage, an der Früh- und Nicht-Christen in wechselseitiger Bereicherung Transzendenz lernten.

2014. 300 pages (est.) (TrC 8).
ISBN 978-3-16-153253-5
sewn paper (September)

Mohr Siebeck
Tübingen
info@mohr.de
www.mohr.de

Custom made information:
www.mohr.de

NEW from OXFORD

THE OXFORD HANDBOOK OF THE PSALMS
Edited by WILLIAM P. BROWN
2014 684 pp. 4 illus.
Hardcover $150.00

ETHICS AND BIBLICAL NARRATIVE
A Literary and Discourse-Analytical Approach to the Story of Josiah
S. MIN CHUN
(Oxford Theology and Religion Monographs)
2014 288 pp.
Hardcover $125.00

THE OXFORD HANDBOOK OF APOCALYPTIC LITERATURE
Edited by JOHN J. COLLINS
2014 564 pp.
Hardcover $150.00

NATURAL LAW
A Jewish, Christian, and Muslim Trialogue
ANVER M. EMON, MATTHEW LEVERING, and DAVID NOVAK
2014 256 pp.
Hardcover $80.00

SEEING THE WORLD AND KNOWING GOD
Hebrew Wisdom and Christian Doctrine in a Late-Modern Context
PAUL S. FIDDES
2013 416 pp.
Hardcover $150.00

A JOURNEY OF TWO PSALMS
The Reception of Psalms 1 and 2 in Jewish and Christian Tradition
SUSAN GILLINGHAM
2014 368 pp. 38 color plates, 5 b/w in-text images
Hardcover $65.00

THE BIBLE IN SHAKESPEARE
HANNIBAL HAMLIN
2013 400 pp. 14 illus.
Hardcover $99.00

THE FATHER'S WILL
Christ's Crucifixion and the Goodness of God
NICHOLAS E. LOMBARDO
2014 288 pp.
Hardcover $99.00

JOSEPH OF ARIMATHEA
A Study in Reception History
WILLIAM JOHN LYONS
(Biblical Refigurations)
2014 208 pp.
Paperback $29.95

UNION WITH CHRIST IN THE NEW TESTAMENT
GRANT MACASKILL
2014 368 pp.
Hardcover $150.00

THE OXFORD ENCYCLOPEDIA OF BIBLICAL INTERPRETATION
Editor-in-chief:
STEVEN L. MCKENZIE
(Oxford Encyclopedias of the Bible)
2013 1164 pp.
Kit $395.00

DEUTERONOMY AND THE JUDAEAN DIASPORA
ERNEST NICHOLSON
2014 208 pp.
Hardcover $99.00

THE OLD TESTAMENT IN EASTERN ORTHODOX TRADITION
EUGEN J. PENTIUC
2014 448 pp.
20 illus. Paperback $35.00

DEBORAH'S DAUGHTERS
Gender Politics and Biblical Interpretation
JOY A. SCHROEDER
2014 384 pp. 6 illus.
Hardcover $74.00

A PROPHET LIKE MOSES
Prophecy, Law, and Israelite Religion
JEFFREY STACKERT
2014 256 pp. 2 illus.
Hardcover $74.00

REMEMBERING PAUL
Ancient and Modern Contests over the Image of the Apostle
BENJAMIN L. WHITE
2014 368 pp.
Hardcover $74.00

FORTHCOMING IN NOVEMBER!

THE JEWISH STUDY BIBLE
Second Edition
Edited by ADELE BERLIN and MARC ZVI BRETTLER
This new edition has over two dozen new and updated essays and updated annotations for nearly the entire Bible.
2014 2400 pp. Full-color map section; 24 b&w illus.
Hardcover $45.00

OXFORD BIBLICAL STUDIES ONLINE
Headed by Editor-in-Chief Michael D. Coogan, Oxford Biblical Studies Online is a comprehensive resource for the study of the Bible and biblical history, with Biblical texts, authoritative reference works, and tools that provide ease of research into the background, context, and issues related to the Bible.

Prices are subject to change and apply only in the US.
To order or for more information, visit our website at **oup.com/us**

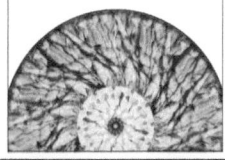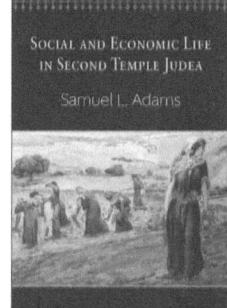

www.ingramcontent.com/pod-product-compliance
Lightning Source LLC
Chambersburg PA
CBHW021826300426
44114CB00009BA/346